Meanings *of* Designed Spaces

FAIRCHILD
BOOKS

Meanings *of* Designed Spaces

Edited by Tiiu Vaikla-Poldma
Université de Montréal

Fairchild Books | New York

Fairchild Books
An imprint of Bloomsbury Publishing Inc

175 Fifth Avenue   50 Bedford Square
New York   London
NY 10010   WC1B 3DP
USA   UK

www.fairchildbooks.com

Library of Congress Cataloging-in-Publication Data
Poldma, Tiiu
Meanings of Designed Spaces
2012946341

ISBN: 978-1-60901-145-1

Typeset by Precision Graphics
Cover Design by Sarah Silberg
Cover Art: © Sølve Sundsbø / Art + Commerce
Printed in the United States by Thomson-Shore, Inc. Dexter, Michigan

Table of Contents

Preface

Meanings of Designed Spaces is a book that considers ideas, theories, provocations, and perspectives about design and spaces. We consider these perspectives from diverse points of view, such as theory, research, practice, and business, and from various domains. Foremost in the book is the link of these spaces with human activity and how people construct meanings of how they live, work, or play, all the while having experiences in diverse types of spaces.

The essential substance of this book comes from the contributions of the authors. This collection of essays and their topics are meant to stimulate thinking, provoke conversations, and generate dialogue about what it means to have experiences in spaces and places, what aesthetic and cultural meanings are created, and what perceptions and responses are constructed through how spaces vehicle meaning.

THE THEORETICAL BASIS AND CONTEXT

No matter where or how we live, people's lives, experiences, and core values are becoming woven within a global economy, transnational contexts, and socially changing paradigms. Physical, virtual spaces intersect with the meanings we make and the experiences that we have, whether social, personal, ethical, or cultural. These diverse spaces and meanings then promote viewpoints and create new boundaries.

Although thinking about complex issues and contexts promotes new emerging frameworks for both theory and practices, we still theorize and conceive of both theoretical and physical spaces as separate, constructed within disciplines and understood within limited frameworks. The various authors who provide essays do so with the idea of challenging these frameworks while remaining respectful of the perspectives that have come before.

This book is about the social, cultural, aesthetic, and multidimensional spaces that are theorized within the design of the built environment. We live increasingly in interior environments where we spend much of our time, and yet the spaces we navigate are at once local, cultural, global, technological, and multilayered interior, exterior, urban, real, virtual, and territorial environments bound by different versions of space and time. More and more we are also changing the very nature of spaces we inhabit through the technological means we have at our disposal. How we communicate and what we do in our daily lives also is affecting our uses and concepts of spaces, be these physical, theoretical, or technological.

The book proposes a dialogue of existing theories and concepts juxtaposed against emerging issues, innovative thinking, and challenges about how spaces generate meanings of various types. By "spaces" we may be referring to the following:

- Theoretical spaces of knowledge and understanding
- Social and cultural spaces
- Management spaces where decision making takes place
- Physical and virtual spaces that act both as places and as environments
- Dynamic spaces that interact with both mind and body

As we become increasingly aware of ourselves, our experiences, and attain a heightened sense of self, we have interactions with others and our body is increasingly interacting with space, environment, others and technology in new and different ways not experienced before in history.

THE OVERALL BOOK CONCEPT

The structure of this book consists of three parts: Part I, Current Design and Inquiry Spaces; Part II, Seminal and Alternate Viewpoints About Design/Spaces; and Part III, Provocations About Spatial Meanings and Future Design and Spaces. Part I lays a foundation of definitions, theories, and concepts. Part II then explores historic, cultural, social, aesthetic, and situational issues and themes. Part III proposes critical and situational contexts of collaborative and ethical spaces, concluding with possible futures.

Each chapter has an overarching grouping of papers organized into three segments: Theoretical papers, Provocation, and Dialogues and Perspectives. These different papers have been selected specifically to convey information and ideas, provoke thinking, and provide forums for dialogue and discussion for the reader. The book hosts an open and constructive dialogue with author essays that provoke and offer theory, experiences, and practical ways to engage in issues about spaces and design, and their meanings. The essays are either theoretically supported by relevant and emerging literature or perspectives from users and designers in diverse parts of the design disciplines and backgrounds.

This is not a book with the specific discipline in mind, but rather it is aimed at understanding how history and philosophical perspectives have influenced certain ideas about design and spaces over time, how meaning is made in current contemporary society, what emerging constructions are shaping values, and what meanings we attribute to how we appropriate and understand various spaces through our understandings.

ORGANIZATION OF THE BOOK

The overall thread of the book is organized with two levels of thinking: (1) In a linear fashion from historic contexts to contemporary issues, and (2) from a perspective of theory and practice, and how practice informs theory and theory provides perspectives for practice.

The diverse articles ground the ideas presented through narrative and visuals. Most articles are original, while a few are carefully selected reprints to give context to particular themes. The contributions range from short, provocative essays and conversations to theoretical papers examining topical issues.

Part I: Current Design/Inquiry Spaces

Part I begins with an overview of the basic definitions and concepts. **Chapter 1** begins with definitions and situating how we unfold concepts within this book. Meaning, design, and space are defined and examined both as ideas and theories, alongside concepts of space, design process, design thinking, design inquiry, practices, knowledge paradigms, and constructions. Chapter 1 structures fundamental concepts of design and spaces, and how these have been understood over time. Inquiry, action, multiplicity of meaning, and changing ideas of intentionality and the nature of experience are introduced through discussions of critical theoretical contexts. We consider how knowledge is generated, and what purpose research and writing have when developing our ideas in the framework of how we evolve meanings in design research.

Chapter 2 continues the development of space and aesthetic, pragmatic concepts of spaces. Theories of modernism, postmodernism, structuralism, poststructuralism, social constructions of spaces and places, phenomenological views, and pragmatism are introduced with examples of how people experience spaces as personal, aesthetic, and cultural places.

Identities, disciplines, and knowledge frame the concepts of **Chapter 3**. Ontology and epistemology of knowledge are explored in greater detail in light of basic concepts of knowledge and as a framework for the discussion on disciplinary knowledge spaces using the example of the discipline of interior design. In Chapter 3 disciplinary identity is juxtaposed with inter- and multidisciplinary contexts and issues of identity and specificity.

Part II: Seminal and Alternate Viewpoints About Design/Spaces

Part II explores seminal viewpoints about spaces, design, and meanings from different contexts and perspectives.

Chapter 4 explores the material contexts of space as a social equalizer, as a social construction, as cultural influence, and as a purveyor of atmosphere through the lens of history. We look at how history forms the framework of how we design—the historic contexts from which we must evolve design thinking and include perspectives that have influenced the evolution of designed space and what influences these have on design in contemporary society. We examine space as ornament, spatial context as an inter-story between artefacts, and space as a construction situated in a weaving together of interior and history. Spaces of gender are introduced within an examination of how gender and power issues play out in a historical perspective of an emerging technological society at the beginning of the twentieth century.

Chapter 5 focuses on alternative spaces of experience considering users, ephemeral spaces, and immaterial spaces. Spaces perceived through experiences of users and what meanings are attributed to these experiences are contextualized through user experience, everyday objects, and the here and now, and how aesthetics frames our surroundings. Whether it is the "Lining Stories" playing out interior spaces of linings or the theatrical interiors of spaces, each proposes feelings about real, lived experiences in spatial contexts.

Chapter 6 considers space of everyday life, self, and social constructions. Spaces of living are explored from perspectives of philosophical thinking, social issues, and gender issues, alongside more fundamental underlying questions about our existence through where we live, the things we live among, and places we live within (as spaces) that give us meaning. What does it mean to live well, and what frames these ideas depending on where one lives? We examine looks the social structures of space and place—how these position our identity, creating political divides or social constructions of places such as home, work, and leisure spaces. Gender issues have an impact on how space is occupied, how it is appropriated, and how it is used. What is boundary making in the home, and how is this framed are issues examined from both historic and contemporary lenses.

Chapter 7 brings spaces into the realm of bodily and aesthetic experiences from the perspective of the visual arts, but framed in how body-space-experiences play out as interrelationships in time and space as dynamic interactions. This chapter examines how bodies, technologies, and art engage with material and immaterial qualities of lived experience intersecting in space in a dynamic manner.

Chapter 8 proposes changing conceptualizations in the real world, using the real-life setting of the corporate environment as the framework for the changing spaces of design innovation and thinking. The service-oriented nature of design and the ways that design thinking transforms business strategies is explored. New dimensional spaces of sensemaking and strategizing using design thinking are considered alongside how designers see the corporate spaces and their evolving workplace cultures.

Part III: Provocations About Spatial Meanings and Future Design Spaces

Part III turns toward emerging contexts of research and practices, exploring new frontiers and developing different ways to consider theory and practice together and how they inform one another.

Chapter 9 explores the emergence of critical design, pragmatism, and collaborative approaches in both research and practice. While in research the person's experiences are taken into account alongside the spaces that affect how he or she lives well, in practice these experiences must be understood to effect change that can be transformative. Examples in research are presented that promote collaborative thinking, communities of practice, and cooperative forms of examining the dynamic spaces of social and physical environmental factors.

Mediated spaces of practice are explored in **Chapter 10**. The impact of technologies adds to the dynamic relationship between people and their environment, and this is examined in terms of how new mediations use design thinking to transform business and environments, and what this means for teaching and learning.

Chapter 11 proposes consideration of ethical approaches in research and practice. Collaborative approaches are explored with a case study of design-led activism, and ethical issues in business are explored. Possible ways to integrate ethics with design practices are examined as spaces of ethical practices.

Finally, we round out the book with **Chapter 12**, which examines researching and futuring in a global world. We pull together the three phases of the book with considerations in academia and practice and through a discussion about possibilities: What is theory and practice in light of these new and emergent meanings? What are possible future scenarios for research, theory, and practice? We conclude with possibilities for continuing the discussion.

This book will be useful for students, professors, those who are interested in asking questions about the designed world and in understanding what constitutes changing ideas about our world, and those who want to explore new ideas about spaces and their meanings. Special features include the interactive nature of the essays and discussion questions in each chapter. These are supported throughout by key words and concepts. The themes explored build from one chapter to the next and yet can be cross-examined within the book on specific topics that span chapters as well. Discussion questions focus on issues within a specific essay within the chapter and may also be used across chapters. Each theme builds on the last throughout the book, and concepts are stepping-stones for discussion in the classroom and among colleagues either through specific essays and their issues or as a springboard to ideas explored in the classroom.

Acknowledgments

This first edition of readings and perspectives is the culmination of over four years of work thanks to many individuals who supported this project from the earliest concepts and ideas.

I would like to thank the contributing authors, all of whom contributed time, stimulating reflections, theoretical papers, provocations, and perspectives willingly and with great collaborations. And thanks to the philosophers whose ideas provided the foundation upon which we all build.

My deepest gratitude goes to my development editor Barbara Price, whose endless hours and constructive criticism, particularly in the earlier stages of the manuscript, honed both my thinking and the subsequent framing of the book. Through her patience and guidance I navigated the waves of writing and consulting with the contributing authors.

Many thanks also to Olga Kontzias, Executive Editor, and Joseph Miranda, Senior Development Editor, for their patience, support, and guidance throughout the process of both organizing the contributors and assisting in framing the essential concepts of the book. Olga and Joe provided much needed guidance and follow-through at essential times in the book development, and for this I am eternally grateful.

I would also like to thank the professors at the Faculté de l'aménagement (Faculty of Environmental Design) at the Université de Montréal for their support and in particular my colleagues who fielded ideas, encouraged the development of specific concepts, and were filters for some of the intellectual ideas that were developed.

Gratitude also goes to the clients and collaborators who supplied conversations, images, and case study examples to support the theoretical elements of the book, and allow the book to visually explicate theoretical and written concepts from the pragmatic perspectives of the real world in both practice and theory.

Much of the book content would not be possible without students who contributed to some of the case study ideas. A special thanks to Doctoral and Master's program students Leila, Sylvain, Virginie, Mariam, Ève, Ramin, and Joumana, with whom I engaged in many discussions on these issues and allowed for reflective thinking to emerge that contributed to the development of the book.

There are many more colleagues, friends, and fellow designers who have contributed in one way or another and are too numerous to mention. In particular, thanks go to those who have inspired or given time and effort to help make this book a reality, including NK, KN, DD, KF, HN, MJ, DV, JAT, MA, and GM, through their ideas and writings as much as our conversations and discussions.

This book was not possible without the views of the many scholars and designers whose engagement with these very issues daily promotes and moves forward these domains, and with whom debates and discussions will continue on.

I dedicate this book to Alar and Julius.

PART I
Current Design and Inquiry Spaces

CHAPTER 1
Knowledge, Meanings, and Spaces of Design

design, meaning, space, design process, design thinking, design inquiry, scientific inquiry, information gathering, design domains, disciplines, practices, knowledge, paradigms, logical empiricism, positivism, postpositivism, critical theory, constructivism, design research, academic research, knowledge in design research, critical thinking, thinking and doing, critical discourse, disciplinary spaces, liquid disciplines, basic research, applied research, clinical research, evidence-based design, empirical knowledge, *apriori* knowledge, *apriori* *assumptions*, BIM, inductive reasoning, epistemology of possession, Body of Knowledge (BoK)

AFTER READING THIS CHAPTER, YOU WILL BE ABLE TO:

- Differentiate between basic definitions of space, meaning, design, and inquiry.
- Understand nuances of design process, design thinking, and design inquiry.
- Discuss fundamental ideas about how we construct meanings.
- Consider different ideas about design and spaces, including what are the multiple, cross-disciplinary, and dynamic ways that we understand spaces of designing and design thinking.
- Consider forms of research, what constitutes design research, and how practice and research intersect in different ways.
- Understand the nature of knowledge from theoretical perspectives in science and design.
- Understand the forms of research in both academia and practice.
- Consider the intersections of design inquiry, scientific inquiry, and positions taken by those who do research.
- Understand a critical design discourse.

BEGINNING

This book is a compilation of papers, provocations, and perspectives about dialogues and meanings of design and spaces. We uncover multiple voices and points of view of scholars and practitioners, businesspeople, and passionate designers, all of whom explore **design**,

meanings, and **spaces** from such diverse perspectives as research, practice, business, and philosophy, and all as drivers of how we mediate experiences within and through various types of spaces. The contributing authors provide theoretical papers, provocations, and perspectives that cross a wide range of ideas about design, about meanings of design and about the various spaces where these concepts intersect.

We live much of our contemporary lives within spaces, and these are designed by many people for various reasons, purposes, and activities. We are surrounded by designed objects, using them to mediate our communication with others and to intersect with others through the virtual and real spaces that we navigate and inhabit. Both designing and spaces are valuable subjects, as these can mediate our activities as human beings in ways we may not even be aware. And yet we make meanings and find value in the ways we interact with others and mediate our various experiences through various spaces.

The construction of the ideas and meanings about design and spaces are centered on the premise that as practice becomes ever-complex in diverse spaces, you need to understand the ways that theory and practice work together in helping to construct meaning. This requires considering different ways we read about and engage in meanings and differentiating between different contexts of spaces and how we construct concepts.

This book is both a compilation of readings and a book about theory, practice, and provocation. You will notice that each chapter is constructed with specific themes, and each author contribution explores theoretical ideas, provokes theoretical or pragmatic ideas, or, through dialogue, provides perspectives on the issues discussed within the chapter.

Design, Meaning, Space

Three overarching themes guide the context of this book: design, meanings, and spaces. We will consider various design and spaces and their meanings, from diverse contexts and from different perspectives. We will examine how designers think and attribute meanings, what users and clients see as important to them in the places and spaces that they experience, and how reflecting on various issues about these subjects is valuable and meaningful.

Change and Complexity: The Context of the Current Moment in Time

Current contexts of spaces are converging with new and emerging ways of working in a global environment, with challenges to world infrastructures and within increasingly socially aware interactions in complex situations. We are living in a moment of time where vast change is confronting political and economic turbulence, and where political and social turbulence are resulting in dramatic change.

Conversely, we are also living in a technologically savvy, changing, and emergent period of time, with the world emerging as a transglobal place in constant and rapid evolution. The dichotomy in this world is that while many are either living with increased standards of living or extreme wealth, others are just struggling to survive. No matter where we live, or within what political, social, or cultural context, people's lives and core values are becoming woven in a global economy, where economies cross transnational boundaries and where societies are experiencing changing paradigms. Public and private domains are shifting as living and working in this global and increasingly interconnected world leads to new ways of understanding space as a lived place.

The Changing Nature of the Designed World

Design, design research, and creating designs within the built environment have changed dramatically even within the past 10 to 20 years. How we live and what we use in our material world locally or globally changes almost daily. Not only are the spaces that we live and work in mutating in new directions, but also our view of these spaces, of our experiences, and of how we organize spaces of varying kinds is shifting, as emerging contexts reveal new spaces daily. Spaces in these contexts may include and are not limited to:

- Spaces of knowledge
- Spaces of culture
- Global interactive spaces
- Virtual spaces
- Physical spaces
- Urban spaces
- Intellectual spaces
- Social spaces
- Spaces of experience
- Geographic spaces
- Narrative spaces

We will examine spaces and their meanings, how designing impacts on diverse types of spaces, and what this means when reflecting on what meanings we attribute to the spaces we use.

We will look at how designing our world and the various spaces within it provides meanings in our lives and ask questions such as:

- What are complex design processes?
- What is designing in traditional contexts?
- What is critical design in contemporary contexts?
- What meanings are constructed around designing within dynamic situations?

- What are social, cultural, and philosophical questions in these contexts?
- What are the contexts of our questions?
- How is this meaning constructed?
- What is design research within this framework?
- How do we use design inquiry as a means to take action, and how is this relevant to how we understand design/spaces?
- How do we balance the innovative nature of design inquiry with the need to build empirical methods to generate new knowledge?
- How do we understand nuances of design inquiry and scientific inquiry?
- How do we understand and respond to the social, political, ethical, and cultural issues in concert with design thinking and decision making?
- What is design and space?

Figure 1.1 View of an atrium space in a hotel from above.
Photo credit: Courtesy of John Sylvester

THE BOOK COMPOSITION

This is a book of ideas and concepts, theories and practices, design meanings and spaces, all emerging within both existing and new contexts. Some of these concepts might be familiar, others not. We would like to walk you through possible ways to use this book.

The purpose of the various papers is to engage you in critical thinking and critical discourse. For this to happen, you need certain intellectual tools, both verbal and visual. We deliberately juxtapose three types of papers for you:

- Theoretical Papers
- Provocations
- Dialogues and Perspectives

Each chapter is composed of theoretical ideas to guide the concepts of the chapter. First, theoretical papers guide the ideas of the chapter. Provocations then contradict the theoretical ideas or support them from a provocative perspective. Finally, the Dialogues and Perspectives provide applications of the theoretical ideas, whether back into theory, as applications in research and practice, or as case studies of real-life settings showing ways that theory and practice come together.

The Language Spaces

The question of languages becomes an important element of this book. By "languages" I am referring to how we explain meanings through written word, and through the narratives we use to express theories and concepts. Three types of languages are used in this book: narrative, vernacular, and visual. Different types of languages support different meanings and ideas that are presented.

First, the theoretical papers are generally narrative in nature, exploring theoretical themes in constructed and synthesized papers. These offer theoretical perspectives for you to develop critical understanding of concepts from diverse perspectives, with suggested readings to broaden the scope of the discussion. Theories range from historical to philosophical to design theory considerations, with multiple views presented about design, about meanings, and about spaces.

Second, the languages in the Provocations and the Dialogues and Perspectives vary from narrative to vernacular to visual language, depending on the issue at hand or the nature of the conversation. The first few chapters include papers, conversations, and perspectives that tackle theoretical issues. Later on, and through both verbal and visual means, we see a shift to pragmatic issues and considerations in practice alongside theories with the ideas applied into examples such as case studies or spaces and places.

The Authors

This book would not be possible without the impressive contributions of the contributing authors, who come from a wide range of backgrounds, and the articles are just as wide-ranging in style and scope. This is done deliberately to enrich the dialogue and provide different points of view for your consideration, critique, and discussion. These varied perspectives sometimes diverge in their views, and this is a good thing!

They also offer different types of languages to you as the reader—theories and practices are explored with different lenses, depending on the stance of the author, his or her professional or academic background, and his or her point of view. It is vital to understand that different people with different backgrounds have different points of view and all contributed to enrich the ideas within this book.

Ultimately, the discussions and questions raised allow you, the reader, to understand and reflect on concepts and to formulate your own critical ideas about spaces, design, and how meanings are made within underlying values and constructs that exist in the world. This will help you hone your critical thinking and inquiry skills.

INTRODUCTION: DEFINITIONS AND CONCEPTS

We begin Chapter 1 by examining several concepts to ground the explorations and discussion that will follow in subsequent chapters. Starting with an introduction to definitions and concepts, the chapter proceeds with the separate theoretical, provocation, and dialogue and perspective segments.

We begin with a brief overview of some basic definitions of design, space, and meanings juxtaposed against discussions about design thinking and design inquiry. This very brief overview grounds concepts used commonly and explores definitions of terms and limitations as well as complexities inherent in the definitions themselves. While meanings of design and spaces seems to clearly indicate spaces with meanings inherent in design, each term is a complex term and requires defining and grounding to prepare you for the chapters that follow.

Later on we will present and examine the nature of inquiry and knowledge. Some of the questions we will tackle include the following:

- What is the nature of knowledge and how is knowledge constructed?
- What is the nature of research in general and design inquiry in particular?
- What are nuances of design inquiry and scientific inquiry?
- What is a design science and how is design knowledge constructed through meanings?

We will present and examine different forms of research, how these forms exist in the world, what paradigms and approaches in both science and design support design inquiry, and what are the diverse knowledge spaces we engage in as both practitioners and researchers.

A BRIEF OVERVIEW OF BASIC DEFINITIONS AND CONCEPTS: DESIGN, SPACE, MEANING, AND DESIGN INQUIRY

We begin with an overview of some basic concepts about design, design process, and design thinking. No matter whether it is information design, design management, designed interior space, architecture, urban design, industrial design, graphic design, digital design; the concept of **design** is at the heart of the designers' preoccupation. We begin with this concept first, as this is often a foundation element in design disciplines who engage in understanding different spaces.

What Is Design?

The Merriam-Webster Dictionary defines design and design subsets as follows:

> *Main Entry:* ¹**de·sign**
> *Pronunciation:* \di-ˈzīn\
> *Function:* verb

Etymology: Middle English, to outline, indicate, mean, from Anglo-French & Medieval Latin; Anglo-French *designer* to designate, from Medieval Latin *designare*, from Latin, to mark out, from *de-* + *signare* to mark—more at **SIGN**
Date: 14th century

transitive verb
1: to create, fashion, execute, or construct according to plan : **DEVISE, CONTRIVE**
2a: to conceive and plan out in the mind <he *designed* the perfect crime> *b:* to have as a purpose : **INTEND** <she *designed* to excel in her studes> *c:* to devise for a specific function or end <a book *designed* primarily as a college textbook>
3: archaic: to indicate with a distinctive mark, sign, or name
4a: to make a drawing, pattern, or sketch of *b:* to draw the plans for <*design* a building>
intransitive verb
1: to conceive or execute a plan
2: to draw, lay out, or prepare a design
—**de·sign·ed·ly** \-zī-nəd-lē\ *adverb*

Main Entry: ²**design**
Function: noun
Date: 1569

1a: a particular purpose held in view by an individual or group <he has ambitious *designs* for his son> *b:* deliberate purposive planning <more by accident than *design*>
2: a mental project or scheme in which means to an end are laid down
3a: a deliberate undercover project or scheme : **PLOT** *b: plural:* agressive or evil intent used with *on* or *against* <he has *designs* on the money>
4: a preliminary sketch or outline showing the main features of something to be executed <the *design* for the new stadium>
5a: an underlying scheme that governs functioning, developing, or unfolding : **PATTERN, MOTIF** <the general *design* of the epic> *b:* a plan or protocol for carrying out or accomplishing something (as a scientific experiment); also the process of preparing this
6: the arrangement of elements or details in a product or work of art
7: a decorative pattern <a floral *design*>
8: the creative art of executing aesthetic or functional designs
synonyms see **INTENTION, PLAN**

Main Entry: **graphic design**
Function: noun
Date: 1935

the art or profession of using design elements (as typography and images) to convey information or create an effect; *also* a product of this art
—**graphic designer** *noun*

Main Entry: **intelligent design**
Function: *noun*
Date: 1847

the theory that matter, the various forms of life, and the world were created by a designing intelligence

----

Main Entry: **interior design**
Function: *noun*
Date: 1927

the art or practice of planning and supervising the design and execution of architectural interiors and their furnishings (Merriam-Webster, retrieved online http:\\www .britannica.com)

The word *design* carries with it many connotations, and even the dictionaries have different meanings. Design is a very broad term used by many fields and disciplines. While in earlier historic contexts designing was in large part a foundation within the built environment disciplines, the scope and breadth of design and designing has expanded greatly in the past 40-plus years, with literally hundreds of domains and fields incorporating *design* within their descriptions.

Designing is actually a complex action verb for a variety of activities representing a wide range of processes including spaces, products, systems, buildings, environments, places, situations, and concepts. These design activities happen in complex situations, for diverse reasons and motives, within multiple contexts, and for people of all walks of life.

Design as a Process—Buckminster Fuller's Idea

Although the dictionary suggests that *design* is both a noun and a verb, I propose here that design is first a verb, an action word. Design is an action that originates in what is known by the "design process," thus giving the concept priority as a verb. Ken Friedman has written extensively about design, design research and theory, and knowledge construction in design research. He defines design as a verb and provides a good analysis of Buckminster Fuller's notion of the design process as a series of steps grounded in search and research. Friedman suggests this is vital to how designers think in that the design process engages the designer in a particular way of thinking that moves ideas and concepts from something unknown toward a design solution.

The subjective process of search and research, Fuller outlines a series of steps:

teleology --> intuition --> conception --> apprehension --> comprehension --> experiment --> feedback -->

Under generalization and objective development leading to practices, he lists:

prototyping #1 --> prototyping #2 --> prototyping #3 --> production design --> production modification --> tooling --> production --> distribution --> installation --> maintenance --> service --> reinstallation --> replacement --> removal --> scrapping --> recirculation

For Fuller, the design process is a comprehensive sequence leading from teleology to practice and finally to regeneration. This last step, regeneration, creates a new stock of raw material on which the designer may again act.

Reference : Freidman, K. (2000). Creating design knowledge: from research into practice. IDATER 2000 Conference, Loughborough: Loughborough University.

Figure 1.2 Friedman's view of Buckminster Fuller's design process.

Designing as an Agent of Change

Design thus is a process that becomes a mechanism by which design thinking (reflection and research) and design doing (practice) transform ideas into viable possibilities and concrete solutions to situations and problems that are identified by a client, user, stakeholder, or any participant in the process. Designing is also the act of thinking and doing, critically understanding the issues, and finding ways to transform situations with multiple stakeholders.

In designing, reflective practice and change inspire, provoke, and charge thinking and doing. In their seminal book *The Design Way*, Nelson and Stolterman (2003) state that design, when understood as a transformative process, means that designs are founded on ideas about purpose, motivations, and change (pp. 3–29). Designing involves questioning the world around you and trying to make it better. To do that, designers must design using inquiry processes such as gathering information, researching the topic at hand, and analyzing that information as a means to identify and solve problems. However, strictly solving problems has not been always useful as a means to develop possibilities beyond the problem in front of us, nor is it in the best interests of change. For example, we may solve a problem yet create new ones that are a consequence of unintended actions. It is precisely this aspect of designing that Nelson and Stolterman discuss:

The focus on problems . . . as the primary justifiable trigger to taking action in human affairs has limited our ability to frame change as an outcome of intention and purpose. (p. 17)

From the perspective of Nelson and Stolterman, design thinking encompasses those characteristics that a designer has that allow for meaningful and thoughtful designs to be created. The designer must become a responsible person who makes decisions that encompass broader issues than the design product or environment alone.

Furthermore, Nelson and Stolterman (2003) develop the idea that:

to be a thoughtful and responsible designer, any general understanding of what design is ultimately about has to be challenged and critically analyzed by you—the individual designer, client, stakeholder—or anyone else affected by the design. . . . any understanding of the design should be the result of reflective practice, intellectual apperception and intentional choice. . . . an individual understanding of design. (p. 25)

Design thinking, according to Nelson and Stolterman, infuses inquiry and action (p. 2) and

the fundamentals of design thinking include: *desirata, interpretation and measurement, imagination and communication, judgment, composition and production, and care taking.* (p. 131)

Each is defined and, in essence, these characteristics are a means to initiate change through designing and initiating design acts.

While designing and design thinking are processes that require inquiry and action, and that infuse both knowledge-seeking with pragmatic issues of the every day, there are nuances when design inquiry is used for practice or when it is used for research in an academic setting. We will explore these ideas later on when we discuss the nature of knowledge and forms of research in academia and in industry.

What Is Meaning?

Another idea to explore is the concept of *meaning*, as in the Oxford English Dictionary definition:

meaning *noun* **1** what is meant by a word, idea or action; **2** worthwhile quality; purpose. Adjective expressive. (Oxford, 2001, p. 804)

Meanings are what we attach to the experiences and objects that we surround ourselves with in our daily lives. In our daily activities, we construct meanings constantly. Whether it is making meaning through simple daily tasks or writing a theoretical paper to explore a concept, we assign meanings to things, experiences, and ideas.

If we consider meaning in the context of design and space, for example, we might attribute values and meanings to the things we create as designers on the one hand, and different (or similar) meanings and values to the things and spaces as those who experience the same place on the other hand. We attribute individual meanings to places we live, to activities that we experience, and to the ways that we work or play, and these are all from multiple perspectives.

We construct meaning both as users of spaces and as the designers that create them, whether it is for ourselves or for others. When creating designs, for example, Nelson and Stolterman (2003) suggest that

> A design has meaning when we can see how it is connected to other things that we value. . . . [T]he meaning of an object can be ascertained by linking it with something of value, and something of value can glean meaning by linking it to something else of value. What really makes the difference is the nature of the linkage. (p. 273)

Both value and meaning are inherent concepts of designing. Nelson and Stolterman continue on to propose that a soulful design is one that is complete and in context with the meaning and value attributed to it. As they note:

> A design with a strong interconnection between value and meaning entertains the necessary conditions for our recognition of it as a conveyor of a soul. In this sense, soul is the animating essence of the original design parti. It denotes a design that has both intrinsic value and relational meaning. We experience this form of soul when we encounter a design with a unified coherence, in relationship to something giving it meaning. . . . [S]uch a design has a depth and complexity that are not easily revealed. Value is not something you can easily see without effort. (pp. 275–276)

This idea of meaning suggests that value is intrinsic to the design being created, and the wholeness of a design, in part, rests in how we receive it as recipients of the design and accept its values through the meanings we understand and appropriate. In essence, we attribute concepts of

- Value
- Meaning
- Wholeness
- Context

to the situations and contexts within which we engage in supporting experiences through the design and spaces that we create.

This implies that both design process and design inquiry are forms of "designerly ways of knowing" as proposed by Nigel Cross (2000) and as Justin Wilwerding examines in this chapter's theoretical paper later on.

What Is Space? Definitions and Prevailing Concepts

Space has many definitions and connotations and is, from the outset, a complex concept. For example, the Concise Oxford Dictionary defines space thus:

> **space** *noun* **1** unoccupied ground or area; **2** a free or unoccupied area or expanse; **3** the dimension of height, depth and width within which all things exist and move; **4** a blank between types of written words or characters; **5** (also **outer space**) the physical universe beyond the earth's atmosphere; **6** interval of time (indicating that it is short): "forty men died in the space of two days"; **7** the freedom and scope to live and develop as one wishes. *verb* position **1** (two or more items) at a distance from one another; **2** (to be spaced out) . . . become euphoric or disoriented, especially from taking drugs. We will explore these ideas in further detail, in particular in Chapter 2, and throughout the book, building on existing concepts and understanding potential alternative perspectives.

Although this definition is clear, it is also limited to framing certain concepts, as, for example, the concept of the limit of three dimensions. This definition limits the idea of spatial dimension as having the limits of height, width, and depth. However, later in the book, we will explore and propose alternate dimensional qualities of space. Some alternative ways of considering space include how space might be at once ephemeral yet real, exist in different ways, and is experienced beyond dimensional qualities that are finite. Space is both a theoretical idea and a physical construct. Space is at once experienced and occupied, used and lived in, theorized and conceptualized. We will explore these ideas in further detail throughout the book, building on existing concepts and understanding potential alternative perspectives.

We will be referring to both Friedman's and Nelson and Stolterman's ideas from time to time, as they are a foundation to how we understand design as a broader critical way to ground our thinking, the nature of design as research, the value of scientific inquiry from a design perspective, and what all this means in terms of spaces and their meanings.

We now turn to a general look at the nature of knowledge and of the paradigms that frame inquiry in general and design inquiry in particular.

THE NATURE OF INQUIRY AND CRITICAL THINKING

The Nature of Scientific Inquiry

There are many views of the nature of design inquiry and scientific inquiry, about how these intersect and how these are divergent concepts. Depending on the discipline and the stance, some scholars suggest that design must be apart from scientific inquiry, while others suggest design inquiry is research by its very nature.

However, as Friedman and others note, the research done to solve design problems is not research of a scientific nature, unless it is informed by scientific inquiry (Friedman 2000; Dickinson and Marsden 2009; Zeisel 2006). What constitutes this nature of scientific inquiry in design is, in part, what we will examine here.

An important goal of this book is to have you become engaged with critical thinking, and with design thinking as critical thinking, and in understanding the differences between scientific inquiry and critical design inquiry, and how these are examined within different disciplinary spaces. How do we go about building knowledge from understanding theoretical concepts, and how might this be understood in the context of the practical things that we may do or experience as designers or various participants in design situations?

Critical thinking requires building theoretical concepts, analyzing and criticizing current ideas, and considering new possibilities. Current ideas include theoretical constructions, or the positions taken over time by researchers and academics about how they understand their lived or natural environment. Theories and assumptions usually frame the way that we understand our particular world, and how we go about constructing a particular world view, whether in science or in philosophy. When we make sense of our world, we undertake to reflect on what goes on around us using critical thinking.

About A Priori Assumptions in Knowledge Creation

A *priori assumptions* are assumptions made or truths believed to be unquestioned that have been gleaned from assumptions. Quite often theories or assumptions are made and proposed, and these are taken to be absolute truth; meaning, that what has been said is accepted as truth without putting the truth into question, or understanding the framework within which the theory or assumption was made. By questioning the way we see the world around us and when we engage in critical thinking, we become engaged with understanding a particular idea or phenomenon and then we question assumptions. *A priori assumptions* are accepted truths about a particular idea, truth, or belief that is then understood to be knowledge.

The Nature of Knowledge

Developing new knowledge is at the core of any work done in science, or in any discipline that develops its foundations. To be able to understand and apply design thinking and doing critically, we need to first understand the role of knowledge and how this is understood in terms of research. We may do research when engaged in using the design processes in various disciplines, or we might engage in research and use research to help us develop a product or service. We may also be interested in understanding the phenomenon of a particular way that people experience space. Each form of inquiry has as its root some form of research.

In this next section we will explore ideas about research and design by considering the nature of knowledge, how research is done, and what this means in considering design/spaces.

Epistemology: How Design Knowledge Is Produced

We begin this discussion with a general development of what constitutes knowledge in a field or discipline. **Knowledge** evolved in many forms and in many ways, from very theoretical and scientific approaches to knowledge-seeking to philosophical and ethical ways of understanding the nature of our world.

What is knowledge in **design research**? Knowledge itself is a term with multiple meanings, and people develop, acquire, or construct knowledge in different ways. The role of research in general is to construct knowledge that informs practice, develops theory, or creates new ideas of the entire range of activities and experiences that create the design considered. The role of **academic research** is, in part, to create new forms of knowledge to innovate, move disciplines forward, and construct ways of knowing, as well as to lay evidence-based design foundations to inform design practice (Friedman 1997; Friedman 2002; Nelson and Stolterman 2003; Nussbaumer 2009).

Types of Knowledge and Knowledge Claims

In a philosophical analysis of the nature of knowledge, Dan O'Brien proposes that knowledge is built upon belief (O'Brien, 2006, p. 11) and that this is based on three suppositions of truth, justification and belief. O'Brien suggests:

> The three conditions are individually necessary for knowledge—knowledge always consists in justified, true, belief—and they are jointly sufficient for knowledge, that is, you always have knowledge when these three conditions are met. (p. 11)

O'Brien suggests that all three aspects must align for knowledge to be true:

> We shall start with the plausible suggestion that we have justified beliefs when we have good reason to think our beliefs are true, that is when we have good evidence to support them. The roots of such an account can be found in Plato, in dialogues that were written some 2,000 years ago. (p. 11)

He continues but proposes that this is a starting point, and that it is a challengeable assumption as well. O'Brien positions two types of knowledge acquisition: (1) the nature of knowledge as derived of reason as *a priori* knowledge and (2) knowledge derived from experience as *a posteriori* knowledge.

Using the example of a book on a shelf, he helps us to understand the notion of knowledge and reason as follows:

Take a rectangular book off your bookshelf and look at the front cover. What is its predominant colour and how many sides does it have? In answering these questions, you now know two things about this book, and these two facts illustrate an important distinction between two ways we have of acquiring knowledge. . . . [Y]ou do not need to look at a book to know how many sides it has. You know that rectangles have four sides just by thinking about what it is to be a rectangle. You acquire such knowledge using only your powers of reasoning: you do not have to consider the evidence of your senses. Knowledge that is justified by experience is called a posteriori or empirical knowledge. Knowledge for which experience does not play a justificatory role is called a priori knowledge. (p. 25)

A priori knowledge is then deciphered in different ways. For example, in her article "Mapping the Meaning of Knowledge in Design Research," Kristina Neiderrer positions *a priori* knowledge as propositional knowledge, that which we know to be true (Neiderrer, 2007), while in a business context, Amin and Cohendet suggest that *a priori* knowledge is that which is possessed (Amin & Cohendet, 2004).

O'Brien offers several examples to clearly help us understand the concepts about truth. He suggests that there are four claims of truth:

Various philosophers have claimed that the following are known *a priori*.
(1) Both simple mathematical truths such as 2 + 2 = 4; and ones more complex such as Pythagoras' theorem. . . .
(2) Truths that are captured by definitions such as: All bachelors are unmarried men.
(3) Metaphysical claims. . . .
(4) Ethical truths such as murder is wrong. . . .

There is a sense in which experience is involved in the acquisition of all beliefs. To know that bachelors are unmarried men, I need to know the meaning of "bachelor," "unmarried," and "men," and such linguistic understanding is acquired through lessons and instruction, practices that involve experience of some kind. Experience, then, does play a certain role in the acquisition of a priori knowledge: it is involved in our coming to understand the language in which knowledge is articulated. (p. 25)

O'Brien then discusses rational philosophers such as René Descartes as those who position *a priori* truths about the nature of knowledge.

Positivism and Rationalism: Creating Dualisms
Each discipline positions knowledge claims when developing a particular knowledge stance. For example, in education, business, or design research, what is considered as valid knowledge is often measured against how René Descartes's proposed knowledge

should be constructed. For example, in education theory, Raymond Horn (2008) argues that Descartes's philosophy is a rationalist view that has as its premise the Cartesian dualism we understand and have inherited in philosophy and science. Using concepts proposed by Cherryholmes, Horn suggests:

> Positivist traditions of teaching and learning found . . . the determination of valid knowledge, appropriate inquiry methods and appropriate knowledge acquisition is grounded in the tradition of Cartesian dualism, empiricism and positivism. Generally, these rationalist traditions promote the assumption that physical and human phenomenon can be objectively studied and manipulated with great degree of certainty when rational thinking and science are used to uncover the causes and effects that underlie the dilemma.
>
> Initially, in a rationalist attempt to reconcile faith and reason René Descartes theorized that the subjective reality of the mind and the objective reality of matter are forever separate. Building upon Descartes' theory, the classical empiricists promoted the idea that the true or objective knowledge can only be uncovered through sensory experience. The radical dualism of Descartes separated knowledge into a binary classification of *a priori* knowledge, or knowledge of innate ideas that is acquired through the mind's employment of reason, and *a posteriori* knowledge . . . knowledge of the objective world that is acquired through observation. Cartesian dualism further resulted in the bifurcation of knowledge and human activity into oppositional categories such as fact/value, objectives/subjective, rational/irrational, analytic/synthetic, schema/content, theory/practice, ends/means . . . that have long characterized modern analytic and scientific thought (Cherryholmes, 1999, p. 42, in Horn 2008, p. 440).

It is this dualism of knowledge that has been at the root of the separation of objective and subjective forms of knowledge, and that has contributed to the oppositions in much theory and knowledge that has been built on the rationalist tradition. This tradition has been exemplified in the scientific method, also originated by René Descartes.

Obstacles of A Priori Knowledge Claims to Knowledge Seeking: Considerations in Business and Design

If we take a contemporary application of these ideas of *a priori* knowledge claims in terms of business management, Amin and Cohendet (2004) suggest that four types of knowledge exist in a "knowledge-reduced-to-information" approach that hampers knowledge seeking, and wherein the actors involved in the process are not considered relevant (Amin & Cohendet 2004, p. 17). These four theoretical obstacles include the following:

(1) . . . the vision of knowledge resulting from the accumulation of information as a linear process; (2) the hypothesis that any form of knowledge can be made codifiable; (3) the vision that knowledge is limited to individuals; (4) knowledge is limited to something that people possess. (p. 17)

In this criticism, Amin and Cohendet contend, for example, that valid forms of knowledge are ones that are codified—meaning that these are forms of knowledge that arise from methods that describe patterns of human activity through codified forms that exist in scientific methods. Codified methods are methods that separate object from subject and are supported by the notion that codified knowledge is somehow more valid than knowledge acquired from subjective, or *a posteriori*, knowledge acquisitions approaches.

However, there are many forms of knowledge that can be documented through other means, such as experiential or tacit forms of knowledge, forms that are not able to be studied in positivist modes per se, just as there are certain types of knowledge that are derived through experiences that are not necessarily codifiable but that can be interpreted as meaningful and trustworthy in philosophical or theoretical terms (Neiderrer, 2007; Poldma, 2003). These more tacit forms of knowledge rely on people's broader intuitive and sensory perceptions and are usually experienced *a posteriori*.

The experiences of spaces, for example, are based on people's intuitive and sensory perceptions in real-life settings, and these cannot be studied *a priori*. Whether or not the experiences can be considered as research and whether these can be documented as such are different questions altogether. Experiences are tacit, and yet very real, for the people who have them. Experiences are also at the foundation of how meanings are constituted by people.

About Empirical Knowledge

In its simplest sense, new knowledge is derived through various forms of research, and in our Western society, we generally have tended to understand research to mean scientific or empirical research that is built from codified knowledge. When we do research in a physics laboratory, for example, we are creating **empirical knowledge**, knowledge based on evidence that we have tested on objects of research for one purpose or another. All knowledge claims fall into one of several paradigms, or categories. Let's examine these constructs next.

PARADIGMS IN SCIENCE AND RESEARCH

In essence, all research done to develop new knowledge falls into two primary modes of research and one of several paradigms. First, research is usually done to search out problems and issues of the real world (Crotty, 2000), from (1) an ontological or an epistemological perspective and/or (2) within paradigms that position the researcher within a particular stance. For example, Egon Guba and Yvonne Lincoln (1994) in their seminal paper "Competing Paradigms of Qualitative Research" outline their view of four major competing paradigms in current research:

- Positivism
- Post-positivism
- Critical theory
- Constructivism

In essence, and as Guba and Lincoln describe, positivism and post-positivism have as their root deductive modes of research derived from empiricism and logical positivism philosophies. These consider the object of research as a separate entity from the subject, thereby separating object from subject in the Cartesian sense. As we explored earlier, this approach is rooted in Descartes and his theories of scientific method and the separation of objective and subjective forms of knowledge-making.

The second two, evolved from postmodern and critical theory philosophies, are critical theory and constructivism. There are multiple modes of constructing research within these paradigms (Guba & Lincoln, 1996, pp. 105–106) because in large part these have evolved, particularly in the latter part of the twentieth century, alongside political and social movements of certain eras, and in response to the need to recognize the value of the subject as part of the research process.

Object and Subject Dichotomy in Research

Deriving from the era of Descartes, the separation of object from subject in scientific modes of research has become an important dichotomy of science (Woolgar, 1988). Design inquiry engages and eludes this dichotomy, as it may engage both empirical/objective and empirical/subjective modes, and thus human activity, when studied as subjectively approached research. But before discussing design inquiry specifically, let's examine each paradigm a little further. There is a dichotomy between design and science that we must understand, and how design inquirers position this dichotomy.

The Nature of Empiricism and Logical Positivism

To understand what dichotomy exists between design and science, we must go back in history and philosophy to understand Descartes's notion of reason-positioned science as objectified knowledge aligned with positivism, and delineate the issue of design as an inquiry space.

What Is Empiricism?

Empiricism is a principle at the root of positivism and positivist modes of science. For example, in *Connected Knowledge*, Alan Cromer (1996) defines empiricism as a principle and its relation to positivism as follows:

> Empiricism is the philosophical principle that knowledge must be based on the evidence of our senses, rather than on the pronouncements of priests and prophets. At its extreme, empiricism denies the existence of any reality beyond the senses. . . . The philosophy of science that emerged from the Vienna Circle is called *logical positivism*. Positivism is another term for empiricism, and the qualifier *logical* softens the pure empiricism of Mach by allowing the theoretical structure of modern physics. (Cromer, p. 20)

This basic idea has defined science in its positivist mode since the time of Descartes, and this becomes the baseline for what we understand to be scientific research.

That being said, and as Friedman notes in some detail (Friedman, 1997), many alternative empirical forms of research have evolved over the last century that counteract these positivist empiricist modes and that account for subjective and tacit forms of knowledge, and we will evolve these ideas a little later on.

The Evolution of Postmodernism and Constructivist Modes of Research

It is impossible in the scope of this book to outline the development of science and philosophy of knowledge that has evolved over the past several hundred years. In the next chapters, authors Melles, Feast, Nelson, and Wilwerding, among others, present diverse perspectives on how the evolution of positivism, postmodern thinking, emergent philosophical views, and alternatives, such as pragmatism and critical theories, has allowed for different ways of understanding the relationship between positivist approaches to research and alternative viewpoints with regard to design and aesthetics. However, to be able to understand the positioning of these modes within the paradigms outlined thus far, we can examine the emergence of critical theory and constructivism as particular forms of theorizing more subjective modes of experience.

About Critical Theory and Constructivist Modes

Lincoln and Guba (1996) provide a clear explication of the emerging paradigms of postmodernism and constructivist modes of thinking that counter positivist modes of thought. They suggest that these emerging views of doing research have sprung, in part, from voices that have brought into question the quantitative approaches that have evolved in science, wherein the object of research is reduced, in a positivist approach, to a comparable variable, or, in essence, "their outcomes can be properly applied only in other similarly truncated or contextually stripped situations: another laboratory, for example." (p. 106)

The essence of constructivist and critical theorist modes of knowledge is the necessity to engage in understanding people and the meanings that they attribute to the activities that they pursue in everyday life, that this happens *a posteriori* in knowledge construction within the situations that these activities occur, and that it is not possible to study by positivist modes in *a priori* situations alone. For example, consider the critical issue that Guba and Lincoln uncover:

> Human behaviour, unlike that of physical objects, cannot be understood without reference to the meanings and purposes attached by human actors to their activities. Qualitative data, it is asserted, can provide rich insight into human behavior. (p. 106)

In essence, it is through the *a posteriori* understanding of the activities, experiences, and narratives of these various activities that we can uncover meaning and purposes that are not possible to grasp through codified knowledge alone. As Guba and Lincoln suggest, qualitative approaches afford this type of study and account for both modes of knowledge acquisition.

Objects and Subjects of Research

While many researchers use empirical modes of inquiry that situate the subject as an object outside the realm of human subjectivity, other paradigms have emerged over the past two centuries to provide alternate modes of inquiry. These include critical and constructivist modes of inquiry as we have discussed thus far. In essence, in these modes of inquiry, the object of research is no longer split from the researcher outside the object of inquiry. In critical and constructivist modes of research, the phenomenon itself becomes the essence of inquiry and includes participants' voices, which may also include the researcher. In other words, a combined subject/object is part of an entire phenomenon of study in an *a posteriori* acquisition of knowledge. Let's define each paradigm in more detail.

About Critical Theory

The evolution of critical and constructivist modes of inquiry has, in simple terms, been an outgrowth of reaction to positivist modes of inquiry that position the human being outside of the scientific mode of inquiry. Guba and Lincoln outline a definition of **critical theory** as follows:

The term critical theory is (for us) a blanket term denoting a set of several alternative paradigms, including additionally (but not limited to) neo-Marxism, feminism, materialism, and participatory inquiry. Indeed, critical theory may itself be usefully subdivided into three substrands: structuralism, postmodernism and a blending of these two. (p. 109)

Critical theory, as defined by Guba and Lincoln, has as its basis the reality of historic context, and the epistemology of an interactivity between the investigator and the object of study, which becomes the investigated, and in essence is at once a subject/object. Guba and Lincoln suggest that research done in this mode provides "findings that are value mediated" (p. 110) meaning that the researcher and the researched are intertwined and separate entities, unlike in positivist modes where they are separated and separate entities.

About Constructivism

On the other hand, constructivism is defined as modes of inquiry that are based on the ideas that our reality is constructed socially and based on our experiences (Guba & Lincoln, 2001, p 110; Vaikla-Poldma, 1999). Investigator and investigated interact and change and transform the subject/object of study. According to Guba and Lincoln (1994), unlike critical theorists whose purpose of inquiry is "the critique and transformation of the social, political, cultural, ethnic and gender structures that constrain and exploit humankind, by engagement in confrontation, even conflict" (p. 112), constructivism's aim of inquiry is "understanding and reconstruction of the constructions that people (including the inquirer) initially hold, aiming towards consensus but still open to new interpretation as information and sophistication improve" (p. 113).

Each paradigm underlies the position of the researcher in research and in practice, values that underlie what designers do and how they do it. In research, value positions guide both the research context and in particular the research methods, and the ways that the objects/subjects of study are framed within methodological choices and research questions as these are formed.

In summary, I defer to Crotty, Guba, and Lincoln specifically due to the simple terms each uses to define these basic concepts in theory-building in the acquisition of knowledge. There are many other perspectives and constructions that may be examined in light of these basic terms and concepts.

We will now turn to an examination of what constitutes the application of these ideas to critical thinking from a design perspective and how we might build a critical design discourse.

DEVELOPING A CRITICAL DESIGN DISCOURSE

To be able to discuss meanings and understand the diverse perspectives in this book, it is useful to understand what constitutes a **critical discourse**. As we have just seen, critical theoretical perspectives provide the backdrop for understanding knowledge, paradigms, and the positions taken by researchers when they engage in investigating particular research questions. If we now apply these theoretical ideas to design inquiry, we might consider how underlying paradigms provide context in theoretical constructions we create and what perspectives we use.

About Theory and Practice

To be able to frame this next discussion with some clarity, we must also define the framework for our ideas. When we design, we do so with the underlying assumption that the designing occurs best when supported by research. However, research when designing is different than research when creating a scientific experiment or when studying people in their lived experiences *a posteriori*.

The third element is how we frame our design activities. Design, by its very nature, is a pragmatic exercise: we design in the real world for practical and pragmatic purposes. As such, we may take a pragmatic stance from the outset, as the research we do about design activities is often grounded in practice-based situations in the real world, when these offer transformational changes as their goals, as we saw earlier with the discussions by Nelson and Stolterman (2003). This type of research is of a different type, grounded in the pragmatic, everyday situations of designing.

Information Gathering versus Research

In practice, when we do research in many **design domains**, we are doing what is more commonly known as **information gathering**, finding out things that inform our designs, that allow the designer to formulate thoughtful solutions, and that allow for alternative possibilities to be envisaged. (Botti-Salinsky, 2009) We understand the various issues and contexts surrounding a project; we make choices with the possibilities we uncover or situate within our work, from whatever perspective we hold and within varying contexts. Each dynamic has its particular characteristics, and every designer intensely researches all the parameters particular to a design problem, no matter what the domain.

Defining Notions of Research in Design Practices versus Academia or Science

One of the problems in understanding research is the very definition and use of the word, particularly in the design disciplines. Practitioners might research products and services and become informed on how to frame the ways that their solutions will fit with the particular needs of the client or user, based on the information that they have gathered. These needs, expressed through the form of a brief or design program, govern how the designer responds to problems and issues both functionally and aesthetically. Research of this nature is usually understood as information gathering (Botti-Salinsky, 2009; Poldma, 2009) wherein information is gathered to inform a design program for a particular context or client-driven need. Critical thinking may (or may not) be a component of this information gathering.

Evidence-based Design

Evidence-based design, on the other hand, is informed design based on empirical research in the form of evidence that has also been done in the search for a more critically constructed picture of the issue at hand. Evidence-based design usually implies that scientific evidence supports the design that is produced, normally statistical data. Some design problems use evidence-based research, while others do not, and some forms of evidence-based design use research methods, while others use information-gathering techniques (Botti-Salinksy, 2009; Nussbaumer, 2009). At what point is a design based on information gathering, informed by evidence, or guided by research, and what forms does this take? At what point is design critical in how it is constructed and framed?

Ideally, design problems are solved using problem-solving methods. As Friedman suggests, "A good design process must embrace the aesthetic as well as the scientific" (1997, p. 5). These stances must be supported by critical theory and inquiry, where problems are constructed and solved using problem-solving methods that are supported by depth of research and questions asked about the issues at hand. What constitutes research, then, is supported by critical inquiry.

Research thus becomes the root of what we do to, in part, inform designing. Next let's look at the concept of research and its definitions.

What Is Research? Defining Types of Research

In his seminal paper "Theory Construction in Design Research: Criteria, Approaches, and Methods," Ken Friedman (2003) proposes that as the complexity of world issues increases, "Design now plays a role in the general evolution of the environment, and the design process takes on new meaning" (p. 509). Friedman suggests that designing has moved from finite creation of artefacts and built environment characteristics toward more complex requirements "requiring systematic and comprehensive understanding."

Defining Research and Three Forms

Friedman (2003) defines and describes the concept of research succinctly as follows:

> The word research is closely linked to the word and concept of search . . . [T]he prefix *re* . . . emphasizes and strengthens the core concept of research. The key meanings are to "look into or over carefully or thoroughly in an effort to find or discover something, to read thoroughly, to look at as if to discover or penetrate intention or nature, to uncover, find, or come to know by inquiry or scrutiny, to make painstaking investigation of examination (p. 1059) (p. 510).

Friedman also identifies three fundamental frames of research: basic, applied, and clinical research and provides the placement of design research done within the context of design practice. According to Friedman:

> **Basic research** involves the search for general principles. These principles are abstracted and generalized to cover a variety of situations and cases. Basic research generates theory on several levels.
>
> This may involve macro level theories covering wide areas or fields, midlevel theories covering specific ranges of issues or micro level theories focused on narrow questions. General principles often have broad applications beyond their field of origin, and their generative nature sometimes gives them surprising power.
>
> **Applied research** adapts to findings of basic research to classes of problems. It may also involve developing and testing theories for these classes of problems. Applied research tends to be midlevel or micro level research. At the same time, applied research may develop or generate questions that become the subject of basic research.
>
> **Clinical research** involves specific cases. Clinical research applies the findings of basic research and applied research to specific situations. It may also generate and test new questions, and it may test the findings of basic and applied research. Clinical research may also develop and generate questions that become the subject of basic research or applied research.
>
> Any of the three frames of research may generate questions for other frames. Each may test theories and findings of other kinds of research. It is important to note that clinical research generally involves specific forms of professional engagement. In the rough and tumble of daily practice, most design practice is restricted to clinical research. (Friedman, 2003, p. 510)

This definition of research clearly demarcates various research forms. In the design disciplines, as in academia, there are many different types of research methods that are used, some clinical, basic, and/or applied, and this compounds our understanding of research in the design disciplines.

Confusing Issues: Why Design Practice Is Not Research

However, problems arise when design practitioners confuse what they do as research. As Friedman (2002) suggests:

> Research is a way of asking questions. All forms of research ask questions, basic, applied, and clinical. The different forms and levels of research ask questions in different ways.
>
> One of the problems in understanding design research emerges specifically from this distinction. Design practitioners are always involved in some form of research, but practice is not research. . . .
>
> Research asks questions in a systematic way. The systems vary by field and purpose. There are many kinds of research: hermeneutic, naturalistic inquiry, statistical, analytical, mathematical, sociological, ethnographic, ethnological, biological, medical, chemical, and many more. They draw on many methods and traditions. Each has its own foundations and values. All involve some form of systematic inquiry, and all involve a formal level of theorizing and inquiry beyond the specific research at hand. (pp. 10–11)

Each form of inquiry uses different paradigms, tools, and research frames, some overlapping with others, and in various domains as Friedman suggests.

Just recently, colleague, architect, and professor Michel Raynaud and I were discussing this issue, and how often design practice research is confused with academic research at a PhD level. We were discussing how practitioners who are interested in developing research questions at the PhD level apply their version of research as opposed to developing a critical inquiry mode. Michel noted that this confusion can be avoided by posing this assumption at the outset:

> Research is not meant to be practical, but to be knowledgeable. It is not what I, as a researcher, want to do, but rather what I want to know.
> (Michel Raynaud, translation from French, conversation 5.7.12)

Critical Design: As Designing

If we think about what we do when we design with a critical perspective, we see that first we collect information to inform us of what possible ideas exist, we then try and implement ideas and possibilities and test them against the data we have collected, and finally we implement solutions based on critical and informed judgment. As designers, we do engage in considering design situations and problems critically, when we use design thinking. The nuance is to know when this is practice and when this constitutes research in the academic sense. And yet, we are confronted with several dilemmas here, such as:

- Designing has as its root information gathering, and this is not research as is understood in academia.
- Problems arise due to designers' understanding *research* to mean "research" as they might do for a project or problem-solving situation.
- Clinical and empirical research have as goals the generating of theories and suppositions to describe and explain the phenomena being studied.
- Design has as its basis the understanding of researched information in order to be able to transform and make changes, or to solve specific problems aimed at improving situations (Simon in Nelson & Stolterman, 2003).
- These propositions make evident the confusion between what we want to do and what we want to know.

Design as Design, Design as Research, Design as Knowledge— Some Possibilities and Ideas

Different forms of research develop different forms of knowledge. While at its root all research is looking into problems, research for the ends of a PhD is not the same as research for the development of products and services in industry, or for designing spaces to solve practical issues. However, one can inform the other and vice versa: theory can be used to inform practice, and practice often allows for reflections in theory. And yet both theory and practice are concepts at the root of research and at the root of design inquiry (Nelson & Stolterman, 2003). What is searched for as an end is also almost as vital as the form or frame of the research itself.

Developing Knowledge Through Different Types of Research Spaces

Industry research is often done through research and development (R&D), whether this is new product design and development of systems and processes for technology or manufacturing. By contrast, traditional academic research has usually been separate from industry in the design fields in particular, and has in fact, lagged behind industry, in part due to business pressure in the design of the built environment that forces change quickly. New spaces of knowledge might include using design research as a means of informing industry through the more pragmatic ways that design provides creative thinking and systematic ways to engage in the problems of innovating that industry requires. Both R&D and various forms of academic research each have a role to play in bringing useful knowledge to industry.

Connected Knowledge in Design Research, Design Inquiry, and Design Thinking

If we return to the fundamental definitions we provided earlier, and in light of these theoretical positions, we can summarize that designing, as in, for example, designing interior spaces, has as its foundation change and transformation through the active engagement and experiences of stakeholders, clients, and users. Sometimes this is grounded in real-time, lived experiences, which are forms of tacit knowledge. To be able to build knowledge through experience, we must think about what philosophical underpinning we want for such knowledge in design research.

There are many forms of design inquiry. The design process might at times use information gathering and at other times, the process may include inquiry, research, analysis, synthesis, designing, problem solving, and numerous actions that are dynamic and changing and all requiring reflection, judgment, and intention-of-action (Jones in Mitchell, 1993; Nelson & Stolterman, 2003; Friedman, 1997; Wiegand, 2006; Vaikla-Poldma, 2003). This design inquiry is usually composed of three components:

1. Designs that result from the discovery of something new or unique using the design process
2. Designs as oriented by systems, ideas, or problems that demand solutions
3. Designs as guided by human psychological or social needs, activities, and experiences

For example, for designers and in the design of interior spaces, all of these components of designs may be part of the design problem, often at the same time. We might be interested in creating new ways of living, working, or playing; solving problems in the workplace; adding economic value through design to the purchase of goods; or creating a more efficient work environment. And finally, we do some or all of these things in response to the intimate needs of users and clients, sometimes one and the same but often not.

Design Inquiry as Transformative Change

When designers use design thinking and design processes combined with inquiry and action, they engage in design as an agent of change. Design thinking, when used in a particular way that encompasses aesthetic/creative thinking, business know-how, problem solving, and a sensitivity to ethical, cultural, or social situations, is broad and ethical as long as these approaches are combined with the designer as being in service to a particular client or user (Nelson & Stolterman, 2003).

Some may refer to this type of process as problem seeking (Pena, 1977; 2006), or inquiry by design (Zeisel, 2006). Nelson & Stolterman refer to the idea of design inquiry as an action-oriented process that encompasses characteristics of "the real, the true and the ideal" (pp. 38–39). For example, they state that

> The real, as a focus of inquiry, is essential to the ultimate goal of creating the *not-yet-existing*. It is about helping to operationalize the creation of the *not-yet-real* and the particular." (p. 39)

This may also be understood as the virtual aspect of design, meaning that we can see problems and issues in diverse types of spaces before others might see them. Designers can understand the meanings of the possibilities we may design, and be able to visualize concepts or solutions for the spaces within which we are working, most often collectively with stakeholders, clients, or users. Design processes are ways of critical and creative thinking that can change the situation we understand requires change. These processes become the means by which we create responses to design situations that require realizing new ways of living, working, or engaging in the physical and sensual world.

Ultimately, design inquiry, whether based on design situated problems, research questions, real-life situations, or specific contexts, relies on search and research, understanding the position of the researcher, and framing both questions and responses appropriately through a critical discourse. This means reading, writing, and developing logical, thoughtful arguments and framing research ideas appropriately.

THE CHAPTER ARTICLES

In the following theoretical papers, provocations, and perspectives, we will examine these ideas in the application of examples. Justin Wilwerding explores design as a metaphysical framework and how theory is built in the design domains. Wilwerding addresses issues of design as a scientific form of inquiry and how knowledge is positioned in the design disciplines, and reviews how theorists account for design as a form of knowledge production in knowledge management and industrial design, as a predecessor to newer disciplinary developments about design inquiry spaces such as those in interior design. Wilwerding proposes six design philosophical foundations to guide the evolution of design as a science for interior design, examining and complementing Friedman's suggestion of a design science as foundational to grounding design inquiry modes.

The Provocation proposed by Hanna Mendoza and Tom Matyók considers how disciplinary boundaries are changing in light of emerging liquidity of disciplinary stances. Mendoza and Matyók dissect issues of disciplinary boundaries, how design disciplines by nature are liquid, what this means, and how both specificity and transdisciplinarity allow for critical and new conceptualizations of how design exists in the real world. They propose a "Third Knowledge Culture" for what could be and discuss how this creates values and meanings that suit the emerging state of the world.

The Dialogues and Perspectives segment is the first part of two conversations with Harold Nelson. Nelson is renowned architect, researcher, and author with Erik Stolterman of the seminal book *The Design Way*. He examines the issue of design inquiry and how this differs from scientific inquiry, and provides a perspective of the role and intention of design inquiry. Nelson proposes that design inquiry infuses components that "results in knowledge for action" and includes tacit forms of *a posteriori* knowledge that lie outside objective scientific inquiry. As Nelson suggests, theory and practice merge together and one supports and is symbiotic with the other.

REFERENCES

Botti-Salinksy, R. (2009). *Programming and Research Skills and Techniques for Interior Designers*. New York: Fairchild Publications.

Cromer, A. (1997). *Connected Knowledge: Science, Philosophy, and Education*. Oxford: Oxford University Press.

Crotty, M. (1998). *The Foundations of Social Research: Meaning and Perspective in the Research Process*. Thousand Oaks, CA: Sage Publications.

Friedman, K. (1997). Design Science and Design Education. In P. McGrory (Ed.), *The Challenge of Complexity* (pp. 54–72). Helsinki: University of Art and Design, Helsinki UIAH.

Friedman, K. (2003) Theory Construction in Design Research: Criteria, Approaches, and Methods. Updated version of a paper originally published in J. Shakelton & S. Durling (Eds.), *Common Ground: Proceedings of the 2002 Design Research Society International Conference* (pp. 388–414), London, UK, September 5–7, 2002, Stoke-on-Trent, UK: Staffordshire University Press. Update printed in Design Studies Vol. 24, No. 6. Great Britain: Elsevrier Ltd.

Friedman, K. (2000). Creating Design Knowledge: From Research into Practice. *IDATER* (pp. 5–32). Loughborough, UK: Loughborough University.

Friedman, K. (2003). Theory Construction in Design Research: Criteria, Approaches, and Methods. *Design Studies 24*, 507–522.

Guba, E. G., & Lincoln, Y. S. (1994.) Competing Paradigms in Qualitative Research, in Denzin, N. K., & Lincoln, Y. S. (Eds.) *Handbook of Qualitative Research* (pp. 105–117). London: Sage Publications.

Horn, R. A., & Kincheloe, J. (Eds.). (2007). *Praeger Handbook of Education and Psychology*. Westport, CT: Greenwood Publication Group.

Merriam-Webster Dictionary. 2012. Merriam-Webster Dictionary. Encyclopedia Britannica Online. URL: http://www.britannica.com/ Accessed 2012 December 12.

Nelson, H., & Stolterman, E. (2003). *The Design Way: Intentional Change in an Unpredictable World. Foundations and Fundamentals of Design Competence*. Englewood Cliffs, NJ: Technology Publications.

Nussbaumer, L. (2009). *Evidence-Based Design for Interior Designers*. New York: Fairchild Publications.

O'Brien, D. (2006). *An Introduction to the Theory of Knowledge*. Cambridge, UK: Polity Press.

Pena, W. (1977). *Problem-Seeking: An Architectural Programming Planner*. Houston, TX: CBI Publishing.

Poldma, T. (2009). *Taking Up Space: Exploring the Design Process*. New York: Fairchild Publications.

Toffler, A. (1970). *Future Shock*. New York: Random House.

Vaikla-Poldma, T. (2003.) An Investigation of Learning and Teaching Processes in an Interior Design Class: An Interpretive and Contextual Inquiry. Unpublished doctoral thesis, McGill University, Montreal, Quebec, Canada.

Zeisel, J. 2006. *Inquiry by Design: Environment/Behaviour/Neuroscience in Architecture, Interiors, Landscape, and Planning*. New York: W. W. Norton & Company,

Some work has already been done in relating the aggregate of design disciplines to determine a philosophical foundation for design as a discipline based upon clear definitions. These disciplines assert that design, while it possesses elements that are related to the natural sciences, social sciences, and humanities, also possesses significant dissimilarities that make the definition of design as a discipline unlike any of these other fields of study. This groundwork seems to be a logical starting point for beginning to address the definitions and concepts that will provide the superstructure for a philosophy of science for the discipline of interior design, a discipline specifically concerned with the interior spaces that people inhabit, and also a very recent discipline in relative historic terms, among the various design disciplines.

Disciplinary Historic Evolution of Design and Designerly Ways of Knowing

Beginning in the late 1970s and early 1980s, several design scholars began to examine the academic trajectory that promoted the humanities and sciences in educational institutions, and how higher education has generally given short shrift to the ontology of other fields of study that, while tangentially related, may have unique ways of defining **disciplinarity** and other approaches to defining the components of a philosophy of science. In the first issue of the journal *Design Studies*, Bruce Archer (1979) initiated a series of articles by various design scholars intended to discuss and define the questions surrounding the disciplinarity of **Design** with a metaphysical definition as a basis for the construction of design as a discipline. Archer noted that between the fourteenth and eighteenth centuries, craft guilds steadily lost their dominance, as universities evolved out of monasteries and became the dominant educational institution. The subjects that were traditional parts of the clerical education became the dominant subjects of study; literacy and the humanities evolving out of biblical translation; philology and hermeneutics, and science evolving out of astronomy and the churches' concerns for cosmology. Left behind was education in the process of making and the development of practical technology originally championed within the guild structure. Archer (1979) proposed that a third academic culture be defined in addition to the sciences and humanities:

> Design . . . is defined as the area of human experience, skill and understanding that reflects man's concern with the apprecia-

tion and adaption of his surroundings in the light of his material and spiritual needs. In particular, though not exclusively, it relates with configuration, composition, meaning, value and purpose in man-made phenomena. (p. 20)

Following Archer's examination of disciplinarity, Nigel Cross (1982) continued to examine the issue in his important work "Designerly Ways of Knowing." Cross (1982) provides more detail regarding the manner in which the academic cultures of the sciences and humanities differ from that of design:

If we contrast the sciences, the humanities, and design under each aspect, we may become clearer of what we mean by design, and what is particular to it.
- The phenomenon of study in each culture is
  - in the sciences: the natural world
  - in the humanities: human experience
  - in design: the man-made world
- The appropriate methods in each culture are
  - in the sciences: controlled experiment, classification, analysis
  - in the humanities: analogy, metaphor, criticism, evaluation
  - in design: modeling, pattern-formation, synthesis
- The values of each culture are
  - in the sciences: objectivity, rationality, neutrality, and a concern for "truth"
  - in the humanities: subjectivity,

imagination, commitment, and a concern for "justice"
- in design: practicality, ingenuity, empathy, and a concern for "appropriateness" (pp. 221–222)

Cross also identifies several unique aspects to the manner in which designers know (epistemology) or the manner in which they study, research and address problems. Cross notes:

I identified five aspects of designerly ways of knowing:
- Designers tackle "ill-defined" problems. (*Metaphysics*)
- Their mode of problem-solving is "solution-focused." (*Epistemology*)
- Their mode of thinking is "constructive." (*Logic*)
- They use "codes" that translate abstract requirements into concrete objects. (*Logic*)
- They use these codes to both "read" and "write" in "object languages." (*Logic*) (p. 226; emphasis added)

Cross's thesis defined major elements of a philosophy of design from metaphysics to epistemology and logic. Beyond the identification of philosophical tenets, there are two further significant contributions in Cross's work. First, he detailed the nature of design problems as wicked or ill-defined, and as such noted that:

They are not the same as the "puzzles" that scientists, mathematicians and other scholars set themselves. They are not problems for which all the necessary information is, or ever can be, available to the problem-solver. They are therefore not susceptible to exhaustive analysis, and there can never be a guarantee that "correct" solution-focused strategy is clearly preferable to go on analyzing "the problem," but the designer's task is to produce "the solution." It is only in terms of a conjectured solution that the problem can be contained within manageable bounds. (p. 224)

This is not to say that some aspects of design may not fruitfully succumb to scientific analysis, but rather that design problems in the main differ from those to which science is normally effectively applied. This is a metaphysical statement of the first order and an important clue to developing a more accurate definition for more contemporary disciplines, especially those concerned with space, such as the discipline of interior design.

The Fundamental Nature of Design

Second, Cross (1982) noted that as a discipline, design is concerned with solutions and innovation; that is, it is a discipline whose orientation is almost entirely constructive. It does not examine what is, but rather constructs what is not presently existing; this means that the metaphysical and epistemological aspects of design are both significantly different in definition and nature from those of the sciences and humanities. This also means that these differences present particularly interesting philosophical epistemological problems, since designers make claims of knowledge with regard to predictions of performance about realities that do not always exist in concrete form (Galle, 2006). Cross (1982) also discussed the notion that the abstract languages of drawing (leveraging elements and principles of design) are a coded or formal language that can and should be studied more carefully; the existence of such a problem-solving language also implies a logic for this language whose structure becomes the topic for philosophical inquiry.

Developing Design as a Systematic Approach from a Philosophical Perspective

In his papers on design philosophy and theory, Terrence Love further develops the themes introduced by Cross. Love (2000) examined the relationship between the development of design theory and the development of a philosophy of science for design. The main thesis of Love's work is that a philosophical structure is needed that provides a means to organizing and linking elements of design theory into an intelligible whole, such that one element of theory can be seen in context and one aspect of design can be seen in relation to another (2000). This holistic or relational structure would provide a means to better understand how one element of theory or practice might be related to or influence another. Love traced at least some of the problems experienced in design theory to philosophical gaps in both metaphysics and epistemology; he noted that the difficulties of design theory are grounded in a conflation of concepts that are the result of a limited philosophical foundation. Love cited the progressive cycling of research and theory development in the absence of a philosophy of design as the cause of a dizzying multiplication of design terminology and theory.

Love goes on to explain why the critical analysis of design theory must be executed from a philosophical perspective:

> "Theories, concepts, assumptions and human values are studied and analyzed as theoretical abstractions. . . . Whilst not at the forefront of academic consciousness, the structuring of abstractions is a basic tool in most disciplines. It can be seen perhaps most clearly in Mathematics—where theorems depend on axioms (both abstractions), and in Philosophy—especially in the field of Logic which is concerned with the manipulation of abstract entities and the verification of logical relationships between them. (Love, 2000, pp. 301–302)

Love then provided a very useful philosophical construct for organizing theory:

> One simple solution to problems of confusion and conflation of the concepts, theories and terminology in design research is to take a meta-theoretical perspective, use a critical framework for analysis, and create a structure that enables elements of different theories and concepts to be located relative to each other. The most obviously useful method is to use a meta-theoretical structure based on levels of abstraction because it offers a means of classification that is hierarchical and relatively independent of the domain-based meanings associated with each theoretical element. This method provides a straightforward means of clarifying and externalizing many of the hidden dependencies between abstractions in Design Theory. (Love, 2000, p. 304)

Love's contributions reify the importance of a philosophy of science for design, to provide a means to shape a body of knowledge possessing internal coherence, and one from which scholars can trace elements of a research program and, most critically, further develop knowledge within the discipline.

The Example of an Evolving Discipline for Designed Interior Space: Interior Design

More recently, similar notions of the need for an integrated model of the interior design body of knowledge have been expressed within the interior design discipline itself. In a paper entitled "Knowledge in Interior Design," Anna Marshall-Baker (2005) envisioned an epistemological structure that is not only internally coherent and integrated but can also trace its relationships to other academic disciplines and professions. Marshall-Baker viewed interior design and its body of knowledge in a larger context of the academy as a whole, and posits that the interactions of various sources of knowledge provide the generative impetus that moves disciplines forward. Stephanie Clemons and Molly Eckman (Clemons & Eckman, M., 2004) also sought to bring coherence to interior design scholarship in their content analysis of scholarship published in the *Journal of Interior Design*. These scholars sought to identify some clearly defined terminology, which is a key structural component allowing scholarship to be cohesively ordered, affording a means to extend and further develop an understanding of the manner in which elements of our understanding of interior design are interrelated. Unfortunately, unlike the epistemological system envisioned by Marshall-Baker, Clemons and Eckman base their epistemological structure not on meta-analysis of what is *understood* about interior design and interior designing, an approach that might lead to a holistic vision of what constitutes the discipline, but instead they only examine the topics of study without further critical consideration of how the conclusions of each fits into a cohesive epistemological system where one element is seen in its relation to another.

Understanding Epistemological Frameworks: What Is the Very Nature of Design?

The elements of an epistemological framework outlined by Archer and Cross are further taken up by Professor Ken Friedman, who enlarged them. Friedman possesses a unique and diverse academic background

with a master's degree in Interdisciplinary Studies in education, psychology, and social science, and a doctorate in Human Behavior. He has been active as a designer and artist and just completed service as the Dean of the School of Design at Swinburne University in Australia. Friedman has written extensively about the development of design as a discipline. Friedman (2000) further extends the ideas of Archer, Cross, and Love, noting that

> Having few historical roots in the philosophical tradition deeper than the last few decades, we have yet to shape a clear understanding of the nature of design. We do not agree, therefore, on whether design knowledge constitutes a discipline, a field, or a science, one of these, two or even all three. (p. 8)

He pointed out the basic epistemological questions that design must address if we are to develop a truly coherent and utile body of knowledge:

> To understand the role of research in knowledge creation, it is ultimately necessary to reflect on what philosophers call "the problem of knowledge." Mario Bunge (1996:104) states that the problem of knowledge is "actually an entire system of problems. Some of the components of this system are: What is knowledge? What can know: minds, brains, computers, or social groups? Can we know everything, something, or nothing? How does one get to know: from experience, reason, action, a combination of two, or

all three, or none of them? What kind of knowledge is best—that is, truest, most comprehensive, deepest, and most reliable and fertile? These five problems constitute the core problematics of epistemology, or the "theory" of knowledge—which is still to become a theory proper. (p. 12)

Friedman's background in knowledge management affords his inquiry into the philosophical aspects of the design discipline, an important advantage in that he is able to examine the difficulties endemic to the development of a body of knowledge from a broad perspective of epistemological study. Friedman notes:

> The challenge of any evolving field is to bring tacit knowledge into articulate focus. This creates the ground of shared understanding that builds the field. *The continual and conscious struggle for articulation is what distinguishes the work of a research field from the practical work of a profession.* (p. 13; emphasis added)

These statements trace both a philosophically epistemological process as well as a metaphysical/ontological one, and explicate once more that the development of the discipline, while it must incorporate professional practice as a frame of reference, nevertheless cannot be driven by the pragmatic exigencies of professional practice. As Friedman notes, a discipline and a research agenda led by practice is likely to fail the long-term interests of practice.

This problem is evinced in the resistance of nineteenth-century medical practitioners to heed the research of Semmelweis, Pasteur, and Lister on the topic of antisepsis; practitioners resisted the conclusions of this research for some time before its efficacy was accepted (Friedman, 2000).

Making Arguments for Design Research: Understanding the Spaces of Design Activity and the Example of Interior Design

To begin to address the question of an epistemological framework that will provide us clear insights into the nature of design, we turn to the works of scholars who have tried to address similar concerns. These fall into two segments: scholars from other disciplines like design that do not fall neatly into categories of either the humanities or sciences, and scholars in the broad field of design (Archer, 1979; Cross, 1982; Love, 2000). The works of these scholars suggested several possible epistemological divisions that may be helpful. Other disciplines have struggled with similar issues, and it might be helpful to first examine one of these as a potential avenue for further study and development.

Interior design as a design discipline suffers from the malady common to its kindred design studies; that is, it belongs neither to the sciences nor to the humanities, yet the culture of universities and the opinions of the informed public demand that its legitimation as a discipline conform to the established standards of systematic inquiry.

Models exist from several other disciplines that have struggled with similar efforts to legitimate their academic standing. The discipline of theology wrestled with this problem beginning in the 1950s. While the object of study in theology may seem at first glance to significantly diverge from that of interior design, on closer examination they have many important similarities:

- Theology deals primarily with questions of the impact of value and culture on individuals and groups.
- The impact of value and culture are encoded in a range of important artifacts (art, architecture, ritual, and texts).
- Historical tradition and precedent are very important to the discipline.
- The manner in which the aspects and structures of the culture are communicated and conveyed to each generation are a significant topic of study.

Thus, theology possesses a range of elements that present difficulties similar to those of interior design in the development and articulation of a disciplinary construct, and that are relevant; the basis of study defined, particularly in epistemology and method, are complex and difficult and the objects of study are not easily addressed within the confines of the scientific method.

In his book *Method in Theology*, Lonergan begins with an examination of metaphysical and epistemological issues in theology in the context of the broad academy. He quotes Sir David Ross's statement regarding Aristotle:

Throughout the whole of his works we find him taking the view that all other sciences than the mathematical have the name of science only by controversy, since they are occupied with matters in which contingency plays a part. So too today the English word, science, means natural science. One descends a rung or more on the ladder when one speaks of behavioral or human science. Theologians finally often have to be content if their subject is included in a list not of sciences but of academic disciplines. . . . Clearly enough, these approaches to the problem of method do little to advance the less successful subject. . . . Nor will recourse to the analogy of science be of any use, for that analogy, so far from lending a helping hand to the less successful, is content to assign a lower rank in the pecking order. (Lonergan, 1972, pp. 3–4)

Lonergan went on to develop an approach to a body of knowledge. He places theological knowledge into a series of interrelated categories he calls the "functional specialties." The purpose of these categories is to afford the discipline a means to organize the objects of study (knowing) into an integrated whole in which one specialty and the objects of its study can be seen in relation to the others, thereby providing a means to understand how one area of study both influences and is influenced by the others. The term *functional specialties* is also particularly apt, as it is expressive of a division of knowledge and practice (specialization) and is also an operative term in that we want to study how each of these specialties function and contribute to the larger body of knowledge.

Lonergan's functional specialties might be viewed as akin to the "knowledge areas" of Martin and Guerin (2005), but their origins are very different. First, Lonergan explains why it is necessary to create these categories:

> To put *method* in theology is to conceive theology *as a set of related and recurrent operations cumulatively advancing toward an ideal goal.* However, contemporary theology is specialized, and so it is to be conceived, not as a single set of related operations, but as a series of interdependent sets. (p. 125; italics added)

He then explained how these functional specialties might be conceived:

> Specialties may be distinguished in three manners, namely (1) by dividing and subdividing the field of data, (2) by classifying the results of investigations, (3) and by distinguishing and separating stages of the process from data to results. (p. 125)

Thus, while we might employ the method used by Martin and Guerin (2005) to distinguish the knowledge areas of interior design—that is, by analyzing the writings of interior design scholars and practitioners for their content areas—there are other approaches. Several seem appropriate in relation to Lonergan's assertions. For example, we might utilize the categories devised by the National Center for Interior Design Qualification (NCIDQ) or the Council for Interior Design Accreditation (CIDA), as these seem to be the regions of knowledge that are commonly agreed and which academics and practitioners alike see as relevant. This would align with Lonergan's notion of "dividing and subdividing the field," since it is often true that as designers mature in their careers, they may focus on one or more aspects of their training, specializing in Environmental Systems and Controls (through an interest in sustainability) or in Regulations (by becoming a code expert) and so on. But while these systems provide us with a set of categories into which we might place various aspects of scholarship and practice, they do not come nearer to providing a holistic and integrated foundation from which we might address metaphysical, epistemological, or other questions related to a philosophy of science for interior design.

Second, in reference to Lonergan's assertion that functional specialties might be derived from "classifying the results of investigations," we might indeed leverage the work of Martin and Guerin (2005) using the knowledge areas they suggested, *provided that we can also trace their interrelationships and make of them what Lonergan referred to as "a series of interdependent sets"* (Lonergan, 1972, p. 125; italics added) of methodological operations. Martin and Guerin (2005) identified 96 knowledge areas, which were then grouped into 6 categories: Human Environment Needs; Interior Construction, Codes, and Regulations; Design; Products and Materials; Professional Practice; and Communication. But the question arises regarding this taxonomy as to whether these categories achieve the epistemological goal that Lonergan has defined here as "classifying the results of investigations." In essence, do these knowledge areas and categories aid the discipline in their understanding of the holistic structure of the practice of interior design? Do they assist both practitioners and researchers to understand the acquisition of knowledge about interior design as "a set of related and recurrent operations cumulatively advancing toward an ideal goal?" While their approach does help us to define elements of knowledge critical to the discipline and profession, it is much more difficult to see how this study provides a vision of a "recurrent set of operations cumulatively advancing toward an ideal goal" (Lonergan, 1972, p. 125), which can help us to better define the *value* of the profession and discipline to the culture, and lead to a comprehensive understanding of the nature of interior design.

Alternately, we might utilize the elements of design process as a means to distinguishing functional specialties. This would align with Lonergan's notions of "distinguishing and separating successive stages of the *process* from data to results" (1972). So we might have functional specialties in programming, planning, or the management of the design process on the whole. Lonergan developed eight functional specialties that very tidily segment the field of theology, but on what basis should we segment the field of interior design? In organizing interior design practice, we can then begin to understand and organize spaces for exploration.

In this regard, let us begin by examination of the works of other design scholars regarding approaches to the segmentation of the discipline into areas of study that meet one or more of Lonergan's criteria for a sufficiently articulated and interrelated epistemological structure—that is, by

1. Dividing and subdividing the field of data
2. Classifying the results of investigations
3. Distinguishing and separating stages of the process from data to results

First, Archer suggests that one of the most significant qualities associated with the activities of designers in contrast to those of scientists or those involved in the humanities is that *their work is aspirational*; it seeks to address problems pragmatically and intervene to change the conditions of reality (Archer, 1979). As an example of how we might begin to define functional specialties for the design disciplines, based on this initial proposition from Archer, we might propose that one functional specialty might be *programming* (or *problematics*), since it is in fact the unique nature of design problems and the unique approach to the manner in which designers define these problems that is a distinguishing characteristic of the discipline. Several scholars (Rittel, H., & Webber, M., 1969; Cross, N., 1982) discuss the nature of design problems as **wicked**, that is, problems that are by nature ill defined and that do not imply right or wrong answers.

Understanding Design Foundations—About Spaces and Designerly Ways

Cross (1982) distinguished several elements that might serve us as functional specialties (more on this subject in Chapter 6, Article 6.2). He begins with three:

> The phenomenon of study . . . in design: the man-made world . . . [This would correlate with Lonergan's distinguishing and separating stages of the process from data to results.]
>
> The appropriate methods . . . in design: modeling, pattern . . . formation, synthesis [aligning with Lonergan's by dividing and subdividing the field of data]
>
> The values . . . in design: practicality, ingenuity, empathy, and a concern for "appropriateness (Cross, 1982, pp. 221–222)

Understanding Designerly Ways of Knowing

Cross (1982) has also defined five "designerly ways of knowing" that may also serve as a basis for the development of functional specialties, especially since they have clear interrelations:

> Designers tackle "ill-defined" problems.
> - Their mode of problem-solving is "solution-focused."
> - Their mode of thinking is "constructive."
> - They use "codes" that translate abstract requirements into concrete objects.
> - They use these codes to both "read" and "write" in "object languages."

Further, Love (2000) discussed a subsequent work by Cross in which he identified themes that represent a chronological development of design research. Love then contributes a further four:

1. The management of the design process
2. The structure of design problems
3. The nature of design activities
4. "Reflection" on the fundamental concepts of design

Two other themes that can be added to Cross's list are as follows:

1. Knowledge about the environment in which designing takes place
2. Knowledge needed for designing, that is, knowledge about objects and design processes (pp. 293–313).

A Proposal for Functional Specialties in Design Research

From the suggestions of these scholars we see a range of possible functional specialties for design research. I suggest the following possibilities in terms of organizing design as ways of knowing:

1. *Design Systematics,* which could address strategic approaches to confronting design problems. This specialty would concern the study of the ways in which interior designers disassemble and manage the processes aimed at addressing problems. Some typical topics might concern project management, business operations, technology management, production of construction drawings, installation of FF&E (furniture, fittings, and equipment),

and construction management. This would seek to define the association between specialties *Design Problematics* and *Design Process.*

2. *Design Problematics*, which would examine both the unique nature of design problems and the manner in which interior designers define those problems so that they can be understood in relation to the design task. Typical subjects of study would consider epistemological constructs, how we define the relationship between programming tools and methods, and how knowledge and an understanding of problems are constructed. For example, in understanding how interior space is constructed, we might use these philosophical constructs to understand the relationships between interior designers, clients and users, and the manner in which they act to define problems collectively. This would also include understanding the designer's relationship to various stakeholders.

   In the example of the interior designer, this means understanding the relationship of the interior designer to the architect, the contractor, the engineer, and others involved in realizing the project outcomes, in relation to solving problems. In essence, this specialty would examine how the relationship between a problem and its resolution is constructed. This specialty would distinguish the relations among specialties that would then become *Design Process, Design Heuristics*, and *Design Logic.*

3. *Design Process*, which would examine both the structures of the interior design thought or creative process and how that process is related to the structure of design problems. Typical topics of study would concern the internal processes of creative and critical thinking; the relationship between verbal, visual, and haptic elements of information that trace the process of design from description to visualization to construction; the associative processes of representation that facilitate the development of a design concept, the encoding of that concept in the built environment, and the interpretation of that concept by clients and users. This specialty would link categories *Interior Design Problematics, Interior Design Heuristics,* and *Interior Design Logic.*

4. *Design Heuristics* would examine the construction of heuristic models by designers. Typical topics of study would concern various models designers construct and through which they come to understand the relationship between a design problem and its solution; models of the manner in which environmental meaning is constructed and altered by designers, clients users, and human culture; and the influences of technological constructs on design processes. This specialty would reflect the conceptual structures that connect specialties *Design Systematics, Design Problematics,* and *Design Process.*

5. *Design Logic* would seek to construct a propositional structure by which designers address design problems. Typical topics of study might concern visual representation and its relationship to the

testing of possible design solutions, the relationship between a program, and the sufficiency of a specific design solution to be considered as fulfilling those criteria. This specialty would support specialties *Design Process* and *Design Heuristics* by providing clarity regarding the validity of design problem solving.

6. *Design History* examines the sociocultural context of design. Typical topics for study might concern the notion of design precedent as a foundation for the development of new solutions and the influence of power, politics, religion, gender, and cultural difference on design. This specialty would provide a context for all other categories and identify influences outside of the discipline that might shape or change it. The specialty would link specialties *Design Process* and *Design Heuristics*.

7. *Design Communications* examines processes and approaches to communicat-ing what designers do. Typical topics of study would concern interior design pedagogy, modes of design communication and design representation, the construction of public messages regarding the profession and discipline, and so on. This specialty would trace the manner in which *meaning* is developed within the other categories and how it is *mediated*. This functional specialty would clarify the relationship between specialties *Design Heuristics* and *Design History*.

This epistemological structure provides an orderly means for both segmenting the subject matter of the discipline and making it manageable, and also for detailing terms and relations among subject matter areas. These categories also seem to achieve the goal Lonergan (1972) suggested: "a set of related and recurrent operations cumulatively advancing toward an ideal goal."

References

Abercrombie, S. (1991). *A Philosophy of Interior Design.* Boulder, CO: West-view Press.

Archer, B. (1979). Design as a Discipline. *Design Studies, 1* (1), 17–20.

Clemons, S. A., & Eckman, M. (2004). Toward A Common Language: Proposed Index. *Journal of Interior Design, 30* (1), 13–30.

Cross, N. (1982). Designerly Ways of Knowing. *Design Studies, 3* (4), 221–227.

Cross, N. (2001). Designerly Ways of Knowing: Design Discipline versus Design Science. *Design Issues, 17* (3), pp. 49–55.

Friedman, K. (2000). Creating Design Knowledge: From Research into Practice. *International Conference on Design and Technology Educational Research* (pp. 5–32). Loughborough, UK: Loughborough University of Technology.

Friedman, K. (2003). Theory Construction in Design. *Design Studies, 16.*

Galle, P. (2006). Worldviews for Design Theory. *Design Research Society*

International Conference (pp. 1–12). Lisbon: The Design Research Society.

Harfield, S. (2008). On the Roots of Un-discipline. *Proceedings of DRS2008, Design Research Society Biennial Conference*, Sheffield, UK, July 16–19, 2008.

Harfield, S., & Burgess, P. (2008). Controlling the Discipline. *Proceedings of DRS2008, Design Research Society Biennial Conference*, Sheffield, UK, July 16–19, 2008.

Love, T. (2000). A Meta-theoretical Basis for Design Theory. *International Conference of the Design Research Society*. La Clusaz, France: The Design Research Society.

Love, T. (2000). Philosophy of Design: A Metatheoretical Structure for Design Theory. *Design Studies, 21* (3), 293–313.

Lonergan, B. (1972). *Method in Theology*. New York: Herder and Herder.

Machamer, P. (1998). Philosophy of Science: An Overview for Educators. *Science & Education*, 1–11.

Marcoux, A. (2008, September 21). *Business Ethics*. (E. N. Zalta, Ed.) Retrieved 2010 from *The Stanford Encyclopedia of Philosophy,* http://plato.stanford.edu/archives/fall2008/entries/ethics-business/.

Markus, T. A. (1993). *Buildings and Power: Freedom and Control in the Origin of Modern Building Tapes* (p. 343). London: Routledge.

Marshall-Baker, A. (2005). Knowledge in Interior Design. *Journal of Interior Design, 1* (1), xiii–xxi.

Martin, C. S., & Guerin, D. A. (2005 edition). *The Interior Design Profession's Body of Knowledge*. St. Paul, MN: University of Minnesota–College of Design.

Pabble, J. (2009). Interior Design Identity in the Crossfire: A Call for Renewed Balance in Subjective and Objctive Ways of Knowing. *Journal of Interior Design* , v–xx.

Parry, R. (2009, September 21). Ancient Ethical Theory. (E. N. Zalta, Ed.). Retrieved 2010 from *The Stanford Encyclopedia of Philosophy,* http://plato.stanford.edu/archives/fall2009/entries/ethics-ancient/.

Poldma, T. (2008). Interior Design at a Crossroads. *Journal of Interior Design, 11.*

"Primary/Secondary Quality Distinction." (n.d.). Retrieved July 25, 2010, from Wikipedia, http://en.wikipedia.org/wiki/Primary_qualities.

Ramberg, B., & Gjesdal, K. (2009, June 21). Hermeneutics. (E. N. Zalta, Ed.). Retrieved August 2010 from *The Stanford Encyclopedia of Philosophy,* http://plato.stanford.edu/entries/hermeneutics/.

Richardson, H. S. (2009, September 21). Moral Reasoning. (E. N. Zalta, Ed.). Retrieved 2010 from *The Stanford Encyclopedia of Philosophy,* http://plato.stanford.edu/archives/fall2009/entries/reasoning-moral.

Rittel, H., & Webber, M. (1969). Dilemmas in a General Theory of Planning. *American Association for the Advancement of Science* (pp. 155–169), Boston.

Rosenberg, A. (2008). *A Philosophy of Social Science.* Philadelphia: Westview Press.

Schroeder, M. (2008, September 21). Value Theory. (E. N. Zalta, Ed.). Retrieved 2010 from *The Stanford Encyclopedia of Philosophy*, http://plato.stanford.edu/archives/fall2008/entries/value-theory/.

Sinnott-Armstrong, W. (2008, September 21). Consequentialism. (E. N. Zalta, Ed.). Retrieved 2010 from *The Stanford Encyclopedia of Philosophy*, http://plato.stanford.edu/archives/fall2008/entries/consequentialism/.

Shapiro, S. (2009, September 21). Classical Logic. (E. N. Zalta, Ed.), Retrieved 2010 from *The Stanford Encyclopedia of Philosophy*, http://plato.stanford.edu/archives/win2009/entries/logic-classical/.

Steup, M. (2010, March 21). "Epistemology." (E. N. Zalta, Ed.). Retrieved 2010 from *The Stanford Encyclopedia of Philosophy*, http://plato.stanford.edu/archives/spr2010/entries/.

Turner, D. L. (2002). Medical facilities as moral worlds. *Medical Humanities, 28*, 19–22.

Yeung, H. W.-c. (1997). Critical Realism and Realist Research in Human Geography: A Method or a Philosophy in Search of a Method? *Progress in Human Geography, 21* (1), 51–74.

van Inwagen, P. (2009). Metaphysics. (E. Zalta, Ed.). Retrieved 2010 from *The Stanford Encyclopedia of Philosophy*, http://plato.stanford.edu/archives/win2009/entries/metaphysics/.

Zalta, E. N. (Ed.). (2009). *The Stanford Encyclopedia of Philosophy*. Stanford, CA: Stanford University, Center for the Study of Language and Information, The Metaphysics Research Lab. Retrieved May/June 2010 from http://plato.stanford.edu/archives/win2009/entries/metaphysics/.

1.2 We Are Not Alone: When the Number of Exceptions to a Rule Exceeds Its Usefulness as a Construct, It is Time for a Change

Hannah Rose Mendoza and Tom Matyók

Provocation

Introduction

Existing models of disciplinary development do not recognize or contribute to a theorization of the multitude of academic responses to changing knowledge landscapes; nor do they accept the emergence of a third, highly integrative, knowledge culture of design. Instead, the focus has been and remains on the struggle to demarcate, define, and deconstruct with the end goal being value created as a result of specialization and elitism. The focus in these exercises of disciplinary map-making has often been to reinforce or advance the power status of one group of knowledge creators over another.

Rather than searching for the boundaries that distinguish one parcel of disciplinary territory from another, design disciplines are created from within and move outward, do not displace or claim exclusive ownership of knowledge territory, and are mutable and always present. Design disciplines, such as interior design, or peace and conflict studies, have internal coherence that arises from the tenets of transformation and are liquid in nature, flowing along information streams sourced from the reservoirs of human knowledge. Design disciplines are distinct from traditional disciplinary modes of scholarship. As a result of their fluidity, design disciplines have been previously rendered invisible in traditional models of disciplinarity, and there has been little or no formal exploration of their disciplinary organization or processes. Evidence for this claim is found in the ever shifting and widely varied location of design programs as each location creates benefits and discomforts but rarely an agreed upon, perfect fit. This inability to accommodate the mutable nature of design disciplines into a rigid structure of disciplinary classification creates a number of anomalies so great as to warrant reconsideration of the current paradigm of disciplinary development and recognition. A revolution in conceptualization is needed in order to allow scholars interested in issues of disciplinarity to address questions previously unavailable because they were "necessarily subversive of [the paradigm's] basic commitments" (Kuhn, 1996, p. 5).

The necessity of reexamining the paradigm of disciplines moves beyond a desire to better understand the ways in which transformative knowledge moves and can be recognized. Rather, the revolution is necessary because of the ongoing struggle, especially in institutions of higher education, to make knowledge transmission more efficient at the cost of effectiveness.

Current models follow a post-Fordist production model in which knowledge and education are perceived as possible to neatly package and monetize. This thinking shifts the academic marketplace away from institutions of learning and inquiry to for-profit corporations focused on transmission and instrumental application. The production model leads to generations of graduates who "possess a finite amount of skills, and an embryonic aesthetic sensibility, with almost no ability to achieve basic insight, and with no tools with which to increase that ability" (Papanek, 1971, p. 64). Students are presented to the world, and expected to engage that world, before they are ready, possibly doing more damage than good (Galtung, 1997).

Our goal in this paper is not to engage in a detailed critique of the accepted cannon of academic disciplines; rather, we call for a revolution in conceptualization that ceases to use the existing disciplines as evolutionary platforms for academic and intellectual growth. We seek to open a dialogue among design scholars in order to recognize, support, and advance new, fluid ways of knowing. The exploration of these concepts and their relationships is a vital part of harnessing innovation, determining competencies, and accessing intellectual capital in design, areas that are vital for creating self-determination.

Our liquid modernity (Bauman, 2000) is not well served in the current system of higher education, which has changed very little from its medieval origins. Using mechanisms developed 500 years ago, we continue educating students who will address social problems that continue growing exponentially (and unabated?) in complexity and depth. Universities as mechanisms for the delivery of information products (Readings, 1996) are not adequate to meet the demands of an unknown future.

We are not naïve; we know our task is difficult. Clearly, the only thing more difficult than getting a new idea into higher education is moving the old idea out. Institutional inertia is a strong force to resist. But we believe we are required to introduce new ways of knowing that will prepare students to confront the complex issues of their time.

Design Disciplines and the Interior Design Example

Interest in formalizing the bodies of knowledge unique to their respective fields of study continues on the part of many members of the design community. It is proposed that this process serves as a marker of the field's privileged place in the pantheon of professions. Interior design is currently involved in a vigorous debate regarding the need for and value of such knowledge capture techniques. The metaphors are of partitioning off, breaking away, and maintaining control. Martin and Guerin advanced the idea that "abstract knowledge defines the interior design profession's jurisdictional boundaries through control of knowledge and skill sets" (Martin & Guerin, 2005, p. 1). And through this codification of knowledge, the authority of interior designers might suggest exercise of control over their profession will be made manifest, and practitioners can then "expect deference from society for the creation and application of their specialization" (Guerin & Martin, 2004, p. 10), something that currently is not the case.

Desire for deference and respect has led many practitioners and educators to seek evidence of interior design's professional and disciplinary status. According to theories developed in industrial sociology, especially Abbott's theory of professionalization, the formalization of a discrete, standardized body of knowledge is one indicator of the transition from an occupation to a profession (Abbott, 1988). Interior design is at that crossroads.

To assist in selecting the correct path forward toward acceptance as a scholarly discipline, *The Interior Design Profession's Body of Knowledge: Its Definition and Documentation* (Martin & Guerin, 2005) was released to members of the interior design profession. This document was the work of a relatively small, closed group representing established institutions and interests, intended to mark out the boundaries that distinguish interior design from other related disciplines. As a result of its creation within a paradigm of specialization, it cannot provide a complete map of the terrain of knowledge traversed in the practice and study of interior design.

The **epistemology of possession** that is currently accepted as part of the process of defining the **Body of Knowledge (BoK)** for interior design denies us the ability to value or even speak about the types of knowledge and knowing that occur in practice (Cook & Seely Brown, 1999). When knowledge is approached as an object that can be gathered together into a whole, the action of knowing and the tacit knowledge connected to it are relegated to a location outside of the formalized framework that privileges explicit, static knowledge over tacit, evolving knowing.

Schön recognized the disconnect between codified knowledge and "the changing character of the situation's practice—the complexity, uncertainty, instability, uniqueness, and value conflicts which are increasingly perceived as central to the world of professional practice" (Schön, 1983, p. 14). This mismatch cannot be resolved through the capture and mastery of increasingly specialized information. Closed systems of knowing cannot propose to constitute the totality of specialized knowledge necessary for the practice and study of interior design.

The discussion of a Body of Knowledge for interior design must be responsive to the constructed, complex, changing nature of design knowledge and designerly ways of knowing (Mendoza, 2009). Learning to recognize design rather than searching for lines that demarcate it presents the "distinct, higher-order pattern of interrelated activities grounded in and emerging from individual actions" that constitutes the activities of interior design (Schön, 1983, p. 374).

The gravitation toward categorization of knowledge that privileges explicit and individual forms of knowledge over others is by no means unique to interior design but rather is part of the dominant mode of Western thought as has been practiced over the last several centuries (Cook &

Seely Brown, 1999). Its origins lie early in Aristotle's epistemological approach that focused on the discovery of the inherent properties of an object that would act to define it and explain its existence (Russell, 1945). Or possibly even earlier in the development of the first need for knowledge dissemination in the Neolithic era where language possibly developed as a method of conveying precise information about the process for turning stone into tools (Burke, 1999). This process for normalizing a series of behaviors in order to attain a specific result was generalized to the way that a process of logic could be applied to understanding the universe. This Cartesian approach serves to institutionalize a compartmentalized conceptualization of knowledge creation, and this disassembly of knowledge into its component parts forms the framework in which science has operated in the West since the seventeenth century.

We live in an age in which more knowledge is more widely available to more people than ever before (Burke, 1999). Any attempt to gather a specific set of that knowledge and claim ownership and control over it is outmoded and, in areas of design, where transformation is both the process and the outcome, self-defeating. The fluidity necessary for the practice of design, the study and practice of what ought to be, is denied. The social and interactive nature of design practice is not well served through the top-down creation of rule sets that cannot possibly take into account the infinite variables present in any given design situation and, therefore,

act only to form design responses rather than to inform design processes.

Design disciplines are liquid in nature. Their purpose is not the capture and maintenance of knowledge; rather, they focus on the creation of new ways of knowing and evolving. Design disciplines are diverse fields of study and practice that have the design of the human condition as their focus.

Disciplinarity

Academic disciplines have traditionally been seen as a milestone along a continuum of progress and as having from three to ten unique characteristics, depending on the theoretical model used. These characteristics, or traits, are often used as a type of checklist against which disciplinary development of any particular subject can be measured. This same approach has been used to determine progress toward professionalization and represents a particular set of beliefs regarding advancement and recognizability.

There are a number of scientific disciplines that fit rather neatly into the existing models of disciplinary development: physics, chemistry, biology, and so on. There are also a number for which the fit is possible but slightly more uncomfortable, generally from the so-called softer sciences such as sociology, anthropology, and psychology. Then there are a growing number of fields that require great contortions in order to be connected to those models in even the most tangential way. Fields of inquiry that focus on gathering information from a variety of locations and examining the connections are often referred to as multi-/inter-/poly-/trans- or some other form of disciplinary structure. This categorization indicates the bringing together of previously disparate information in a way that the connections can be examined. It also indicates the potential absence of a single strong central core or shared paradigm.

The perceived absence of this set of agreed upon practices has led to criticism of these fields as lacking rigor, being purely derivative (in other words, engaging in work that can be or already has been performed in other disciplines), and being unsuitable for academic engagement. These arguments are tendered not against the bringing together of information, but rather, are couched in the belief that those who can most appropriately do so are currently engaged in its production within their specific disciplines. Making appropriate connections then becomes simply a matter of actively pursuing information produced by others within their disciplinary environment and engaging in some form of synthesis.

The idea that information from disparate disciplines will somehow spawn new, connected knowledge simply as a result of being proximate is equivalent to assuming that racial integration will occur simply by overcoming physical distance. There are structures of thought and interaction that must be cultivated in order for the proximity to even be seen as desirable and then explored and cultivated. Just so, there is an art and a study to bringing together information, of moving in liquid knowing,

in order to create a transformation, and it is that art that creates the coherence of a design discipline. These disciplines are part of the movement from the information age to the conceptual age, from the service economy to the creative economy, and from a binary understanding of knowledge cultures (science and humanities) to a multivariate understanding of knowledges and intelligence.

Multidisciplinarity is the act of building bridges between distinctions; it is a particular structure that is constructed leaving the two connected entities separate but with opportunities for communication. It is an artificial structure that has to be re-created each time a new connection is desired. The bridge gives the illusion of rigidity, but only from a distance. In actuality, the bridge is flexible (it must be in order to not fracture), and depending upon the scale at which you examine it, wildly so. The bridge is maintained as long as it is useful, but without careful maintenance, it falls into disrepair and cannot be easily realigned as a response to new information or possibilities. The river, however, continues to move and flow between the connected points without any need for boundaries or discrete moments of contact; it is a natural form— and an appropriate metaphor for the way that we truly think. Reexamination of this metaphor is important because we live in our conceptualizations of reality: rethinking the way we imagine the world actually changes the world as we experience it. Liquid knowing engulfs, carrying along what advances us toward more complex understandings and leaving behind what no longer helps.

Following are features of liquid design disciplines:

- Liquid scholars may have a disciplinary/research professional organization, but in addition to institutional unit affiliations, members are involved in an extremely broad spectrum of organizations.
- Liquid scholars often publish and present research findings in journals and at conferences representing a wide variety of disciplines.
- Liquid scholars engage in cross-disciplinary, collaborative research with partners from a wide variety of academic disciplines.
- Institutional units make sense in nearly every location within academic institutions—it is very difficult to argue out of the connection.
- Liquid design disciplines are transformation focused and engaged in the creation of novel mental images.
- Liquid design scholars and educators come from a wide variety of disciplinary backgrounds.
- The faculty in academic departments engaged in liquid design scholarship are often from multiple disciplines.
- Members of liquid design disciplines are often viewed as being everything and everywhere.
- Liquid design scholars and departments value group work and collective development.
- There is an emphasis on holistic learning—portfolios are often used to tie together the entire educational experience.
- Design scholars value learning, knowledge, and experience, tacit and explicit, gained inside the classroom and in alternative venues (life experience counts).

The theorization of scientific revolutions (Kuhn, 1996), and their role in the history of the development of scientific thought, has led to any number of scholars attempting to measure their own area's progress leading not only to some appropriate generalizations but also to some wildly tenuous and overly artificial metaphors. The intellectual acrobatics performed by scholars as they use this respected work to demonstrate the development of their own field could be viewed as evidence of the very anomalies that Kuhn himself addressed.

The Third Knowledge Culture

The culture of scientific inquiry is one that relies upon an ability to very clearly define the problem to be addressed, the ability to replicate experiments, and the generation of knowledge that describes as accurately as possible what *it* is. The framework for data generation and analysis requires breaking the object or process under study into its smallest component parts, deconstructing, in order to examine the object at a close and detailed scale. And there is an assumption within the scientific community that this is an appropriate way to understand which problems are available for inquiry, and how to understand the methods and results of that inquiry. Inquiry within the culture of the humanities looks for meanings and metaphors. The focus of inquiry in the humanistic tradition is undertaken in order to provide frameworks for description and to discuss why and how in terms of contexts and relationships attempting to explain what *it* means. While the agreements regarding practices and interpretations are not as closely defined as in areas of scientific inquiry, there is a shared core. These two knowledge cultures should not be conceived of as opposites; nor as a yin and yang that creates a whole.

A third knowledge culture exists that addresses ill-defined issues in an attempt to determine and create knowledge regarding what *it* could be. This third knowledge culture is design and includes disciplines such as industrial design, interior design, peace studies, and creative. They are disciplines that address wicked problems in which the pinpoint accuracy of problem definition required by science cannot be achieved (Buchanan, 2000). The complexity of the context means that it is never possible to fully understand all of the tools required to create any given solution prior to beginning. Further, the mode of inquiry is one that is transformation focused and requires **inductive reasoning** processes in which the question and the solution are reworked in light of each other until an appropriate response is encountered. It is not so much about arriving at a solution as it is about asking better questions. These fields focus on studying and analyzing an issue until there is no answer; analysis, intervention, and transformation merge.

It is in understanding this third knowledge culture that we begin to recognize, and appropriately utilize, the mutability that creates unique value. Rather than understanding design disciplines as being simply locations for encountering information from a variety of areas, there is an acknowledgment of the knowledge, scholarly activities, and skills scholars are required to perform, and that also shape the academic core, separate and unique from other disciplinary structures. Like education, design is valuable though it cannot be defined directly. Instead, an understanding of design and liquid knowing is inferred through its effects, interactions, and performances, and its value is understood as inherent rather than instrumental (Peters, 1965). This type of disciplinary activity is visible when:

1. Worthwhile products of value are created.
2. The processes and circumstances of knowledge creation are as important as the product and meaning (in other words, products created accidentally, or processes engaged in without interest, lie outside of its realm).
3. Acts are fully conceived and the actor perceives the connections within a larger pattern.

Liquid Knowing

The valuable and venerated practices of the sciences have led to the generation of vast quantities of increasingly refined, but also fragmented, knowledge. Combined with exponential increases in humanity's capabilities for storing and disseminating that information, the amount of information being circulated, produced, and reproduced is beyond the imagination of even the largest minds. As a result of the close scale at which much information is currently being examined, a scholar may spend a lifetime generating data about a single item or a very particular phenomenon. That type of closely refined information is vital, but it can also be produced in such a way that it does not reach outward to make new and highly valuable connections.

The emergence of design as discipline in response to a need for moving more freely among knowledge territories is not a wholly new phenomenon but rather a continuation of the work begun by geographers in the last half of the nineteenth century when they found themselves in the uncomfortable position of justifying their wide-ranging and personal products and processes against the standard practices of scientific discipline (Livingstone, 1992). The fractured nature of knowledge specialization created an environment in which "integrative subjects like geography seemed to lack the specialized scientific rigour that was required to provide a coherent disciplinary identity. It [became] clear, then, that if the newly professionalized geographers wanted to retain the subject's traditional concerns, some fresh conceptual foundations had to be found that would render their project intellectually plausible" (1992, p. 177).

Academic geographers lamented the lack of a coherent methodology and the conceptualization of the field as one engaged in the production of data rather than the creation of knowledge. Rather than relying on an ability to draw a boundary around a particular area of knowledge over which they could claim dominion, an argument for validity was constructed based on the possibilities for geography to bring knowledge together. Geography has become a study of the connections and relationships between societies and natures. In embracing this model, geography moved from a "science of description [of] distribution" to a discipline engaged in inquiry with regard to causality and interaction (Mackinder as cited in Livingstone, 1992, p. 190). Rather than abolishing specialized disciplines and focused areas of finely tuned inquiry, the discipline of geography is built upon examining connections between bodies of knowledge regarding space, and bodies of knowledge regarding societies. In that sense, its disciplinary domain exists in the examination and theorization of the spaces between, around, and through more discrete disciplinary areas.

Geography and other disciplines are trans/multi/inter/poly in the sense that the data and information they collect comes from any number of external areas of inquiry, and the nature of their disciplinary framework creates a web of coherent connections as the context for the production of novel mental images. Design disciplines provide opportunities to reconstruct the world from the pieces deconstructed for intense and focused scrutiny. However, this reconstruction is not simply mimicking some original form, but aims to innovate and address the future, to create what *it* should be. The production of novel mental images results from the reorganization of meaning within previously unconnected contexts and in light of newly proximate knowledge (Sik-Wah Fong & Ka-Yan Ip, 1999).

While geography has been engaged in this type of disciplinary activity for over 150 years, many scholars engaging liquid knowing did not gain recognition in institutions of higher education until much later. As a result of the open and engaged nature of these disciplines, and the newness of their existence as part of academic culture, many of the scholars who have provided and/or continue to provide significant contributions to the fields have arrived from a wide variety of disciplinary foundations. This has resulted in the expression of theories, methods, and content areas that are likewise varied. This variety of scholars and practitioners are vital in fields that embrace holistic approaches to complex, mutable, and ill-defined issues. This diversity has also led to the misperception that there is no disciplinary core and to the belief that anyone can engage in the area's un-scholarly activities.

Proponents of liquid knowing recognize the following:

- They should not engage in turf battles.
- It is not possible to either usurp other areas or be usurped by them.
- They should gather data from a vast number of sources.
- They should recognize that the number and location of those sources are unknowable at any given moment and are only measurable in movement and momentum.
- They should utilize multiple and variable frameworks for creating connections.
- They should relate the knowledge created to the discipline specific artifact and its net.
- They should view "multidisciplinarity" not as in weaving together threads but holistic in producing an entirely new substance.
- Not a super-discipline or hierarchically superior to traditional disciplines.

A difficulty encountered in the literature attempting to explain the positions and multiple vehicles for scholarship in liquid design disciplines is the manner in which authors have consistently redrawn the map of knowledge, placing their specific discipline at the center, where all other disciplines converge. This conceptualization creates a definite hierarchy in which other disciplines are seen as existing at a level inferior to that of the one belonging to the author; and if not inferior, certainly pushed to the periphery. For example, Alger in "Reflections on Peace Research Traditions" locates peace research "at the crossroads where all disciplines interact, so it can draw on the relevant knowledge of all" (Alger, 1996, p. 2). This unidirectional benefit acts to colonize the lesser disciplines and mine them for their resources in an attempt to put their knowledge in context. At various times, interior design, architecture, and any number of other disciplines have also located themselves at the center of the disciplinary universe, alone holding the keys to the kingdom of knowledge.

The struggle within current disciplinary divisions focuses on discovering and staking claim to that central point. This activity has actually been more damaging than beneficial to these design disciplines, as they possess no clearly defined, rigid center. Any determination that such a center must exist in order for there to be the production of valuable research necessarily devalues the products and processes of these investigations. What is the benefit of determining the center of something as vast and ever-changing as knowledge? In order to determine the center of the Pacific Ocean, we must determine its boundaries; we must always know that those boundaries are an artificial and somewhat arbitrary construct. The act of determining where the middle point between those boundaries lies is purely middle school geometry. How does any of this help us to actually know or understand the workings and state of the Pacific Ocean itself?

These types of claims are partly based on egoism, and are also partly created by the failure of the vocabulary of disciplinarity to speak in any language other than space and control. Stepping away from colonizing metaphors available through geographical or architectural expression and into the language of liquidity presences the mutability and unique values provided through the connections created in a knowledge culture of design. This conceptualization makes irrelevant acts of boundary defense or aggression, as disciplinary movement does not displace or claim exclusive rights to territory. Instead, the attention paid in these design disciplines touches and transforms the knowledge landscape through constant movement, picking up and leaving behind, finite but not constricted.

A New Center

Disciplinarity is irrelevant and moving toward extinction; it's an evolutionary dead end. Academic disciplines have persisted despite evidence that they have outlived their abilities to respond to the needs of society or provide platforms from which to do so. Instead, their presence has continued because of institutional inertia. The recognition of liquid design disciplines is not undertaken in order to force open a position within the university or elicit acceptance by an antiquated, medieval academic structure. Rather, it should change our very ways of knowing.

We seek a change that creates a new center not occupied by discrete disciplines, but rather by new forms of liquid knowing. Liquid design disciplines offer avenues of study and research coherent with the complexity of post- and post-postmodern problems. They are our way forward.

It is our hope that this can serve as a point for in-depth examination and reimagination of current models of disciplinary inquiry and the process of university education. Interior Design and Conflict Resolution and Peace Studies have been pulled together here to prove a point, but this is not a call for a discipline-by-discipline review in which each area is held up to be measured. The renaming or recategorization of areas is not sufficient if the deconstructed pieces remain autonomous and unaffected. Instead, the very foundations of fractured and defended knowledge must be overthrown and replaced with a tectonic shift that allows us to celebrate and participate in the holistic, integrated, and mutable nature of human knowledge. Let us emerge from Plato's cave and into the blinding light of day, to look upon the face of the idea.

Discussion Questions

1. What is the reconception of the disciplines that Mendoza and Matyók advocate and why is this liquid?
   a. How are liquid disciplines changing the knowledge landscape?
   b. What are the characteristics of these liquid disciplines?
   c. What are the new liquid discipline spaces?

2. What is a knowledge culture of spaces in the context of what Mendoza and Matyók are discussing?
   a. What is a knowledge culture in the example they give of interior design?

3. What is a third knowledge culture?

References

Abbott, A. (1988). *The System of Professions: An Essay on the Division of Expert Labor*. Chicago: University of Chicago Press.

Alger, C. (1996). Introduction: Reflection on Peace Research Traditions. *International Journal of Peace Studies*, *1* (1), 1–5.

Bauman, Z. (2000). *Liquid Modernity*. Maldern, MA: Polity.

Buchanon, R. (1992). Wicked Problems in Design Thinking. *Design Issues*, *8* (2), 5–21.

Burke, J. (1999). *The Knowledge Web: From Electronic Agents to Stonehenge and Back—And Other Journeys Through Knowledge*. New York: Simon & Schuster.

Cook, S. D., & Seely Brown, J. (1999). Bridging Epistemologies: The Generative Dance Between Organizational Knowledge and Organizational Knowing. *Organization Science*, *10* (4), 381–400.

Galtung, J. (1997). Peace Education Is Only Meaningful If It Leads to Action. *UNCESCO Courier*, *50* (1), 4–8.

Guerin, D. A., & Martin, C. S. (2004). The Career Cycle Approach to Defining the Interior Design Profession's Body of Knowledge. *Journal of Interior Design*, *30* (2), 1–22.

Kuhn, T. S. (1996). *The Structure of Scientific Revolutions* (3rd ed.). Chicago: University of Chicago Press.

Livingstone, D. N. (1992). *The Geographical Tradition*. Malden, MA: Blackwell Publishers.

Martin, C. S., & Guerin, D. A. (2005). The Interior Design Profession's Body of Knowledge. Interior Design Educator's Council. Retrieved from http://www.careersininteriordesign.com/idbok.pdf.

Mendoza, H. R. (2009). The WikiD: An Alternative Approach to the Body of Knowledge. *Journal of Interior Design, 34* (2), 1–19.

Papanek, V. (1971). *Design for the Real World*. New York: Pantheon Books.

Peters, R. (1965). Education as Initiation. In R. Archambault (Ed.), *Philosophical Analysis and Education*. London: Routledge and Kegan Paul.

Readings, B. (1996). *The University in Ruins*. Cambridge, MA: Harvard University Press.

Russell, B. (1945). *The History of Western Philosophy*. New York: Simon & Schuster.

Schön, D. A. (1983). *The Reflective Practitioner: How Professionals Think in Action*. New York: Basic Books.

Sik-Wah Fong, P., & Ka-Yan Ip, D. (1999). Cost Engineering: A Separate Academic Discipline? *European Journal of Engineering Education, 24* (1), 73–82.

Dialogues and Perspectives

1.3 How Is Design Inquiry Different from Scientific Inquiry?

Harold Nelson

The following article is the result of a recent conversation I had with Harold Nelson to glean some of his thoughts about what constitutes design inquiry. I posed the following questions:

- How is design inquiry different from scientific inquiry?
- How are technology and intention vehicles for imaging change?

Harold Nelson: Design inquiry is different from scientific inquiry in that it is inclusive of analytic reasoning—i.e., determination of that which is true—but it is also inclusive of determining that which is real, that which would be ideal, and that which ought to become real. Design inquiry results in knowledge for action. Knowledge for action is different from scientific knowledge of what is true universally, contingently, and predictably.

Scientific inquiry is, at its essence, focused on developing descriptions and explanations of phenomena and events in the world, but descriptions and explanations do not prescribe action. Design inquiry prescribes action based on inputs from clients, decision makers, and other stakeholders. Design action is based on both sound rational decisions as well as professional judgments. A concern arises when design is scientized. The justifica-

tion for action, particularly action through design, cannot rest on formal logic, objective rationalization, and mathematical measure alone. Design inquiry includes inputs from nonobjective sources such as empathy, emotion, imagination, holistic reasoning, and a host of other approaches residing outside of the scientific methods of inquiry.

Design in architecture, for example, is becoming driven by **BIM**—building information modeling. BIM is a computer technology predicated on objective scientific thinking—prediction and control—that too often displaces or limits professional agency. Professionals are removed from accountability and responsibility when a science-based form of artificial intelligence in the configuration of software technology replaces human judgment. These science-based algorithms are at the basis of computer-aided design processes that rightly provide an excellent means for describing and explaining aspects of complex socio-technical designs. However, description and explanation cannot prescribe which choices or judgments ought to be made in design situations.

Such technologies are also great aids in helping to predict and control the behavior and consequences of complex designs, but prediction and control do not replace ethical judgments and moral responsibilities. Technologies like BIM can augment but certainly cannot replace professional designers, their judgments, or fiduciary responsibilities to all stakeholders including the natural environment and future generations. Ethics must be included as a balanced counterpoint to rationality and technology in order to ensure that the right kind of design action is taken for the right reasons for the right people.

Design inquiry is different from scientific inquiry in other ways as well. Every design is either a system or a part of a system. Designs and designers do not exist in a vacuum. As Russell Ackoff says, you can't optimize a solution for a part of a system without running the risk of suboptimizing the performance of the whole system. You have to design for the whole system while making trade-offs in and among the parts for the benefit of the whole. Scientific analysis assumes that the parts can be dealt with independent of one another. Descriptions are made in this way but not explanations. Explanations require that the whole system be taken into account, which is the realm of systems science. But again, analytic science even with the addition of systems science cannot prescribe what actions ought to be taken either in reforming, transforming, or forming systems. Design knowing is the possession of knowledge for such actions.

Knowledge for action is different in that it is comprised of making judgments that cannot be separated from the judgment maker in the way that decisions can be separated from decision makers as bits of knowledge. Judgments are revealed through action. In order for designers to take action, judgments are a necessary and legitimate way to bring closure to design deliberations as they occur throughout any design process.

When we engage in design inquiry, we cannot separate thinking from acting. In design schools we cannot learn how to practice without learning how to think and reflect on what we create, who we create for, and why we create this particular thing in this place at this time in this way and how it will be made real.

In addition, a traditional Ph.D., a Doctorate of Philosophy in Science, cannot create knowledge for action or even guides for action because the degree process was not designed to be that kind of inquiring system. We cannot determine "what ought to be" made real using research methods. We can only determine what is universally or contingently true using accepted research methods.

It is understood generally that values, in distinction to facts, come from clients and stakeholders. When designers practice, they ideally enter into a contract of service and they become part of a design conversation about "what ought to be made real in the world." Values, including ethical, aesthetic, and spiritual, are part of a holistic conversation of "what ought to become or be made real."

Source: Conversation/Interview with Harold Nelson—personal correspondence January 20, 2011.

References

Ackoff's Keynote Address at ICSTM 2004 Conference

Dr. Russell Ackoff on a systems approach to the mess the world is in. Keynote delivered May 19, 2004, at the International Conference on Systems Thinking and Management (ICSTM), University of Pennsylvania. Accessed July 8, 2012, at http://ackoffcenter.blogs.com/ackoff_center_weblog/2009/02/ackoffs-keynote-address-at-icstm-2004-conference.html.

Video of the conference available at:
Part 1: http://www.youtube.com/watch?v=ZLU3aoQ7t7c.
Part 2: http://www.youtube.com/watch?v=VsF32GAHVfI.
Part 3: http://www.youtube.com/watch?v=_Z3hJIGHdfk.

SUMMARY

We have introduced in this chapter basic definitions of space, meaning, and design, while also examining the paradigms and theoretical constructions that accompany these ideas. We have also laid a fundamental groundwork for the next two chapters. In Chapter 2 we explore specific theoretical and philosophical views of space and expand on the basic definitions provided in this chapter. In Chapter 3 we expand on the knowledge spaces that frame design thinking and concepts of space themselves.

SUGGESTED READINGS

Crotty, M. (1998). *The Foundations of Social Research: Meaning and Perspective in the Research Process*. Thousand Oaks, CA: Sage Publications.

Friedman, K. (1997). Design Science and Design Education. In P. McGrory (Ed.), *The Challenge of Complexity* (pp. 54–72). Helsinki: University of Art and Design, Helsinki UIAH.

Friedman, K. (2003). Theory Construction in Design Research: Criteria, Approaches, and Methods. *Design Studies 24*, 507–522.

Guba, E. G., & Lincoln, Y. S. (1994). Competing Paradigms in Qualitative Research. In Denzin, N. K., & Lincoln, Y. S. (Eds.), *Handbook of Qualitative Research* (pp. 105–117). London: Sage Publications.

Nelson, H., & Stolterman, E. (2003.) *The Design Way: Intentional Change in an Unpredictable World. Foundations and Fundamentals of Design Competence.* Englewood Cliffs, NJ: Technology Publications.

O'Brien, D. (2006). *An Introduction to the Theory of Knowledge.* Cambridge, UK: Polity Press.

OVERVIEW QUESTIONS FOR DISCUSSION

1. What constitutes knowledge in research versus knowledge in the design disciplines?

   a. What are the traditional forms of research, and how does design research position itself relative to scientific modes of research?

   b. What are alternate paradigms and ways of knowing as compared to more traditional scientific modes of inquiry?

   c. What are the values of critical design and research?

2. Explore Wilwerding's proposal for design specialties as foundations for knowledge.

   a. What are design functional specialities?

   b. How might we consider these for diverse concepts of design and space?

3. What is design inquiry in the context of what you have read in this first chapter?

   a. What are the differences between design inquiry and scientific inquiry in light of Cross, Friedman's and Nelson/Stolterman's ideas?

   b. How does Harold Nelson distinguish between design inquiry and scientific inquiry in his conversations?

   c. How does Wilwerding unfold these ideas as compared with Friedman and Nelson/Stolterman?

   d. Are there distinctions of design research and research about interior spaces? Why? Why not?

4. Define and articulate design research and critical thinking

   a. What is Desiderata?

   b. How do we initiate design thinking using Nelson and Stolterman's ideas?

   c. What are liquid disciplines, according to Mendoza and Matyók?

CHAPTER 2

Aesthetics, Poststructuralism, and Pragmatic Spaces

space, context, meaning, place, relative space, absolute space, aesthetic meaning, beauty, social construction of space, space as place, aesthetics, critical material space, (new) pragmatism, atmosphere, fragmented space, dialogue spaces, space as a medium

AFTER READING THIS CHAPTER, YOU WILL BE ABLE TO:

- Differentiate between different philosophical and theoretical views of space.
- Define space in terms of relative or absolute space, space as place, space as atmospheric, space as aesthetic, space as beyond container, and so on.
- Discover philosophical and theoretical perspectives about space from diverse disciplines such as philosophy, cultural geography, aesthetic theory, architecture, and design.
- Consider contexts of phenomenology, structuralism, and poststructuralism, and how knowledge is constructed.

INTRODUCTION

Spaces are what we make of them. We create them, or they exist when we arrive. Just as we do, they change, engage, and live, in part, as a response to our interactions. Spaces are illusory yet real, tangible yet intangible, and ever-changing depending on our point of view. Whether it is expressed in visual image, in spoken language, or through text, spaces reveal qualities that manifest meanings. And yet space is also historically grounded in both philosophical constructions and multiple meanings influenced by historic contexts and philosophical arguments.

We will explore meanings of space as these are traced over time and within the philosophical frameworks of structuralism, poststructuralism, phenomenology, semiology, and aesthetic theory. Space has been understood within history in particular contexts that are changing with new meanings in current contemporary theory emerging, such as the contexts of aesthetics of experience and lived pragmatic contexts. Whether it is dissecting concepts of space through language or living experiences within spaces as dynamic and changing entities, space becomes a dynamic place of lived experience.

We examine the evolution of these constructs over time and through various theories and concepts in such diverse disciplines as architecture, sociology, philosophy, cultural geography, and aesthetics. Philosophies and theories about space, space as place, aesthetic theories and concepts, and the intersection of spaces are all examined through the lenses of theoretical papers, provocations, questions from a perspective of "place as place," and the context of lived experiences.

Justin Wilwerding begins with "A History of Aesthetics and the Structuring of Space," exploring how definitions, philosophical ideas, and concepts about space are constructed theoretically. Space is examined in terms of relative and absolute space, space as place, and spaces as social constructions, and he tackles perspectives ranging from Aristotle and Plato to Baudrillard, Foucault, and Merleau-Ponty, among others. Spatial contexts are also defined by aesthetics. Wilwerding considers aesthetic judgment and how semiotic representations of spaces affect the things that compose the experienced environment. Objects, volumes, and meanings are coexisting aspects of space; Wilwerding proposes ways to critically examine these in terms of place, aesthetics, aesthetic judgment, and meaning.

Melles and Huppatz unfold theoretical perspectives about space derived from architectural theory and practices within a (new) critical pragmatism that they propose supports the emerging ways we understand interiors. In explaining the ways that philosophies have guided our views of space in modern times, they juxtapose theoretical concepts of modernist spaces with emerging arguments about phenomenological spaces as pragmatic poststructuralist places. These are places of meaning and context, grounded in social constructions, and made possible through meaning making. Spaces are explored as either outgrowths of structuralist modes wherein spaces are decoded and universalized or as poststructuralist places of human meaning contextualized in the experiences of the spaces. They propose that the interior is ill defined and usually understood as a "contained architectural space" and thus linked inextricably to architecture. Alternatively, they propose that experience and different understandings of space as multidimensional, temporal, and informed by pragmatic stances force new meanings of space, influenced by pragmatism and the ideas of Dewey, among others.

Spaces become dynamic and lived places with the subjective and local experiences of the people who use them. The Provocation explores what is meant by poststructuralism in the context of spaces, by suggesting that phenomenology and lived experience are fundamental components of the ways that spaces engage in the construction of meaningful experiences. How is this meaning made? Why is this knowledge useful and necessary to examine? Through Drew Vasilevich's perspective, the Provocation examines issues of those aesthetics and the question of how we live. He proposes what contexts of meaning we attach to the places and things we hold true in our lived experiences.

Travis Mann's Dialogues and Perspectives places these concepts into narrating pragmatic experiences from the standpoint of "place as place." Mann considers place as place through a view of life experiences, how spaces converge and diverge largely based on the human experience of travel, and the places experienced along the paths that we take. Whether it is the 7-Eleven store in the United States or the Australian Outback, the perspective of the aboriginal or the white man, places are anchors of subjective experience for each individual as they appropriate them, grounded by cultural identity. Identity, social interactions, and subsequent memories often reside in the places visited, experienced, or frequented. Experiences build on previous ones, whether individual or in a social context, including culture and identity, and all are anchored in the concept of place.

Space has been variously defined as political currency (Markus, 1993), as a medium of communication (Thiis-Evensen, 1990), as a pedagogical system (Markus, 1993), and even as a sacramental artifact (Eliade, 1987). The semiotic power of interior space is one of the least critically analyzed components of human culture (Hardwick, 1977). This essay examines the history of notions of space beginning with the metaphysics of Aristotle (Zalta, 2009) and concluding with modern questions of the significance of space as examined in sociology, anthropology (Turner, 2001), archeology, and cultural geography (Tuan, 1990).

The Development of the Idea of Space

It has been said that the medium in which interior designers work is space. But space is a notion that has a long history in a range of disciplines, all of which have influenced each other, beginning in ancient cultures and extending through the present era. To work in the medium of space, in a thoughtful and effective manner, designers and architects should be expected to examine the history of concepts of space, including its purpose and meaning. Yet from an educational and disciplinary perspective, little effort has been devoted to the study of this

important element of our profession. In this paper we propose to examine the history of theories of space, both aesthetic and metaphysical, in an effort to explicate the conceptual history of space and, in so doing, uncover the origins of our notions of modern space as a social medium and as a cultural construct within which designers shape our perceptions of an environment and our understanding of its intentions.

To begin to understand the context in which we understand space within the built environment, we must search cultural history for the development of ideas of space as a broad metaphysical category. Clearly, various cultures have treated space and place in vastly differing ways. The most ancient notions of space are cosmological—that is, they concern myths of the creation of the universe. The great historian of religions Mircea Eliade makes clear that for ancient human culture the sacred was the organizing principle that provides a means to order space:

There is, then, a sacred space, and hence a strong, significant space; there are other spaces that are not sacred and so are without structure or consistency, amorphous. Nor is this all. For religious man, this spatial non-homogeneity finds expression in the experience of opposition between the space that is sacred—the only *real* and *real-ly* existing space—and all other space, the formless expanse surrounding it. (1987, p. 20)

Even in our present time we see remnants of these notions of sacred space, the notion of one's *sanctum sanctorum*, one's most private space, as the groundwork for organizing the remainder of our experience and keeping chaos at bay. In Eliade's words:

It is not a matter of theoretical speculation, but of a primary religious experience that precedes all reflection on the world. For it is the break effected in space that allows the world to be constituted, because it reveals the fixed point, the central axis for all future orientation. (1987, p. 21)

For modern man still, we can identify the basis of the horror of homelessness as a loss of sacred space, the loss of a fixed point—what Eliade later refers to as the *axis mundi*, or the tent-pole of the universe, that provides a means for us to locate and ground our day-to-day existence. Thus without a foundational ordering principle around which we can order the remainder of space, we are literally lost.

Cosmologies begin with order and chaos, and work to make sense of these two entities. This is important because space, unbounded and seemingly limitless space, represents chaos. Space without an ordering principle is equivalent to nothingness, and human beings (at least in Western cul-ture) are uncomfortable with nothingness; in essence without a something to provide a foundation for our understanding nothingness, space can be terrifying.

These cosmologies, developed through the ages of human culture, form our first orientation to the production and segmentation of space. Thus, these orientations begin with two places: home and temple. The organization of these places are representations of both our understanding of the ideal ordering of the universe and the stable basis by which all other aspects of life are ordered. Emerging from this ordering we will see that human culture seeks an ordering principle that is representative of the ways in which human beings have envisaged their relationships to nature, to other human beings, and to cultural and political institutions.

As human culture progressed, the cosmological views of the organization of space evolved from a perspective in which humans sought to identify divine principles of order to one that sought to clarify the operational structures of order itself (divinely ordained or not). Beginning with Aristotle's metaphysics, we can identify the development of abstract notions about space as an entity. These notions have a number of elements or, using Aristotle's term, "categories." As regards our subject, there are two relevant categories: substance and place (Bodnar, 2010). Space can also be examined in relation to other concepts that Aristotle examines, change and motion. In some real sense, Aristotle sees space/place as an entity, not as mere emptiness. Space is a constant that allows substance to change through motion. The essence of space for Aristotle might be conceived of as void in that it represents a location that can be filled by a substance. In this context, the nature of space is locational—that is, it identifies both one place in relation to another, as well as to the movement implied between spaces and the time it takes to move from one place to another. Aristotle begins by denoting the meanings of the notions up and down— upward movement and downward movement—by identifying these directions with the center of the universe (which was coincident with the center of the Earth) (Huggett & Hoefer, 2009). Aristotle sees space as something rather than nothing.

Space as It Becomes a Place

Aristotle's views mark the beginning of a long dichotomous tradition of the way we conceive of space. Space may be something, particularly when it becomes a place, a location for something; this theory is called *relative space*. In contrast, space can be conceived of as nothingness, pure potential without form or substance or meaning—a theory known as *absolute space*. The opposing pole of this argument begins with the ancient Greek mathematician Euclid, who defined space from the perspective of the distance between some point of origin and an infinite number of points lying along a straight line. This definition implies that space is unrelated to substance and is limitless. The dualistic argument continues through the medieval period, in which scholars developed arguments for both points of view:

While some philosophers, such as Telesio, Campanella, and Bruno, held space to be always filled with matter (i.e., a plenum) yet somehow independent of matter, others, like Patrizi and Gassendi, endorsed a more absolutist notion that allowed spaces totally devoid of matter (i.e., vacuum). (Slowik, 2009)

The argument continued through the seventeenth century. Proponents of the locational relativist perspective included Descartes (1596–1650), who held that the primary characteristic of matter (substance) was "extension" and likewise that the primary characteristic of space was also "extension." Thus, he concludes that matter and space were one and the same. Descartes is also notable for extending and modifying the Euclidean notion of space. However, Descartes conceived of this system as a means to precisely describe physical geometries (from an algebraic perspective) rather than as a means to describe empty and limitless space. Descartes's coordinates did, however, have another result in the definition of space: the capacity to impose a locational device upon space (particularly the land) that would provide a means to define specific and definite locations of boundaries and to therefore segment space in a prescriptive manner. We will return to this notion of a defined and specific boundary later.

Relative versus Absolute Space

The dichotomy of relative versus absolute space continues in the next generation with

Newton (1643–1727), who, in examining the manner in which Descartes defines the ways in which a body moves through space, concluded that space must not in fact be a substance and should therefore be considered as absolute (Huggett & Hoefer, 2009). At the same time Newton modified this perspective slightly by also concluding that space is not literally nothing. As Huggett and Hoefer write:

> In De Gravitatione, Newton rejected both the standard philosophical categories of substance and attribute as suitable characterizations. Absolute space is not a substance for it lacks causal powers and does not have a fully independent existence, and yet not an attribute since it would exist even in a vacuum, which by definition is a place where there are no bodies in which it might inhere. Newton proposes that space is what we might call a "pseudo-substance," more like a substance than property, yet not quite a substance.

In contrast to Descartes and Newton, who attempted to examine space as a real entity, Newton's contemporary Leibnitz held the view that space is a construction of the mind, a heuristic device, if you will, that allows us to track the movement (motion) of bodies relative to other bodies. This again represents the "relativistic" perspective of space as a set of relations rather than as empty void (Norberg-Schulz, 2001).

From the eighteenth until the late nineteenth century, Newton's views of absolute space dominated intellectual debate over the nature of space. Beginning in the 1880s and continuing until the mid-twentieth century, we see a series of scholars in both philosophy and physics develop assertive positions in which they develop very convincing views that space must be viewed relatively, as opposed to in absolutist terms. Both Mach and subsequently Einstein held views that space, time, mass, and energy are inexorably linked and that space is an entity and that it is not merely a void. These scholars convincingly assert (and experimental data affirms) that space is not merely space but is in fact space-time—that is, a set of relations between bodies and forces that can only exist relative to ·one another. It is from this perspective that Einstein develops the Theory of General Relativity, in which space and motion cannot be separated as entities and, hence, space is tied to time and distance and their relationship.

While this argument seems rather lengthy, it is important to understand that our notions of space as designers are grounded in both the philosophical and scientific development of how we understand the concept of space. The philosophical examination of space has a long and vigorous history, but from this history we can see the development of three ideas relevant to our culture and to the practice of designers who design spaces:

1. Space is a substance—Relativist perspective (Aristotle, Mach, Einstein).
2. Space is a void—Absolutist perspective (Euclid, Newton).
3. Space is a relativist mental construct (Leibniz).

These ideas form the foundation of thought regarding notions of space within our culture and provide the basic orientation for the study of space and place in various disciplines.

Space versus Place

In contrast to philosophy, psychology and the social sciences do not broadly examine the question of "What is space as an entity?" but rather propose to build on the orientation proposed by Leibniz, that space is a mental or social construct. Nevertheless, how place and the production of place is studied continues to draw upon a variety of notions of place as space—that is, place can be studied as a substance that is socially constructed and place can be studied as a space that possesses infinite social potential but begins as pure undifferentiated void. An understanding of place begins in this theoretical perspective with the individual, where each person's experience influences his or her views of place and behavior in relation to it. In this view, our understanding that space and ultimately place is the product of an active search for the meaning of our environment, and equally importantly, that place is not an object to be known but is in fact the result of our intentional act of knowing and the search for meaning. In his paper, Moore (1974) proposed that

> [I]t is argued that in as much as there is no way for us to know the nature of "reality" except through the minds of persons, it is impossible to separate the process of knowing from the resultant knowledge, and, more importantly, it is impossible to separate what is known from what is "real." Thus, what is "real" is in fact what is only taken to be "real," i.e., a construction of reality, a product of an intentional act of knowing. In as much as this "reality" can only be known through the efforts of particular minds, it follows that knowledge of "reality" in general, and of the environment in particular, is the product of an active construction of thought. (Moore, 1974, p. 184)

This notion of space and place is enormously important, since it implies that our understanding of space and place, while influenced by the data of sense provided by our experience, is almost entirely an artifact of our processes of knowing, in essence, that reality as such does not exist "out there" but within the human mind, and it is constructed on the basis of our desire for meaning. Moore and other psychologists have taken the view that the process by which we know about our surroundings is an active one and one that is "mediated" and altered by our ongoing collection and categorization of environmental experiences.

Psychology as a discipline has developed a wide range of theories regarding both how individuals understand the built environment and how they respond to it. According to Kopec (2006), these theories fall into two groups: theories of environmental perception and theories of human environment relationships. Although designers have leveraged these theoretical constructs heavily, too little inquiry has taken place regarding exactly how these notions have influenced the manner in which designers either conceive of or manipulate space as a medium. While we have studied the artifacts that result from the processes of design, we have not gone very far in our study of the processes by which designers use psychological theories to inform their manipulation of space within the design process. Psychologists like Hall (1966) and Sommer (1967, 1969) explore environment and behavior theories as these relate to space, but how these theories are applied to the development of spatial solutions by designers remains problematic. Obviously theories like those introduced by Hall and Sommer help to shape the quantities and arrangements of space, but we are left to work out theories related to the qualitative nature of spatial composition. Some theories developed by psychologists do give us clues regarding the aesthetic elements of spatial composition. These are helpful and may inform design process, yet the manner of direct application of these theories in the context of process remains unclear.

Similarly, sociologists have been instrumental in helping both designers and society in general understand the manner in which space is defined for groups and cultures. Sociological theory may in the end be somewhat more useful in defining the nature and use of space as place, a conceptual definition of location that embraces the relationship between people, objects, and their surroundings as a meaningful and interactive structure. As Gieryn (2000)

noted in his paper "A Space for Place in Sociology":

[T]he three defining features of place—location, materials form and meaningfulness—should remain bundled. They cannot be ranked into greater or lesser significance for social life, nor can one be reduced down to an expression of another. Place has a plenitude, a completeness, such that the phenomenon is analytically and substantially destroyed if the three become unraveled or one of them is forgotten. (p. 466)

In the case of sociology, the conceptual construct originated by Aristotle is followed, space/place is a substance and must sustain its internal coherence. Gieryn goes on to note that space is *not* the same as place. He discusses space in various forms and notes that space is characterized by geometrical form and is often represented by "geographic or cartographic metaphors (boundaries, territories) that define conceptual or analytic concepts." Perhaps most importantly Gieryn related that

Space is not place[;] space is what place becomes when the unique gathering of things, meanings and values are sucked out. (Gieryn, 2000, p. 456)

These defining features seem eminently important to the understanding of space and place as they relate to the design of interior spaces. It is clear that at some level of the design process, designers are entirely concerned with space, its geometry, its quantity, and its relation. But at some other point in design process, professional interior designers are extremely concerned with the transition of space to place; we work to invest the cartographic quantities we have defined with deeper meaning and intent. The question becomes how and when does this transition properly occur in order to attend to the significance of space in potentiate and that of place in specificity? Yet further, how is the appropriateness of both space and place defined in relation to both the mathematical and meaningful goals of design process? Finally, what are the factors that affect the composition of both space and place within the design process from the interior designer's perspective?

The final question is perhaps the easiest to answer from both a sociological and design perspective. The factors affecting the composition of space and place are varied, they are certainly functional, related to the physical constraints of the activities proposed for space, and they are quantified by the requiring of modern technology and its constant march of innovation. Yet more complexly, the factors affecting the composition of the built environment are political, they are economic, and they are gendered. Interior design research has examined the more quantifiable aspects of space and place, but the discipline continues to struggle with the deeper and in many cases more potent determinates of spatial and place design. There has been too little examination of the manner in which the design process can or should address the conflicting political, economic, and social agendas that are virtually ever-

present in the design of interior environments. Only recently have we begun to see articles regarding the complex issues of the "social compact" (Barbara G. Anderson, Peggy L. Honey, & Michael T. Dudek, 2007; Stauffer, 2007). Gieryn noted:

> It is, at once, the making of a place and the negotiation, translation, and alignment of political and economic interests, technical skills and imperatives, aesthetic judgments and societal futures (Stieber, 1998). The finished places that we see, inhabit, visit and suffer are as much the consequence of decisions made by place-professional as of the wishes of clients upon whom they depend for their livelihood. (Gieryn, 2000, p. 471)

and further Gieryn states:

> as the profession patrols its porous boundaries from encroachments by engineers, developers, amateurs, and U-design-it software. All of these struggles—melded with emergent constraints from clients' preferences and budget, local building codes, the terrain of the physical site—get materialized in the built-form of a place. (Gieryn, 2000, p. 471)

Gieryn's thesis is that the role of place in sociology is not described by the study of place, but rather in an explicit and conscious awareness of the role of place in the broadest possible range of sociological studies that are "informed by a sense of place" (Gieryn, 2000, p. 468). He has noted that virtually all sociology is location related and that the framework of place becomes the context for any sociological study.

One of the most notable sociologists to study space and place from the perspective of interior design was Jean Baudrillard. In his book *A System of Objects* (1996), Baudrillard takes a different tack regarding how space is composed and defined. Beginning with the interior design object of furniture, Baudrillard first notes that traditional interior spaces were defined in an almost centrifugal manner—that is, the object, the piece or arrangement of furniture, defined the composition and arrangement of space and that this composition and arrangement both reflected and reinforced the roles of the members of a household who occupied those spaces. This approach is also critically important both to the interior designer's understanding of space/place and, more broadly, to our understanding of the impact of societal roles on space and of space on societal roles. Baudrillard also notes that modern furniture is largely freed from its symbolic social convention, but it is pared down to its most basic composition, pure function. In turn, this frees space and the role of the individual in that space to explore a broader and more pragmatic self-definition, Baudrillard noted:

A bed is a bed, a chair is a chair, and there is not relationship between them so long as each serves only the function it is supposed to serve. And without such a relationship there can be no space, for space exists only when it is opened up, animated, invested with rhythm and expanded by a correlation between objects and a transcendence of their functions in this new structure. In a way space is the new object's true freedom, whereas its function is merely its formal freedom. The bourgeois dining-room was structured, but its structure was closed. The functional environment is more open, freer but it is destructured, fragmented into its various functions. (Baudrillard, 1996, p. 18)

Baudrillard saw a distinct shift in our approach to furnishings/objects and spaces; whereas traditional furnishings were invested with complex social meaning, modern objects and furnishings are more often systems of function, divested of ritual and almost sacramental significance. In this regard, Baudrillard identified the role of interior design in modern culture:

We are beginning to see what the new model of the home-dweller looks like; "man the interior designer" is neither an owner nor a mere user—rather, he is an active engineer of atmosphere. Space is at his disposal like a kind of distrusted system, and by controlling this space he holds sway over all possible reciprocal locations between the objects there, and hence over all the roles they are capable of assuming. (It follows that he must be "functional" himself: he and the space in question must be homogeneous if his messages of design are to leave him and return to him successfully.) What matters to him is neither possession nor enjoyment but responsibility, in the strict sense which implies that it is at all times possible for him to determine "responses." . . . He discovers himself in the manipulation and tactical equilibrium of a system. (Baudrillard, 1996, p. 27)

For Baudrillard, there seems to be a duality in the way that interior designers, and indeed the culture, compose and appreciate the value of spaces. Traditional objects and the spaces that contained them were laden with highly structured meaning; this tied the appreciation of objects to a social and moral structure and bound the users of spaces and objects to that order. Modern interior designers, by contrast, are freed from much of the social and moral hierarchy of previous generations, and users are freed of the hegemony of these symbolic systems. At the same time, this forces both modern designers and users of the built environment into an endless organizational game of manipulating objects and the spaces that are a reflection of their composition into an endless series of possible expressions, but expressions that are no longer a dialogue between object space and user, but rather one of the control of the system of meanings. Thus, the contrast is between participation in a system of meaning and one of continuous control over ever-shifting meanings. This perspective represents both an important structural vision of objects and spaces as well as an exploration of the way in which spaces and objects shape social meaning through their composition, inherent meaning, and visual heritage (or lack thereof).

Another prominent sociologist, Henri Lefebvre, elaborated on Baudrillard's notions regarding space in his book *The Production of Space*. In this book Lefebvre leverages Marxist theory (much modern sociology is influenced by Marxist thought emerging out of an important sociological tradition begun at the University of Frankfurt am Main, in Germany) of production to examine space as an entity.

First, like Baudrillard, Lefebvre considers space to be the product of a system of individuals and objects that occupy it. This idea is not generally foreign, but Lefebvre elaborates on this theme, differentiating between the traditional *composition* of space as a work that emerges over time as a set of relationships shaped by those who live in the space; and *production*, which again reflects Baudrillard's views that modern space is systematized, modualized, and preplanned. Lefebvre's approach changes the manner in which spaces and the objects that animate them emerge. In essence, modern space that is reduced to a standardized commodity is both more mutable and more subject to the manipulations of those who seek to exert power over social relationships. The meaning of space does not emerge from the working out of social relations, but is rather constructed in an intentional and calculated manner. This process of producing/constructing space also implies that, according to Lefebvre, space is not a real thing that has any actual permanence but is constructed, destroyed, and reconstructed as a set of meaningful relations over and over again (1995).

About Critical Science and Critical Thinking

Lefebvre's thesis seems related to the methodological structure of Critical Science. This is a likely association since Critical Science also developed out of the Frankfurt School of social theory, of which Lefebvre is a descendant. Jürgen Habermas, the progenitor of Critical Science, posited that, unlike empirical positivism and interpretive approaches to research, in which the researcher stands at various degrees of removal from the subject of study, it is impossible for a researcher (particularly one who studies or is engaged in the production of human meaning) to stand apart and objectivize the subject of study, but rather the researcher (or in the case of the present argument the interior designer) has no choice but to be a full participant in the production of meaning along with the objects, space, users, and clients involved. A foundational principle of Critical Science is to eliminate distortions of meaning that are the result of tacit and unexplored understanding of the people involved in the production of meaning; to examine the sociopolitical assumptions of various groups in an effort to find consensus surrounding what the meaning of a particular social construct should be. Interior designers encounter these distortions of meaning on virtually every project they encounter—the divergence of a husband and wife regarding the level of formality of their living space; the divergence of upper management, middle management, and workers regarding the most effective design of the workplace; the conflict between security

and openness in a public government center. The question that remains however is, what is the most appropriate and effective role for the professional interior designer in this context?

Human Ecosystem Theory

Another framework in which we might view this notion of the creation of meaning is Human Ecosystem theory (Guerin, 1992). Human Ecosystem theory also holds the view that our culture is organized through an interrelated structure of the human organism, the natural environment, the social environment, and the built environment. Unfortunately, here too we are left to struggle with an effective theory of process that provides designers of the built environment with an understanding of how to apply this paradigm to the process of creating meaningful environments, such as those interior designers attempt to create.

About Social Justice, Meaning, and Social Construction

From the sociological perspective, we see that space is an ever-shifting set of relations and as a standardized commodity of value that is often held under significant control by interior designers. This raises the question regarding how those who design spaces both mediate meaning and control the distribution of space as a commodity in the service of clients and users. Here again we are confronted by the extremely problematical social justice role of interior design. We are also presented with a second challenge regarding the impact of our role in directing that selection of objects and the shaping of spaces that valorize some social relationships at the expense of others. Do we as interior designers possess an adequate understanding of the effects of our roles in this process of social construction? I think we must admit that we do not. We can certainly examine our history as arbiters of what might euphemistically be called *taste*, but in reality was the reinforcement of a set of highly structured power relationships within society, but that role now seems a quaint artifact of an outdated professional definition. The question that remains is how do we now function as arbiters not of taste, but of the process by which social relations are constructed, altered, or disassembled?

Cultural Geography and Meaningful Space Structures

Cultural geography is a related discipline (or subdiscipline) to sociology, which is even more closely tied to notions of place and space. Let us examine this academic discipline for clues regarding how to examine and clarify the medium of space and its aesthetic nature. Perhaps the most notable academic in cultural geography in the last 25 years is Yi-Fu Tuan.

Tuan's work also examines the meaningful structures of space, but unlike Baudrillard and Lefebvre, he takes a more historical and culturally diverse view of space and place. Tuan asserts that a defining characteristic of place (as opposed to space) is one of scale; that the size of a place

is typically scaled such that it is within the full range of human perception, that it is in some sense perceptually and conceptually digestible. Much as we would cut a morsel of food in order to make it easy to consume, so space is segmented into place to provide a delimiting frame within which to grasp the fullest possible range of meanings (Tuan, 1990).

Tuan looks at place from the perspectives of spatial perception and phenomenology, seeking to understand how space becomes place. Tuan introduces the idea that biology, specifically the biology and organization of our perceptual systems, is the superstructure by which we organize meaningful sensory information (2001). Thus the physical experiences of the body and perception are important influences in the further development of conceptual meaning:

> The direction upward, against gravity, is then not only a feeling that guides movement but a feeling that leads to the inscription of regions in space to which we attach values, such as those expressed by high and low, rise and decline, climbing and falling, superior and inferior, elevated and downcast, looking up in awe and looking down in contempt. (Tuan, 2001, p. 395)

Thus, our creation of space and objects is intrinsically tied to the proportions of the human body. This provides both an elaboration on, and confirmation of, the notions introduced by Baudrillard and Lefebvre that space/place does not exist without human presence.

Tuan also locates the meaning of space and place temporally. Our experience is not isolated in the present but is also mediated by our past experiences and our imagined future ones. According to Tuan, we tend to view the space that we occupy in the frame of the present, but the spaces that are immediately about the space serve as tropes both past and future, our experience invests these secondary or, as Tuan calls them, latent spaces, with both memories of the past and the imagined possibilities of the future.

Tuan's contributions indicated that as much as a system or construction of social meanings and hierarchies, space also represents more basic sets of human meanings of experiential history. It translates physical meanings into a broader meaningful context in which physical sensation is transferred to a social context, one in which there is an intermingling of discrete physical sensory information that is interconnected, where the physical sensation of sharpness is transferred to the olfactory in a sharp smell and in which the implications of physical height are conferred onto social concepts such as upper class. The ideas that Tuan introduces are also directly related to semiotic and phenomenological constructs that will provide an important possibility in terms of a theoretical framework for the manner in which interior designers and others shape and compose space and place.

Space, Place, and Aesthetics from the Interior Design Perspective

The expressive nature of space and place beg the question regarding the expressive goals of interior design as a discipline. Clearly, interior designers seek to guide spatial composition toward an expressive structure appropriate to the individual and social intentions of each environment. Further, our examination of space and place indicates that space is by its very nature a meaningful structure, and in this context it is appropriate to ask by what standards interior designers may judge the appropriateness of expressive composition. Here again we must identify a means to discovering what aspects of meaning are foundational in human culture. The study of value and meaning have a long history in value theory and aesthetics, and we will leverage this lineage to begin to identify a basis for making judgments regarding spatial composition.

The Nature of Aesthetics

Aesthetics is concerned with three primary concepts: beauty, the pleasure that beauty elicits, and so called *aesthetic judgment* associated with the capacity for human beings to seek and discover meaningful beauty. We could say that beauty is purely subjective, that there are no commonalities to the perception of and the pleasure taken in beauty. Conversely, we can say that aesthetic beauty is grounded in an authoritatively determined standard; this, however, returns us to standards of environmental beauty associated with taste and locates the role of interior designers as tastemakers. Further, viewing aesthetic judgment authoritatively is contradictory to the understanding we have developed thus far—that is, that space and place are dynamic systems of meaning constructed in an interaction between designers, objects, the space they define, users, and clients. Aesthetic judgment as taste implies that aesthetics is an independent structure that can be authoritatively determined.

This still leaves us with the problems of how this system of aesthetic judgment and meaning functions, and what is the role of the interior designer in this system. We can draw from our examination of psychology, sociology, and cultural geography as well as from the history of aesthetics that aesthetic judgment possesses a strongly normative foundation; that it is both grounded in social norms as well as in biological and perceptual structures. But in order for these norms to be effective as an element of interior design practice, we need to discover, if possible, a more concrete set of standards by which we might judge the correctness of our aesthetic judgments. From an interior designers' perspective, it seems clear that aesthetic judgment is directly related to questions of meaning and the construction of meaning in the built environment. It also seems clear that aesthetic judgment cannot find clarity in a subjective context, but that aesthetic judgment is dialectical as well as normative; that is, we seek to affirm aesthetic judgment in a dialectical system that engages the critique and confirmation of others. This is in alignment with both what we have established in the examination of psychological, sociological, and geographical examinations as well as in the normative processes of those who frame aesthetic judgment in the context of the

responses of users and clients. Finally, we can say that the most basic constructs of aesthetic judgment are to be found in the structures of our perceptual systems, in the Gestalt principles from which we derive basic rules of design composition through the elements and principles of design. It is also clear that while we have some grasp of the foundational principles of aesthetic judgment (the need for environmental meaning, the satisfaction of perceptual structures), there remains much that is unclear regarding an approach to design process that offers standards of meaning and beauty upon which interior designers can agree.

We can fairly safely assert that there are two levels at which we make aesthetic judgments: the ones that Emanuel Kant termed *judgments of agreeability*. An example is a statement such as, "I like the taste of blue cheese and you do not, but I do not think your judgments are defective by your dislike nor you mine for my preference." Alternately, we make judgments of what we would commonly refer to as taste, such as, "A Mozart sonata is beautiful, and if you do not think so, I can believe that your judgments are defective and that you are mistaken." Thus, in some important way, judgments of beauty/taste are different than judgments of like or dislike, and we can also say that judgments of taste are different from empirical judgments based upon evidence. Nick Zangwill in his article "Aesthetic Judgment" explained it well:

> [J]udgments of taste occupy a midpoint between judgments of niceness

and nastiness, and empirical judgments about the external world. Judgments of taste are like empirical judgments in that they have universal validity; but, they are unlike empirical judgment in that they are made on the basis of an inner response. Conversely, judgments of taste are like judgments of niceness or nastiness in that they are made on the basis of an inner subjective response or experience; but they are unlike judgments of niceness and nastiness, which makes no claim to universal validity. (Zangwill, 2010)

Zangwill goes on to provide a basis for aesthetic judgment that will afford those interested in designing spaces with a pathway (or perhaps more than one) for developing standards for an aesthetics of space. Zangwill posits that aesthetic judgments are dependent on non-aesthetic qualities:

This dependence relation implies (but is not identical with) the supervenience relation or relations: (a) two aesthetically unlike things must also be non-aesthetically unlike; (b) something couldn't change aesthetically unless it also changed non-aesthetically; and (c) something could not have been aesthetically different unless it were also non-aesthetically different. (Zangwill, 2010).

In other words, our perception of the beauty of a thing or space is dependent on other characteristics of that thing or space. There are many possible characteristics or elements of the built environment that might support this kind of dependent structure. These might include other semiotic elements that provide meaningful cues related to the environment, the use or type of space—that is, the purposes for which the space is intended—and several other possible relations.

Space, Place, Meaning, and the Design Process

What we have discovered from our examination of space thus far is that space exists as pure potential until it is occupied by people and objects, and that the relationships and symbolic value of these objects and the space that envelopes them are locked in a phoenix-like structure of meaning circuiting through creation, emendation, destruction, and re-creation. Thus, the first notion that we must emphasize is that while space may be a medium in that it mediates meaning, its reality (and even the reality of the objects that generate its shape and volume) is not that of an object. This implies a possible shift in the way we as designers of interior spaces must consider that which makes space visible; that is, we must make a radical conceptual shift from the understanding of floors, walls, ceilings, and furnishings as things and find a way to see and understand these elements of our work as elements in a set of meaningful relations. Thus the compositional development of space both as an enveloping structure of meaning surrounding a set of objects and relations, and as the development and meaning of those spatial, *objective*, and human relations, becomes the object of our study and of our process. We have also identified some criteria and structures of aesthetics and aesthetic choices that can help to establish criteria for beauty and meaning in interior environments.

Theorizing within a Practice: The Example of Interior Design

In the example of interior design practice, what we are lacking is a theory of design process that provides a means to understanding of the composition of spaces as sets of relations between objects, volumes, and human meaning. We also lack a formal set of procedures and criteria for making judgments of beauty and meaning. Environmental psychology, sociology, and cultural geography give us theoretical frameworks that help us to understand spaces, objects, and beauty human meaning, but they do not provide a means to understand the interior designers' role participating in a process of the composition of space as a set of meaningful relations.

There exist several theoretical frameworks that approach these notions of the composition of spatial meaning and beauty. Gestalt psychology—from which we derive the elements and principles of design—spatial syntax theory, and pattern language theory all provide some insight regarding how we might approach beauty and meaning. Perhaps the most fruitful theoretical prospect that will allow interior designers to understand how the meaningful systems of space and object might be composed and a process of composition in which the interior designers partici-

pate in a process that legitimately shapes a relevant system of meaning are the theoretical frameworks offered by semiotics and architectural phenomenology, as seen through the methodological construct of critical science.

Semiotics as the study of linguistic construction is relevant because interior designers generally consider the artifacts they produce, interior environments, as communicative systems composed of a range of elements including space. Architectural phenomenology provides various approaches to a grammar of design that afford a compositional structure that in relation to an understanding of spatial typology can function as an approach to design process. Finally, critical science offers clues to a process by which interior designers might participate in the construction of a meaningful system of expressive relations and normative beauty that embraces an egalitarian process that is inclusive of the symbolic lineage of objects and spaces, and the views of users and clients.

Semiotics and the Visual Reading of Spaces as Significant

Semiotics provides an important perspective on the manner in which meaning is encoded in visual structures. The theory identifies three types of symbolic communication that explain the relationships between the author: the signifier, or the physical form that the communication takes; the signified, which is the message or meaning that is intended to be expressed; and the author. There are three types of expression: *symbol, icon,* and *index.* Table 2.1 explains some of their characteristics.

The language of design typically operates on the second level, that of *icons* (though occasionally it can also operate on the level of an index). This means that the form of the signifier possesses some important characteristics of the thing or quality signified. This notion is strongly related to the precepts of Gestalt psychology. For example, if an interior designer is charged with creating a space that is ener-getic or active, the designer might begin by selecting angular and irregular shapes and lines that mimic the motion of the body in space when it moves actively, and so on.

However, we must be careful regarding how we view semiotics and the construction of meaning in the built environment. Meaning is neither univocal nor is it stable. As we have noted previously, meaning is constantly re-created in an interaction between objects, the space that they generate, users, designers, and clients. With

TABLE 2-1

The Three Types of Symbolic Communication of Semiotics

	Relation to an Author	Signifier (form of the communication)	Signified (meaning to be communicated)
Symbol	The author is recognized as a specific person; the message is encoded by an author. (Specific)	The form or the signifier is arbitrary and unrelated in any way to the message encoded. (Numbers and letters)	The message encoded is abstract and not related to the form of the signifier. (Written language and numbers; abstract ideas)
Icon	An author is recognized but the author may be unspecific; there is no explicit claim of authorship.	The form of the signifier is not arbitrary; it directly resembles some qualities of the signified. (Drawings and diagrams)	The messages encoded are the most critical perceptual characteristics related to that which is being communicated. (Design generally operates in this area most often.)
Index	An author is not necessarily recognized.	The form of the signifier is not arbitrary; the form of the signifier is inferred by a relationship to or characteristic of the signified.	("Where there is smoke there is fire."), Medical Symptoms

the design in interior spaces, for example, designers leverage a range of constructs by which they intend to invest spaces with meaning and aesthetic beauty. There are also other elements in the construction of meaning that are outside of the immediate control of designers. First, the elements with which designers work often possess a lineage of multivalent meanings that the designers may or may not be aware of (Tuan, 2001), If the designer is aware of these inherent meanings, the designer must work to frame the desired meaning in the context of other design elements, reinforcing one meaning and deemphasizing others. This is a common semiotic approach to meaning; in written language, the sentence gives meaningful context to particular meanings of the words contained in it, promoting some meanings and deemphasizing others. Further, the message that the designer selects must be supported by the agreement of the client who is financially supporting the design of the project. Thus, the client may modify the meaning of the space in one or more of several ways. They may not understand the manner in which the interior designer has constructed the particular aesthetic and its meaningful intentions and may therefore reject it outright. The client may understand but disagree with the meaningful aesthetic construction proposed by the designer and may prefer their own notions of what is appropriate, sometimes at the expense of the preferences of users. Conversely, they may base their decisions on their detailed understanding of the preferences of the users of that space. Clients may also seek to modify the aesthetics construction of meaning based on personal

research. Finally, users may accept, reject, or modify environmental meaning and or aesthetics through a range of similar actions.

It is also important to note that each time people occupy a space, the meaning of that space is re-constructed through interactions with the space, objects, and others in the environment (Lefebvre, 1995; Kazmierczak, 2003). Take, for instance, the simple example of a classroom. At one point the space is a lecture hall, at another point it is a meeting room intended for discussion, and at another it is a laboratory in which people experiment with concepts and procedures. Each of these settings alters the immediate and collective meaning of that space.

Theories of Design Intention and Aesthetic Meaning

The understanding of the processes by which meaning is constructed, modified, destroyed, and reconstructed gives us some insight into the role of the interior designer in this meaningful construction, but it does not give us many clues into the actual concrete processes of meaningful aesthetic construction undertaken by interior designers. We have noted that the basic iconic components of interior design arise from the discoveries of Gestalt psychology and are imbedded in our perceptual systems. We have also noted that aesthetic beauty is associated with nonaesthetic components and with the normative nature of social meaning. Thus, the concrete processes by which interior designers operate are tied to these considerations—that interior design vocabulary is semiotic, iconic, and normative, and that its acceptance is linked to nonaesthetic considerations.

The Work of Christopher Alexander and Pattern Language

In this regard, the work of architectural phenomenologists is the most relevant means to filling the concrete components of design process, which can provide a clearer understanding of the processes by which both architects and interior designers shape space and aesthetic meaning. From an architectural perspective, the most prominent in this context are the works of Christopher Alexander and Thomas Thiis-Evensen. Christopher Alexander's works, *A Pattern Language: Towns, Buildings Construction*, *A Timeless Way of Building*, and *The Oregon Experiment*, propose a series of meaningful elements of the built environment (based on studies conducted through the University of Oregon) that can be combined and recombined to generate a larger meaningful construct. Building on his original thesis, Alexander has since gone on to develop a more flexible approach to semiotic construction, which he calls "generative sequences." In both cases, Alexander's research has developed an approach that reflects our understanding of the manner in which meaning is produced.

Thomas Thiis-Evensen and the Nature of Structures and Meaning

Thomas Thiis-Evensen takes a similar approach to the problem. Thiis-Evensen locates the nature of the meaning of the structures that generate and define space in three qualities of experience "motion, weight and substance." What is particularly interesting about these qualities is that they are nonaesthetic in nature and yet in his book *Archetypes in Architecture*, Thiis-Evensen leverages them to great effect in defining the manner in which the structuring of the elements that bound space communicate (Thiis-Evensen, 1989). Thiis-Evensen discusses the manner in which these experiential qualities of the physical world are translated into meaningful structures of the built environment; he develops an interesting and useful taxonomy of the elements that define space and their relationship to motion, weight, and substance.

This taxonomy could be a particularly useful way to discuss how designers define a meaningful and aesthetically pleasing spatial structure. Thiis-Evensen examines the influence of motion, weight, and substance in each of the defining elements of the built environment, floor, wall, and roof (or more preferable for interior design, *ceiling*). For each element, he examines the expressive qualities in relation to typical perception of motion, weight, and substance. While this work is not particularly well supported by research, it does present interesting possibilities regarding ways we might approach an understanding of meaningful spatial structure.

This assertion is further supported by the work of an interior design scholar, Jan Jennings in her work "A Case for a Typology of Design: The Interior Archetype Project." Unlike Thiis-Evensen's archetypes, Jennings and her graduate students have developed more complex historical and contemporary constructs that connect spatial compositions with meaningful implications for designers and users. Jennings's examples of wall and lighting typologies are particularly interesting in their examination of surface and composition of lighting, conveying particular constructs of meaning as a framework through which interior designers may explore an aspect of environmental meaning in a specific project. The value of archetypal constructs are that they provide interior designers with a series of elements that connect perceptive constructs with meaningful ones, and provide a common vocabulary that can be used as a point of reference between interior designers, users, and clients in the construction of meaning.

Conclusion

The spatial characteristics of meaning and aesthetics in the built environment have a long and complicated history. It is hoped that this work has provided some analysis of the problem and potential benefits that a more systematic study of aesthetics and meaning can offer. We have endeavored to provide both a lineage and exegesis of the problem of spatial meaning, examining both its historical roots and definitions as well as assembling a group of theoretical perspectives, which while not comprehensive, can aid in the development of our understanding of space.

This work is obviously only a signpost pointing to the need for much thoughtful and creative scholarship. It must be hoped that what we have examined will offer a range of possible directions for further study; of particular interest and moment would be studies that examine the design of space from a semiotic and phenomenological perspective and that provide a range of typological structures offering a framework of environmental meaning to practitioners. Finally, further study is needed in the area of decision theory and the manner in which designers, users, and clients leverage objects and spaces as meaningful constructs and the processes of collaborative decision-making leading as regards the built environment.

Discussion Questions

1. Discuss the concepts of space and space-time as these are developed by Wilwerding.
2. What is space in terms of both physical and philosophical definitions?
3. What is space-time in physics?
4. Examine the concepts of space as proposed by Wilwerding and the theorists:
   a. Space is a substance—Relativist perspective (Aristotle, Mach, Einstein).
   b. Space is a void—Absolutist perspective (Euclid, Newton).
   c. Space is a relativist mental construct (Leibniz).
5. Wilwerding suggests, "An understanding of place begins in this theoretical perspective, where the individual, that is, each person's experience influences his or her views of place and behavior in relation to it. In this view, our understanding that space

and ultimately place is the product of an active search for the meaning of our environment, and equally importantly, that place is not an object to be known but is in fact the result of our intentional act of knowing and the search for meaning."

a. Discuss this idea in light of the previous ideas about space.

b. How is our understanding of space created by intentional acts and the search for meaning?

6. Discuss Lefebvre's concept of "space as entity" and Baudrillard's concept of space as a place, such as home. How are these different from the previous ideas about space? Similar?

7. How is space and place temporal as theorized by Tuan? Situate his approach in terms of phenomenological ideas about what constitutes lived experiences?

8. What is semiotics? How does semiotics play a role in how we read space as a visual representation?

References

Alexander, C. (1977). *A Pattern Language.* Oxford: Oxford University Press.

Alexander, C. (1996). *The Origins of Pattern Theory.* Retrieved August 2010 from Pattern Language, http://www.patternlanguage.com/archive/ieee/ieeetext.htm.

Baudrilliard, J. (1996). *A System of Objects.* (J. Benedict, Trans.) New York: Verso.

Barbara G. Anderson, Peggy L. Honey, & Michael T. Dudek. (2007). The Interior Designer's Social Compact: The Missing Aspect of Our Quest for Professional Legitimacy. In J. C. Pamlea Evans (Ed.), *Design and Social Justice* (pp. 91–98). Austin, TX: The Interior Design Educators Council.

Beecher, M. A. (2007). No Unimportant Folk: Lessons from the Social Justice Agenda of Martha Van Rensselaer. In J. C. Pamela Evans (Ed.), *Design and Social Justice* (pp. 107–114). Austin, TX: Interior Design Educators Council.

Bodnar, I. (2010, March 21). Aristotle's Natural Philosophy. (E. N. Zalta, Ed.). Retrieved August 2010 from *The Stanford Encyclopedia of Philosophy,* http://plato.stanford.edu/archives/spr2010/entries/aristotle-natphil.

Eliade, M. (1987). *The Sacred and The Profane: The Nature of Religion.* San Diego: Harcourt Brace Jovanovich.

Genz, H. (1998). Nothing: The Science of Empty Space. New York: Perseus Books.

Gieryn, T. F. (2000). A Space for Place in Sociology. In *Annual Review of Sociology* (Vol. 26, pp. 463-496). Bloomington, Indiana: Indiana University.

Guerin, D. A. , (1992). Interior Design Research: A Human Ecosystem Model. In Home Economics Research Journal, Volume 20, Issue 4, pages 254–263, June 1992.

Habermas, J. (1984). The Theory of Communicative Action. Boston, Massachusetts, U. S. A.: Beacon Press.

Hall, E. T. (1966). The Hidden Dimesion. Garden City, NY: Doubleday.

Hardwick, C. S. (1977). Semiotic and Significs. In C. S. Hardwick, Semiotic and Significs.

Huggett, N., & Hoefer, C. (2009, September 21). Absolute and Relational Theories of Space and Motion. Retrieved August 2010 from *The Stanford Encyclopedia of Philosophy*, http://plato.stanford .edu/entries/spacetime-theories/.

Jennings, J. (2007). A Case for a Typology of Design: The Interior Archetype Project. *Journal of Interior Design, 32* (3), 48–68.

Kazmierczak, E. (2003). Design as Meaning Making: From Making Things to the Design of Thinking. *Design Issues, 19* (2), 45–59.

Kopec, D. (2006). *Environmental Psychology for Design* (1st ed.). New York: Fairchild Books.

Lefebvre, H. (1995). *The Production of Space.* Cambridge, MA: Blackwell.

Loustau, J. (1988). A Theoretical Base for Interior Design: A Review of Four Approaches from Related Fields. *Journal of Interior Design Education and Research, 14* (2), pp. 3–8.

Norberg-Schulz, C. (2000*). Architecture: Presence, Language, and Place.* Illustrated ed. Milan, Italy: Skira Editore.

Markus, T. A. (1993). *Buildings and Power* (p. 343). London: Routledge.

Moore, G. T. (1974). The Development of Environmental. In T. L. D. Canter (Ed.), *Psychology and the Built Environment* (pp. 184–194) New York: Wiley/Halsted.

Pabble, J. (2009). Interior Design Identity in the Crossfire: A Call for Renewed Balance in Subjective and Objective Ways of Knowing. *Journal of Interior Design, 34* (2), v–xx.

Port, R. (2010, August). Icon, INDEX, and SYMBOL. Retrieved August 2010 from *L101–Introduction to the Study of Language*, http://www.cs.indiana .edu/~port/teach/103/sign.symbol. short.html.

(1974). Course in General Linguistics. In C. B. Sechehaye.

Slowik, E. (2009, September 21). Descartes' Physics (E. N. Zalta, Ed.). Retrieved 2010 from *The Stanford Encyclopedia of Philosophy*, http:// plato.stanford.edu/archives/fall2009/ entries/descartes-physics/.

Sommer, R. (1967). Sociofugal Space. *The American Journal of Sociology*, 654–660.

Sommer, R. (1969). *Personal Space.* Englewood Cliffs, NJ: Prentice-Hall.

Stauffer, R. (2007). The Poché: The Intersection between Ethics and Design. In J. C. Pamela Evans (Ed.), *Design and Social Justice* (pp. 315–326). Austin, TX: The Interior Design Educators Council.

Tuan, Y.-F. (1990). *Topophilia: A Study of Environmental Perception, Attitudes, and Values.* New York: Columbia University Press.

Tuan, Y.-F. (2001). *Space and Place* (pp. 387–422). Minneapolis, MN: University of Minnesota Press.

Turner, V. (2001). *From Ritual to Theater: The Human Seriousness of Play.* New York: PAJ Publications.

Thiis-Evensen, T. (1989). *Archetypes in Architecture*. Oxford: Oxford Univesity Press/Norwegian University Press.

Yanow, D. (2005). *How Built Spaces Mean: A Semiotics of Space*. In D. Yanow & D. Y. Schwartz-Shea (Eds.), *Interpretation and Method: Empirical Research Methods and the Interpretive Turn* (pp. 3-47). Armonk, NY: M.E. Sharpe.

Zalta, E. N. (Ed.). (2009). *The Stanford Encyclopedia of Philosophy*. Stanford, CA: Stanford University, Center for the Study of Language and Information, The Metaphysics Research Lab. Retrieved May/June 2010 from http://plato.stanford.edu/archives/win2009/entries/metaphysics/.

Zangwill, N. (2010, September 21). Aesthetic Judgment. (E. N. Zalta, Ed.) Retrieved September 2010 from *The Stanford Encyclopedia of Philosophy*, http://plato.stanford.edu/archives/fall2010/entries/aesthetic-judgment/.

2.2 From the Philosophy of Architecture to Architecture + Philosophy: New (Critical) Pragmatism and the Architecture of (Interior) Space

Gavin Melles and DJ Huppatz

Philosophical intersections with architecture and design, particularly postmodern European speculations, have been a constant topic in recent scholarship of aesthetics and space. Lead by practitioners such as Rem Koolhaas, architectural theory, along with that of other built environment disciplines, has begun to move beyond a speculative aesthetics of observation to one more attuned to the material construction of space. Under the banner of (new) pragmatism, a critical approach to constructing space provides an alternative means of acknowledging the social, ideological, aesthetic, and material constraints of the design process. Transcending the often unnecessarily abstract reflections on the act of designing and the discourses of space, critical pragmatism provides a potential philosophical foundation for contemporary architecture and design that breaks with widespread intellectual and alienating reflections on aesthetics and space. Following a brief overview of recent and existing philosophical engagements with architecture and design, this essay explores the current critical pluralism and pragmatism informing a new generation of architectural practitioners and students, a new stream that has potential for contemporary interior design theory, as it establishes a more solid theoretical basis.

Architecture, Design, and Philosophy

To say that practical knowledge is devoid of significant theoretical contents is as false as to say that theoretical knowledge lacks pragmatic purpose. We would prefer to describe their assemblage as two epistemological tendencies within a particular discipline and a particular domain of reality, one toward virtualization (i.e., theory), the other toward actualization (i.e., practice) (Zaera-Polo 2007, p. 1).

Philosophy is a notoriously slippery term that is often recruited into discourses beyond the autochthonous discipline. Traditionally, philosophy defines itself from the Archimedean viewpoint, as transcending the particularities of practice and other local disciplinary logics, for example, of science, to give the philosophy of science, education, and so forth. In this context, philosophy's engagement with fields such as architecture and design tends to operate as a meta-discourse, generalizing above local material concerns. This article will first explore the borrowings from philosophy by architectural and design theorists and then introduce a new critical model for synthesis between the two disciplines.

Postwar Developments in Philosophy, Architecture, and the Interior

The postwar era in architectural theory saw both the continuation of an earlier modernist legacy as well as the emergence of new theoretical paradigms from philosophy that would challenge that legacy. The modernist emphasis on space—and more particularly, an abstract, homogenous, and universal space—continued (for example, see the extremely influential Giedion, 1967) and could be adopted in the design of everything from postwar corporate office towers to large-scale urban projects (an approach exemplified by the functionally and technologically driven work of a firm such as Skidmore, Owings and Merrill). However, alternative philosophical currents, particularly from Continental philosophy, suggested other possibilities for engaging with architectural and interior space. In philosophy, phenomenology, structuralism, and poststructuralism offered various challenges and alternatives to the modernist architectural legacy, while postmodernism and eclectic borrowings from cultural studies offered further dimensions—phenomenology in its reinstatement of human experience and subjectivity; structuralism in its highlighting the meaning of design; poststructuralism in its critique of meta-narratives and a self-reflexive questioning; and postmodernism in its questioning of the political, social,

and economic dimensions. This section briefly traces these threads through to the present.

If modernist space was frequently understood as abstract, homogenous, and universal, phenomenological thinking, derived from philosophers such as Maurice Merleau-Ponty, reinstated the importance of human (that is, *subjective*) experience into our perception of space—spatial design could no longer be understood as empty, but inhabited by bodies, and no longer homogenous and universal, but invested with particular qualities of its own. Phenomenological space was based upon the reception to the wholeness of lived human experience, an experience of space that engages with the senses and the body. Against the rationalist theories of the prewar generation, architects were drawn to Heidegger's emphasis on dwelling "poetically" in the world (see Heidegger, 1971). The critique of the privileging of the visual and the objective mind in representations of architectural space and re-engaging the senses is best developed in a book such as Pallasmaa's *The Eyes of the Skin: Architecture and the Senses* (2005). Alternatively, Gaston Bachelard's *Poetics of Space*, drawing upon psychoanalysis and literary theory, offered an understanding of "the intimate values of inside space" (1994, p. 3), focusing on the effects of memory, imagination. and dreams on our experience of space. The rich, sensual understanding of space through the body (rather than simply the rule of the eye and the rational mind emphasized by modernist functionalism) was the legacy of phenomenological thought on architecture/the interior.

A further theorist of space from out of this phenomenological tradition, Henri Lefebvre, a philosopher and Marxist critical theorist, added a social dimension to this understanding of subjective or lived experience. In *The Production of Space*, Lefebvre criticized the modernist privileging of visual space, which he argued emptied space of any social dimension and abstracted it. For Lefebvre, "The user's space is *lived*—not represented (or conceived). When compared with the abstract space of the experts (architects, urbanists, and planners), the space of the everyday activities of users is a concrete one, which is to say, subjective" (Lefebvre 1991: 362).

An alternative philosophical thread that developed in architectural theory, particularly in the 1960s, was the impact of French structuralism. The symbolic function of architecture was a key theme, a theme derived from writers such as Roland Barthes, whose writings analyzed how people attach meaning to artefacts. In this understanding of architecture as artefact, there was a focus on interpretation and the politics of form. Architecture was read and decoded as a visual sign—Kevin Lynch's reading of the city, for example, or Aldo Rossi's *Architecture of the City*, both understood the city as a work of art (Lynch, 1971; Rossi, 1982). For structuralists, the world was understood as signs to be decoded, and there was a tendency to universalize and create systems of meaning. For architecture, this reinstated an emphasis on the semantic meanings of architecture as form (though the symbolic value of monumental architecture was as well understood

by the ancient Romans as by the Imperial British). Unlike phenomenology, with its emphasis on the subjective, for structuralism, the individual subject was effectively liquidated, an effect of the signifying system (see Hays, 1998, p. xiii). However opposed in their approaches, both structuralism and phenomenology were used through the 1960s and 1970s in order to go beyond the received wisdoms of modernist functionalism advocated by the prewar and immediately postwar generation of architects and theorists.

Following the structuralist challenge, poststructuralism attempted to go beyond form in order to challenge the universalizing tendency of structuralism to focus on difference and play. Derrida's work had a significant impact upon Bernard Tschumi, particularly his well-known Parc de la Villette—an interpretation of deconstruction as architecture—play of meaning as Derrida does with text here done by Tschumi in built form. Poststructuralist theory often referred to as the *linguistic turn* in architecture, typically defined architectural forms as text, the meanings of which are never fixed but constantly deferred. The work of philosopher Michel Foucault on power was also influential in architecture, as was Deleuze on repetition and difference, plurality and flux. In Deleuze's essay on Foucault, "Postscript to the Societies of Control," he writes: "We are in generalized crisis in relation to all the environments of enclosure—prison, hospital, factory, school, family. The family is an 'interior,' in crisis like all other interiors—scholarly, professional, etc. The administrations in charge never cease announcing supposedly necessary reforms: to reform schools, to reform industries, hospitals, the armed forces, prisons. But everyone knows that these institutions are finished, whatever the length of their expiration periods. It's only a matter of administering their last rites and of keeping people employed until the installation of the new forces knocking at the door. These are the *societies of control*, which are in the process of replacing the disciplinary societies" (in Leach, 1997, p. 309). Foucault's work on the exercise of power through spatial division and surveillance has continued to be a useful thread in understanding contemporary interior space (especially Foucault on Panopticism, 1979, 195–228).

This line of philosophical thought and its relationship to architecture has been most productively mined recently by philosophers Elizabeth Grosz and Andrew Benjamin (Grosz, 2001; Benjamin, 2000). Grosz (2001), for example, has argued that architecture and philosophy require a "third space" within which to interact, specifically posing the idea of this third space as one of experimentation that might render space more active and mobile, as well as a space for dialogue and transdisciplinary interactions.

Nina Last offers a particular example of how this third space might work in examining Wittgenstein's house in Wien. Last (2008) shows, for example, how "the house bears the signs of spatial questioning and questioning in many of the ways that became apparent in the late philosophy's examples of visual and spatial thinking" (p.

2). Highlighting how architecture as practice became a lens through which Wittgenstein's view of language could highlight everyday practice, Last suggests, "Architecture thereby becomes that through which philosophy looks, a look which transforms the specific understanding of the functioning and locating of language, shifting it from a basis in logic to being formed in everyday practice" (p. 4). In her text, Last shows that most discussions of the relations between philosophy and architecture subsume the practice to the discourse of philosophy (or vice versa), while what is required is a third discourse that does not subsume one to the other. The practice of ordinary language as the common territory of philosophy and life and ordinary people becomes a site in which the relationship between philosophy and architecture can be reexamined (p. 18), and approached this way, "architecture needs to be understood not as an autonomous discipline but more broadly as a spatial or spatio-visual practice" (p. 21).

Running parallel to these theoretical approaches, postmodernism offered another potential path for architecture and interior spaces. Cultural theorist Fredric Jameson and urban geographer David Harvey's defining texts offered the idea of thinking through how architecture is determined by social, political, and economic conditions (one of the best examples of this applied specifically to architecture is Mary McLeod's "Architecture and Politics in the Reagan Era: From Postmodernism to Deconstructivism," in Hays, pp. 678–702). For Jameson and Harvey, there was no escape from capitalism, little room for critical maneuver, or more precisely, the utopian impulse in architecture, based on individual agency and the architect as artist, needed to be radically rethought. From this postmodern perspective, architecture arises out of broader social, political, and economic forces—and such writers offered an understanding of the underlying conditions in which architecture is built, rather than simply treating architectural forms in isolation as symptoms. Jameson's disorientating Bonaventure Hotel, for example, was described as an exemplary postmodern interior space: "the Bonaventure aspires to being a total space, a complete world, a kind of miniature city; to this new total space, meanwhile, corresponds a new collective practice, a new mode in which individuals move and congregate, something like the practice of a new and historically original kind of hypercrowd" (Jameson, 1997, p. 40). This, and Harvey's interventions into understanding the postmodern city in its economic and political context, has much potential for theorists of the interior (Harvey, 1989).

From this postmodern perspective, the sociohistorical and economic contexts of architectural production are seen to be impossible to separate from resultant buildings. Another understanding of architecture that emerged with postmodernism was the building as a vehicle of meaning rather than a neutral, abstract form. In architectural theory, exemplified by Charles Jencks's *Postmodernism and Architecture* and Robert Venturi's *Complexity and Contradiction in Architecture* (Jencks 1997; Venturi 1977), aspects of structuralism (particularly semiotics) insisted on meaning, but emphasized façades, aesthetics, and a resultant flattening of architecture into a series of screens, and at its worse, socially and politically indifferent. Visual narratives in space have potential future direction, but these approaches in general seemed analogous to structuralism in that they emphasized the building as exterior form, and offered little new for an understanding of the interior. However, out of the broader postmodern critique came a range of alternative approaches to understanding space drawn from other disciplines, most notably for the interior, the impact of feminist theory. The role gender and identity play in our understanding of, and construction of, space is an important outcome of this, and crucial for going forward in terms of understanding the interior (of the many 1990s publications on the subject of gender and architecture, see Borden et al., 2000 for a good introduction and survey of the field).

The Interior

While philosophical thought, particularly what is often referred to as Continental Philosophy, has long informed architectural discourse, the interior lagged behind, picking up some of the threads suitable for theorizing the interior as a distinct space beyond architecture, but in general lacking a strong theoretical bent until very recently (examples include *Intimus: Interior Design Theory Reader*, 2006; Penny Sparke's *The Modern Interior*, 2008; Sparke, et al.,

Designing the Modern Interior: From Victorians to Today, 2009, the new journal *Interiors*, Berg Publishers, 2010; and Charles Rice's *The Emergence of the Interior: Architecture, Modernity and Domesticity*, 2009). Interior design histories have tended to emphasize the discipline as simply an inside version of architectural history and followed a series of formal period styles derived from architecture (see Pile, 2005; Abercrombie, 1990). For example, this sense of the interior as a contained architectural space is emphasized by design historian John Pile in the introduction to his pioneering book, *A History of Interior Design*: "interior design is inextricably linked to architecture and can only be studied within an architectural context" (Pile, 2005, p. 11). However, more recently, the interior has become the subject of more theoretical interest. The pioneering *Intimus: Interior Design Theory Reader* embraced an interdisciplinary approach—drawing upon a broad range of contemporary and historical sources including philosophy (Baudrillard, Thoreau, Bachelard, de Certeau), anthropology, architectural historians and theorists, interior design practitioners (including the decorating tradition) and architects, tastemakers, and critics—and, further, included an excerpt from a novel. This in an effort to survey the various approaches to the interior and "to defend the field as plural, multiplicitous and interdisciplinary" (Taylor, p. 10). The eclectic collection stretches beyond architecture and design into other considerations that impact upon the interior environment—taste, bodies in space, identity politics, gender, histories, spatial theories.

In his book *A Philosophy of Interior Design*, Stanley Abercrombie (1990) argues that while architectural histories tend to focus on the façades of buildings (the exterior), understanding the containers within (the interior) requires a different experience: "We do not merely pass them on the street; we inhabit them. When we enter a building, we cease being merely its observer; we become its content" (p. 3). Importantly, the interior is defined by Abercrombie as inseparable from the people who inhabit it, so an interior history that simply catalogues and analyzes empty architectural containers seems inadequate. For design historian and theorist Suzie Attiwill, this flattening of three-dimensional space into a two-dimensional image suppresses the interior's temporal aspect: "Interior design histories have . . . ignored temporality in the design of interiors through a focus on objects and built space as static form" (Attiwill, 2004, p. 6).

Importantly, in the modernist architectural theories, space was typically understood as abstract, homogenous, and universal. And the interior as simply an architectural container filled with furniture, decorative objects, and people. For the interior this means beyond thinking the interior from the enclosure of architecture, enclosed and encapsulated within a larger discourse. New concepts of space and inhabitation derived from cultural and visual studies, feminism, gender and identity politics, urban geography, media studies, and design history. As yet, however, new pragmatism has yet to inform interior's history and practices.

Toward a Pragmatic Compromise

[Richard]Rorty, the neo-pragmatist philosopher, said that regardless of what inspires a particular design, in the end the building must speak for itself. Yeats may have been inspired to write poetry because of a philosophy of gyres and moons, but in the end we are "'bowled over" by the poems themselves. What matters, Mr. Rorty said, is not the philosophy behind a building but what he calls its "'imaginative novelty,'" whether it shakes things up (Boxer 2000).

Before considering what (new) pragmatism might mean for interior space, it is necessary to look at how a new generation of architects has found pragmatism to define an attitude consistent with a socially and aesthetically sensitive approach to meaningful work. This critical Pragmatism (with a capital P) is distinct from a naïve or vulgar instrumentalism—pragmatism (with a small p). The sense of pragmatism developed here begins with William James and John Dewey, who themselves borrow some inspiration from Charles Sanders Pierce's original work at the end of the nineteenth century.

Dewey's concern with democracy, human experience, and art are critical to pragmatism's contribution to architecture and design. Spector (2004), for example, suggests that Dewey's *Art as Experience* holds lessons for architects no longer content with a commodified aesthetics of art and a Platonist *judicial* separation of the object from experience: "The pragmatist aesthetic experience tracks the subject's engagement with the work of art; it is neither solely derived from the physical properties of the work nor from the imaginative experiences of the subject, but from something forged from the prolonged encounter" (p. 136). This broadly phenomenological account of the experience of design focuses on the embodiment and effect of experience on human beings, rejecting the idea of the inherent aesthetics of objects, buildings, and spaces. It is thus an experiential embodied aesthetics in that "Deweyan pragmatism asserts against the metaphysics of the judicial approach that it is senseless to posit aesthetic qualities that exist independently of perceiving, thinking beings able to mentally assemble such qualities out of sense experience" (p. 137). This pragmatism also rejects the elitism associated with art, since Dewey's "belief in democracy extends to an insistence that perfectly valid aesthetic experience doesn't require elite guidance and it need not to occur in a gallery or museum" (p. 138). This democratic everyman's account of art and the aesthetic experience resists the canonizing of objects in art galleries and other spaces as requiring elite intellectual guidance. Thus, pragmatism is an action-oriented aesthetics of engagement; one that critiques an objectified contemplation as useful or meaningful. As Spector writes, "Pragmatic regard for the aesthetics of action helps account for Dewey's distaste for 'museum art' which is not only put on a pedestal to serve the interests of an elite, but also thereby becomes revoltingly inert, dead, incapable of fostering further action" (p. 146). This democratic sense of artistic and aesthetic experience is prescient of current practices of socially responsible design, illustrated recently, for example, in MOMA's Small Scale: Big Change Exhibition (see http://www.moma.org/interactives/exhibitions/2010/smallscalebigchange/).

Until recently, architecture schools have often preferred to ground their theoretical and material work in speculative postmodern philosophy. Some 25 years ago, Mayo (1985), for example, suggested that technical reasoning and an avoidance of the politics and ethics of architecture reigned in architectural schools through the overarching influence of postmodern speculation in architecture. The move into the postmodern and the importation of continental philosophers shunted aside pragmatic questions, replacing them with a pseudo-intellectualism that is being challenged by a new generation of architects and designers. The title of Michael Speaks' (2003) article summarizes this shift nicely: "Theory Was Interesting . . . But Now We Have to Work."

In the theoretical literature of architecture and design disciplines, there has been a recent move away from a focus on postmodern speculation toward a growing recognition of the value of pragmatism and a critical pluralism. The latter term referring to the generation of solutions or responses to briefs, and issues, which themselves serve as conversation starters through engaging with users and the human collective in general. Lamenting a lack of work in architecture in this tradition, Guy and Moore (2007), for example, point to "those who are productively blurring the distinction between critical theory, pluralism, and pragmatism—James, Dewey, Hickman, Feenberg, Haraway, Latour, Schlosberg, and Rorty (pp. 21–22). Linking pragmatism with concern for sustainability in the built environment, the authors suggest that sustainable architecture will not be achieved without civic participation and that critical pluralism can provide the theoretical motivation and justification for such work in design. The authors exemplify their proposal with the story of the Norman Foster design of the Commerzbank of Frankfurt, originally rejected as "a degenerate American architectural form associated with urban decay" (p. 20) and the public participation in its reinterpretation as part of a regenerated city skyline, now signaling not postwar decay but renewal. The authors claim that pluralist practice is "seeking out the synthetic opportunities that are latent in the conflicting imaginations of citizens" (p. 21). According to this interpretation of architecture's pluralism, architecture can participate in this conversation of conflicting imaginations over time. In a follow-up piece, Farmer and Guy (2010) claim, rightly in our view, that Pragmatism's embrace of contextual pluralism, its emphasis on experience and practice, and its high regard for the political worth of the community can move discussions in architecture away from a narrow focus on predefined and universal codes and toward a sociotechnical process that engages a wide range of human (and non-human) actors in the production and use of complex architectural artefacts.

This connection to imagination, as Collier (2006) points out, bridges the actual with the virtual:

> Pragmatism and the work of John Dewey in particular, create a new role for imagination. Whereas classical thinking viewed imagination as the facility of "imaging" sensible objects, and the romantic tradition saw it as the ability to generate entirely new objects, pragmatism treats imagination as the capacity to understand the actual in the light of the possible. (2006, p. 313)

Rem Koolhaas is one of the signal voices of this new pragmatic attitude to architecture. Graafland (2000), for example, describes Koolhaas's approach as design without a master plan: "Koolhaas, although the same is true of Tschumi, is focused not so much on the architecturally significant characteristics in the plan as on its operational and pragmatic possibilities—where time is an essential characteristic . . . Koolhaas's pragmatism is determined more by the tensions between standardization and homogeneity versus the wish to allow relatively random 'streams' to flow freely . . . The architect has long since lost control over the future of his design" (2000, p. 115). Architecturally this entails a structuring that avoids the social mimesis of existing social chaos while enabling flow, "and then within that structure allowing the Deleuzian flows to flow into each other"

Figure 2.1 OMA/Rem Koolhaas housing, Nexus World, Fukuoka, Japan: Exterior view.
Photo credit: Image Courtesy of OMA: photographed by Hiroyuki Kawano.

(pp. 119–120). One interpretation of the effect of this structuring with flow and its connection to pragmatism is in the work of Albena Yaneva (2009), who conducted ethnographic fieldwork in Koolhaas's studios. The author offers her own action-oriented construction of Pragmatism and its intersection with architecture, rejecting the idea of architecture as just service to society conditioned by circumstances, but rather following the proactive power of architectural projects to mobilize heterogeneous actors, convincing, persuading, or deterring them. Architecture and building will be tackled here, as becoming social (instead of hiding behind or serving the social), as active participants in society, design—as a process of recollecting, reinterpreting, and reassembling the social (p. 18). Such agency for architecture comes from a critical realism that structure without a master plan leaves space for interpretation. Bullivant (2007), for example, refers to "progressive architectural practices" in the UK, where public collaboration is invited, in these terms: "Reflecting social change without being socially determinist and allowing the process of production to transform the initial idea for the project—these are some of the design parameters that distinguish the finest work of this rising generation from that of any generation that asks too much or too little from architecture" (p. 88).

Future Directions

As a shortcut to a new style, it offers little; it will be a sad day when we see "pragmatism" used to put a glamorous gloss on pipe rails or exposed steel. But as a method to reinforce skepticism, to erase credulity, to verify through action new ideas that work, it may be just what architecture needs. (Nobel 2001)

The interest in the pragmatist (read: Deweyan) and neopragmatist (read: Rortian) potential for a new generation of architects is at least a decade under discussion, and centers on our relations to things in the making and public and private spheres and questions (see Ockman, 2000). The effect of the importation of continental philosophy into architectural schools in the United States in the 1990s is characterized as follows by Saunders (2007):

The "discourse" at leading architectural schools and intellectual publications in this period was amazingly muddled by pseudo-intellectuality, by dazed and confused attempts to import the language and ideas of arcane philosophy and cultural studies. (Saunders 2007, p. ix)

Such a characterization remains true in many areas and a new generation of anti-intellectual architects has emerged, led by figures such as Koolhaas, to point at the emperor's new clothes of the former period.

Dorrian (2005; see also Saunders 2007) rightly identifies the fact that the new pragmatism could simply be a "quietistic liberalism" in disguise that leaves critical interrogation aside:

To affirm that practice is performative and that we aim to produce divergent multiplicities does not necessarily call for, or entail, a questioning of the limits within which they operate, or indeed for having a strategy to assess what is (or will be) produced and its concomitant effects (2005, p. 232).

While this is true, it presents an impoverished view of critical pragmatism.

Tom Fisher suggests that architecture should engage with pragmatism to avoid an overemphasis on idealistic focus on intentions:

> The architectural community would greatly benefit from a more serious engagement with the ideas of pragmatism, which can illuminate some of the blind spots in architecture today. Pragmatism is not against theory, nor is it an "imperialist gambit" by American thinkers. Pragmatism urges us to look to the consequences of what we do, which the discipline of architecture, infused with an idealistic focus on intentions, frequently resists (Fisher 2000).

Pointing to both empathy and dramatic rehearsal as key elements in the architect-user relationship, Collier notes that design research traces consequences in the ways that James (1907) suggested for all potential propositions addressing ideal futures. In my recent (Melles, 2008) plea for pragmatism in design, I suggest that

> What new (critical) pragmatism offers is scope for the self-creative and public projects of individuals to be achieved through appropriations and transformation of the past in built and designed forms. Such an approach accepts the inherent wicked nature of design problems, and accepts the creative quality of the theory-practice interaction that Schön proposes as distinctive for design in general. It also sees neither the humanities nor the sciences or design as having special purchase on truth, but equally pursuing truths whose merits must be judged by their consequences. (100–101)

Where does this leave interior architecture/design and its engagement with the philosophy of aesthetics and space?

First, interior needs begin treading a path already blazoned by architecture—to read and learn. Second, an interior perspective and attention to interior spaces—to the retrofitting of existing structures—will require some thought about how such practices can engage with the premises of a pragmatic approach to design, as outlined here. Third, the implicitly closer engagement with people that interiors often have in comparison to architecture offers possibilities for material engagement with pragmatism that is not easily afforded to mainstream architecture. Implications for students of (interior) architecture are a closer and more intense engagement with pragmatism's literature and material manifestations, and a move away from postmodern (French) speculation on the meaning of space. The current century faces global and local crises of different dimensions and meanings, and recent responses to these suggest that the turn to pragmatism has already occurred. Critical pragmatism offers an intellectual platform for envisioning the ideological and material consequences of future practice and solutions.

Discussion Questions

1. Define John Dewey's idea of pragmatism in more detail.
   a. Unpack the concept of Pragmatism and pragmatism as Melles and Huppatz suggest.
   b. How is design pragmatic in nature?
   c. What is a pragmatic stance when understanding design meanings?
   d. How is this rooted in values and underlying values we use to make design decisions?

2. What are the spaces of the physical and the virtual as discussed here?

3. Melles and Huppatz suggest that the understanding of architecture and philosophy allows for understanding intimate spaces of interiors. How? Why is this important?

References

Abercrombie, S. (1990). *A Philosophy of Interior Design.* New York: Harper & Row.

Abercrombie, S., & Whiton, S. (2008). *Interior Design and Decoration* (6th ed.). Upper Saddle River, NJ: Pearson.

Attiwill, S. (2004). Towards an Interior History, *IDEA* (Interior Design/ Interior Architecture Educators Association). Brisbane, Australia: QUT Publishing.

Bachelard, G. (1994; original 1958). *The Poetics of Space.* M. Jolas (Trans.). Boston: Beacon Press.

Benjamin, A. (2000). *Architectural Philosophy.* London/New Brunswick, NJ: Athlone Press.

Borden, I., & Rendell, J. (2000). *Intersections: Architectural Histories and Critical Theories,* London: Routledge.

Borden, I., Rendell, J., & Penner, B. (2000). *Gender Space Architecture: An Interdisciplinary Introduction.* London/ New York: Routledge.

Boxer, S. (2000, November 25). The New Face of Architecture. *The New York Times.* Available at http://www.nytimes.com/2000/11/25/arts/the-new-face-of-architecture.html.

Bullivant, L. (2007). No More Tabula Rasa: Progressive Architectural Practices in England. In W. Saunders (Ed.), *The New Architectural Pragmatism: A Harvard Design Magazine Reader* (pp.

75–88). Minneapolis, MN: University of Minnesota Press.

Collier, J. (2006). The Art of Moral Imagination: Ethics in the Practice of Architecture. *Journal of Business Ethics, 66*(2–3), 307–317.doi: 10.1007/s10551-005-5600-4.

Farmer, G., & Guy, S. (2010). Making Morality: Sustainable Architecture and the Pragmatic Imagination. *Building Research & Information, 38*(4), 368–378.

Fisher, T. (2000, December 1). Pragmatic Architecture. *New York Times.*

Foucault, M. (1979). *Discipline and Punish: The Birth of The Prison.* Alan Sheridan (Trans). New York: Vintage Books.

Graafland, A. (2000). *The Socius of Architecture: Amsterdam, Tokyo, New York* (p. 256). Rotterdam, Germany: 010 Publishers.

Leach, N. (Ed.). (1997). *Rethinking Architecture: A Reader in Cultural Theory.* London/New York: Routledge.

Lovejoy, A. (1920). Pragmatism as Interactionism. *The Journal of Philosophy, Psychology, and Scientific Methods, 17*(23), 622–632.

Giedion, S. (1967; original 1941). *Space Time and Architecture: The Growth of a New Tradition.* (5th ed.). Cambridge, MA: Harvard University Press.

Grosz, E. (2001). *Architecture from the Outside: Essays on Virtual and Real Space.* Cambridge, MA: MIT Press.

Harvey, D. (1989). *The Condition of Postmodernity: An Enquiry into the Origins of Cultural Change.* Oxford, UK, and Cambridge, MA: Basil Blackwell.

Hays, K. M., ed. (1998). *Architecture Theory Since 1968.* Cambridge, MA/London: MIT Press.

Heidegger, M. (1971). "Building Dwelling Thinking." In A. Hofstadter (Trans.), *Poetry, Language, Thought* (pp. 145-161). New York: Harper & Row.

Jameson, F. (1997). *Postmodernism, or, The Cultural Logic of Late Capitalism.* Durham, NC: Duke University Press.

Jencks, C. (1977). *The Language of Postmodern Architecture.* New York: Rizzoli.

Lefebvre, H. (1991). *The Production of Space.* Donald Nicholson-Smith (Trans). Malden, MA/Oxford, UK: Blackwell Publishing,.

Lynch, K. (1971). *The Image of the City.* Cambridge, MA: MIT Press.

Mayo, J. M. (1985). Political Avoidance in Architecture. *Journal of Architectural Education, 38*(2), 18.doi: 10.2307/1424814.

Moore, K. (2003). Overlooking the Visual. *The Journal of Architecture, 8*(1), 25-40.doi: 10.1080/1360236032000068497.

Nobel, P. (2001, July). What Pragmatism Ain't. *Metropolis Magazine.* Available at http://www.metropolismag.com/html/content_0701/far/.

Ockman, J. (Ed.). (2000). *The Pragmatist Imagination: Thinking About Things in the Making.* Princeton, NJ: Princeton Architectural Press.

Rice, C. (2009). *The Emergence of the Interior: Architecture, Modernity, and Domesticity.* London/New York: Routledge.

Rossi, A. (1982). *The Architecture of the City*. D. Ghirardo & J. Ockman (Trans.). Cambridge, MA: MIT Press.

Pallasmaa, J. (2005). *The Eyes of the Skin: Architecture and the Senses*. Chichester, UK: John Wiley & Sons.

Pile, J. (2005). *A History of Interior Design*. (2nd ed.). Hoboken, NJ: John Wiley & Sons.

Proto, F. (2007). Between Pragmatism and Theory. *Architectural Design, 77*(3), 16–17.doi: 10.1002/ad.447.

Saunders, W. (2007). Introduction. In Saunders, W. (Ed.) *The New Architectural Pragmatism: A Harvard Design Magazine Reader* (pp. i–xvii). Minneapolis, MN: University of Minnesota Press.

Speaks, M. (2003). Theory Was Interesting . . . but Now We Have Work. *Architectural Research Quarterly, 6*(03), 209–213.

Sparke, P. (2008). *The Modern Interior*. London: Reaktion Books.

Sparke, P., Massey, A., Keeble T., & Martin, B. (2009). *Designing the Modern Interior: From Victorians to Today*. Oxford, UK/New York: Berg.

Taylor, M., & Preston, J. (2006). *Intimus: Interior Design Theory Reader*. Chichester, UK: John Wiley & Sons.

Venturi, R. (1977). *Complexity and Contradiction in Architecture*. London: Architectural Press.

Yaneva, A. (2009). *The Making of a Building: A Pragmatist Approach to Architecture*. Bern, Switzerland: Peter Lang AG International Academic Publishers

Zaera-Polo, A. (2006). A Scientific Autobiography 1982–2004: Madrid, Harvard, OMA, the AA, Yokohama, the Globe. In W. Saunders (Ed.). *The New Architectural Pragmatism: A Harvard Design Magazine Reader* (pp. 1–21). Minneapolis, MN: University of Minnesota Press.

Provocation

2.3 Poststructuralism, Phenomenology, and Lived Experience: About Meanings Held within Design and Spaces
Tiiu Vaikla-Poldma with Drew Vasilevich

I begin this provocation with a vignette by Drew Vasilevich,* who talks about how we use interior space both through design thinking and through a construction of our human abilities and meanings. Vasilevich offers some provocative examples and thoughts.

A Vignette by Drew Vasilevich

To generate any idea, you must be inspired by someone or something that stimulates you to think. The designs of objects and spaces are just ideas generated by our human ability to think. As designers, we often take for granted that our ideas create design and we feel at ease when we unconsciously attach our own meaning to what we have created, whether it is a space or an object. Fortunately, for designers this unconscious attachment of meaning within the design process allows us not to be intimidated by the notion that design has power.

The construction of meaning within the design process is a human imperative and is therefore unavoidable. In the real world, designers attribute meaning to what they

design because design requires them to understand the real purpose of objects and spaces. But is there truth in meaning in any context? Can that truth be honest and consistently relevant in the real world? If the context within the design process changes, do people change and adapt? The context does change when there is an alteration of circumstances or events that form the environment in which something exists or takes place. This is a simple morphism. Do we adapt or do we feel dislocated?

As designers, we plan with intent and assign purpose to satisfying the functional and spiritual needs of users. We invest meaning in things only to understand their relationship to us. When we repurpose objects or spaces, does the meaning change?

In today's economy the large churches that were built decades ago as places of worship have become financially unmanageable for shrinking congregations. Many of these churches have been repurposed as retail spaces or condominiums. Has the meaning changed? Does a repurposed church remain spiritual?

The railway roundhouse in downtown Toronto has been repurposed as a brewery and a furniture store. The roundhouse in Vancouver is now a community centre. Some industrial buildings have become

---

* Drew Vasilevich is retired professor, School of Interior Design, Ryerson University, Toronto, Canada.

places of worship, and various office buildings are now condominiums. We can see new meaning in repurposed spaces regardless of the cleavage. When we accept that this split exists, it can be normalized and we may be either challenged or pleased by this change of purpose and meaning.

When we design a living space, we consciously attempt to attach the meaning of home to the space. We construct meaning in a pragmatic, philosophical, and spiritual sense in an attempt to understand the purpose of the home. Meaning and the attachment of purpose have many social implications. In the TV sitcom *Frasier*, Frasier lives in an expensively furnished condo, complete with an Eames chair. When his father Martin moves in, he brings his comfortable battered and duck-taped recliner chair. The meaning of home changes for both Frasier and Martin, and the original assignment of purpose violates social norms. Does home in this case have a meaning in the philosophical sense, or do we construct new meaning in an attempt to understand the purpose of the home?

As designers, we have accepted the virtue of good design in Frasier's home due to the tasteful objects in an attractive room. His home reflects pleasure, refinement, and personal fulfillment, and yet the manner in which Frasier assigns meaning to his home could be construed as hedonism. Contradiction arises because Frasier's home reflected fine taste and intellectual interests before the arrival of his father, the recliner, and his blue-collar ideas. This contradiction exposes Frasier's moral truth as hedonism. Does contradiction change meaning?

If there is meaning, is there logic? Is it folly to assign meaning to the purpose of design? The concept of design is an objective meaning. It always has a goal or outcome whether intended or not. In the world of human-based endeavours, "you cannot not design" and there are always consequences.
May 25, 2011

Vasilevich proposes a dualism of design intent (design thinking and process) versus the way that we receive, appropriate, and use the designed intentions. What Vasilevich describes is a creation of meanings of design/spaces on two levels: (1) the poststructuralist idea that what we experience is intrinsically tied to our understanding of how we express what we experience in terms of meanings we attribute to objects and things (Csikszentmihalyi & Rochberg-Halton, 1981; Belsey, 2002) within the fundamentally phenomenological perspective of lived space as a social construction of reality (Berger and Luckmann, 1966; Poldma, 1999); and (2) the nature of the everyday as a source of value construction and vehicle through spaces and objects to what we attribute social value and significance (Csikszentmihalyi & Rochberg-Halton, 1981; Barthes in Belsey, 2002). As Csikszentmihalyi and Rochberg-Halton suggest in discussing both the sociological view of Berger and Luckmann and the social construction of things: "it becomes possible to see how interactions with objects results in socialization" (1981, p. 50), and that which is situated within our senses or experiences is thus independent of another's intention.

Is Frasier's disdain for the chair a personal issue or a social issue influenced by the modern design of his environment? Are Frasier's and Martin's ideas of home within the same space that different from socially constructed values in conflict?

Poststructuralism and Meanings of Spaces

First, let's examine the poststructuralist idea that what we experience is intrinsically tied to our understanding of how we express what we experience in terms of meanings and the fundamentally phenomenological way we experience spaces in lived lives. As we have noted, not only are spaces experienced in the moment, they are experienced through time and within our personal and social lived contexts. When we interact, these experiences formulate the social constructions that we accept as part of how we live. As Vasilevich mentioned, the changing vocation of churches and cathedrals are also statements of changing social norms and values. The trouble is, spaces may impact on us in ways we are not even aware, and quite often deliberately through the design intent.

Second, if we think about the everyday, we are tempted to propose that society and culture are social constructions; this implies we only understand what is around us when socially constructed norms provide meaning. Alternatively, we might suggest that our social construction of reality manifests itself within the spaces that we live in a fundamentally intersubjective experience of space through places,

objects, and the signifiers of things that are meaningful to us in any given moment. It was Berger and Luckmann in their seminal book *The Social Construction of Reality* who initially defined this intersubjective experience of the everyday world. As they wrote, the "reality of everyday life further presents itself to me as an intersubjective world and a world that I share with others" (1966, p. 23).

Parallel to this concept is the emerging concept that it is in the everyday, within the lived experiences we have daily, that meanings are made, that values are formed (Steeves, 2006; Belsey, 2002). For example, within our lived spaces, we construct meanings moment by moment and over time and space, often (but not always) independent of intention and more often dependant upon the intersubjective interactions that shape our experiences of spaces and places in the moment that we navigate them.

Regarding poststructuralism, Catherine Belsey (2002) writes:

"[The] poststructuralist names a theory, or a group of theories, concerning the relationship between human beings, the world, and the practice of making and reproducing meanings. On the one hand, poststructuralists affirm, consciousness is not the origin of the language we speak and the images we recognize, as much as the product of the meanings we learn and reproduce. On the other hand, communication changes all the time, with or without intervention from us, and we can choose to intervene with the view to altering the meanings—which is to say the norms and values—our culture takes for granted (p. 5)."

Belsey goes on to ask the fundamental question "What is meaning?" (p. 7) and proposes that in a poststructuralist view, "The answer seems to vary with the context" (p. 7). Using the example of language, Belsey suggests that Barthes proposes signifiers in language through a semiotic interpretation of language of commonplace everyday meanings. Genders, symbols, and contexts change with culture and vary from one language to another. And yet with spaces, we engage them as places depending on our own cultural location.

As we consider spaces and our occupation of them, this mutability is revealed through the intentions of those who created them and of those who occupy them. However, whether we are aware of it or not, the social construction of space and place is our way of interlacing our meanings held in the real world with spaces and our appropriation of them. We engage in activities and interact with others or things within spaces:

> Spaces impact on us as humans, and create the social constructions that govern social and power relations between men and women. Not only do these value constructions influence how we see spaces and how designers create spaces for people, they also contribute to the reproductions of the values through the spaces that vehicle them (Poldma, 1999, p. 2).

Considering Voice

If we consider that interior spaces are intrinsically linked to human perception, action, and social intersubjective experiences, then we should also consider how voices might be heard. Languages include the voices of all people in all situations. In a poststructuralist world, aesthetic choices within spaces would be grounded with the voices of the various people who will be a part of the construction of the spaces.

These voices are many and also vary by context and situation. The designer has a voice of a particular type, as do users, actors, participants, stakeholders, and others who engage with spaces and their situations. There are alternative ways of making meaning through vehicles such as constructed knowledge (Berger & Luckmann, 1966; Code, 1997; Field Belenky et al., 1997). Voices are made known, acquire skills, are made silent, depending on the situation at hand (Field Belenky et al., 1997). As Field Belenky et al. note, there are ways to "understand other people's ideas in the other people's terms rather than in their own terms " (p. 124) and that this form of connected knowledge accounts for voices in context of their meanings and within environments that represent the views held from a constructivist perspective (p. 152).

Understanding intersubjective experiences requires considering how spaces act on our perceptions and perpetuate our social relations. For voices to be uncovered, we must understand the ways that design decision making and intentions also affect the ways that we construct our realities.

Ultimately these experiences are phenomenological, understood through the lens of the person living the experience. Phenomenology and lived experience are fundamental components of the ways that spaces engage in the construction of meaningful experiences. Spaces become dynamic and lived places with the subjective and local experiences of the people who use them. In Vasilevich's example of Frasier and Martin at home, we return to the dualism of their individual constructed meanings. We may understand, as designers, the meaning and value of the Eames chair, while for Frasier the entire space was a symbol of a life well lived. For Martin, the chair he loved and coveted spoke to his values and the meaning of the chair from his perspective. All three are valuable perspectives, and no one is right or wrong. In the end, however, it is Frasier and Martin who engage in their views: both had their ideal space as a place, and their ideal objects within the space. It was their social construction that was the source of difference, and yet each one, within their particular context, constructed what was meaningful to them. The space supported both.

References

Belsey, C. (2002). *Poststructuralism: A Very Short Introduction.* Oxford, UK: Oxford University Press.

Berger, P. L., & Luckmann, T. (1966). *The Social Construction of Reality: A Treatise in the Sociology of Knowledge.* White Plains, NY: Longman Publishers.

Csikszentmihalyi, M., & Rochberg-Halton, E. (1981). The Meaning of Things: Domestic Symbols and the Self. Cambridge, UK: Cambridge University Press.

Code, L. (1991). What Can She Know? Ithaca, New York: Cornell University Press.

Field Belenky, M., McVicar Clinchy, B., Tarule Goldberger, N., & Mattuck Tarule, J. (1997). *Women's Ways of Knowing.* New York: Basic Books.

Poldma, T. (1999). Gender, Design and Education: The Politics of Voice. Unpublished Master's thesis. Montreal, QC: McGill University, author.

Steeves, P. L. (2006). The things themselves: phenomenology of the everyday. London: Routledge.

You get a strange feeling when you're about to leave a place . . . like you'll not only miss the people you love, but you'll miss the person you are now at this time and this place, because you'll never be this way ever again.

—Azar Nafisi, *Reading Lolita in Tehran: A Memoir in Books,* p. 336.

On a recent fall vacation trip to Rhode Island from Texas, my wife, Christine, and I revisited a long-running debate we have about the concept of place. This ongoing discussion began more than four years ago when I said to her that the convenience store, 7-Eleven, says many things to those who stop in to buy various things in the way it's designed, created, stocked, and marketed. "You know you're crazy," she responded. "It's only a convenience store. It doesn't 'say' anything beyond 'I'm a store in which to buy stuff and leave.'" I countered that the store's design, lighting, color schematic, and layout speak volumes. The colors, I argued, predominately green, red, and orange, clearly represent a stop-light effect for stopping quickly, pausing to buy a few items, then heading on down the road. The corporation, I suggested, thought through the choice of colors to connect this idea to their customers. The interior design of most 7-Elevens allow a fast perusal of offerings and items, and suggest to visitors that they make a quick decision—and, through marketing and design, the decision is always to buy something and keep moving. The entire structure, I argued, says that this is not a place to linger. Its design differs significantly from, say, a Starbucks, which has comfortable chairs and tables (and sometimes couches) in which to sit, and lighting and music that asks visitors to stay. 7-Elevens rarely have places to sit, and one certainly wouldn't linger.

But Rhode Island sparked the conversation anew as I began noting various things about architecture and design. When I go off unpacking my ideas about place and how we understand the idea of place, Christine usually placates me with a smile, sometimes a pat, and allows me to ramble on. Her idea or understanding of place runs more Dr. Seussian in nature: A place is a place, as simple as that. My research and ideas about place tend to complicate ideas for a simple reason: Place and places *matter*. Places represent anchors for individuals, communities, societies, cultures, and nations. This grounding affects self-identity as well as distinctions and delineations from others. It provides boundaries for social and cultural groups from which collective identity springs forth. Place also defines individuals and groups, offering identifiable characteristics or traits. For instance, consider Paris. Many French identify themselves with their nation's capital. And by proxy, those who think of the French tend to think of Parisian landmarks: the Eiffel Tower, the Louvre, the Seine, small cafes and restaurants that line the streets, the Champs-Élysées. These places are France and represent the nexus of power for the French population. Paris matters as a cornerstone of French identity. In her essay "Language of Place and Discourses of Power: Constructing a New Sense of Place," Patricia Stokowski argues that places represent "dynamic contexts of social interactions and memory" and the importance of place cannot be understated (p. 369). As the Parisian example demonstrates, place-linked geographical anchors reflect individuals and cultures in a way that binds a collective history with a particular spot on the globe. Stokowski argues that a "sense of place is important both individually and socially and only through analysis of the collective, constructed potential of place will social and cultural power be made manifest" (p. 369). Places represent that location where human history converges with geographical coordinates to define both individuals and cultures.

The impetus for this paper might have started in a 7-Eleven, but the idea of place constantly evolves, moving and changing and complicating as the concept of place changes from individual to individual, culture to culture. Our approach to understanding, analyzing, and occupying places connects directly to our cultural values and how we reflect those values in particular spaces. Space manifests into real places only through the cultural lens that individuals and societies bring to the understanding of space versus place. This article explores both cultural and individual understanding of the concept of place by focusing on specific texts that interrogate the notion and brings diverse voices into understanding the idea of place. It also explores other media and how changing ideas about place further complicate our understanding of place. The long-term goal of my exploration of place has always been to clearly and concisely affix place somewhere between a common-sense notion of place and the more complicated ideas surrounding place and its affect on us—if, in fact, that grounding is even possible.

Anchoring Place in Place

The best way to begin situating place within an understandable framework appears to be by establishing a clear and concise definition of the term. A seemingly simple endeavor, but according to Tim Cresswell (2004) in *Place: A Short Introduction*, getting to a clear understanding of how the word is and has been used quickly becomes quite a messy affair. He writes:

> Place is a word that seems to speak for itself. . . . Place is not a specialized piece of academic terminology. It is a word we use in the English-speaking world. It is a word wrapped in common sense. In one sense this makes it easier to grasp as it is familiar. In another sense, however,

this makes it more slippery as the subject of a book. As we already think we know what it means it is hard to get beyond that common-sense level in order to understand it in a more developed way. Place, then, is both simple (and that is part of its appeal) and complicated. (p. 1)

Cresswell's onion-peeling dissection of the term leads into a deeper and more complex understanding both in the sense of our relationships to places as well as how we delineate the term in reference to geography. For a common understanding, Cresswell begins by exploring how the term is used in everyday life where place represents the "ownership or some kind of connection between a person and a particular location" (2004, p. 1). My place, your place, our place, a place at the table—these phrases encapsulate the simple notion of ownership, either temporary or permanence, or an individual's particular portion of space. Cresswell acknowledges diverse distinctions of the term (for example, the word suffices as both a noun and a verb), but the goal of his book targets the unpacking of place in relation to a geographical location primarily, defining the difference between space and place. His simple statement that "places have spaces in between them" serves as a crux for this chapter's exploration of geographical anchored places as well as socially constructed places (Cresswell, 2004, p. 8).

Cresswell's text serves as an interesting focal point for an initial exploration of place. When I used Chapter 1 of his book as the first reading assignment of a sophomore writing course focused specifically on unpacking the idea and relationship of individuals and societies to place, my students immediately rebelled, noting that they did not care to think and write about place for an entire semester. They thought (like most first- and second-year students think) that they already knew how to define the term without experiencing the need to delve deeper into nuances of meaning. Yet after reading Cresswell's introductory chapter and other place-based texts, my students began to have deeper discussions, focused more and more on how individuals think about, talk about, and write about place. By semester's end, their understanding of place as well as their individual connections to specific places appeared to change. They had engaged ideas about place and, as Cresswell wrote earlier, began "to understand it in a more developed way" (p. 1). Almost without exception, they agreed with Robert Sack's argument in "The Power of Space and Place" that "People are always in a place, and place constrains and enables" (paragraph 12). These students had spent 16 weeks in the same place exploring ideas and concepts about place only to stumble to the conclusion that defining place remains a complex and messy task, even the seemingly simple idea of describing place geographically.

Cultural Considerations of Place

One aspect of place that invites unpacking is how different cultures view themselves in relation to particular places. In the 2002 film *Rabbit-Proof Fence*, place plays a seminal role in conceptualizing the understanding of how one culture views its place compared to another. The story, set in Western Australia in 1931, focuses on the Anglo government's policy of removing culturally mixed Aboriginal children from their families and sending them to what are essentially re-education camps to teach them how to be servants for the Anglo population. This policy, articulated throughout the film by the main white character, A. O. Neville, chief protector of Aborigines in Northwest Australia, seeks to "save them from themselves," as the prevailing conventional wisdom at the time suggested that these children would not fit in with Aboriginal families. These children, white society said, would in effect be "out of place." Educating them to be servants would offer them a better life in a better place. The plot focuses on three Aboriginal and white mixed-race girls, Molly, Daisy, and Gracie, who were forcibly taken from their mothers and moved 1,500 miles to a white settlement named Moore River. Here, they were dressed in white clothes, housed in white buildings, taught how to clean and care for white people, and inculcated into white cultural traditions, such as religion and language. Neville argues that this rehabilitation will ultimately extinguish the native ways out of the children, removing all vestiges of their former lives. But viewers clearly see that the policy essentially seeks to erase the girls' connections to their families, as well as their sense of place.

The film contrasts Anglo and Aboriginal sense of place by juxtaposing cultural ideas about what constitutes place. The Anglo sense of place suggests that the Australian Outback simply represented open and unoccupied space without name or cultural context. The transformation from space to place only occurs with the building of settlements. Anglos needed to construct fences and build homes, shops, and churches as a means to impose their idea of place on space. They viewed the Aborigines as essentially place-less due to their ability to migrate throughout the Outback without a specific location to call their own. In Moore River, the girls were forced to live in a foreign place (a dormitory) and spent much of their time within white-constructed structures. The girls, noticeably out of their place, decide to escape, finding and following the continental-wide fence that runs from Moore River to their land of Jigalong. The fence, built to control the rabbit population and keep them from destroying farmland, divides places as well as cultures, but the girls use this invention of the Whites to find their way home. Depiction of Aboriginal life suggests that living outdoor in open places more clearly allows the natives to feel connected to their place. Scenes at the film's beginning depict Molly's mother showing her places to hunt and find water and shelter. In one foretelling scene, her mother points to a large bird flying, telling Molly that the Spirit Bird will always look after her. This symbol of connection to place reappears as the girls begin to find their way home.

Western histories display commonalities of one culture's misunderstanding of another and how the difference in the understanding of place plays a role in cultural clashes. In his critically acclaimed 1991 book *PrairyErth: A Deep Map*, William Least Heat-Moon attempts to understand the prairies of Kansas, and specifically Chase County, a place situated a few miles from the United States' geographic center. An explorer of both cultural and natural landscapes, Heat-Moon works his way through his understanding of what the defined place of the prairie means to him as well as the residents who occupy the sparsely populated land. In thinking about the white culture's understanding of the place, he constantly returns to the land's original occupants, uncovering stories and traditions that seem to run counter to our understanding of what places means. He writes:

> To them attach this old Indian story: The white man asked, *Where is your nation?* The red man said, *My nation is the grass and rocks and the four-leggeds and the six-leggeds and the belly wrigglers and swimmers and the winds and all things that grow and don't grow.* The white man asked, *How big is it?* The other said, *My nation is where I am and my people where they are and the grandfathers and their grandfathers and all the grandmothers and all the stories told, and it is all the songs, and it is our dancing.* The white man asked, *But how many people are there?* The red man said, *That I do not know.* (p. 16)

This story demonstrates that Native American understanding of their place or nation appears to be tied more with historical experiences within a broadly defined geographic location without specific boundaries rather than the notion of ownership of a specific place. This understanding of place differs from Anglo conceptions of place that appear to be understood only in a more physically bounded, tangible realm: Place requires ownership (many times based solely on written texts that dictate ownership) and well-defined boundaries.

In Cresswell's *Place*, he explores this apparent difference in the understanding of place between traditional cultures as compared to Western culture. Cresswell analyzes ideas presented in Jonathan Raban's 1999 book *Passage to Juneau* that demonstrate a fundamental difference in the definition of place between the natives, the Tlingits, who live along the Northwest Coast of what is now Washington and Oregon, and early explorers seeking to name and ultimately occupy empty spaces for the expansion of the English Empire. These explorers were mystified as they learned that the Tlingits "read the sea as a set of places associated with particular spirits and particular dangers. While the colonialists looked at the sea and saw blank space, the natives saw place" (Cresswell, 2004, p. 9). Raban notes that one German geographer

was astounded by what he saw as the local Tlingit's ignorance of their place in the world, which to him was dominated by the enormous mountains that towered behind the small strip of land they inhabited by the sea (Cresswell, 2004, p. 9).

The natives had myriad names for places on the sea, but their culture saw little need to name areas of land. The explorers held the exact opposite notion for understanding place. Cresswell analyzes this distinction, drilling down to a fundamental essence that we seem to understand about place:

> Space, then, has been seen in distinction to place as a realism without meaning—as a "fact of life" which, like time, produces the basic coordinates for human life. When humans invest meaning in a portion of space and then become attached to it in some way (naming is one such way) it becomes a place (p. 10).

Place-Making Rituals

In Western cultures, we create places through various rituals as a way to sort and understand the world(s) in which we live. Our sorting of world(s) into understandable chunks allows individuals and societies to make sense and adapt to our environment. During our earlier hunter and gatherer phase, groups or tribes traveled from place to place, each place delineated by designations based on use: best area to hunt game, or the place that roots and tubers grow, or the salt-gathering place, or places to find flint or rocks for tools. The significant places became spots on the collective internal map that offered our early ancestors a way to sort their world into livable, manageable ideas. As societies evolved and became more connected to place, evidence suggests that place-making activities led to the continued growth of specific places as cultural sites of power. Writing in "Place, Landscape and Environment: Anthropological Archaeology in 2009," Christopher Rodning suggests "It is cultural activity—and cultural knowledge—that gives meaning to particular spaces in the landscapes and makes them places" (p. 180). One tool that cultures use to unpack space is the idea of naming places. By employing language as a cultural artifact to identity a place, we, in essence, create metaphors of places, instilling powerful significance on strategically bounded places. These place identifiers become richer as they move down through cultural timelines, adding history and knowledge. Perhaps, then, Western culture has adapted part of traditional culture's conceptions of historical experiences combined with our need to own places, in order that we might clearly define how we think about place.

However, Western culture also attempts to understand that which we do not know by employing metaphors to stand in for empty spaces. Take, for example, the idea of the Pacific Ocean as a place. Unlike the Tlingits, most Western observers see the broad expanse of open water merely as open space with no boundaries or identifiable structures; however, by agreeing to name it the *Pacific Ocean,* we fill it with the sense of place. Again, we do this as a cultural ritual in order to adapt to our environment as well as to sort worlds into manageable chunks. Then we begin to drill further down to make the place of the Pacific Ocean more understandable, and, by definition, more

Figure 2.2 Windansea Beach in LaJolla, California, draws surfers and beach lovers alike. The name functions as both a place identifier and a cultural designation important to those who use and occupy the space. One only has to mention Windansea to seasoned Southern California surfers to demonstrate the significance of this place.
Photo credit: Courtesy of Travis Mann

of a place. We begin to chunk that huge expanse into demarcations: the Southwest Pacific Basin, the East Pacific Rise, the Aleutian Trench, the Clarion Fracture Zone—all identifiable, boundary-enclosed places. One cannot see the boundaries, but by naming and separating places with names, we continue those place-making activities in order to comprehend what the Pacific Ocean represents. Still, these named places are under vast stretches of open water (undefined space?), a cultural acknowledgment that our society struggles to see the expanse of ocean as anything more than open space. It seems we need hard, geographical surfaces in order to imbue a place as place.

For generations, cultures have explored the idea of geography as a way to docu-ment and understand both places and open spaces that lie in between particular places. Old World cartographers created detailed maps of new discoveries, as intrepid explorers returned with tales of new worlds and landscapes. But explorers also told of lands not yet seen, perhaps only heard of in tales and traditions. Cartographers needed to add structure to these unknown places and lands yet to be discovered. Early maps from the great empirical ages of discovery show imagined coastlines complete with mountain ranges, seas, and even creatures that may occupy those places. In those instances of imagining a yet-undiscovered or explored place, these individuals created landscapes as a way to understand something that was as yet not understandable. This cultural adaptation recognized that creating words and images about places—even places that were unseen and unexplored—imbued human understanding and meaning onto and into a particular chunk of space. Using drawing and words to convey meaning about place allows the place to become important in the realm of ideas, a metamorphosis from blankness into something with meaning, even without setting foot in a given area. Knowledge of a space facilitates the movement from unknown space to knowable place.

Natural landscapes seem somewhat easy to map, but in what way can we map culturally created landscapes? Technology allows us to create places that, until only a decade or a few years ago, would have never been considered places to begin with. Look at the rise of social media and its relationship to the idea of personal space. When individuals delve into the most talked about social space, Facebook, they become their own explorers and cartographers, finding new places in which to attach individual, social, and emotional significance. Facebook users upload photos; comment on each other's photos; and write about their life, their status, and their relationships with and to other people. In essence, we carve from space a place and stake our individual flags, saying "This is my place." In fact, we designate it as "our" Facebook page. However, this place represents one place that we own where we invite people to change our place, offering comments and critiques and posting thing to our place. Almost without excep-

tion, we would not allow people into our homes or apartments or condos and allow them to change our places, move furniture about, hang their photos on our walls, and the like. Yet in the Facebook landscape, we combine our individual sense of place with the collective idea, allowing people to change our place. This social phenomenon changes our perceptions of places as a site where individualism clearly combines with the larger collective. Facebook is more than merely a place for community; rather, it represents a matrix of constantly shifting and evolving interconnected personal places that only function because we are changing our ideas about what constitutes community or collective places.

People connect themselves to places through physical and emotional attachments. A trip to New York or London or Toronto involves visiting sights, eating at various places, buying artifacts of places, staying in various places, and moving through unknown spaces to finally touch down in places that sometimes have strong emotional attachments. For instance, during my trip to Rhode Island, I created places for myself from spaces that before that trip only existed in an imagined world. Having never ventured to the Ocean State before, my curiosity led me to explore the place before I even arrived. I read reviews of what to do during our trip, what places I had to see, where the best bird-watching places were, and what natural areas held the most promise for long hikes and explorations. I began imbuing the place with parts of myself before I even landed. After my online explorations, had my trip been suddenly cancelled, I would have wanted to explore Rhode Island in the future, but my connection to the place called *Rhode Island* would have been limited at best. But once I began interacting with places, I began to form emotional attachments. On a side trip to Block Island, a small island a few miles off the southern coast, one of our activities riveted a particular place to me. After a few hours of bicycling around the island, my wife and I noticed a secluded beach marked on the visitor's map that seemed like a promising spot to take time to relax. After working our way downhill, we discovered a rocky beach protected from the wind, with crashing waves and sun-drenched spots to take the cool from the autumn afternoon. We walked for a while, but finally found a small stretch of sand where we could pitch a blanket and prop ourselves on backpacks to spend time listening to the waves and thinking vacation thoughts. After I while, I began to feel myself unwinding, letting the stresses associated with everyday life melt away and, for the first time, really feel like I was on vacation. The place changed me. Or, maybe a better way to say it is that because I had formed an emotional connection to the place, my understanding of it changed. No longer did it represent merely a place on a map or a sign at the top of the hill; this cliff-lined, rocky beach became a significant place to me. I'd created an important emotional attachment to this place and for me the place became real. I'd created place.

A cultural practice we subscribe to reinforce place is to tell stories about places, making them real, or as close to real as they can become to our family, friends, and colleagues who have not seen or experienced these places. My beach place became a collective experience with others when, over dinner that evening, I told my father-in-law of our treks across Block Island. When we arrived at the narrative that included our beach experience, I found myself focusing not so much on how the beach looked or the views or the scenery, but rather on the experiences we had and the feelings that the place generated. My wife's experiences were different: she remembers lightly snoozing on the blanket, how the cliffs blocked the wind, and the warm feel of the sun on her skin. Yet both stories wove together to form the collective experience of a particular place. Individually, we had each created a specific personal experience of the same place; yet collectively, our experiences and new histories added to our cultural understanding of a place.

But is place an end or some part of the means? Christopher Rodning draws a conclusion that continues to complicate the idea of place and our relationships to it. He writes, "Places are not just backdrops to cultural activity. Places are outcomes of that activity, and they shape practices of domestic and ritual life" (p. 187). He argues that specific sites do not merely serve as static landscapes, but our collective construction of places demonstrates that places affect us as individuals and societies. Cultural activity and the use of histories of people in specific spaces establish place markers, but they also show that places can change much beyond the physical characteristics of geography. But understanding and identifying place involves much more than simply saying cultural activity imbues space with a distinction of place. Our emotional attachment to a place signifies the human construction of place.

In most Western cultures, our collective understanding of particular places is directly connected to our emotional experiences of specific places. For instance, take two American places that are laden with strong initial emotions: The site of the Alfred P. Murrah Building in Oklahoma City, which was bombed in 1995, and 9/11's Ground Zero in New York City. For most Americans, our connection to these places includes horrific memories of burning buildings, the sights and sounds of catastrophic mayhem, and of children, women, and men dying. Many people can remember where they were—the exact places—when these places were attacked. Yet as time and distance from these events happen, our collective understanding of these places has changed since the horrific events sealed those places to us. Visitors to these sites see how our place-making activities have changed our connections to these places. Instead of wreckage, we now see memorials and tributes that honor all those who died in the attacks. Instead of pain and suffering and death, our emotional attachments slowly change to notions that these places represent hallowed ground, sites that clearly solidify our sense of ourselves as Americans. Our individual attachments weave together to create a collective tapestry of a place that defines our sense of selves as Americans.

Figure 2.3 The author and his wife sink into place, looking out to sea from Block Island, Rhode Island. They ultimately named the beach "Serenity Beach," and drift back to the place in stories and thoughts when they need a mental break. In essence, they created place from space.
Photo credit: Courtesy of Travis Mann

Has Place Been Anchored or the Idea Merely Exploded?

A colleague of mine proffered an interesting definition of place during an online conversation. He described place as the intersection of dirt and the human narrative. His description struck me as an exact, expressive way to describe place based on geographically bound constructs. Cultures interact and rely on place as a way to understand and identify ourselves within specific contexts. Our individual and collective stories reinforce the concept of place and places, digging us deeper into our individual and collective dirt. These stories or histories of interactions with dirt compel us to continue identifying ourselves with concrete places. After all, those modern cultures that do not have connections to their own dirt (the Palestinians come to mind) appear placeless and lack a significant cultural understanding of their collective and individual identity.

But ideas about place continue to change when the concepts expand beyond connections to physical places. We're moving toward distinctly more complex understandings of how we look at place, and these avenues of exploration require us to continue the work of unpacking place in light of changing cultural adaptations to our environment. Technology expands our comprehension of space through sites of social interaction on the Web, yet expansions of how we use various spaces will also change our relationship and understanding of what place represents. Cloud computing, for instance, will undoubtedly change how

we think about place and locations in space. The paradigm shift we will experience (some of us will not be able to understand how connecting computers and shared resources creates new places) will change what and where information is shared, saved, and changed. This shift makes our concept of place both grow and shrink: expansion of where we can do things shrinks the spaces between the places that we occupy, drawing us closer to a more shared place.

On some level, however, we seem conflicted about understanding our sense of self within places. That thought seems well encapsulated in Alain de Botton's notion from his book *The Architecture of Happiness*. He writes, "We seem divided between an urge to override our senses and numb ourselves to our settings and a contradictory impulse to acknowledge the extent to which our identities are indelibly connected to, and will shift along with, our locations" (p. 12). Many of us choose not to consider the role that place plays in our individual and collective identity, yet at the same time almost all people seem to have specific places that in some way anchor them. Within this messiness about place lies the expanding complexities that require us to continue explorations surrounding our understanding of place. Per Linde et al. acknowledge this notion in their article "Interaction Design as Understanding and Transforming Place" when they write: "What constitutes place is a complex totality of social engagements with other people, use of artefacts, information and lived experience that is hard to pinpoint" (Linde, p. 198).

Discussion Questions

1. What is cultural meaning for Travis Mann in terms of place?
2. How do different cultures "unpack space as place"?
   a. Look at the examples given by Mann.
   b. Provide new examples familiar to you.
3. Discuss and compare/contrast the experiences of the culture and how identity is woven around the meaning of *place*.
   a. What does *place* mean to you?
   b. Why do you think Mann's students would rebel against the idea of studying *place* all semester?
   c. What are "place making rituals"?
4. Discuss how place and space are for you
   a. Similar.
   b. Different.
   c. Culturally bound.

References

Cresswell, T. 2004. *Place: A Short Introduction.* Malden, MA: Blackwell.

de Botton, A. (2006). *The Architecture of Happiness.* New York: Pantheon Books.

Heat-Moon, W. L. (1991). *PrairyErth: A Deep Map.* Boston: Houghton Mifflin.

Linde, P., et al. (2004) Interaction Design as Understanding and Transforming Place. *Digital Creativity, 15*(4), 197–208.

Nafisi, A. (2003). *Reading Lolita in Tehran: A Memoir in Books.* New York: Random House.

Noyce, P. (Director). 2002. *Rabbit-Proof Fence* [DVD]. Miramax Home Entertainment.

Rodning, Christopher. (2010). Place, Landscape, and Environment: Anthropological Archaeology in 2009. *American Anthropologist 112*(2), 180–190.

Sack, R. D. (1993). The Power of Space and Place. *Geographical Review 83*(3), 326.

Stokowski, P. A. "Languages of Place and Discourses of Power: Constructing New Senses of Place." *Journal of Leisure Research* 34.4 (2002): 368. *Academic Search Complete.* EBSCO. Web. 11 Nov. 2010.

SUMMARY

Through a philosophical and theoretical examination of space and its diverse meanings over time, we can consider different types of theoretical structures, both theoretical and pragmatic, of concepts about space, of meanings held, and of how experiences broaden aesthetic concepts of space. These theories challenge *a priori* concepts of space as a container, propose interiors as intrinsically tied to intimate human experiences, and propose alternate ways for how spaces intersect with activities and experiences beyond purely physical constructions.

We frame meanings through theoretical concepts and constructions that we use and that change with time and with the increased knowledge we have of our perceptions and views of spaces. We also consider the different ways that space is constructed as a concept in diverse paradigms and cultural historic contexts. For example in structuralist and poststructuralist modes, these viewpoints reframe assessments of how the social constructions that we create when designing spaces vehicle human activity. These current views consider space in its multiple contexts.

SUGGESTED READINGS

Belsey, C. (2002). *Poststructuralism: A Very Short Introduction*. Oxford: Oxford University Press.

Lefebvre, H. (1991). In D. Nicholson-Smith (Trans.), *The Production of Space*. Malden, MA/Oxford, UK: Blackwell Publishing.

Baudrillard, J. (1996). In J. Benedict (Trans.), *A System of Objects*. New York: Verso.

OVERVIEW QUESTIONS FOR DISCUSSION

1. Trace the various definitions and positions about relative space, absolute space, and other ways that space is defined through time. What is salient in these definitions? How has our concept of spaces changed in just the past few years?

2. Consider the various meanings of modernist spaces, constructivist spaces, and alternative spaces as proposed by both Melles and Huppatz and by Wilwerding. What do these diverse perspectives reveal about:

   - Different ideas about space.
   - Space as a container.
   - How people perceive spaces.

3. Examine these different definitions in light of the various theories and perspectives proposed by each author.

4. Analyze Wilwerding's views of relative and absolute space in light of what we consider space to be.

5. Compare Wilwerding's view of space as place with Mann's exploration of "place as place" as an experiential space.

6. How do Melles and Huppatz propose that "interior as a contained architectural space" no longer is enough to account for how spaces are perceived and conceived?

7. What is the aesthetic experience that Rorty proposes and that is presented by Melles and Huppatz?

8. What contribution does Dewey's idea of aesthetic experience make to Melles and Huppatz's ideas about pragmatic approaches to lived experiences in diverse spaces?

9. What is poststructuralism? Compare the provocation view of spaces as products of lived experience within a poststructural framework with Melles and Huppatz's definition of architectural form in the context of poststructural thinking. What possibilities exist for interiors to be considered from these perspectives? How does a phenomenological understanding of space fit in?

10. What are social constructions of reality according to Berger and Luckmann? How would we consider subjective and intersubjective experiences people have when considering spaces?

CHAPTER 3
Identities, Disciplines, and Knowledge Spaces

disciplinary space, knowledge space, identity, practice, pragmatic knowledge, design inquiry, design research, knowledge domains, designing, ontology, epistemology, methodology, methods, body of knowledge, paradigms of knowledge, inquirer stance, professional identity, hermeneutics, heuristics, oxiology, deontic

AFTER READING THIS CHAPTER, YOU WILL BE ABLE TO:

- Understand the nature of knowledge.
- Analyze the components of designing as a practice, as a research form, or as knowledge acquisition.
- Differentiate concepts of identity of a discipline.
- Understand issues in the ways that knowledge is defined in different contexts.
- Understand the broad issues of design as a discipline of practice, research, and knowledge.
- Situate the context of a body of knowledge for a discipline.
- Compare the issues of spaces of interior design as a discipline.

INTRODUCTION

Disciplines are spaces of knowledge construction and evolution. Spaces are considered by and designed by a multitude of people from such domains as architecture, interior design, industrial design, landscape, urban designers, and many others that challenge spaces as having specific disciplinary boundaries. Add to this emerging context the rapidly changing ways that we evaluate and judge what constitutes the nature of spaces, be these physical, virtual, context, or knowledge-driven. Each profession must develop new knowledge to advance its own specificity as a discipline, while positioning itself amongst other professions/disciplines and working in transdisciplinary contexts. The design and creation of interiors as spaces is in the domain of architects, interior designers, industrial designers, psychologists, anthropologists, sociologists, and a host of others who have interests in the design and conception of spaces for people and their experiences.

The spaces of interiors fall into a muddy category of disciplines, where multiple stakeholders develop knowledge about the built environment. Add to this dilemma the fact that interior design as a discipline is rapidly developing new knowledge and adding to its body of knowledge almost daily, as a result of and as documented by Guerin and Martin. (2005)

These realities are compounded by emerging ideas about spaces, their meanings, and design spaces of changing dynamics. As we noted in Chapter 2, meanings of design/spaces connotes understanding how space is defined, how spaces evolve with time, what meanings are attributed to the subjective experiences of space, and how spaces have moved beyond physical attributes alone. The creation of spaces for living, working, or playing includes complex relationships with diverse actors who engage in the process of making, whether this happens in virtual realms or by combining the real and the virtual. Each exploration is done in a practical world, while reflection on practices and understanding stances requires reflection on the actions that have occurred.

To be able to contextualize the discussions on knowledge spaces and discuss the case of interior design as a particular knowledge of the space disciplines, we will summarize very briefly some basic theoretical concepts about knowledge: designing, ontological and epistemological stances of knowledge, and paradigms of knowledge as required to position discussions about knowledge construction.

Defining Design and Knowledge Spaces: The Case of Interior Design

At the heart of interior design and spaces is the act of design itself. Designing, as we have seen in Chapter 1, is first a verb. This denotes an engagement of the act of designing spaces with making meanings that involve people who engage in designing. Spaces are designed in multiple contexts and by various disciplines and, in particular, by those interested in interiors and who have designing at the root of their conceptualizations.

We return to this definition of design with a mind to frame the concept with the development of knowledges within disciplines and design fields and how this impacts our understanding of spaces. For example, Ken Friedman elaborates how the definition of *design* is grounded both as a discipline and a profession and with certain broad domains of knowledge. He provides Merriam-Webster's definition of design as "to conceive or plan in the mind, b: to have a purpose; intend, c: to devise for a specific function or end" (Friedman, 2003, p. 508). Friedman then suggests six domains of design knowledge framed as:

[T]he frames within which a design must act. Each domain requires a broad range of skills, knowledge and awareness. Design is the entire process across a full range of domains required for any given outcome. The field organized around design can be seen as a profession, a discipline, and a field. The profession of design involves the professional practice of design. . . . one model of the design field represents six general domains. These domains are (1) natural sciences, (2) humanities and liberal arts, (3) social and behavioural sciences, (4) human profession and services, (5) creative and applied arts, and (6) technology and engineering. (Friedman 2003, p. 508, from Friedman 2001, p. 40)

For design, as Friedman proposes, these domains of knowledge suit the purposes of understanding the knowledge spaces where these concepts of design exist. If we apply this same exercise to spaces of interior design more specifically, we would see these domains represented among other domains.

As we can note from these relatively straightforward definitions, *design* as a noun connotes certain meanings, while *design* as a verb connotes other meanings. In this book we have referred to designing as a verb, grounded in the process of generating a possible vision of something that was not conceived before the design act was used to create a new situation, solution, idea, concept, or space.

We return to these definitions again when we speak of knowledge spaces and disciplinary identities and as we examine how these ideas revolve around interior spaces and their design. When exploring spaces and their meanings, we must also understand the disciplinary perspectives that give rise to certain theories and points of view. What knowledge is developed or put forth is necessary to understand, in equal measure to understanding the perspective from which this knowledge is produced.

Defining Knowledge Sources

When defining a position or stance as a form of knowledge within a discipline, we might begin by defining the type of knowledge we are interested in developing. In the past, theoretical constructs about spatial knowledge have been situated in more pragmatic concerns as these relate to the built environment disciplines such as architecture, interior design, engineering, and so on. As such, the knowledge we construct has been based in large part on practical, pragmatic issues we find in the environments we construct and within concepts of spaces as containers or within aesthetic concepts of visual art and aesthetic beauty in the Kantian sense. However, ideas and theories are emerging that contradict the constructs and defy these ideas while adding new knowledge, and these ideas are forcing discussions about what constitutes designed space.

We might then view *design* in the professional sense of business, as inquiry, as in the evolution of research, or design as knowledge in the sense of developing new knowledge for disciplinary evolution. Each meaning is a different one and dependent on the person's professional (design as design), researcher (design as inquiry), or philosophical (design as knowledge) stance.

Ontological and Epistemological Knowledge

Finally, we also understand our world from an ontological or epistemological perspective. In terms of knowledge, quite often we confuse our knowledge acquisition and construction by not being aware of our relative ontological or epistemological stance. In Chapter 1, we examined the nature of knowledge and how researchers take positions that are situated in particular world views. We reviewed the four paradigms of knowledge as proposed by Guba and Lincoln as ways to construct knowledge: positivism, postpositivism, critical theory, and constructivism. We return to these paradigms to locate how these concepts answer questions about how knowledge is constructed as either ontological or epistemological. Each paradigm must answer the three foundational questions as Guba and Lincoln propose:

> Inquiry paradigms define for inquirers what it is they are about, and what fall within and outside the limits of legitimate inquiry. . . . The basic beliefs that define inquiry paradigms can be summarized by the responses given by the proponents of any given paradigm to three fundamental questions . . . : (1) the ontological question; (2) The epistemological question; (3) the methodological question. (1994, p. 108)

Alternatively, in the book *The Foundations of Social Research*, author Michael Crotty helps to further define these questions by restating them as four different questions. He asserts that the answers to these fundamental questions are the basis of research:

> What methods do we propose to use?
> What methodology governs our choice and use of methods?
> What theoretical perspective lies behind the methodology in question?
> What epistemology informs this theoretical perspective? (1998, p. 2)

Ontological Knowledge

While Guba and Lincoln include the ontological question in the situating of paradigms, Crotty, referring back to his four inquiries, clarifies the ontological question as one asked alongside the epistemological question, thus:

> In the research literature there is frequent mention of ontology and you might be wondering why ontology does not figure in the schema (4 questions) at this point.
> Ontology is the study of being. It is concerned with "what is," with the nature of existence, with the structure of reality as such. Were we to introduce it into our frame-

work, it would sit alongside epistemology informing the theoretical perspective, for each theoretical perspective embodies a certain way of understanding what is (ontology) as well as a certain way of understanding what it means to know (epistemology)....

. . . to talk of the construction of meaning is to talk of the construction of meaningful reality." (p. 10)

While Crotty argues that Lincoln and Guba position ontology as a positivist position, Guba and Lincoln clearly position ontology as a construct that is independent of a particular position in their work. Even in theory positions and definitions are argued with different meanings! Whatever the inquirer's perspective, it is the position of the knower in relation to the type of knowledge to be constructed that reflects a particular paradigm, be this positivist, postpositivist, critical, or constructivist. No matter what the position, we must remember, as Lincoln and Guba suggest, how research develops and how knowledge is constructed, as a means of constructing a meaningful reality of the situation or phenomenon being examined. Crotty goes on to say:

Not too many of us embark on a piece of social research with epistemology as our starting point. "I am a constructionist. Therefore I will investigate..." Hardly. We typically start with a real-life issue that needs to be addressed, a problem that needs to be solved, a question that needs to be answered. (p. 13)

This is an important point: questions asked, whether for designing or for solving a real-life issue that needs investigating, are at the foundation of finding and constructing meaning and knowledge.

If we summarize the construction of theorizing knowledge, this must begin with a positioning of the constructs that the inquirer uses to construct new knowledge. Knowledge spaces inform new knowledge construction and build knowledge within a discipline. Without understanding the foundations of how new knowledge is constructed, discussions about knowledge are not complete nor useful.

IN THIS CHAPTER

In this chapter we apply these ideas to an examiniation of interior design. We begin the chapter with Justin Wilwerding, who defines the philosophy of science for interior design as a new space of considering knowledge and examines how this might be constructed. The issue of interior design as an epistemological construct is explored, exposing the problems with its current nature.

In the Provocation Jo Ann Asher Thompson suggests that interior design is interdisciplinary by nature, and submits that knowledge spaces for interior design are transdisciplinary. She explores the disciplinary nature of interior design knowledge that includes several domains of expertise alongside the integration of both theoretical and pragmatic perspectives.

In the Dialogues and Perspectives, we engage two author perspectives, Justin Wilwerding and John Weigand, who each discuss how to go about building knowledge in one discipline concerned with the design of interior spaces: interior design. Wilwerding briefly proposes a philosophy of design, followed by Weigand, who engages us in a dialogue about how an identity for the discipline of interior design might be constructed. Weigand proposes how this idea of scale and identity are situated in a project example, and how other professions deal with relative disciplinary distinctions and convergences. Wilwerding suggests that interior design needs a philosophy to ground the discipline; otherwise, definitions remain vague and contribute to a lack of clarity of specificity.

REFERENCES

Crotty, M. (1998). *The Foundations of Social Research: Meaning and Perspective in the Research Process.* London: Sage Publications.

Friedman, K. (2003). Theory Construction in Design Research: Criteria, Approaches, and Methods. *Design Studies, 24*, 507–522.

Guba, E.G., & Lincoln, Y. S., Eds. (1994). Competing Paradigms in Qualitative Research. In *The Handbook of Qualitative Research.* London: Sage Publications.

Guerin, D. & Martin, C. (2005). *The Interior Design Profession's Body of Knowledge: Interior Design Educator's Council.* Retrieved from http://www.careersinteriordesign .com/idbok.pdf.

It is frustrating when interior designers must struggle with the common perception of interior design as simply icing on the proverbial cake, particularly when in this era of economic privation, most people feel they can't even afford the cake, much less the icing. Our most difficult disciplinary question then becomes, "Why is this simplistic view of the interior design profession so dominant?"

One common notion is that interior design is merely a business and as such, should be defined by those characteristics concerned with commerce. But medicine also has aspects that are related to business, yet it has defined itself as a profession concerned with the welfare of the public and has effectively communicated how it delivers these defining values. Promoting the welfare of the public is also a characteristic value of the definition that interior designers include in their vision of professional practice. Our frustration thus derives from our seeming inability to convince the public that the values that characterize the interior design profession are at best incomplete, and at worst inaccurately communicated to the public at large. Poldma (2008) proposes that we alter the definitions most commonly associated with interior design:

In its current epistemological form, interior design is considered primarily a visual act. This value assumption poses limitations on what designers can actually do when creating spaces. Interior designers must be prepared to question and uncover underlying philosophical values that affect the social activities that determine spatial relations. (p. ix)

In essence, we have allowed our profession to be defined by those aspects of interior design practice most easily marketed as decorative. The intimations of this definition are enormously problematic, since they limit the outcomes of interior design practice to those who can afford the highest level of cultural aesthetics, while also diminishing the goal of the profession to a "nice to have" outcome. We as a professional body have failed to develop a clear, concise, and thoughtful definition of the interior design profession that provides the public insight into the true value of the profession.

Our frustration is derived, therefore, from a failure of definitions. The recent efforts of the academy to find a pathway toward identifying the boundaries and values of our profession is a significant step forward in the effort to more accurately define the profession. (Martin & Guerin,

2005; Marshall-Baker, 2005; Poldma, 2008). However, a discipline driven primarily by the pragmatic exigencies of practice fails to address important questions implicit in the creation of artificial environments that are socially, politically, and culturally significant, questions only a philosophy of science for the interior design discipline can address.

This essay will discuss the development of a philosophy of science for interior design, whose purpose is to provide a structure to define the discipline by offering defining philosophical arguments of metaphysics, epistemology, axiology, logic, and ethics and by proposing an outline for a clearer paradigm for the future development of the discipline.

Defining the Importance of a Philosophy of Science for a Discipline: Interior Design

A philosophy of science for interior design begs the question regarding the characteristics of a philosophy of science per se, and the general usefulness of the endeavor to develop a philosophy of science. As a discipline, we seek to base our work on an evidentiary foundation; most academic disciplines would aver that such an evidentiary foundation must be developed based upon scientific principles. Yet before we can adequately address the development of a scientific/evidentiary foundation, we must define our terms—that is, what is *science* itself and how is it constituted? As Machamer (1998) noted in his paper "Philosophy of Science: An Overview for Educators":

[T]here remain inadequately answered questions about what science is, how to characterize the nature of its practitioners' activities, and what is the significance of the whole enterprise. . . . Philosophy of science is concerned with the methods that scientists use in discovery, and to elaborate and confirm theories. Also, the philosophy of science is concerned with the effects of science on the activities and interests of nonscientists and nonscientific institutions and practices that are part of society—past and present. . . . Philosophy of science, like philosophy in general, is a discipline that tries to expose the underlying presuppositions that structure important practices and institutions of life. It subjects the structures of life and thought to critical examination. In short, it makes us think about what we are doing and why. It scrutinizes the goals and purposes of human activities, then questions the methods and procedures by which those goals and purposes are attained. In doing so, it attempts to justify the goals and improve the procedures. (pp. 1–2)

Interior Design Scholarship and the Development of a Philosophy of Science

As we try and understand the foundations of a design science, we might examine the evolution of interior design toward a discipline. The study of interior design presently suffers from a serious gap in the development of a set of structures and principles through which we might organize the existing body of knowledge into an articulated and intelligible whole. The work of Martin and Guerin (2005) proposed a means to begin the process of establishing a borderland for the discipline; however, the development of a conceptual foundation for the discipline cannot be grounded in empirical research, as this is incapable of offering a holistic paradigm guiding interior design research and practice. The time is ripe for the Academy to reexamine interior design scholarship, critically and holistically evaluating its ontology from a philosophical perspective. If we are to flourish as a discipline, we must find a way to direct research, theory development, and ultimately design process toward an integrated vision, connecting large conceptual constructs (knowledge areas), like those identified by Martin and Guerin (2005), into a flexible framework that reveals ways in which one area of knowledge in the discipline relates to, influences, and is influenced by the others. This effort would provide the discipline the means to organize and structure the research agenda that it can advance our understanding of the salient issues related to interior design. It would also allow research to be more thoroughly integrated into design praxis within the community of practitioners, as well as afford a clearer perception of the location of interior design among our sibling design disciplines, and move us from what is too often a defensive posture to a proactive and generative position.

The notion proposed by Martin and Guerin (2005) of developing a body of knowledge structured around a research process is unfortunately untenable; this is simply a function of the fact that the construction of the kind of coordinated and flexible framework, which a body of knowledge must be, is largely a project concerned with carefully identifying and articulating the values upon which the discipline is based. The articulation of a set of defining values guiding the development of the discipline is a philosophical enterprise. Value is not a construct that can be developed through the application of empirical methods; empirical research describes what is, while ideas about value direct our aspirations toward what is better or best, and thus questions of value fall outside of the purview of empirical research. Yet the most basic questions supporting a body of knowledge are defined by a philosophy of science—values of truth and knowledge defined through the philosophical epistemology, values of the ontology of a discipline defined by a metaphysics of interior design, values of education clarified again through epistemology as well as logic, and values of praxis clarified through philosophical pursuits of logic and ethics. Broadly, the project of a philosophy of science—that is, providing a larger and more complete definition of value—is also the surest way to firmly ground the interior design body of knowledge and to clarify the value of the profession to the larger public.

Grounding Concepts of Values in Philosophy

These are not questions for science. Science can tell us what is but has no capacity to tell us what should be. This project is one that falls in the domain of philosophy and philosophy alone. The systematic nature of philosophical reasoning provides intellectual rigor to the products of this process, as well as offering a means to identify and model a structure of knowledge and inquiry for the discipline. This will allow scholars to more thoroughly understand the multiplicity of concerns and elements associated with research and praxis. Much as the natural and social sciences have established a rational and thoughtful philosophical structure that identified distinct but interrelated domains encompassing biology, physiology, chemistry (and its sub-domains), physics, and so on, for the natural sciences, and sociology, anthropology, psychology, cultural geography, and archeology in the social sciences, so too interior design must identify and interlace its multiplying subspecialties. A well-defined philosophy of science for interior design can provide this type of framework

The Importance of Philosophy of Science to the Development of the Interior Design Discipline

In some respects, it seems odd that we would only now be examining the question of a philosophy of science for interior design; the basis of most academic disciplines is the critical and self-correcting relationship between philosophy, theory, and research. Interior designers have been concerned with the latter two for several decades, but there has been precious little discussion of philosophy until the last several years. One can only suspect that this is a function of the fact that while academics may be trained in research methods and the development of theory that accompanies them, few if any are well trained in philosophical argumentation. Nevertheless, without some philosophical foundation, the development of a discipline cannot progress. A philosophy of science provides the basic tenets for approaches to research (interpretive and empirical orientations are philosophical positions) and based on these tenets theory emerges and is corrected. Without an explicit examination of the philosophical underpinnings of academic inquiry, however, there is a sense of "un-discipline" (Harfield, 2008; Cross, 2001), that is, a lack of common terms, structures, standards, and methods of inquiry by which the discipline coordinates the development of the body of knowledge. Sadly, this is a malady from which many design disciplines suffer. Un-discipline allows for ungrounded research and provides no standard by which research and the knowledge it produces might be evaluated and critiqued.

So what is the philosophical enterprise as regards interior design? It is perhaps easiest to begin answering this question by identifying the aspects of philosophy that are most useful and relevant in supporting the activities of the discipline. Traditionally there are a number of basic branches of philosophy, each having as an object of study some element of thought or reasoning structure that is relevant to the intelligibility of the discipline as a cohesive body. The traditional aspects relevant to a philosophy of science are metaphysics, epistemology, logic, axiology, and ethics. The following looks at each of these.

Metaphysics

Metaphysics is the hardest philosophical notion to simply define, but it is of critical importance, broadly asking the question "What are we doing when we do interior design (as opposed to, let's say, architecture)?" or "How do we identify and understand both the activities and results of interior designing?" In other words, what is it that uniquely defines the activities and questions endemic to the study and practice of interior design? A metaphysics of interior design would seek to identify the most elemental aspects of the study and practice of interior design, and the nature of design activity itself. To some it may seem elementary and unnecessary to ask these kinds of questions, but Galle (2006) in his paper "Worldviews for Design Theory" notes that we ignore questions of metaphysical clarity at our peril:

> When I call our metaphysical assumptions treacherous, it is because we cannot help making them, any more than we can help eating. But just as food may cause infectious diseases if contaminated so, I submit, our metaphysical assumptions may be incoherent without our knowing, and thus cause undetected inconsistency in our "body" of theory. (p. 2)

Thus, it seems likely that some of the problems related to the lack of clarity in a definition of Interior Design are related to either a poorly defined or uncritically examined metaphysical groundwork. Galle (2006) further explicates the problem of operating as a discipline without explicit metaphysical theory:

> [A] "worldview" should provide design theories with "low-level" means for understanding reality (conceptions of properties, agency, time, etc.), and enable us to express knowledge and understanding of various aspects of design in a principled manner, so as to ensure internal and mutual consistency of our theories. (pp. 3–4)

Galle also develops an analogy explicating the need for a philosophy of science in terms similar to the need for a computer to have an operating system platform. The platform of an operating system allows programs to seamlessly share data. Problems occur when a program is not available on the platform that you are using. Galle notes that this is similar to problems in research and theory when metaphysical assumptions of two researchers make connections between two studies difficult or impossible though they share subject matter, because the terminologies used are uncoordinated, and more importantly that competing metaphysical world views under which theories are being developed may be too diverse to allow any coordination of theories into a meaningful body of knowledge. Since questions of metaphysics affect the manner in which we conceive of the propositional structures under which we reason, how we define a metaphysical worldview for the study of interior design will affect research, theory construction, and ultimately design reasoning (logic) and thus practice.

Questions that might be endemic to the metaphysics of interior design relate to definitional notions with which the discipline grapples; for example, notions of the definition of space as an abstractly or socially defined concept. Specifically, how do human beings manage perceptions of space when they have no direct experience of physical artifacts (except through sensory filters) (van Inwagen, 2009)? These larger questions then devolve into more specific issues related to a metaphysics of interior design; if the constitution of space is the general issue, then interior design must address questions of the ways in which spaces constituted by interior designers are different (better than?) space constituted by, lay people, contractors, architects, and so on.

Epistemology

Epistemology deals with belief, knowledge, and truth. It seeks to establish standards for knowledge, or knowing, within a discipline, or why we should believe a particular assertion to be true (Steup, 2010). For interior design, epistemology addresses questions of the definitions and limitations of qualitative and empirical research methods. Thus, epistemology would question whether the basis of empirical methods as grounded

in observable facts can overcome the concern that humans have no direct contact with the factual information in question, but that all facts must be derived from our perceptual system and thus filtered and in some way interpreted by that system. Or it might address the question of intersubjectivity, related to interpretive/qualitative methods, and whether or not one human can accurately understand the meaning communicated by another, particularly if the observer has a significantly different frame of reference and life experience.

There are also two important subelements to epistemology for interior design: **hermeneutics**, the study of interpretation, and **heuristics**, the study of theoretical models that facilitate problem-solving strategies. Hermeneutics is a very old thread of academic inquiry. Originally developed as a structure for the interpretation of biblical documents, the structures and methods of hermeneutics were expanded in the nineteenth and early twentieth centuries by philosophers such as Schleiermacher, Heidegger, and Gadamer, (Bjørn Ramberg, Kristin Gjesdal, 2009) from merely being concerned with the interpretation of texts to the much broader questions of symbolic communication. The study of a hermeneutic structure for interior design would provide the discipline with a larger and more developed understanding of the grammar and syntax of communication conveyed by the built environment. A hermeneutics of interior design would address the question of interior environments as texts to be interpreted by users, investigate the manner in which meaning is constructed in these environments, and develop formal approaches to meaningful environments and to educating future designers in an understanding of how environments communicate.

Heuristics is the study of mental or abstract models that facilitate problem solving. The word heuristics derives from the expression of "*Heurika*" (later altered to Eureka) uttered by Archimedes upon discovering the principle of volumetric displacement in his bath, which provides some insight into the study of this set of phenomena. An examination of heuristic devices used by interior designers would aid in the refinement of design process as well as in design pedagogy.

Logic

Put simply, formal logic offers rational structures (proofs) of thought wherein it can be determined if one proposition provides sufficient reason to be related to another (inferences). Many of us took formal logic as undergraduate students ("If a then b," "If b then c," "If a then c"); the constructs of a logical system provide truth conditions that allow us to trace the relationships between argumentative propositions. In other words, logic allows us to think through problems.

Interior design has always described itself as a "problem solving discipline," and as such, it has begun to develop problem-solving structures (logics) that formalize conditions under which an argument for one approach to the resolution of a design problem is favored over another. Examining these sets of discursive rules from a

philosophical standpoint would offer three benefits. First, it would allow the discipline to better trace complex design arguments and discern their validity as rational assertions. Second, it could provide the discipline with a paradigm for the development of improved design strategies. Third, it would provide a more consistent teaching tool by providing students with insights into design thinking by formalizing the propositional structures much like formal logic, and help them to build strategic tools to approach design problems. Logic is related to epistemology in that it provides a formal structure assuring that the criteria for knowledge also derive truth through correct reasoning.

Based upon this model, we might develop a more formal understanding of the manner in which diagrammatic representations of environments allow designers to test the truth of particular design solutions, since diagrams could be considered a formal language. Drawing/diagramming has as its purpose, to leave out (distill) aspects of the information contained in a discussion of real space and focus attention on specific issues that form the propositions of the argument for a particular design solution. Just as mathematical models are used by scientists to represent and test notions about the behavior of the natural world, so too the interior designer's use of drawing has a formal structure used to test models of reality. Unfortunately, this type of formal language has not been examined enough as a critical structure within the discipline regarding how arguments are constructed (reasoned) and how their premises (in drawn form) are related to, and produce a valid and derivable conclusion.

Axiology

Axiology or value theory concerns three philosophical issues: moral philosophy, social and political philosophy, and aesthetics. In all three instances, interior design could benefit from the application of philosophical principles. The built environment can be construed as a moral issue in that it provides value. Thus, it is of serious concern who defines, controls, and benefits from that value. Interior design is clearly a social and political construct and involves issues of social relations and power (Markus, 1993). In this way, it is often a politically driven medium. Interior design is inexorably linked to aesthetics, its evocative power and capacity to deliver values of pleasure and comfort. Ultimately, the axiologically (or value theory) driven aspects of interior design are concerned with the "evaluative" nature of interior design. That is, from where/whom do the products of interior design derive their value/goodness, and how is that value determined (what is "good" and what is "better") and defined (reasons for that value to be esteemed). These are so called *deontic* aspects. **Deontic** refers to "what ought to be done," or "what are interior designers obligated to do in order to provide the greatest value users and clients"; aspects of interior design as a process; and the teleological aspects of interior design, that is, what choices should interior designers make in order to lead to specifically valuable outcomes?

Ethics

While it might seem that the most relevant area of philosophical ethics related to interior design would be business ethics, a brief examination of the impact that the products of both interior design scholarship and interior design practice have on individuals and society indicates a much broader scope for the application of the principles of ethical philosophy to the discipline. Philosophy of business ethics and the treatment of business ethics as an academic subject has, from both the practical and academic perspective, focused on both the policy issues of corporate governance, decision making, and the dynamics of employment; far too little work has been done examining the ethical obligations (deontic nature) of the manner in which the activities of business affect the broader community of stakeholders (Marcoux, 2008).

Over and above the concerns of policies regarding corporate governance and employment, interior design engages in a wide range of decisions that have moral and ethical significance. Interior design may empower or limit people and their choices; the application of interior design process is often fraught with ethical questions related to the distribution of value and social and political power and authority. The products of interior design can reinforce cultural norms or modify them. Interior design often impacts questions of justice, gender, power, value, property and ownership, privacy, and so on, all of these issues either directly or indirectly related to an ethical system, either by intent or, more sadly as is largely the case presently, by default.

Clearly the philosophical constructs of ethics are directly related to those of axiology; the equitable distribution of social and human values is a central concern for designers who seek to ensure the life, health, safety, and welfare of users. Ethical behavior entails "individual or collective practical reasoning about what, morally, one ought to do" (Richardson, 2009). Much of value theory and therefore much of ethics is based on a definition of a standard or a set of standards of value—most traditionally the notion of human happiness or good as embodied in the practice of "human excellence; human excellence includes the moral virtues (courage, moderation, and justice), which are implicitly or explicitly other-regarding" (Parry, 2009). It seems clear that much as medicine has developed an extensive body of scholarship to guide the ethical behavior of a discipline whose stated purpose is to attend to the health and well-being of individuals, interior design is a discipline that purports to also attend to the health, safety, and welfare of individuals as regards the built environment. It also needs to develop a significant body of scholarship that can guide inquiry and decision making to ensure that appropriate values are equitably delivered to the users of the environments we design. In an article in *Medical Technologies*, "Medical Facilities as Moral Worlds, " Turner (2002) links the two disciplines in an illustrative manner as regards ethical decision making, wherein the author discusses his role as a medical ethicist in a long term care facility, noting that:

Focusing upon the ethos of place draws attention to the way in which architectural design features of buildings, the interior design of hallways, common areas, bedrooms, and recreation areas, places for plants, pet programmes, arts and crafts programmes, music, and art contribute to the everyday moral life of a particular place . . . , creating a moral place can be recognized as a matter of fostering specific practices and affording the opportunity for particular human experiences in specific habitats. (p. 19)

In this context there is clearly a need for the development and application of principles of philosophical ethics to interior design. Professional standards are only a beginning; the character of the decisions made by interior designers has the potential to either promote or devalue human welfare, it can be a force for equity and justice or it can promote the hegemony of the moneyed and powerful, it can promote human connection and communication or it can hobble it. For professionals in such positions of power and importance, interior designers can ill-afford to make decisions casually; the profession will not be taken seriously without the thoughtful training of professionals in the processes of ethical thought and decision making.

Philosophy of Science and a Holistic Definition of Interior Design

The components of a philosophy of science form a coordinated whole that is the superstructure of a discipline. Metaphysics identifies elements of significance to the discipline *in toto* and frames inquiry in the context of world views, which are then clarified by the development of an epistemological framework affording a manner in which beliefs about these concerns can be understood and to which standards of truth can be associated. Logic provides an approach to investigate truth claims established under epistemology as well as a means for grounding deontological decisions (decisions about what "ought to be done" under particular design conditions, and directing the ethical behavior of the discipline). Axiology defines the values that the discipline provides to the culture at large and also offers the basis of ethical decision making regarding how the profession and academy distribute those goods to individuals, and so on. This articulated structure is key to providing a focused and detailed definition of the discipline and profession. It is evident that the elements delineated above form an integrated whole in which we can begin to see how one area of the discipline influences another.

This integrated structure is critical to the continued development of interior design as a discipline and a profession. It affords an *articulated,* that is, interrelated and flexible, system that allows us to evaluate the rigor of existing knowledge, assemble various elements of knowledge in a holistic manner, and trace the influences of one area of our understanding upon others, and it provides the standards and definitions that indicate how new elements of knowledge may be woven into the greater body of knowledge. In truth, the philosophy of science is the disciplinary foundation that compiles, evaluates, and coordinates elements of knowledge, allowing a cumulative acquisition of knowledge that enlarges and enhances our understanding of what interior design and interior designing are, and provides a basis for enhancing the efficiency and efficacy of practice.

Discussion Questions

1. What is the value of understanding a philosophical approach for interior designed space?

2. How does philosophical thinking in understanding how spaces are framed by how designers think?
   a. Discuss the concepts Wilwerding proposes for a philosophy of science for interior design.
   b. What is fundamental to framing a philosophy for space-based thinking?

3. What are metaphysics, epistemology, axiology, and ethics?
   a. Unpack each concept and define its main characteristics.
   b. How might we apply each to designed spaces?
   c. What is the role of ethics here?

4. What are knowledge areas of interior design as defined by Guerin & Martin?

5. How do we understand space in terms of these concepts and what is design thinking in light of these ideas?

References

Abercrombie, S. (1991). *A Philosophy of Interior Design.* Boulder, CO: Westview Press.

Archer, B. (1979). Design as a Discipline. *Design Studies, 1* (1), 17–20.

Ramberg, B., & Gjesdal, K. (2009, June 21). *Hermeneutics.* Retrieved August 2010 from *The Stanford Encyclopedia of Philosophy,* http://plato.stanford.edu/entries/hermeneutics/.

Clemons, S. A., & Eckman, M. (2004). Toward a Common Language: Proposed Index. *Journal of Interior Design, 30*(1), 13–30.

Cross, N. (1982). Designerly Ways of Knowing. *Design Studies, 3*(4), 221–227.

Cross, N. (2001). Designerly Ways of Knowing: Design Discipline versus Design Science. *Design Issues, 17* (3), pp. 49–55.

Friedman, K. (2000). Creating Design Knowledge: From Research into Practice. *International Conference on Design and Technology Educational Research,* (pp. 5–32). Loughborough, UK: Loughborough University of Technology.

Friedman, K. (2003). Theory Construction in Design. *Design Studies,* 16.

Galle, P. (2006). Worldviews for Design Theory. *Design Research Society International Conference* (pp. 1–12). Lisbon: The Design Research Society.

Harfield, S. (2008, July 16–19). *On the Roots of Undiscipline.* Proceedings of DRS2008, Design Research Society Biennial Conference, Sheffield, UK.

Harfield, Steven, and Burgess, Peter. (2008, July 16–19). *Controlling the Discipline.* Proceedings of DRS2008, Design Research Society Biennial Conference, Sheffield, UK, 2008.

Horst W. J. Rittel, & Melvin M. Webber. (1969). Dilemmas in a General Theory of Planning. *American Association for the Advancement of Science* (pp. 155–169). Boston.

Love, T. (2000). A Meta-theoretical Basis for Design Theory. *International Conference of the Design Research Society.* La Clusaz: The Design Research Society.

Love, T. (2000). Philosophy of Design: A Metatheoretical Structure for Design Theory. *Design Studies, 21* (3), 293–313.

Lonergan, B. (1972). *Method in Theology.* New York: Herder and Herder.

Machamer, P. (1998). Philosophy of Science: An Overview for Educators. *Science & Education,* 1–11.

Marcoux, A. (2008, September 21). *Business Ethics.* E. N. Zalta, Ed. Retrieved 2010 from *The Stanford Encyclopedia of Philosophy,* http://plato.stanford.edu/archives/fall2008/entries/ethics-business/.

Markus, T. A. (1993). *Buildings and Power.* (p. 343). London: Routledge.

Marshall-Baker, A. (2005). Knowledge in Interior Design. *Journal of Interior Design, 1* (1), xiii–xxi.

Martin, C. S., & Guerin, D. A. (2005). The Interior Design Profession's Body of

Knowledge. St. Paul, MN: University of Minnesota–College of Design.

Pable, J. (2009). Interior Design Identity in the Crossfire: A Call for Renewed Balance in Subjective and Objctive Ways of Knowing. *Journal of Interior Design*, v–xx.

Parry, R. (2009, September 21). *Ancient Ethical Theory* (E. N. Zalta, Ed.). Retrieved 2010 from *The Stanford Encyclopedia of Philosophy*, http://plato.stanford.edu/archives/fall2009/entries/ethics-ancient/.

Poldma, T. (2008). Interior Design at a Crossroads. *Journal of Interior Design*, 11. "Primary/secondary quality distinction." (n.d.). Retrieved July 25, 2010, from Wikipedia: http://en.wikipedia.org/wiki/Primary_qualities.

Schroeder, M. (2008, September 21). *Value Theory*. (E. N.Zalta, Ed.). Retrieved 2010 from *The Stanford Encyclopedia of Philosophy*, http://plato.stanford.edu/archives/fall2008/entries/valuetheory/.

Sinnott-Armstrong, W. (2008, September 21). *Consequentialism*. (E. N. Zalta, Ed.). Retrieved 2010 from *The Stanford Encyclopedia of Philosophy* http://plato.stanford.edu/archives/fall2008/entries/consequentialism/.

Shapiro, S. (2009, September 21). *Classical Logic*. (E. N. Zalta, Ed.). Retrieved 2010 from *The Stanford Encyclopedia of Philosophy*, http://plato.stanford.edu/archives/win2009/entries/logic-classical/.

Steup, M. (2010, March 21). *Epistemology*. Retrieved 2010 from *The Stanford Encyclopedia of Philosophy*, http://plato.stanford.edu/archives/spr2010/entries/.

Richardson, H. S. (2009, September 21). *Moral Reasoning*. (E. N. Zalta, Ed.). Retrieved 2010 from *The Stanford Encyclopedia of Philosophy*, http://plato.stanford.edu/archives/fall2009/entries/reasoning-moral.

Rosenberg, A. (2008). *A Philosophy of Social Science*. Philadelphia: Westview Press.

Turner, D. L. (2002). Medical Facilities as Moral Worlds. *Medical Technologies 28*, 19–22, doi:10.1136/mh.28.1.19.

van Inwagen, P. (2009). *Metaphysics*. (E. Zalta, Ed.) Retrieved 2010 from *The Stanford Encyclopedia of Philosophy*, http://plato.stanford.edu/archives/win2009/entries/metaphysics/.

Yeung, H. W.-c. (1997). Critical Realism and Realist Researching Human Geography: A Method or a Philosophy in Search of a Method? *Progress in Human Geography, 21* (1), 51–74.

Zalta, E. N. (Ed.). (2009). *The Stanford Encyclopedia of Philosophy*. Stanford, CA: Stanford University, Center for the Study of Language and Information, The Metaphysics Research Lab. Retrieved May/June 2010 from http://plato.stanford.edu/archives/win2009/entries/metaphysics/.

What is interior design? Ask this question to the general public and it soon becomes evident that confusion runs rampant. At one extreme are those who think of interior design as a hobby—essentially a simple activity that anyone with a bit of artistic flair can do well. At the other end of the spectrum are those who argue that interior design is a profession backed by a solid underpinning of critical thinking, theory, and research—a profession that requires several years of higher education to qualify. Given this state of confusion, what does the future bode for interior design as both a discipline and as a profession? What can we do to lessen the confusion and ensure a positive future for the discipline and profession of interior design? How can we position interior design as relevant for future consumers? Can design research serve as a catalyst for change and innovation?

Addressing such questions as these is critical to the future direction of the discipline and profession of interior design. In this article, I will argue that in order to predict answers to these questions, it must first be acknowledged that the discipline of interior design is, by its very nature, interdisciplinary. As a discipline, interior design draws from various other disciplines that focus on the human condition (e.g., social sciences, psychology, etc.). At the same time, it integrates tacit knowledge of production that changes ideas into intuitive thinking, visual representation, and conversations that can then be changed into viable, thoughtful, and service-based intentions (Nelson & Stolterman, 2003).

Friedman proposes an extension of this argument by suggesting that design (as a field) involves more skill, knowledge, and awareness than one designer can provide and that most successful design solutions require several kinds of expertise (Friedman, 2000). In other words, the conclusion can be made that interior design, in its essence, is an interdisciplinary discipline and profession that draws from various domains of knowledge and then applies this information into a creative design process.

Herein lies the problem. The notion that interior design is an interdisciplinary discipline (i.e., requiring the application of various domains of knowledge) flies in the face of most academic institutions, which promote the idea of disciplinary (rather than interdisciplinary) endeavor as supreme. According to the literature, within academic institutions:

A discipline is literally what the term implies. When one studies a discipline, one subjugates the ways one learns about phenomena to a set of rules, rituals, and routines established by the field of study. A student learns to study according to these rules, classifying phenomena according to commonly adopted terms, definitions, and concepts of the major field. Relationships among phenomena are revealed through the frames provided by the discipline, and the researcher or student arrives at conclusions based on criteria for truth or validity derived from the major field (Radcliff, 2008).

The idea of subjugating how one approaches a design problem to only one set of rules as dictated by one field of study is alien to the way designers think and work—limiting the creative process necessary to achieve interior spaces that successfully address the human condition. As a result, many university administrators are perplexed by interior design and unsure about how it fits into a traditional academic hierarchy—oftentimes resulting in interior design being assigned to units that have little relationship to the discipline itself (e.g., agriculture, home economics, human ecology, etc.). By the same token, interior design research that is undertaken at institutions of higher education is often perceived as second-class to that of other disciplines, which better fit the traditional disciplinary mold. Given the identity crisis that interior design faces within most institutions of higher education, it is no wonder that as a profession, interior design continues to face many of the same issues of credibility and acceptance.

How can we change this picture? Although I don't believe there is a simple remedy that will solve all these problems in one fell swoop, I do believe progress is being made toward a positive future for interior design in both the academic and professional communities at large. I suggest that an interior designer's task for any given project is to integrate theoretical and philosophically reflective practices with pragmatic everyday design problems situated within a specific project. This being the case, it can be argued that design and the creation of knowledge are both intensely human acts—the meaning of which is dependent upon the utility and cultural location or "situatedness" of the environment as proposed by Laurel (Laurel, 2003). As such, interior design is dependent upon the situatedness of the people within the environment. Once the situatedness of the environment is understood, interior designers can create spaces that mediate human responses using functional and visual design processes. When this truth is universally accepted, then many of the issues that have been outlined in this article will become moot. Although overcoming these issues may seem daunting, as pointed out by Nissani, "Being truly interdisciplinary is rarely easy, as it is all about boundaries and being in-between established categories" (Laurel, 2003).

I'm encouraged by the trend to create new shared, interdisciplinary homes for various disciplines (Simpson et al., 2008), by the increase in funding opportunities for interdisciplinary teams, and by efforts to restructure university reward systems to encourage interdisciplinary scholarship. I am further encouraged by the continuing effort of interior design scholars and practitioners to build interior design's body of knowledge as distinct and separate from other disciplines and professions. This, in combination with an intensified effort to perform meaningful research, will underpin the discipline and serve as a catalyst for the discovery of new knowledge. By recognizing the interdisciplinary nature of interior design, we can capitalize upon the networks established between interior design scholars and practitioners, and individuals from other disciplines and professions—all of whom can speak to the importance of interior design practice and research in today's world. Efforts such as these will help solidify and define interior design as a discipline and profession, and lessen the confusion currently surrounding it.

Discussion Questions

1. What is the difference between interior design as a discipline and interior design as a profession? Why is this distinction important?

2. If interior design's body of knowledge is separate and distinct from other disciplines, how can it be argued that it is interdisciplinary?

3. What role can/does research play in the future of interior design?

References

Friedman, K. (2000) *Creating Design Knowledge: From Research into Practice*, Loughborough, UK: IDATER.

Laurel, B. (2003). *Design Research: Methods and Perspectives*, Cambridge, MA: MIT Press.

Nelson, H., & Stolterman, E. (2003). *The Design Way: Intentional Change in an Unpredictable World*. Englewood Cliffs, NJ: Educational Technology Publications.

Radcliff, James A. *The Academic Major: The Rise of the Disciplines and Majors, Structure, Interdisciplinary Majors, Academic Majors Students, and Disciplinary Knowledge*. Retrieved January 23, 2009, from http://education .stateuniversity.com/pages/1726/ Academic-Major.html.

In this article we will engage in two specific points of view about developing interior design knowledge: Justin Wilwerding (Perspective I) and John Weigand (Perspective II). Each perspective offers counterpoints to ideas already discussed and how we might go about the construction of the domains of knowledge needed to fulfill what has already been done in the field.

Perspective I
Case Study: Developing Interior Design Knowledge
Justin Wilwerding

As we have seen in my essay in Chapter 1, "Meanings of Design and Space: A Metaphysical Groundwork," and from the line of inquiry developed by various design scholars examined in the essay over the past 30 years, we can begin to identify the primary issues that presently hamper the further development of understanding interior space. For example, in trying to define the discipline of interior design, the discipline would be considered as having the following:

- A lack of clarity regarding the metaphysical nature or the worldview(s) within which the discipline operates
- Inexplicit or tacit epistemological assumptions under which methods of

inquiry are constructed, research is conducted, and a body of knowledge can be constructed.
- The lack of an organizing structure within which the interrelationships of theoretical concepts can be seen, and into which new research and knowledge can be integrated.

The Example of a Profession in Evolution: Interior Design

Many of the notions suggested here are obviously preliminary and speculative and thus they only begin to sketch out issues of significance to the development of a design philosophy. If applied to the example of designed interior space and the emerging interior design discipline, one notion is less preliminary than the others—that is, without the development of a philosophy of science for the interior design discipline, there is little hope of constructing a pathway that will allow academics and practitioners alike to envision an intelligent and intelligible course leading to a clearer definition of the value of interior design. To date, interior design has relied upon the philosophical underpinnings developed by related disciplines to shape our approach to research, theory development, and knowledge. This approach has allowed us to move forward quickly and develop a significant body of interior design research, but because the assumptions (and as Galle puts it, "worldview") that undergird the research methods, epistemological structures, and other aspects of this research are largely borrowed from others, the approach lacks a cohesive and coordinated framework through which we may identify those concerns and interests uniquely significant and valuable to interior design.

The preliminary nature of this work is intended to initiate a dialogue critical to the future of interior design. Tiiu Poldma (2008) stated the problem in a very clear fashion:

> I submit that interior design is a profession moving toward becoming a discipline that has stalled in the manner in which knowledge and its acquisition are understood and translated into perceptions in society. In interior design, unfortunately, part of the problem is that quite often the realms of education, academic research, and practice are worlds apart (Thompson, 1992; Vaikla-Poldma, 2003). Education strives to create new professionals capable of entering the workforce as practicing interior designers, while in academic research we aim to form new educators who study the methods and processes of interior design empirically. (Poldma, 2008)

Without a robust philosophy of science we have little hope of clarifying, "the manner in which knowledge and its acquisition

are understood and translated into perceptions in society" (Poldma, 2008, p. vii), and without this foundational orientation, we have little hope of unifying the worlds of academia and practice. And without a unified approach to the definition of interior design, we have little prospect of conveying the value of interior design to the larger culture.

Perspective II
Rethinking Professional Identity in Interior Design
John Weigand

During the past couple of decades, the interior design profession has made it a priority to define and articulate a knowledge base. This effort makes sense. Any profession—in order to establish its legal and jurisdictional boundaries—must be able to clearly communicate what it does and what it knows, and (more importantly) how that knowledge base is distinct from other professional groups. Any group claiming professional legitimacy must be able to define what it does uniquely in addition to what it does specifically. As interior design licensing efforts and resultant legal challenges have both intensified, the need to clearly define these jurisdictional boundaries has become critical.

So what is it that interior designers do? On the surface, the answer might seem obvious. Interior designers design. And yet, design is not a proprietary skill. Architects also design. As do product and graphic designers, and landscape and fashion designers. When the thing being designed is less tangible, the list grows to include such groups as organizational designers, systems designers, environmental designers, and experience designers. The digital revolution has contributed software designers and web designers. And the list goes on. The link is design; each of these disciplines—or professional groups—designs something. The differentiator is the thing being designed. So in order to better define the proprietary contribution of the interior designer, the definition needs to become more specific.

The *Body of Knowledge* project (Martin & Guerin, 2005), released to the public in 2005, attempted to do just that. The idea was logical—to assess distinct knowledge through a careful examination of academic accreditation standards, testing standards, and licensing requirements. Endorsed by all constituent interior design professional groups, the *Body of Knowledge* document clearly articulated the array of skill sets required to competently engage in interior design practice. The process for determining these skill sets was systematic—comparing and contrasting knowledge standards across the stages of a professional career.

The *Body of Knowledge* project was not uniformly embraced, however. Many in the academic community, especially, challenged the idea of defining interior design as a detailed list of knowledge areas or skill sets. The argument was that design, by definition, is more than the sum of its component parts. It is complex and gestalt, and also process-based, and so cannot easily be deconstructed into any sort of list. Further, by defining proprietary knowledge in terms of its component parts, the *Body of*

Knowledge document implies that interior designers own this knowledge, when in fact various professionals educated outside the discipline can and do contribute higher levels of expertise within any specific knowledge area. For example, interior designers turn to lighting consultants, material specialists, psychologists, acoustical engineers, and others on a regular basis for the specialized knowledge needed to complete a project. Clearly, the interior design knowledge base is broad, but it is not very pure in the sense that it intersects frequently with other disciplines.

Rethinking the Knowledge Base

A more holistic definition of the knowledge base, one that is centered on the act of design but informed by a unique understanding of the factors impacting design at the interior scale (the interior design skill sets), likely comes closer to capturing what interior designers really know and do. In order to achieve successful design solutions, designers must have a breadth of knowledge across the range of skill sets, and these skill sets must be brought to bear on the design process and also anchored in a holistic understanding of design theory. This argument is supported in the academic setting, where the design studio is placed at the core of student activity, and where students are required to synthesize content knowledge learned across a range of support courses into coherent interior design solutions. Take away the studio component, and the various support areas fail to stand on their own.

Design is not just another skill. It is fundamentally different, and (even as designers) we too often underestimate its complexity. Again, by definition, design is a process, one that begins with a careful consideration of a problem to be solved and a willingness to challenge or redefine this problem. It requires some amount of research, so that possible solutions to the problem are well informed and grounded in what we already know. It requires an understanding of precedent, or how similar problems have already been solved. It is grounded in a theoretical understanding of the discipline (its principles and methods). And it requires of the designer a willingness to take creative leaps and to pursue divergent solutions. Designers must continually critique their work, redirect their thinking, try new ideas, and be willing to fail often. Thus the process is not linear. As possible solutions emerge, they must be refined or eliminated until only one best solution remains. And even then the process continues, through ongoing critique or more formal assessment of a built project.

Design is also highly synthetic and gestalt. Integrative thinking is required because design solutions must succeed on many levels and across multiple disciplines. Consider the act of drawing a single line on paper to indicate a wall on a floor plan. In the interior designer's mind, this wall has thickness and height, material qualities, and structural properties. If the line is curved, the implications for how the wall is built will change. For the user who will touch the wall, or see it, or walk along it, it will have tactile qualities and aesthetic qualities and emotive qualities. It will relate to its architectural context and draw from historical precedent. It will mediate sound and light. The wall will meet—or fail to meet—egress and fire code requirements, as well as requirements for sustainable construction. Hopefully, it will be perceived as beautiful or possibly innovative. In the second it takes to make the mark on paper, the trained designer is able to understand the mark for all that it implies and in all its complexity. This is design.

Learning to design is not dissimilar from learning to ride a bike. In the academic setting, design is anchored in the studio, where students are confronted with, and asked to solve, a wide variety of design problems. Design skill is not mastered, however, upon completion of any given academic studio. The student must learn from mistakes, get back on the bike, and revisit the process all over again. Only after completing a lengthy studio sequence, typically spanning several years and characterized by problems that increase in complexity and vary in type, does the student begin to have some mastery over the process. This learning continues, and very likely becomes more specialized, throughout the subsequent professional career.

Arguably, then, an accurate definition of interior design knowledge is anchored in a facility with the design process along with a comprehensive understanding of factors specifically relevant to the interior scale. This definition does a good job of characterizing what interior designers do and know. And yet, it still fails to adequately distinguish interior design from architects and other professionals who lay claim to the same work. Architects design at the interior scale, so do kitchen and bath designers, and others. If the real motivation in defining the knowledge base is to construct clear and defensible boundary lines for interior design practice, then we are left at an impasse.

Constructing an Identity Based on Scale

The reason that clear boundaries cannot be established between these allied professional groups is that their distinction is not based as much on content knowledge as it is on the scale of the work. Professional boundaries are not defined by what one knows as much as by the scale at which one applies this knowledge. It's commonly accepted that the architect's domain includes the design of the building. Since the interior is a significant component of any building and can't be separated from its architecture, it's logical that architects lay some professional claim to the design of the interior environment. Good architecture is grounded in a sound understanding of the interior, just as good interior design is (or should be) grounded in a sound understanding of its architectural context. Yet as interior environments have become more complex and specialized, this work has—to a greater or lesser extent—been removed from the scope of the architect. A building and its interior are integrally connected but also distinct, based on the scale of work. Imagine here a Venn diagram, with intersecting circles.

This contention is supported in the academic context, where students of architecture and students of interior design are similarly grounded in the arts and humanities, in compositional theory, design history, the behavioral sciences, graphic communication, building technology, and other foundational studies. As this knowledge is applied to more complex problems, and as the scale of work diverges, the academic studies similarly diverge. Here again, the knowledge base is both shared and distinct.

Consider the example of a small restaurant project. The client may first secure the services of an architect to design a building. The architect very likely will require the specialized expertise of an interior designer, whether this individual is employed directly by the architect or retained as a consultant. Both professionals presumably demonstrate expertise in hospitality projects or specific experience with restaurants. Other specialists may be required, including a kitchen designer or a lighting designer. Of course, a variety of engineering consultants will join the team as technical designers, and (if energy performance is a priority) a LEED-accredited designer may be needed. Finally, a team of behind-the-scenes individuals will contribute to the project as designers of furniture, millwork, light fixtures, textiles, and a variety of products incorporated into the final design solution. The project is ultimately accomplished by a team of designers. Each works at a different scale and each contributes a different expertise.

In this example, the architect may choose to exclude the interior designer (or others on the team), claiming that he or she has the knowledge and experience to accomplish this aspect of the project. In some cases, this may be true; in other cases not, if a more specialized knowledge of interior-scale environments is required. By extension, this argument is made in the legal arena, where lobbyists argue against interior design licensure, claiming that architects—as evidenced by education, examination, and experience—demonstrate the ability to design the interior environment. Interior designers push back, of course, and the battle for professional turf continues.

Interestingly, the same scenario plays out with the kitchen designer. This (sub-) specialist contributes focused expertise related to the design of the kitchen, and as such intersects the domain of the interior designer. Interior designers claim that this work falls under their jurisdiction; thus, the kitchen designer must first jump through the educational and professional hoops of the interior designer before developing any specialization at the level of the kitchen. This, of course, is the same argument made by the architect. Only the scale has changed. Again, imagine a complex web of intersecting (and nested) circles within a Venn diagram—each representing a unique contribution to the design of the built environment and vary-

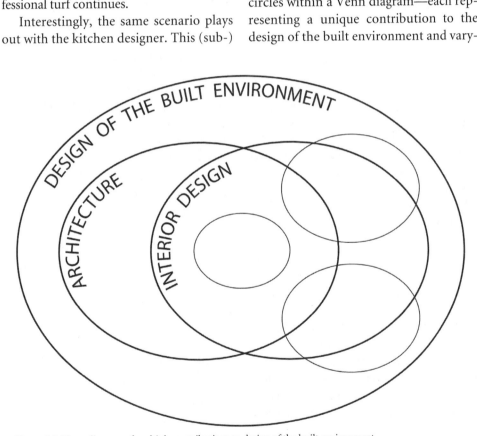

Figure 3.1 Venn diagram of multiple contributions to design of the built environment.

ing based on the scale of work and the level of specialization.

The challenge in defining professional distinction, then, requires that the professional domain be enlarged to include multiple contributions to the design of the built environment. This can be represented by a single, larger circle that surrounds all other circles within the Venn diagram, defined as the "design of the built environment." We might call this larger domain architecture, for clarity, or not. But such a holistic profession is inclusive of all sub-professions that are more or less specialized or that focus at a specific scale of work.

Other Professional Models

This model exists elsewhere, notably in the medical and legal professions. In medicine, the heart surgeon performs a very different kind of work than does the orthopedic surgeon or the pediatric specialist. And yet all are doctors. Each is grounded in core knowledge—defined by education (medical school), testing, and experience—and by the fundamental tenet of providing medical care. Within that broader framework, each pursues distinct knowledge and makes a unique contribution. More specialized testing ensures competency within the advanced specialty area. Where the knowledge base of the heart surgeon and the orthopedic surgeon might intersect, they do not need to compete for professional legitimacy.

It's also worth noting that not all medical professionals achieve the same minimal level of education, testing, and experience. Nurses, technicians, and a host of contributing sub-

specialists establish different (and somewhat less rigorous) benchmarks for professional competency. Yet all make important contributions to the broader medical profession. Similarly, the law profession casts a wide net over the various areas of legal practice and also recognizes the need to establish less rigorous benchmarks for other contributors, for example, paralegals or clerks.

The medical and legal professions can serve as models for a more holistically defined profession centered on the design of the built environment. Clearly, as the design profession has increased in complexity and as multiple subspecialties characterized by distinct knowledge, contribution, or scale of focus have appeared, it has become critical to expand the professional domain. For interior design, this should not be threatening. The need will continue and likely intensify for legal certification of interior designers, for rigorous academic accreditation of professional programs, and for the testing of professional competency. Similarly, the need for interior design professional organizations should only intensify as interior scale work becomes more complex. Finally, just as in medicine or law, if the competencies required for some types of design practice are deemed to be less rigorous, benchmarks for education, examination, and licensure can be established differently.

A Collective Solution

The challenge, then, is to redefine a broader and more inclusive profession that unifies the various contributors rather than pitting them against one another. This won't happen by continuing to focus on the knowledge base for interior design, especially if the subtext is to construct this knowledge base as unique and detached from that of other allied design professionals. And it can't happen if interior design practice is understood as a prize to be claimed by one professional group or the other. A more collective and unified profession can only be realized by increasing dialogue between all groups (specifically architects and interior designers) that contribute to the design of the built environment. This dialogue needs to underscore both the inherent shared knowledge across the range of design scales and the distinct contribution of knowledge required at the scale of the interior. The interior design profession is at a point in its young history where it can now engage and promote this dialogue from a position of strength. Failure to do so will only postpone real progress. On the other hand, the potential for such a unified and multilayered profession to not only improve its own status in the world but to also have a profound impact on the world is exciting!

Discussion Questions

1. What are Weigand and Wilwerding saying about
   a. Disciplinary perspectives on the built environment?

2. How might interior design build specificity and pluralism?

3. What is identity and how might a philosophy of interior design be constructed? How is this congruent with meanings of design/spaces?

Discussion Questions: Part I—Wilwerding

1. What is Wilwerding defining when he means a design philosophy?

2. What is Wilwerding proposing about a philosophy for interior design?

3. How might we begin to construct philosophy?

Discussion Questions: Part II—Weigand

1. How do we identity what constitutes designed interior space?
   a. What is an identity based on scale?
   b. What is the dialogue that needs to happen with allied design professionals, according to Weigand?

2. What core knowledge is specific to one discipline or another?

3. What challenges is Weigand issuing to the professions?

References

Martin, C. S., & Guerin, D. A. (2005). *The Interior Design Profession's Body of Knowledge. Interior Design Educator's Council.* Retrieved from http://www.careersininteriordesign.com/idbok.pdf.

Poldma, T. (2008). Interior Design at a Crossroads. *Journal of Interior Design, 11.*

Weigand, J. (2006, Winter). Defining Ourselves. *Perspective.* IIDA.

SUMMARY

In this chapter introduction we have explored spaces of knowledge as these exist, and what is understood by a particular disciplinary approach to space, that of the discipline of interior design. Various perspectives offer ways to identify and issues regarding stances, definitions, and positions in how knowledge is constructed.

Knowledge is constructed in research and to evolve disciplines and perspectives grounded in the reality of things in everyday life situations. The example of interior spaces is used explicitly to provide a perspective about the profession of interior design; and how this young profession is struggling with its identity and as current trans-disciplinary realities compel the development of a clear identity. Wilwerding, Thompson, and Weigand each propose alternative ways to construct meaning in knowledge-building. Philosophy, interdisciplinary stances, and identities all are suggested as ways to help give interior design its disciplinary character.

SUGGESTED READINGS

Piotrowski, A., & Williams Robinson, J. (2001). *The Discipline of Architecture.* Minneapolis, MN: The University of Minnesota Press.

Grosz. E. (2001). *Architecture from the Outside: Essays on Virtual and Real Space.* Cambridge, MA: MIT Press.

Rice, C. (2009). *The Emergence of the Interior: Architecture, Modernity, and Domesticity.* London/New York: Routledge.

Weigand, J. (2006, Winter). Defining Ourselves. *Perspective.* IIDA.

OVERVIEW QUESTIONS FOR DISCUSSION

Review in more detail knowledge construction in research at the level of master's and doctoral work in your particular field, and examine issues related to knowledge in your particular domain. Discuss with peers the following issues:

1. How is knowledge constructed in research?

2. What is "professional research" versus "academic research" in the social sciences? In the built environment disciplines? How do these differ? Are similar?

3. Why is the construction of knowledge important for a discipline? How is this bounded by values of particular people and why is this important to know?

4. Examine the two positions of Wilwerding and Weigand in more detail.

5. What is an identity for interior design?

6. How do concepts of spaces include other domains and why is this of value?

7. How does interior design intersect with other disciplines of the built environment? In the natural sciences? In the social and human sciences? Why does this add complexity to the construction of interior design as a discipline with specificity?

8. How is interior design interdisciplinary in nature? What makes the design of spaces uniquely specific to interior design? Examine Thompson's ideas about the knowledges that contribute to interior design knowledge

PART II
Seminal and Alternative Viewpoints about Design and Spaces

CHAPTER 4
Space as History, Ornament, and Story

material culture, immaterial contexts, interior as artefact/atmosphere, container, artefacts, space as inter-story, space as social signifier, space as social equalizer, gender, power, meanings of objects/things, historic lens, social construction, existing meaning, atmosphere, ornament, ornament as presence, absence of ornament

AFTER READING THIS CHAPTER, YOU WILL BE ABLE TO:

- Understand the ways that history adds context to the meanings we attribute to spaces and things.

- Discuss how social and cultural contexts are built into historic aspects of space.

- Illustrate how the context of material culture, artefacts, and forms as physical elements affect how space is conceived.

- Examine how cultural meanings come to bear on historical perspectives of space.

- Assess how history and interiors might be reconsidered as intertwined and not opposing constructs.

- Distinguish issues that are interlaced with historic context in terms of gender, social standing, and political or social structures in society

INTRODUCTION

In Part I we have examined theory and knowledge construction and now we turn towards the various spaces that emerge in Part II. Later in the book we will expand the notions of disciplinary spaces as these relate to research and theory building of diverse types of spaces.

In the design of interior spaces, there has always been a struggle to reconcile **material culture** with immaterial aspects of space. This struggle first is engaged in the historic aspects of:

- Space as a "container"
- Space as a place of decoration
- Space as absence of decoration

And yet how we frame what we know and understand in design thinking and about spaces depends on historic contexts and on notions of what constitute artefacts, material culture, and space as a place of artefacts and things.

In this chapter the meanings and contexts of spaces are explored using the historic lens that frames the evolution of space through specific examples, with implications on contemporary considerations of space, artefacts, objects, and material culture both from material and immaterial perspectives. When we attribute contexts to spaces and situate meanings of design from historic perspectives, we take into account the ways that what has been done in the past can offer perspective to future ideas and possibilities for understanding the here and now, as well as into the future. We also consider our position as designers of spaces from the perspective of what came before and what affects how we actually see and understand spaces as we perceive them today.

Perspectives explored in this chapter include the idea of ornament and culture in the design of interior spaces (Turpin) and reframing space notions using both interiors and historic context simultaneously (Attiwill). These theoretically ground the considerations of the divergent ways that historic perspectives are understood in spatial contexts. First, John Turpin explores an understanding of space framed within ideas about ornament. Turpin examines ornament as a cultural and historic entity over time and how ornament frames our perceptions of design. Turpin bases his essay on Wharton and Codman's *Decoration of Houses* (1897) and Adolf Loos's *Ornament and Crime* (1908) to articulate the polar approaches to both ornament and space that defined the twentieth century.

Turpin examines the concepts of ornament as historically grounded in technology and structure, while masking concepts of power and social position. He then moves into how, from the Victorian era and into the Modernist movement of the earlier part of the century, ideas about ornament shift and thus also the ways that space is understood as a place of ornament.

In "Practices of Interiorization: An Inter-Story," Suzie Attiwill proposes a view of history that challenges the assumptions of the dichotomy between artefacts and spaces, an approach bringing interior and history together to foster design thinking and experimentation. Attiwill suggests an altogether different way of creating spatial context through the idea of *space as inter-story*. Her concept suggests that the weaving together of interior and history allows for a different way to understand interior space as a malleable entity.

We then turn to a Provocation from Lisa Tucker, who talks about the value of the historic perspective. This provocation is a counterpoint to the theories we have seen, as Tucker proposes that the idea of artefact as a place for historic expression must be tackled from a holistic perspective.

Finally, in the Dialogues and Perspectives, Ronn Daniel presents a pragmatic example examining the relationships of space, gender, and Victorian society in the workplace through a historic interior. Daniel looks through the lens of the past in Victorian America, from an understanding of the historic contexts that align spaces as they were created in the late nineteenth and early twentieth centuries as place of gender and social stratification, taking us well beyond space as a physical container. In doing so, he addresses the relationship between interior space and technological modernization, with allusions to gender and power issues.

4.1 Ornament: A Physical Language of Design and Culture

John C. Turpin

or·na·ment

A thing used to adorn something but usually having no practical purpose, esp. a small object such as a figurine.
Something that lends grace or beauty[1]

The Great Exhibition of 1851 became the touchstone for the debate regarding ornament as critics in a wide range of disciplines commented on the Victorian era's predilection toward excess in the areas of ornamentation. More often than not, the result was a rather severe censure of English pretentiousness. In his 1851 prize winning essay "The Exhibition as a Lesson in Taste," Ralph Nicholson Wornum (1812–1877) noted that "Another great fact displayed, perhaps unavoidable where true education is absent, is the very general mistake that quantity of ornament implies beauty" (p. xvii). Wornum recognized that the enthusiasm surrounding machine technology as opposed to the educated taste of the designer influenced many of the design decisions. This coming from a critic who embraced ornament and considered it "an absolute necessity . . . for there is a stage of cultivation when the mind must revolt at a

---

[1] It is worth noting that the Merriam-Webster definition begins with the archaic definition: *a useful accessory*.

mere crude utility" (Wornum, 1851, p. xxi). In one essay, Wornum identified the two foundational arguments that would define the discourse of ornament for the next 150 years: ornament as excess, and ornament as necessity.

Ornament, its application and utility, has been and continues to be a highly debatable concept within the framework of architecture and interiors. The two definitions above—randomly pulled from different sources—reveal the undertones that evoke intense positions on the subject and reflect the critiques offered by Wornum in the nineteenth century. The first definition articulates the idea that ornament has no practical purpose. One does not do anything with ornament. The authors of this definition focus on what is not. The second definition takes a more positive approach by stating what ornament provides—grace or beauty—which the author embeds in the first definition's reference "to adorn." These definitions represent the two most general positions on the subject matter. The first suggests that ornament is not necessary; it is a form of excess. Embedded within the idea of ornament as excess grows concerns of health, management, and democracy relative to the interior environment. The second believes that beauty and grace, which are criteria driven by personal values and social norms, are necessary components of the human experience—essentially, to provide pleasure. At the turn of the twentieth century, ornament stimulates the mind and demonstrates one's taste and place in society, but it had rules that must be followed. Class and ornament, consequently, became irrevocably linked in the domestic environment.

The debate over ornament during the last two centuries has had major impacts on the design of the built environment, and many have participated in the discourse. Ornament is discussed more vociferously within the discipline of architecture and its application to the exterior than within the discipline of interior design, in part, because of architecture's struggle to negotiate its position between two powerful forces—art and engineering—during the twentieth century. The subtext of much of the discourse reveals a slippery slope that challenges architecture's autonomy as a clearly defined discipline that is neither fine art nor engineering, but a unique combination of the two. However, architecture's attention to the concept of ornament has had a significant impact on the development of the interior because relatively few interior designers have entered the conversation. Their focus on client needs and preferences typically outweighs a philosophical approach on the subject. Consequently, the motives for the application of ornament on the exterior and the interior are generated from two completely different places: the realm of theory versus the realm of consumption.

As a profession, architecture has been dealing with ornament far longer than the comparatively youthful profession of interior design. Their discussion of ornament inevitably relates to the structure of the building. In 1869, Robert Kerr (1823–1904), a Scottish architect and writer, articulated four possible relationships between ornament and structure.[2] The first, "structure ornamented," was surface ornamentation historically derived. Designs based in classical systems from the Renaissance forward, with the exception of the exuberant and misdirected Victorian revivals, fall into this category. The second category, "structure ornamentalized," required the designer to render the structure itself as ornamental. The modernists preferred this approach above all others due to their reductive approach to design. "Ornament structuralized," according to Kerr, was not an opposite of the previous. In this category, ornament and structure blended into a unifying experience. The final option, "ornament constructed," privileged ornament above structure, and usually obscured all other aspects. Those who have invoked Kerr's definitions continue to critique ornament based solely on its relationship to the structure—the tension between art and engineering. I wish to view the role of ornament not as product solely defined by its relationship to the structure, but instead consider ornament's role in the manifestation of social relationships.

---

[2] See Peter Collins, "Aspects of Ornament," *Architectural Review* 129 (June 1961): 375–376.

Ornament became a tool to visually articulate wealth and power in the development of the western tradition. Those with money could purchase the skilled labor of craftspeople to create elaborately carved, sculpted, woven, or painted objects.[3] And, since most Western societies lacked a well-defined middle class, ornament became a luxury for the wealthy. Following the Civil War, the United States produced a remarkable number of millionaires. Lacking the birthright of the existing upper class, the *nouveaux riches* looked to existing models within the built environment that communicated both wealth and social standing—two new aspects of their lives. This new leisure class's conspicuous consumption, as noted by Thorstein Veblen, author of *The Theory of the Leisure Class* (1899), provides a framework for our consideration of ornament as reflecting certain social constructs. The fact that ornament reveals something about the inhabitant is a concept grounded in Mario Praz's (1896–1982) discussion of *stimmung*, which he introduced in his historical analysis of art depicting interior environments.[4]

By examining examples of nineteenth- and twentieth-century texts and projects using this lens of social inquiry, I will propose that ornament is a useful means of communicating social relationships— sometimes consciously and intentionally, and sometimes not.

Ornament as Social Qualifier

Ornament has a rich history that predates the twentieth century. In fact, the concept of ornament, its application, and utility consume much of the criticism about design during the nineteenth century. The ever-maligned revivals of the Victorian period produced firebrands that resulted in a number of critics, if not reform movements. Even those who championed ornament recognized a need for greater regulation.

Edith Wharton (1862–1937), a novelist and designer, and Ogden Codman, Jr. (1863–1951), an architect and interior decorator, collaborated on one of the most influential decorating books of the early twentieth century. *The Decoration of Houses* (1897) framed the discussion of ornament as evidence of good taste, which revealed their target audience: the wealthy, who followed aristocratic European examples, and the middle class, who closely looked up to their social superiors and emulated them to the best of their ability. For the wealthy, taste became a commodity during the latter part of the nineteenth century, especially for women who were indoctrinated at an early age in decorum and decoration. The upper class wielded both as a means to substantiate their heritage and place in society. In fact, the existing upper class used it as their last great defense against the *nouveaux riches* whose

---

[3] Vernacular objects often received ornament. However, the discourse surrounding the topic of ornament in this paper is focusing mainly on the designed interior—an interior that has been designed by professionals—thus excluding the vernacular.

[4] See Mario Praz, *An Illustrated History of Interior Decoration* (London: Thames & Hudson, 1964).

new money often dwarfed their own bank accounts, and thus threatened greatly their social authority.

A battle of social control waged as America's elite manifested its warfare through the construction of extravagant and extraordinary domestic spaces. Following the guidance of Wharton and Codman, who claimed good taste as anything of Italian, French, or English design from the Renaissance forward, the upper class competitively built villas, chateaux, and castles in New York, Southampton, and Newport. Ornament was perhaps their most effective tool in communicating their wealth, and hopefully their social status.

The interiors in *The Decoration of Houses* celebrated the geometry embedded in classical design. The function of ornament not only provided pleasing detail, but also articulated the geometry and symmetry of the space. Cornices and baseboards delineated the wall planes and brought attention to intersections. Moldings on the walls framed doors and windows, locating each within a logical rhythm of the room. The ornament, in short, made visible the mysteries of space and proportion, while simultaneously tapping into the pleasure center of the brain. Wharton and Codman (1897) suggested "Structure conditions ornament, not ornament structure" (13). Ornament became a means to an end; it articulated proportion and provided repose and distinction to a room, "which the ancients called the soul" (Wharton and Codman, 1897, p. 31).

To speak of specific examples is difficult, for unlike the exterior, the interiors of the grand homes built in this spirit utilized numerous stylistic languages. The Gothic, Renaissance, Baroque, and Rococo were just a few of the revived styles used to ornament the space. Coffered ceilings, arched windows, and hooded fireplaces required the work of countless craftsmen in stone, wood, and glass. The interiors of Rosecliff (Newport, 1898–1902), Old Westbury Gardens (Nassau County, NY, 1903), and Vicaya (Miami, 1914–1919) are just a few examples.

The ballroom at Rosecliff is an exemplar. Stanford White (1853–1906), the principal architect, created a space three bays wide by five bays deep. White articulated each bay with an arch framed by Corinthian pilasters. Bolection molding further divided the wall plane, and plaster cartouches emphasized the central line of each of the three bays directly beneath the arch. The ceiling responded accordingly to the other elements with the exaggerated cove of the ceiling matching the widths of the outer bays. The *trompe l'oeil* ceiling spanned the width of the central bay and stretched accordingly the length of three bays on the other walls. White's lavish embellishments responded to the structure and the architectural elements (e.g., windows and doors), and yet provided pleasure to the mind while articulating the abstract mathematical beauty of the space's proportions.

Wharton and Codman's approach to ornament falls under Kerr's category of structure ornamented, which is essentially surface ornamentation historically derived. However, the social relevance of this relationship, as demonstrated above, regards ornament as a social qualifier. Ornament speaks of a social hierarchy in which the inhabitant intentionally separates him- or herself not only from the other classes (lower and middle) but also from their social peers. The ornament communicates a social hierarchy through its material, craftsmanship, and, perhaps above all, quantity—albeit controlled. The guests of the host locate their own social position relative to the social status of the host by quietly admiring or critiquing the home. Ward McAllister (1827–1895), attorney and author, wrote extensively about his interactions with the social elite. Even though he was from a prominent family in Savannah, he recognized his position when in the presence of society's matriarchs. When asked why he eagerly attended the events at one leader's house, he replied, "Because I enjoy such refined and cultivated entertainments. It improves and elevates me" (McAllister, 1890, p. 128).

Within the larger structure of society, the ornament represents the American capitalist system where the consumer purchases the product to display their wealth, a craftsperson receives compensation to create the product, and a member of the lower class (the servants) maintains the ornament by dusting and cleaning on a daily basis for very little money. Ornament as social qualifier is the most evident in this example; however, the American middle class valued progress and their potential to make it rich. Their avid emulation of their social superiors gave birth to etiquette and decorating books. Emily Price Post's

(1872–1960) *The Personality of a House: The Blue Book of Home Design and Decoration* (1930) was one of the most popular and influential.

Post, a member of the upper class herself, provided substantial advice in the various aspects of designing, building, and decorating the home. Her guiding premise was that the home must reflect the personality of the inhabitant lest it be perceived as a "dress shown on a wax figure," indicating a disconnection between the inhabitant and the home (Post, 1930, p. 3). Although Post attempted to stay neutral when presenting both historic and modern styles, her upper-class biases entered the discussion. In the chapter addressing the modern home, Post (1930) stated "one value of old furniture is that quite inevitably it imparted the quality of ancestry" (p. 492). Post's ancestry belonged to a privileged class. She lived in Tuxedo Park, New York, one of the most exclusive enclaves in the United States that boasted families like the Harrimans, Juilliards, and Lorillards. The "old furniture"—complete with historical ornament—conveyed a deep, rich ancestry that located Post as an important figure connected to American history, and as for many upper-class families, a descendent of a royal family in England.[5] Because

---

[5] The families in Tuxedo Park, home to Emily Post and Dorothy Tuckerman Draper (another woman of renowned taste), were well-known anglophiles due to their ancestries that linked them to prominent, well-established names in England. See George M. Rushmore's *The World with a Fence Around It: Tuxedo Park—The Early Days* (New York: Pageant Press, 1957).

the upper class relied heavily on their heritage as a validation of their wealth or station in society, the home became a display of ancestral artifacts and treasures.[6] The middle class certainly possessed a general pride in heritage, but heirlooms became far more valued for their mnemonic purposes than claiming a significant ancestry.

Post's text was a natural continuation of *The Decoration of Houses*. The fashion of the upper class had made it to the masses. The meaning of the ornament changed little as the middle class used ornament to separate themselves from their social inferiors or reconfirm their status by following excepted measures of good taste.[7] The tradition required the addition of ornament in response to the structure—a recognition of their relationship—but its effect remained true: it provided visual pleasure and made claims of social status, real or imagined.

Ornament as Social Equalizer

Just over a decade after Wharton and Codman's *The Decoration of Houses*, Adolf Loos

(1870–1933), an Austrian architect, wrote an essay that redefined design for much of the twentieth century. "Ornament and Crime" (1908) dismissed the relevance of historically grounded ornamentation for modern twentieth century Viennese culture. Loos argued that design should reflect the current culture, not the ghosts of the past. "The evolution of culture is synonymous with the removal of ornamentation from objects of everyday use" (Loos, 1908, p. 167). He called upon criminals and aboriginal cultures, known for their tattooing practices, as a means to defend the lack of congruency between ornament and the current society. Cultured, upstanding citizens of Vienna did not ornament their bodies. They should not do the same to their buildings. The stylings of the Gothic, Renaissance, Baroque and Rococo had run their course, and were henceforth irrelevant.

Relative to Wharton and Codman, Loos stood at the other end of the spectrum. Ornament was not to be a social qualifier; its absence was to indicate a social equalizer. Loos condemned the social positioning announced by highly decorative details. Ornament for the sake of beauty was insufficient. Ornament represented a waste of human labor, money, and material (Loos, 1908, p. 169). It lacked social responsibility.

Loos's design work manifests his philosophy. The Villa Moller (1928) and Villa Müller (1930) symbolize the rejection of ornament as anachronistic. The white cube dominates the composition of each design, lacking any definition other than another

---

[6] See Clive Aslet, *The American Country House* (New Haven: Yale University Press, 1990), and Lucy Kavaler, *The Private World of High Society* (New York: D. McKay Co., 1960). Both address the emulative practice of the Olde Guard and their relationship with seventeenth- and eighteenth-century England. See also Cleveland Amory's *The Proper Bostonian* (New York: E. P. Dutton, 1947) for a discussion of the Bostonians reliance on English customs, manners, fashion, and interiors.

[7] See John Turpin's "The Doors of Dorothy Draper: Vestiges of Victorian Manners with a Middle-Class Sensibility" in *In.Form: The Journal of Architecture, Design, and Material Culture 1*, no. 1 (2000): 8–15.

white cube protruding from the front façade in order to provide shelter above the front door, a subtle indentation framing the upper story windows, or the simple punctures of window openings. However, Loos views the exterior and the interior as separate in so far as "the building should be dumb outside and only reveal wealth inside" (Loos, 1914). As a member of a civilized culture, one does not boast of their wealth publicly; that is inappropriate. However, within the confines of the home, the inhabitants are free to express themselves as they wish. Because Loos's design work does not extend to furniture selection or placement in residential projects, the interiors appear almost schizophrenic as the inhabitants are free to select objects replete with ornament; but what is perhaps even more significant is the impact of Loos's theory of *raumplan* on the interior.

Loos freed space vertically once he started to think of it as a continual entity moving through the interior. No longer fettered by the self-contained volumes of classicism, Loos embraced the plasticity of space, allowing it to flow and wrap inside his otherwise harshly geometricized shells. Containing space was not his goal; consequently, walls took on new roles, guiding the flow of space. Instead of defining the space, interior walls became objects within the space. With such a fluid interior, a system of ornament that grew from the construction was an overwhelming task. The classically based ornament Loos banished had previously articulated the volume of the space, enhanced its proportion and geometry, and provided variety (pleasure) for the eye. Loos's new design strategy did not offer the long uninterrupted surfaces that welcomed ornament. Asymmetry was a natural characteristic of his interiors. Envisioning the successful application of traditional ornament was almost futile. Moldings and trim would have been running rampant along walls, over ledges, around corners, and through openings. The interior would have looked more like an Escher painting, complete with its disorienting effects. The only form of ornament responsive to this system of design is the material cladding Loos introduced. The solid sheets of material (whether marble or wood) communicated the complexity of the space, made visible the intricate layers, and enhanced the movement of the volume. The cladding was the ornament; in fact, James Trilling (2003), author of *Ornament: A Modern Perspective,* calls it "modernist ornament" (135). Nonetheless, just like Wharton and Codman's ornament, it was useful because it aided the viewer in reading and appreciating the space, as well as providing a pleasurable experience.

Walter Gropius (1883–1969) adopted Loos's theory of ornament by instigating an anti-historical approach to the curriculum he crafted for the Bauhaus:

The first task was to liberate the pupil's individuality from the dead weight of conventions and allow him to acquire that personal experience and self-taught knowledge which are the only means of realizing the natural limitations of our creative powers. (Gropius, 1965, 71)

Gropius and his colleagues expunged history from the curriculum, which was the first step in presenting his rational approach toward design. With the added emphasis on technology and standardization as core values of the Bauhaus and its founders, excess became antithetical to modernist philosophy. Le Corbusier (1925) stated the relationship quite clearly: "Trash is always abundantly decorated; the luxury object is well-made, neat and clean, pure and healthy, and its bareness reveals the quality of its manufacture." His Villa Savoye (1929) followed suit.

Le Corbusier stripped the interior of any ornament, creating an almost museum-like space with the sculptural service stair to the left and the graceful ramps straight ahead paralleling the hallway for the first floor. The overtly white interior announces the interest in hygiene, as does the sink located in the hall; however, the simplicity of the space, the absence of ornament, combined with the multiple methods of circulation, challenges the guest to know how to use the space. Historically, designers rendered service stairs in a manner to communicate their use by the staff, and the public stair, or grand stair, readily indicated use by the owners and the guest. The democracy of the space eliminates the necessary hierarchy needed to understand a space. But, at the same time, there is no clear hierarchy of class manifested in built form.

Underpinning the design philosophy of Loos, Gropius, Le Corbusier, and future modernists like Charles and Ray Eames was a distinct desire to provide good design for all. Modernists rejected ornament as a symbol of social division and classism. Even Post (1930) commented on modernism's equalizing effect on society: "The Modern style is a medium of amusement for the very rich, and one of practical value to the fairly poor" (p. 497). She continued by acknowledging "one great advantage of the modern interior's intentional emptiness, is that those who are furnishing for the first time with few possessions can feel as if their home is complete" (p. 508). Verging on a backhanded compliment, Post recognized the benefits of the application of the modern aesthetic across class boundaries.

Even though many iconic homes across America were built in the modern style (Eames House, Glass House, Farnsworth House), the majority of Americans did not embrace modernism prior to 1945, finding it too cold and impersonal during a period of American history that was fraught with stress and anxiety due to World War I, the Depression, and World War II. A glance through popular shelter magazines like *Better Homes and Gardens* and *House & Garden* provides all the necessary information. However, interior design had its modernist champions. In 1942, Mary Davis Gillies, *McCall's* Interior Decorating Editor, published *All About Modern Decorating*. In the preface, she expressed her opinion quite definitively:

[This book] is intended for that "forward-looking" group who recognize the fallacy of clinging to worn-out modes. It is intended for realists, who face life as it is and who see the underlying strength in building a background and a home which is an out growth and expression of the day in which we live. (Gillies, 1942, p. ix)

Gillies and other designers who referred to the realities of the time faced an uphill battle with the majority of the American public. Between 1930 and 1945, the reality of American life was unpleasant, to say the least. The Great Depression and World War II hindered the pursuit of the American Dream as the populace turned their efforts toward physical, emotional, and psychological survival.

The desire for escapism or fantasy manifested itself in many aspects of daily life. The most obvious was the explosive popularity of movies. The relatively new media became the "space of supreme illusion" during the 1920s and 1930s (Fischer, 1942, p. C10).[8] Interior designers like Dorothy Draper (1888–1969), understood the needs of the populace and consistently created escapist experiences in public spaces, such as The Orangerie, a restaurant in the Hampshire House (New York City, 1937) that transported the guests to a southern plantation complete with a fruit orchard.[9]

Modern interiors did not provide the distraction the American public required. Upon reflection, Robert A. M. Stern (1986)

stated "the modernist movement had declared its greatest ambition the public good but had never shown much interest in the reality of the public's world as it was and openly despised the public's dreams and fantasies . . . of the world as it had been or might be" (p. 35). The rational designs spawned by the German modernists left little to the imagination. The efficient use of industrial materials such as tubular steel and the stance against ornamentation produced machine-like furnishings, famously referred to by Le Corbusier as "equipment." The architecture of the interior became a blank backdrop in which human activity, furniture, and accessories were privileged, according to Gillies. Not until the 1950s did a shift occur in American preferences due to a phenomenon of newness.

> All of the postwar suburbs proclaimed the advantages of newness, an American tradition especially attractive to the young. Newness promised freedom from crust, dirt, prior owners, and vandals, and offered material objects and social relations that people could embrace as their own from the start. (Baritz, 1989, p. 197)

Shunning the past because of its harsh realities, the middle class finally had an opportunity to live in the present and start afresh. Heirlooms became less desirable, while affordable mid-century modern furniture promised a hopeful future. But the middle class did not abandon historicism completely; a desire to be "rooted" still existed (Baritz, 1989, p. 180). Suburban

---

[8] According to Kathryn Weibel, movies became more escapist during the 1940s due to the psychological stress of the war. Kathryn Weibel, *Mirror, Mirror: Images of Women Reflected in Popular Culture* (Garden City, NY: Anchor Books, 1977).

[9] See John Turpin's "The Life and Work of Dorothy Draper, Interior Designer: A Study of Class Values and Success" (PhD diss. Arizona State University, 2008).

developments such as Levittown offered a number of model homes inspired by historic styles complete with ornamentation modernists thought unessential and antidemocratic. Middle-class homes often revealed a rather awkward desire for the inhabitant to selectively negotiate past and present, the traditional and the modern, within their interiors.

The argument for the absence of ornament as social equalizer has its merits. If fashion dictates that architectural planes are stripped of ornamentation, then the most basic wall required to construct a home allows all classes to participate in the fashion of the time. However, the social phenomenon of taste shifted the perception of modernism as a reflection of social equality. At the beginning of the twenty-first century, the modern classics such as Mies van der Rohe's Barcelona chair and Le Corbusier's lounge chair carry hefty price tags. Our culture identifies them with office interiors of powerful business executives. The pure modern aesthetic in architecture are also expensive homes. The absence of ornament that can hide construction flaws requires a level of craftsmanship that does not come cheap, which is why virtually all new suburban developments rely on traditional stylings; they cost less to build, cover poor craftsmanship, and still tap into the romantic desires of the middle class.

Ornament as Social Sensitivity

Historicism and modernism demarcate the ends of the spectrum when looking for relationships between ornament and society. One embraces ornament; the other calls for its absence. Each philosophical approach toward ornament has been grounded—at least partially—in discussions relating to class. Historic ornament participated in the American social structure as a measure of ancestry and wealth, while modernism championed a more socialistic strategy that removed conspicuous consumption from the equation. Searching for examples of applied ornament that fall between these two benchmarks is more challenging. However, Frank Lloyd Wright's approach to ornament may offer some options.

Frank Lloyd Wright (1867–1959) was situated tenuously on the margins of modernism during the first half of the twentieth century, at least according to Henry Russell Hitchcock (1903–1987) and Phillip Johnson (1906–2005), authors of *The International Style: Architecture Since 1922* (1932). Their publication corresponded with "Modern Architecture: International Exhibition" at the Modern Museum of Art. Conspicuously absent from the exhibit was American architect Frank Lloyd Wright. His "individualism . . . and relation to the past" marked him as one of the "last representatives of Romanticism" (Hitchcock and Johnson, 1932, p. 27). Wright's conviction to unify the structure to the site sat in direct opposition to the International Style that believed their designs were essentially site-less, meaning they were appropriate anywhere.

Wright worked on the margins of the Arts and Crafts, the Art Nouveau, and the Modern Movement, as evidenced by the difficulty historians have had in categorizing his work. His Prairie Style reflected his Arts and Crafts training through his appreciation of natural materials, especially the use of wood on the interior. He abstracted the surrounding nature and incorporated it thoughtfully in the design of his window or tiles on the exterior in the spirit of the Art Nouveau designers. He rejected the academic styles of the past, noting that "no ideal seems to have power enough or beauty to resist the fateful law of change in any of its many manifestations" (Wright, 1970, p. vii). In short, architects should not force academic styles upon society, as it is unnatural.

Like Wharton and Codman and Loos, Wright framed his discussion of architecture in sociopolitical terms. His four presentations for the Sir George Watson Lectures in 1939 addressed the "place Architecture must have in Society if Democracy is to be realized" (Wright, 1970, p. vii). Wright referenced democracy as a freedom of individual expression. He believed "beauty" (i.e., architecture) should be more spontaneous, "true to time, place, environment and purpose" (Wright, 1970, p. vii). The development of his Prairie Style expressed a connection to site through form and materiality, and responded to the growing wave of simplified ornamentation in recognition of modern life. Wright spurned the "arty-pretense" of classical ornamentation, naming the Parthenon as an example (Wright, 1957). This, however, was not a general rejection of ornament. In fact, Wright believed ornament was "intrinsic to the being human of the human being"

(Wright, 1957, p. 158). But it must be organic—a natural expression of the architectural form. The result was ornamentation as social sensitivity.

The interior of the Robie House (1908), a quintessential example of Wright's Prairie Style, expressed a social sensitivity whether or not Wright created it consciously with this intent. Wright ornamented the living room of the Robie House by structuralizing ornament, according to Thomas Beeby (1977). The simple linearity of the wooden moldings that spanned the ceiling and dropped briefly on to the wall emerged from the constructive techniques and the emphasis on the horizontal line, a defining characteristic of the style. The ornament enhanced and challenged the geometry of the space simultaneously.

Wright's moldings grew organically from the construction of the space by articulating both the vertical and horizontal members hidden behind the finished surfaces, as well as the overall forms— the vertical central fireplace that staked the composition to the site and the horizontal planes that extended outward like branches. Although the part of the Robie House is essentially two rectangles slid together, Wright attempted to break apart the box that he had created in order to demonstrate a greater unity with nature and the site. He positioned his molding in a manner that negated the juncture of architectural planes (walls and ceiling). The molding recognized the change in dimension by dropping onto the surface of the soffit, where it returned mid-plane before paralleling its course back across the ceiling.

Unlike the ornamentation described in *The Decoration of Houses*, Wright's ornament consciously challenged the viewer's perception of the spatial geometry while, in fact, still reinforcing it. According to Beeby (1977), Wright "blurred the line which had separated ornament and structure" (p. 19).

To suggest that the Robie House is an example of ornamentation as social sensitivity requires that it be evaluated comparatively to the two previous sections. During the early twentieth century, historic ornamentation designated wealth for reasons already stated. German modernism was still in a nascent state; however, a general movement against the excess of the Victorian movement played out all over Europe and the United States in a number of different styles. Wright's design for the Robies did not express their wealth in the typical design language of historic revivals. Its modern aesthetic made a statement, but the interior did not carry the cultural cues of pretense that had been established in the nineteenth century. While beautiful and elegant in its own way, the interior communicated a comfortable ease to all visitors. The warmth of the wood and the masterful craftsmanship tapped into people's memories and perceptions of a vernacular life, simple and easy.

The Robies opted not to display their social status in a traditional manner. Geometric patterns replaced highly carved details on pediments, fireplaces, and door surrounds. Wright's interest in eighteenth-century American architecture resonated, even if subliminally, with those who visited the Robie House. He reinterpreted the exposed wood beams and central fireplace, masterfully creating a nostalgic experience in a modern form.

The Arts and Crafts movement in the United States possessed a similar approach toward ornamentation. The work of the Green Brothers comes to mind, which resulted in an explosion of bungalows across the United States. Ornament as social sensitivity is difficult to find during the rest of the century, especially as taste shifts its preference to the modern. Traditional ornamentation never went out of style, and continued to be the other dominant choice for Americans. The hybrid experienced by the middle class in the suburbs suggested that choice and self-expression were part of the American Dream.

Ornament as Individual Expression

During the socially turbulent years of the 1960s and 1970s, Americans of all walks of life struggled for freedoms not yet realized. Women, ethnic minorities, homosexuals, and even the youth protested passionately for social change. At stake was indeed the ability to express the self without fear of social retribution. Designers sought a similar release from the grip of modernism.

Modernism's momentum began to wane in the 1960s. Robert Venturi (b. 1925) challenged some of the core elements of modernism with the turn of a single letter. Mies van de Rohe's "Less is More" became Venturi's "Less Is a Bore." Throughout *Complicity and Contradiction*, Venturi (1966) promoted both/and scenarios over modernism's either/or, thus opening the floodgates of expression. Historical references returned to the designer's toolbox unfettered by any rules. Charles Moore's (1925–1993) Piazza d'Italia (1978) in New Orleans demonstrated an exuberant design vocabulary articulated by bright colors, shiny metallic surfaces, lighting, and exaggerated classical ornament.

The postmodern movement ushered in opportunities for the individual expression of ornament. Charles Moore's own house is indeed an expression of the individual. Some of the interior rooms are blanketed with his collections. Both decoration and ornamentation obscure the shell. The structure's role has been relegated to a support system for the display of the individuality of the inhabitant—very much in the spirit of Mario Praz's concept of *stimmung*.

The exaggerated ornament found in Moore's interior is an individual expression. With the rules of modernism banished, although not completely forgotten, designers began to play with ornament relative to scale, proportion, and color/material presentation. Other designers like Michael Graves (b. 1934) participated in this postmodern approach, but his domestic interiors were more restrained in their use and interpretation of classical principles. Other architects, like Charles Gwathmey (1938–2009), continued following a more modernist tradition. Essentially, the last quarter of the twentieth century became an opportunity for experimentation. Pluralism is alive and well.

What is perhaps more interesting is how architecture as an object has become

the ornament to the landscape. Frank Gehry's (b. 1929) work is an excellent example. He employs computers to produce algorithms that have resulted in the Experience Music Project in Seattle (2000), the Disney Concert Hall in Los Angeles (2003), and the Guggenheim Museum in Bilbao (1997). The complex, twisting planes defy a viewer's ability to understand the structure. These projects are almost baroque in their vigor and exuberance compared to the surrounding cityscapes. The interior of the EMP takes ornament to a new level. Light, color, materiality, and what appear to be structural elements are transformed into a series of unrelated patterns collaged in space that change with time due to the movement of light and the digital screens displaying an ever-changing array of images. Illusion underscores the interior experience as Gehry subsumes visitors in spaces that challenge perceptions of reality. The blurring of structure and ornament in Wright's Robie House was to achieve unity and clarity; the blurring of structure and ornament in Gehry's EMP was just the opposite. One comforts, the other excites.

Interiors like those of the EMP are not yet feasible, or considered tasteful, for residential living spaces. The EMP seems to be more an opportunity for Gehry to express himself as a designer, in a way similar to the designers of the Memphis Movement, who were also challenging the conventions of taste and design but focusing more on interior furnishings and decorative accessories. When ornament is "constructed" in the manner that Kerr spoke of, the outcome will inevitably be extremely personal, but for who? Is it the designer, the client, or perhaps society as a whole?

Summary

Ornament is a cultural symbol that expresses individual and/or group values. It adorns objects, making them more beautiful, and can also reveal the structure that is hidden behind. However, historically speaking, ornament is rarely discussed as a manifestation of social relationships or structures. At the turn of the twentieth century, ornament participates in the hierarchical structuring of an elite group, not so subtly making claims for power and authority. This tradition is deeply rooted in the development of Western design thinking. Those who have the resources can purchase the material and labor to create extraordinary works of art.

With the Industrial Revolution, societies begin to reconsider new ways of living that take advantage of the machine and its time-saving abilities. The middle class grows in financial power and sheer numbers, separating themselves from the labor class, but still clearly distinguished from their social superiors. Socialist ideologies evolve, and some designers vanquish ornament as a representation of a past that is no longer relevant or ideal. The absence of traditional ornament reflects new social views.

Not all designers agreed on the complete rejection of ornament. Some embraced a more restrained approach that perhaps unintentionally presented a compromise between the two extremes. Democracy took on new meaning as it was applied to the built environment, from which inevitably grew a desire of choice, and stylistic pluralism indicated a time of experimentation, fostering great advances in technology and a global community whose boundaries deteriorated with each decade.

Ironically, technology—once the reason for the rejection of ornament—is perhaps one of the reasons for its return. Andrea Gleiniger (2009) states that "now ornament is being postulated as a type of emerging phenomenon, as an excess of algorithmic patter production, which accrues from its apparently infinite number of notions of possibility" (p. 14). At the end of the twentieth century, the computer has revolutionized the design professions. Hernan Diaz Alonso (b. 1969) has inspired a new generation of designers by introducing terms long since absent from design vocabulary: exuberance and excess. Alonso (2008) defines exuberance as an adjective that might describe his work, while excess is logic. Alonso's designs follow in the tradition of Gehry, but take the formation of the building to an entirely new level—one that seems to be more ornament than structure—but this is indeed just one approach.

The range of philosophies surrounding ornament is evident in popular texts and scholarly discourse. Cuito champions the traditions of the Modern Movement in her text *Minimalist Spaces*. All of the projects have forced aside ornamentation in an attempt for architecture's search for essential elements (Cuito, 2001). In *Structure as Design*, Allen (2000) demonstrates the advancements in construction techniques and the corresponding possibilities for structure to be ornament. Trilling (2003) argues that ornament should provide visual pleasure above all else. Betsky (1997) believes that ornament is simply an inherent component of the human condition: "to decorate is human" (p. 25). While Levit (2001) values it for its materiality and symbolism, Moussavi demands ornament must be fundamental, and Domeisen (2008) finds it essential to reveal the content of a structure. Ornament will likely continue to be one of the most debatable aspects of the built environment for decades to come.

Aside from the physical implications of a designed space, designers and critics have framed ornament within the discourses of social relevance and responsibility. In order to situate ornament within a socio-logical context, the perceptions of people at a variety of scales (from the individual to the group) must be explored. Extrinsic (e.g., technology, social conditions) and intrinsic (e.g., taste, finances) factors weigh heavily on the outcome. Ornament is many things (reality/fantasy, male/female, public/private, rational/irrational, intellectual/emotional, art/science, past/present), but I would argue that neither of the definitions provided at the beginning of this essay are entirely accurate—they are a reflection of the twentieth century's obsession with binary oppositions. Both/and seems to be more appropriate, and I would argue, accurate.

Thus, I close with a proposal:

or•na•ment—A physical language of design and culture.

Discussion Questions

1. How is an ornamental perspective about space useful and of value when you are discussing meanings of design?
   a. What constructions do "concepts of ornament" create?
   b. What is your idea of ornament, and how do you experience ornament in your everyday life as a person? In the interior spaces that you live in?
   c. What is Turpin saying about the role of ornament in our spaces?

2. Unpack some of the fundamental concepts Turpin outlines in more detail with readings. These include
   a. Ornament as social qualifier
   b. Ornament as equalizer
   c. Ornament as social sensitivity
   d. Ornament as individual expression
   e. How would you understand ornament in contemporary spaces with these concepts?

3. Discuss modernism as a historic period in light of concepts of ornament and space. Why and how are these concepts political as much as physical?

4. Turpin suggests alternative ways to understand ornament. He notes Frank Lloyd Wright, who believed "beauty" (i.e., architecture) should be more spontaneous, "true to time, place, environment and purpose" (Wright, 1970, p. vii). What do you

think? How might you examine these ideas in light of Wright's architecture and the spaces that he creates?

5. Turpin closes with a proposal: How is ornament a "physical language of design and culture?" Unpack this idea by looking at the examples Turpin proposes, and perhaps crucially suggests, engaging in a debate about ornament as a language of design and culture. What are these possibilities? What are other ways that we define our personal or cultural spaces?

References

Allen, I. (2000). *Structure as Design.* Gloucester, MA: Rockport Publishers, Inc.

Alonso, H. D. (2006). *Xefirotarch.* San Francisco, CA: San Francisco Museum of Modern Art.

Amory, C. (1947). *The Proper Bostonians.* New York: E. P. Dutton.

Aslet, C. (1990). *The American Country House.* New Haven, CT: Yale University Press.

Baritz, L. (1989). *The Good Life: The Meaning of Success for the American Middle Class.* New York: Alfred A. Knopf.

Beeby, T. (1977). The Grammar of Ornament: Ornament as Grammar. In S. Kieran (Ed.), *Ornament: The Journal of the Graduate School of Fine Arts* (pp. 11–12). Philadelphia: Falcon Press.

Betsky, A. (1997). Ornament is Fine. *Blueprint* 145, 24–25.

Collins, P. (1961). Aspects of Ornament. *Architectural Review*, 129(772), 373–378.

Cuito, A. (2001). *Minimalist Spaces.* New York: HarperCollins.

Domeisen, O. (2008). Communicating Content. *Volume 17,* 72–75.

Fischer, B. E. S. (October 28, 1942). Dorothy Draper, Designer, Ties Up Her Hotel Decorations All in One Package. *Christian Science Monitor.*

Gillies, M. D. (1942). *All About Modern Decorating.* New York: Harper & Brothers.

Gleiniger, A. (2009). New Patterns? Old Patterns? On the Emotional Appeal of Ornament. In A. Gleiniger & G. Vrachliotis (Eds.) *Pattern: Ornament, Structure, and Behavior* (pp. 13–24). Basel, Switzerland: Birkhäuser.

Gropius, W. (1965). *The New Architecture and the Bauhaus.* Cambridge, MA: MIT Press.

Hitchcock, H. R., & Johnson, P. (1932). *The International Style: Architecture Since 1922.* New York: W. W. Norton & Co.

Kavaler, L. (1960). *The Private World of High Society.* New York: D. McKay Co.

Le Corbusier. (1925). The Decorative Art of Today. *L'Espirit Nouveau.*

Levit, R. (2008). Contemporary Ornament: The Return of the Symbolic

Repressed. *Harvard Design Magazine* 28(13), 70–85.

Loos, A. (1914). *Heimatkunst.* Innsbrook, Austria.

Loos, A. (1908). *Ornament and Crime: Selected Essays.* Riverside, CA: Ariadne Press.

McAllister, W. (1890). *Society as I Have Found It.* New York: Cassell Publishing Company.

Moussavi, F., & Kubo, M. (2006). *The Function of Ornament.* Barcelona: Actar, Harvard University, Graduate School of Design.

Post, E. (1930). *The Personality of a House: The Blue Book of Home Design and Decoration.* New York: Funk & Wagnalls Company.

Praz, M. (1964). *An Illustrated History of Interior Decoration.* London: Thames and Hudson.

Rykwert, J. (1982). *The Necessity of Artifice.* London: Academy Editions.

Rushmore, G. M. (1957). *The World with a Fence Around It: Tuxedo Park—the Early Days.* New York: Pageant Press.

Stern, Robert A. M. (1986). Charles Moore: The Architect Running in Place. In E. Johnson (Ed.), *Charles Moore: Buildings and Projects 1949–1986* (pp. 35–38). New York: Rizzoli.

Trilling, J. (2003). *Ornament: A Modern Perspective.* Seattle, WA: University of Washington Press.

Turpin, J. (2000). The Doors of Dorothy Draper: Vestiges of Victorian Manners with a Middle-Class Sensibility. *In.Form: The Journal of Architecture, Design, and Material Culture, 1*(1), 8–15.

Turpin, J. (2008). The Life and Work of Dorothy Draper, Interior Designer: A Study of Class Values and Success. Unpublished Doctoral Dissertation. Arizona State University.

Venturi, R. (1966). *Complexity and Contradiction in Architecture.* New York: Museum of Modern Art.

Weibel, K. (1977). *Mirror, Mirror: Images of Women Reflected in Popular Culture.* Garden City, NY: Anchor Books.

Wharton, E., & Codman, O., Jr. (1897). *The Decoration of Houses.* New York: Charles Scribner's Sons.

Wornum, R. N. (1851). The Exhibition as a Lesson in Taste. *The Art Journal Illustrated Catalogue: The Industry of All Nations,* i–xxii.

Wright, F. L. (1970). *An Organic Architecture: The Architecture of Democracy.* Cambridge, MA: MIT Press, 1970.

Wright, F. L. (1957). *A Testament.* New York: Horizon Press.

Inter-Story

Highlighting interior design as the *designing* of interiors focuses on practice as distinct from artefact, and process as distinct from outcome. Interior, then, is something designed and, as such, open to potential new ways of thinking what is an interior, how is an interior, and when is an interior. This re-posing responds to emerging qualities and characteristics in the practice of interior design at the beginning of the twenty-first century, such as digital technologies and environmental issues around sustainability, which are transforming understandings of space and time. *Inter-story* is a tactic to bring interior and history together, inter + story, to foster experimentation. Invented to augment new ways of practicing, thinking, and discussing the discipline of interior design, inter-story highlights the criticality of the concept of interior as a condition that is not assumed as a given but to be designed, and it acknowledges the value of history in this process (Attiwill, 2003, 2004).

Inter-story developed as a pedagogical tactic from a desire to engage interior design students as emerging practitioners with the past, and to stimulate their design thinking and designing of new kinds of interiors. The tactic is an invitation to work in the middle, where "it is necessary to distinguish what we are (what we are already no longer), and what we are in the process of becoming: the historical part and the current part" (Deleuze, 1992, p. 164).

Inter-stories are arrangements that bring ideas, techniques, and things together to experiment and see what emerges. The idea of a collection is critical to an appreciation of different ways of thinking and doing at various times, and the effects of forces such as technology. The method here is curatorial in much the same way history is defined in relation to Michel Foucault's method, as "a practice, as a particular set of actions brought to bear on a particular material" (Dean 1994, p. 15). One of the main criteria for evaluation for any inter-story is usefulness—useful in the designing of interiors and mobilization of ideas and practices to foster creativity and inventiveness. The pedagogical approach shifts from what? to how?, from a focus on knowing the past to a question of how to work with the past.

Existing histories of interior design present a collection of precedents that focus on outcomes rather than processes, entities rather than practice—"whats" as distinct from "hows"—and define interior design as that which occurs inside buildings. An example of such an approach is

John Pile's *The History of Interior Design.* In this history, an interior is defined as inside a building: "Interiors are an integral part of the structures that contain them—usually buildings. This means that interior design is inextricably linked to architecture and can only be studied within an architectural context" (Pile, 2009, p. 11). This places the interior designer in a dialectical relation where an exterior is positioned as existing and to be understood prior to, and as part of, the interior design; hence, the activity of designing becomes one of negotiation, representation, identification, and even transgression. Inter-story is a tactic to engage students in the potential of an emerging critical thinking addressing the question of interior and interior design where the role of architecture as "the primary 'space provider' in culture" is brought into question (Rice, 2007, p. 113). Inter-story is an invitation to experiment and invent new interiors through a focus on relations between interior and exterior as distinct from space and enclosure.

One of the provocations for the invention of inter-story was my experience as an undergraduate interior design student. The history course I experienced focused entirely on artefacts, mainly furniture and buildings, and where relevant/possible, the designer's intention. This was in stark contrast to the precedents encountered in the design studio. Here references were made to artists such as James Turrell as a way of opening up the question of the idea of interior in relation to techniques of production, spatial experience, and relational conditions. At that time I was curious why interior design history and its discourse did not connect with ideas emerging in the design studio. I was also concerned about the division between what we were engaging with as future interior designers and the idea encountered in existing interior design histories that interior design happened inside buildings. The tension and difference between an object/product approach and one concerned with spatial production, experience, and atmosphere seemed like different practices.

This was 20 years ago, and I continue to wonder where are the histories of interior that articulate this other trajectory. As a coordinator of history and theory of an undergraduate interior design program from 2000 to 2010, I responded to this challenge by designing the curriculum content of courses where inter-story is presented to students as one approach to engage with the past. Inter-stories are not concerned with a rewriting or a re-righting of history. Instead, inter-stories are "adventures of ideas" and frame "a speculative scheme of ideas" (Whitehead, 1933, p. 6); tools for experimentation in the production of the new.

In this sense, inter-stories come between, in the middle, to offer up a provisional composition as a platform for the arrival and departure of thinking and doing. Each inter-story assembles practices of interiorization where interior is the focus of enquiry as a relational condition of interior/exterior produced through imagining, selecting, and projecting different exteriors and interiors. "The interior is only a selected exterior, the exterior—a projected interior: (Deleuze, 1988, p. 125). Students are encouraged to consider these as experiments rather than exemplars and through an appreciation of the diversity and richness of potential relations and ways of working to experiment and take risks with their own designs. Per Colebrook:

"The world we see is one possible world, one expression or actualization of a world of power and potential that hold other worlds, or "lines of flight"; these lines can be released . . . by creating new relations, new actualizations of the potentials . . . (2006, p. 7).

This inter-story selects and arranges some examples to invite new ways of thinking and practicing interior design. Aaron Betsky, director of the 11th Venice Architecture Biennale, 2008—picks up the idea of interior design as a relational condition in a text he contributed to a book on contemporary architecture and digital technologies. He writes:

I have long argued that the interior, and especially the domestic interior, might be understood as such an intersection of forces and the source for a new approach to architecture . . . an open system that can accept objects and images from the outside and make sense out of them by the way they are integrated through use and arrangement (Betsky, 2005, p. 253).

And to push this idea even further, to consider relations not just as the relation *between* objects in space but to consider relations as dynamic forces that *produce* subjects and objects. This shifts from a position that privileges entities and enclosures as preexisting to a consideration of process, movement, and duration in the production of interior.

Interior

During the twentieth century, the profession of interior design was defined in distinction to both interior decoration and architecture. In contrast to a practice concerned with decoration and soft furnishings, the practice of interior design was, and is still, described as one concerning space and spatial experience. In fact, a number of interior design programs have been renamed as spatial design programs to better express the nature of their course content. The term "interior architecture" has also been adopted in recent times to further distinguish a practice concerned with interior space and the built environment. Increasingly, interior design is defined within this context and hence as a practice of negotiating existing architectural space. Per Brooker and Stone:

Interior architecture, interior design and building reuse are very closely linked subjects, all of them deal in varying degrees, with the transformation of a given space . . . One of the fundamental principles of interior design is that the discipline is concerned with the understanding and the subsequent reuse of existing spaces. Objects and spaces are "valued" for their previous meaning and retained or re-used in a space" (Brooker & Stone, 2011, pp. 228, 231).

Here the concept of "interior" is implicated in a dialectical relation with architecture and one that requires the interior designer to understand the previous meaning of existing space as part of the process of designing. This kind of relation, however, is only one of many possible relations between interior and exterior. "Interior design," unlike interior architecture, keeps the question of "interior" open as a creative proposition and problematic in response to contemporary forces. Positioned in this way, the concept of interior as addressing existing space within architecture is one example and as such is useful to examine in terms of what it manifests—and includes and excludes—as distinct from accepting it as a definitive statement.

An exhibition held at the beginning of the twenty-first century investigates the potential of engaging with the concept of interior as a dynamic relational condition. Titled *InterieurExterieur: Living in Art,* the curatorial approach mapped and presented modernity's rethinking of

the traditional separation between interior and exterior: the interior opens itself up to the outside, expands out into it ... Conversely the exterior everts itself into the interior like a glove. . . . The co-dependent term "inside-out" has been construed for this phenomenon which has developed into one of the most efficacious paradigms of modernity and

one which has wound its way into many other areas (Brüderlin & Lütgens, 2008, p. 14).

This is exciting in terms of offering up a trajectory that gathers what has happened in terms of interior/exterior relations and contributes to thinking about interior design as a relational condition and highlights the concept of "interior" as a problematic. Deleuze identifies this problematic at the end of the twentieth century as one where "we are in a generalized crisis in relation to all the environments of enclosure . . . in crisis like all other interiors" (1997, p. 309); and at the end of the nineteenth century, Walter Benjamin observed "the liquidation of the interior" (Benjamin 2002, p. 20).

In *The Emergence of the Interior,* Rice defines the interior as "a conceptual apparatus" (2009, p. 132) involving a relational condition of doubleness between image and space:

"Considering the emergence of the interior means entertaining the idea that it is not what 'we' know it to be. The effects of its emergence have been more diffuse, yet more pervasive, than those highlighted when it is defined in terms of what is already assumed, or what seems to be essential" (Rice 2007: 113).

A shift from examples of artefacts to practices of interiorization activates a connection with the past that highlights modes of practicing and thinking as well as style where differences are foregrounded. Students are invited to *think through* these practices as distinct from developing a position of *knowledge about* precedents. They are encouraged to take risks with their thinking and engage with the plethora of possibilities, to follow lines of interior thinking across different practices and disciplines, to experiment and invent rather than worry whether they are right or wrong, or know enough.

Towards an Inter-Story

Assembled here are four interior designs where each is a distinctive expression of a practice of interiorization and interior as a relational condition. It will become apparent that an architectural lineage is not being traced and there is not an attempt to produce a sequential narrative. Instead, these examples cross disciplines and spatial types in the pursuit of different practices of interiorizations. In their selection, collection, and arrangement, a curatorial approach is present; however, it is not one that attempts to establish a meta-narrative so much as to mobilize connections and potential in the current. The examples are not based on a typology of space such as domestic or retail but attend to the question of interior/exterior relations and practices of interiorization. Each is presented as an example of interiorization where interiors are produced through techniques that engage with exteriors—selecting, projecting, transforming, interiorizing.

Walter Benjamin's writings are replete with reference to "interior." Two models of interiorization are identified in Benjamin's writings: "one based on contraction and the other on expansion" (Fuss, 2004, p. 12). The contraction model is manifested by "the window mirror," which attempted "to pull the exterior wholly inside itself." Set into window casements, these mirrors reflected the outside inside in an attempt to pull and absorb "the whole world inside" (Fuss 2004: 12). The act of collecting artefacts and arranging them within the nineteenth-century bourgeois home is another example of interiorization as a practice of contraction. Like the window mirror, an exterior is gathered and folded inside; interiorized. The living room becomes "a box in the theatre of the world" (Benjamin, 2002, p. 19). Benjamin makes analogies between this interior and a shell as both involve an ongoing process of fabrication through accumulation. As Benjamin noted:

> Perhaps the most deeply hidden motive of the person who collects can be described in this way: he takes up the struggle against dispersion (2002, p. 211).

Surfaces of plush and violet velvet manifest traces of inhabitation, both inhabitant and collection. Here ideas commonly associated with interior design such as comfort, intimacy, privacy are equated with a desire for stability and security achieved through a slowing down of movement encountered in the perceived chaotic exterior of industrialization.

The other model of interiorization is one of expansion, which "pushes the inside out so that the internal expands without limit"

(Fuss, 2004, 13). The example referred to here is Benjamin's description of the covered arcade inhabited by the flâneur. Quoting Theodor Adorno, Fuss describes this as a "spatial inversion . . . 'the flâneur promenades in his room; the world only appears to him reflected by pure inwardness'" (Fuss, 2004, p. 13). These two examples manifest an interior/exterior relation as a relation of selection and projection where "the interior is only a selected exterior, the exterior—a projected interior" (Deleuze, 1988, p. 125).

The Futurists engaged with a different interior/exterior relation to the inner reflective models above. Umberto Boccioni's request of "Let's split open our figures and place the environment inside them" (Kern, 2003, p. 197) turns the relation inside out. The selected exterior here is also one of industrialization, speed, and transformation, yet the projected interior was not one of retreat and refuge. Expressing a desire to abolish "quietness and stasism," Boccioni claimed the Futurists "documented the new conception of space by confrontation of interior and exterior. For us gesture will not any more be a fixed moment of universal dynamism: it will decidedly be the dynamic sensation eternalized as such" (Boccioni, 1925, p. viii). Instead of defined forms outlining objects and subjects, force fields and energies rendered form plastic and elastic. Dynamic sensation is made visible. Movement, change, and duration are understood as "the interior force" of all things, both animate and inanimate. In the text *The Exhibitors to the Public*, which accompanied the

first *Exhibition of Italian Futurist Painting* in London, 1912, the Futurists incited the public to participate *in* the action: "In painting a person on a balcony, seen from inside the room, we do not limit the scene to what the square frame of the window renders visible; but we try to render the sum total of visual sensations which the person on the balcony has experienced . . . This implies the simultaneousness of the ambient, and, therefore, the dislocation and dismemberment of objects, the scattering and fusion of details, freed from accepted logic, and independent from one another" (Boccioni et al., 1912). The "spectator" should not "be present at, but participate in, the action." Boccioni's *Fusion of Head and Window* 1911–12 literally fuses interior and exterior, person and architecture. The desire to celebrate dynamic sensation through a reconceptualization of interior/exterior dissolved boundaries and form. Here, practices of interiorization produce an immersive condition where the environment is *in* the spectator as much as the spectator is *in* space and time. This is not a dialectical relation between interior and exterior so much as one that is co-extensive and dynamic that produces subjects and objects.

Artist and founder of De Stijl, Theo van Doesburg's proclamation "We are in need of a new interior" is a direct address to the potential of "interior" through a reconceptualization of interior/exterior relations. This declaration was made in a letter to the architect J. J. P. Oud inviting his "collaboration" in the production of "an atmosphere" (Troy 1982: 165). Detailed in his theory of

Elementarism, van Doesburg's concept of a new interior was one of expansion beyond the given architectural frame to engage the temporal:

> non-balanced counter composition as a phenomenon of a time-space tension of color, line or plane always in opposition to the natural and architectural structure . . . to destroy completely the illusionistic view of the world in all its forms . . . and yet at the same time construct an elementary world of exact and splendid reality. (1927, pp. 85–87)

The Cinema-Ballroom in the Café L'Aubette, Strasbourg, 1928, was one of the few opportunities van Doesburg had to actualize his theories. In amongst the diagonal composition of color planes, the cinema screen, and music, bodies were immersed in an atmosphere of moving image, light, sound, and dance. The surface was transformed by the oblique and color. Techniques of interiorization produced a dynamic environment, an interior that was extended beyond the limits of three-dimensional space to fold in an exterior of perceived universal laws without the mediation of symbolic representation:

> . . . the architectural space must be considered as shapeless and blind emptiness until color brings real shape to space. The creative space-time painting of the twentieth century enables the artist to realize his great dream to set man in the painting instead of in front of it (1928, p. 26).

Alexander Dorner, the director of the Hannover Landesmuseum from 1923 to 1936, used the term "atmosphere." In his "manifesto," *The Way Beyond "Art,"* Dorner defined his vision for a new museum as "a kind of powerhouse, a producer of energies" (Dorner, 1958, p. 147). Dismissing the desire for 'certainty-giving space,' Dorner advocated processes of becoming, which engaged with life, growth, energies, and time, and hence were transforming rather than fixed and eternal. In the redesign of gallery spaces and hanging of art, Dorner attempted to actualize this becoming through an encounter with an historical past that was neither representational in terms of presenting the past as static and contained nor as an experience produced wholly by the viewer but one of atmosphere, of life and energies that enfolded the present as part of an ongoing process of becoming. Renaissance, Baroque, and Medieval galleries were redesigned by Dorner as "atmosphere rooms" produced through an attention to design aspects such as layout, sightlines, circulation, lighting, color, and arrangement. Dorner commissioned El Lissitzky's famous *Abstract Cabinet* as one of these atmosphere rooms. Dorner described it as "the first attempt to overcome the fixity of the gallery and the semi-stasis of the period room and to introduce modern dynamism into the museum" (Dorner, 1958, p. 115). This was achieved by covering the walls with vertical tin strips of different colors on each side. As the viewer moved through the exhibition, the walls became dynamic with color oscillating and shimmering (Attiwill, 2008).

A Conclusion as an Invitation

Inter-story is offered as a tactic to enable an encounter with history in relation to thinking and practicing now. Privileging the criticality of the concept of interior and acknowledging the value of history in this conjunction, inter-story invites experimentation with what can be thought and said in relation to interior design with a view to connecting current forces and inciting future practices. This highlights the concept of interior as a contemporary problematic and invites consideration of other examples shaped by different ideas and practices of interiorization.

There is a sense of urgency with this pedagogical project and its contribution to the discipline of interior design, as it is apparent there is an increasing emphasis on interior design as a practice addressing the inside of buildings and existing conditions in relation to issues of environmental sustainability and the reuse of buildings. While this is a relevant and exciting trajectory, the discourse associated with this trajectory is producing essentialism in relation to the concept of "the interior," with the imperative to reflect "what *it* is" as distinct from loosening and opening "interior" to invention and a contingent exterior.

An inter-story happens in the middle with the current; it doesn't have a start and an end but *becomes* through writing and encounters. As a provisional platform—an interiorization of a temporary consistency—examples are selected and assembled to make apparent the plethora of different selected exteriors and projected interiors, and to invite experimentation in the pursuit of the new.

Discussion Questions

1. Discuss Attiwill's ideas on the context of inter-story. What is this? How does the concept of interior differ here, and what is the way that history informs interior space?
   a. How is the concept of inter-story an invitation to understanding interior spaces differently?
   b. How are interior-exterior relations dynamic and not limited to existing conditions in spaces?

2. What constitutes interior spaces in your mind? What is happening when people engage in activities in changing spaces and for various reasons?

3. What challenge does Attiwill lay out in the conclusion ?
   a. Why is this vital to explore?
   b. How can the dynamic nature of interiors become played out in a broader understanding of other design spaces? How can meaning occur in these contexts?

References

Attiwill, S. (2011). Between Representation and the Mirror—Tactics of Interiorization. J. Fleming, F. Hay, E. Hollis, A. Milligan, & D. Plunkett (Eds). *Interior Tools, Interior Tactics: Debates in Interior Theory and Practice* (pp. 159–169). Faringdon, UK: Libri Publishing.

Attiwill, S. (2005), Inter-story. In T. Nairn & M. Kalantzis (Eds.). *International Journal of the Humanities. Vol. 1.* Altona, Australia: Common Ground Publishing.

Attiwill, S. (2004). Towards an Interior History. *IDEA Journal 1*(5), 1–8.

Benjamin, W. (2002). *The Arcades Project.* H. Eiland & K. McLaughlin (Trans.). Cambridge, MA/London: Harvard University Press,

Betsky, A. (2005). From Box to Intersection—Architecture at the Crossroads. In George Flachbart & Peter Weibel, (Eds.) *Disappearing Architecture: From Real to Virtual to Quantum,* Basel, Switzerland: Birkhäuser.

Boccioni, U. (1925/1990). Futurism. In El Lissitzky & Hans Arp (Trans.). *The Isms* (p. viii). Zurich, Switzerland: Verlag/Lars Müller.

Boccioni, U., Carra, C., Russolo, L., Balla, G., & Severini, G. (1912). The Exhibitors to the Public. Retrieved January 12, 2009, from http://daemon.dyne.org/?page_id=17.

Brooker, G., & Stone, S. (2011). Spolia. In J. Fleming, et al. (Eds). *Interior Tools, Interior Tactics:.Debates in Interior Theory and Practice* (pp. 223–232). Faringdon, UK: Libri Publishing.

Brüderlin, M., & Lütgens, A. (Eds.). (2008). *Interieur, Exterieur: Living in Art: From Romantic Interior Painting to the Home Design of the Future.* Ostfildern, Germany: Hatje Cantz Verlag.

Colebrook, C. (2006). *Deleuze: A Guide for the Perplexed.* London/New York: Continuum,

Dean, M. (1994). *Critical and Effective Histories: Foucault's Method and Historical Sociology.* London/New York: Routledge,.

Deleuze, G. (1997). Postscript on the Societies of Control. In N. Leach (Ed.) *Rethinking Architecture: A Reader in Cultural Theory* (309–313). London/New York: Routledge.

Deleuze, G. (1988). R. Hurley (Trans.) *Spinoza: Practical Philosophy.* San Francisco: City Light Books.

Dorner, A. 1958. *The Way Beyond "Art."* New York: New York University Press.

Fuss, D. (2004). *The Sense of an Interior: Four Writers and the Rooms That Shaped Them.* New York/London: Routledge.

Kern, S. (2003). *The Culture of Time and Space. 1880–1918.* Cambridge, MA/London: Harvard University Press.

Pile, J. (2000). *A History of Interior Design.* London: Laurence King Publishing.

Rice, C. (2009). The Geography of the Diagram: The Rose Seidler House. In P. Sparke, A. Massey, T. Keeble, and B. Martin (Eds). *Designing the Modern*

Interior: From the Victorians to Today (pp. 131–143). Oxford, UK/New York: Berg,

Rice, C.. (2007). *The Emergence of the Interior: Architecture, Modernity, Domesticity.* London/New York: Routledge.

Troy, N. (1982). The Abstract Environment of De Stijl. In *De Stijl: 1917–1931. Visions of Utopia.* Walker Art Center Minneapolis, MN/New York: Abbeville Press.

van Doesburg, T. (1927). Schilderkunst en plastiek Elementarisme. *De Stijl VII,* (78), 82–87.

van Doesburg, T. (1928). Farben im Raum und Zeit. *De Stijl* VIII, 87/89 26–27.

Whitehead, A. N. (1933). *Adventures of Ideas.* Harmondsworth, UK: Penguin Books.

This essay discusses the importance of history to the design professions. A comprehensive knowledge of history informs the present and is a crucial tool to a good designer. A key difference between someone with a good eye or knack for design and a trained design professional is a knowledge and command of historical precedents and other key areas of knowledge. Like excellence in painting, in order to abstract an image, you must first be able to draw it correctly with a mastery of perspective and line. Similarly, to reject history in design, you must first know it.

It is my contention that one of the primary things that distinguishes the novice from the professional designer is education. A key component of a design education necessarily includes history—a history of the profession and a history of designed buildings. Knowledge of the past provides a foundation upon which to build through the continuation of a tradition or through its rejection. Either way, the knowledge of history is required. For example, the manner in which new knowledge is formed within architectural or design history falls under the domains of architecture/design and history. Using the example of architectural and design history, let us expand on these ideas.

Traditionally, in the United States. architectural history has been housed within academic departments of architecture or art history. The first architectural historians were actually architects or the relatives of architects. As the discipline has become more formalized in the last century, architectural historians have most often been taught art historical methods for research.

Architectural history, like all history, relies on interpretation by the historian and seeks to explain some phenomenon. In this way, the historian theorizes explanations for buildings, events, and circumstances. Taking a holistic view of a particular building, movement, professional body of work, or trend, the historian tells the story from which others can learn.

In their publication *Intersections: Architectural Histories and Critical Theories*, Iain Borden and Jane Rendell (2000) argue against the position held by some historians that theory is not necessary to the writing of history. "The question of whether to use theory or not is an irrelevance. Rather the question must be, first, which theory to use, and second, how to relate it to the ostensible objects of study." Borden and Rendell outline nine epistemological frameworks through which architectural historical inquiry can be conducted: theory as objects of study, new architectures, framing questions, critical history, interdisciplinary debates, disclosing methodology, self-reflexivity, re-engagement with theory, and praxis. They title the section that describes these nine frameworks the "nine challenges."

Since some historians do not overtly evoke any epistemological framework in their research, it is important to review each of the nine frameworks that Borden and Rendell discovered in their research prior to proposing one for this work. Each framework takes a different approach to the study of architectural history. "Theory as object" is the architectural history approach that describes the historic use of theories in architecture as a way to organize the architecture itself. "New architectures" employs the understanding of things outside architecture as a way to return to architecture. "Critical history" occurs within the domain of criticism and uses criticism as a tool for interpreting architecture. "Interdisciplinary debates" seek to put architecture in a broader context within which it becomes more meaningful to those who know very little or too much about architecture. In the "disclosing methodology" framework, the historian describes the complete process through which the historical narrative is written and thus reveals the decision-making process that led to the ultimate result. "Re-engagement with theory" involves the use of critical theory to look at architecture anew. A "praxis" approach takes into account how history shapes the practice of architecture.

While not all historians agree with the need for theory, Borden and Rendell (2000) reinforce the need for theory in history when they summarize the reason for the nine frameworks (or any theoretical framework in history research):

> If architectural history ignores the kinds of theoretical explorations undertaken by other disciplines, it runs the risk of doing something that, while perhaps perfectly enjoyable, will be meaningful only as a self-referential exercise and thus irrelevant to anyone else. (p. 15)

This implies that there is a reason for history and that it is relevant. The question then becomes, how? And, perhaps, why? How can history assist us today? And why do we need it at all?

I would propose that the answer to one question provides the answer for the other. History shows us where we come from. It demonstrates both success and failure in the past. With regard to design, history provides a record of the time, social issues, political concerns, and ethos of a given place. We can learn from others and thus invent anew in an informed and knowledgeable manner. One of the most prominent applications of history comes in the form of case study research common to most designers. Precedent studies form a basis for new work. There is no need to repeat the problems of the past if we can learn from them.

TABLE 4-1

Borden and Rendell's Nine epistemological frameworks

Theory as object	Architectural history approach Describes historic use of theories in architecture A way to organize the architecture itself.
New architectures	Employs the understanding of things outside architecture A way to return to architecture.
Framing Questions	New meaning can be given by posing new questions.
Critical history	Occurs within the domain of criticism and uses criticism A tool for interpreting architecture.
Interdisciplinary debates	Seek to put architecture in a broader context within which it becomes more meaningful to those who know very little or too much about architecture.
Disclosing methodology framework	Describes the complete process through which the historical narrative is written and reveals the decision making process which led to the ultimate result.
Self reflexivity	Makes historian conscious of what they are doing, and able to consider not only the study of the object of also the development of the frilled that focuses on and helps create the object. Seeks to revise the grounds of knowledge as well as what historical knowledge might say about a particular architectural event or space.
Re-engagement with theory	Involves the use of critical theory to look at architecture anew.
Praxis	Takes into account how history shapes the practice of architecture.

A Personal Perspective

One example of how history can inform us today comes from my own research on the Architects' Small House Service Bureau. In this research about the ASHSB organization, I became aware of a rela-
tionship with the American Institute of Architects and the ASHSB in the early twentieth century. I have written about this relationship previously (*Journal of Design History*). What is relevant to this current essay is how architects have proceeded to coalesce their own profession

over the last 150 years and what interior designers might learn from this. Many of the struggles over territory, multiple professional organizations, infighting among professionals over legislative issues, and the progressive loss of responsibility in the building and design process experienced by the architecture profession in the United States in the late nineteenth and early twentieth century are being repeated by the interior design profession. I contend that interior designers should understand the lessons learned from architecture. As much as we as interior designers want to differentiate ourselves from architects, we are making the connection to the profession of architecture by the very act of resisting it. Additionally, we are both professionals dedicated to the design of spaces and buildings and it is, in my view, pointless to pretend otherwise. Just as architects spent a lot of time in the early twentieth century trying to educate the public about their own importance, interior designers are seeking to educate the public about their importance. The public would more than likely understand the value of design once they have experienced it. The time wasted trying to educate the public could be better put to use in service of people, the planet, and the future of all design—which, ironically, also educates the public about the power and importance of design.

Reference

Borden, I., & Rendell, J. (2000.) *Intersections: Architectural Histories and Critical Theories* (p. 7). London: Routledge.

At first glance, the most remarkable thing is the ordinariness of the picture (Figure 4.1), a straightforward photograph of people at work. Identical desks are arranged neatly in rows, the hands of hundreds of typists, most in white blouses, addressing themselves to hundreds of identical typewriters. Circular concrete columns, also in rows, rise unadorned. Electric lights hang down while windows at the far left and right provide secondary light. It is a picture of female clerical workers in the industrial era.

This is a photograph of the most commonplace of moments. Whatever its origins, it is an ordinary picture—nothing majestic, nothing beautiful.

Except . . . the image haunts (Barthes, 1982). It is a glimpse into a world that is both commonplace and yet utterly strange.

High in the left corner stands a solitary man, underscoring the femaleness of the women who sit. He is singular; the women overseen number in the hundreds; the scale of the crowd catches the breath.

Figure 4.1 The massive order entry department in Chicago's Catalog Distribution Center began the process of filling customers' purchases in 1914.

Photo credit: © Sears Holdings + Historical Archives

How did so many women come to be in this one room? Can we imagine a business massive enough to require so many typewriters? The orders processed in this room exceeded 100,000 per day (Sears, Roebuck, & Co, 1908, plate 23). The clatter of so many typewriters must have been deafening.

The presence of so many women begs the question: where are all the male clerical workers? Two generations earlier, in the middle years of the nineteenth century, the world of business belonged exclusively to men.[1] Accountants, bookkeepers, clerks—all were men. It was the world of Dickens' *Nickleby*, Melville's *Bartleby*, and Poe's *Man of the Crowd*. It was an era of small offices in small rooms, merchants and their clerks, crowded together into dimly lit counting houses, and a time of ledger books, quill pens, black coats, and top hats. How disorienting this crowd of women would have looked to those punctilious scriveners. But our contemporary eyes understand at once—the Sears photograph was taken inside an office building.

About Historic Contexts of Interior Spaces

Although our contemporary cities are built of office buildings, seemingly as natural as the cars and streetlights, they did not even exist in Revolutionary-era Philadelphia, or steamboat-age St. Louis, or pre-fire Chicago. In that sense, the eyes of the black-suited clerk, raised in a city before office buildings, would have understood the Sears photograph more clearly than we do. He would have recognized its profound strangeness. He would have marveled at its scale and scarcely have recognized the work that was happening within. Typewriters? Women clerks? An open floor-plate? To say nothing of the invisible camera that captured the view. He would have seen them all as shocking, foreign, and radically transformative.

Standing in his place, we can begin to see this entire scene—its architecture, the hundreds of female workers, the electrical lamps, the identical typewriters, desks and chairs, even the absent Dictaphones, time clocks, and streetcars—as gears of a giant machine. This was a machine assembled for the singular purpose of the manipulation of an avalanche of paper; a "visible hand" (Chandler, 1977) of hundreds to coordinate the capitalist armies of business.

A New Typology

The office building in which the typists sat was the *Sears Administration Building*, designed by George C. Nimmons in 1905. It was but one piece of Nimmons' larger Sears, Roebuck & Co. campus on the west side of Chicago.[2] Although clad in columns and pilasters, and topped with

---

[1] The first documented employment of women clerical workers was in 1862 by the U.S. Treasury Department (Schlereth, 1992, p. 150).

[2] An incredible set of images of the Sears complex can be found in Sears, Roebuck & Co. (1908).

Figure 4.2 Guarantee Building.
Photo credit: © G.E. Kidder Smith/CORBIS

a pediment, this building was no expression of a timeless or ancient typology. The Sears Administration Building was an invention of the industrial age. Like all office buildings, it belonged exclusively to the modern world.[3]

Administrative tasks like bookkeeping, contracts, and correspondences are as ancient as bureaucracy. However, the spaces in which that administrative work took place, at least since the Renaissance, had been accommodated within other types of buildings—a minister's room in the royal palace, a back room in the merchant's warehouse, a front parlor in the lawyer's residence, a cathedral's chapterhouse, or the public space of a coffee-

house (Gatter, 1982, p. 14). The idea of a purposely designed, freestanding building in which a corporation might centralize clerical and administrative operations did not exist in the United States until the 1880s (Pevsner, 1976; Hill, 1901; Chandler, 1988).

In this sense, the Sears women shown in Figure 4.1 were subjects in a grand social experiment. Although their bodies appear doubly static, frozen both in a photograph and into a fixed spatial grid, they were in actuality on the vanguard of great social and spatial changes. The office interiors in which they labored, emerging in the absence of established precedents of "correct" design, were sites of profound experimentation and rapid change. The interior spatial logics shifted as quickly, as did the innovations in paper-processing machinery.

The early office interiors revealed themselves to be no more (and no less) than undisguised factories for the production of paper. Just as Ford was revolutionizing and deskilling labor on his assembly line, the theorists of the early office buildings were systemizing and deskilling clerical tasks. Clerical work was quantified, broken into small pieces and steps, and industrialized. To each task would be joined a machine; between the machines a frictionless flow. The Sears typists sat on the front line of this change, heroically weaving a paper web made from "a billion slips of paper that gear modern society into its daily shape" (Mills, 1951, p. 189). In that nascent moment of clarity, the early office interior was truly a filing cabinet in the sky.

---

[3] Influential architectural histories of the office building include: Condit (1964), Rowe (1976), Willis (1995), Landau and Condit (1996), and Bruegmann (1997).

Gender

The photograph of the Sears Order Entry Department captures a stark moment of gender segregation—hundreds of female typists inspected by a solitary male supervisor. He is the only man visible in the room, observing hundreds, himself nearly unseen. To modern eyes it is a shocking scene, how did such extreme segregation come to be?

To make any sense of it, it is necessary to abandon the deceptively "self-evident" notion that the Sears room was once empty.

Before the first worker arrived, before the first piece of furniture had been ordered, even before Nimmons had finished his first sketches, the space that would become the Sears Order Entry Department was *already* deeply striated by determinative social and gender rules. As the historian Robin Evans reminds us, "Ideas about the nature of things are built into the structures of our surroundings"[4] (1997, p. 41). We inhabit our spaces only within a matrix of pre-articulated social relationships. There are no spatial vacuums; space is already full, already saturated. It is social before it can even be space. As the twentieth-century theorist Michel Foucault put it:

> . . . we do not live in an homogeneous and empty space, but in a space that is saturated with qualities . . . The space

Figure 4.3 Employment of Women?
Photo credit: © Mary Evans Picture Gallery

[4] Robin Evans, "The Rites of Retreat and the Rites of Exclusion: Notes Towards the Definition of a Wall" in *Translations from Drawing to Building and Other Essays* (Cambridge, MA: MIT Press, 1997) 41.

in which we live, from which we are drawn out of ourselves, just where the erosion of our lives, our time, our history takes place, this space that wears us down and consumes us, is in itself heterogeneous. In other words, we do not live in a sort of a vacuum, within which individuals and things can be located, or that may take on so many different fleeting colours, but in a set of relationships that define positions which cannot be equated or in any way superimposed (1997, p. 331).

The presence of hundreds of women typists in an office interior is inescapably a question of how contested gender relationships materialized into a "heterogeneous" space (Foucault, 1997) during the emergent years of the early corporate office.

For most of the nineteenth century in the United States, it would have been unthinkable for a young woman to work in any office in any capacity. To the gender ideology of the time, it was thought obvious that the supposed natural and complementary differences between men and women should correlate to different and complementary social roles (Fines, 1990). Men were believed to be strong, aggressive, rational, and practical (although vulnerable to vices), while women were considered to be frailer, more aesthetic, religious, emotional, and more moral. These characteristics suggested that men were naturally well equipped to operate in the public world of the emerging industrial economy as tradesmen, professionals, merchants, clerks, and laborers. Conversely, women

were thought to be ideally suited for private and domestic life, entrusted with the education of children, food production, household tasks, and the moral upkeep of the family. There existed for the two genders two clearly distinct and separate realms: men in public and women at home.[5]

The physical, economic, and cultural space of the nineteenth century office was structured in a dozen different ways to preclude the possibility of female clerical workers. It was unthinkable for a woman to be paid the same wages as a man;[6] likewise, it was equally unthinkable for a woman to supervise a man's labor. Traditionalists and progressives alike both feared the licentious consequences of men and woman comingling in public.[7] Had women been permitted to work, the situation would have been further complicated by the restrictions

---

[5] With that said, there existed three discrete circumstances in which upstanding women might perform paid labor outside of the home. First, women might act as domestic workers for hire— jobs such as housekeepers, maids, nannies, and other forms of domestic service. Second, a woman might work temporarily during a time of family crisis in order to protect the family structure. Finally, young women were generally permitted to work outside of the home before marriage.

[6] From an 1886 newspaper article: "Without anyone but herself to maintain, except in very rare cases, a woman can naturally accept a lower wage than a man. For instance an advertisement asks for a female book-keeper to take a wage of sixteen shillings and a woman speaking German asks for employment at ten shillings a week. How can a man compete with that?" (Anderson, 1976, p. 59).

[7] There are many excellent histories and analyses of the early typewriter, including: Richard Current (1954), Davies (1982), Kittler (1999), Orbell (1991), Yates (1989), and the unaffiliated The Early Office Museum (n.d.).

that nineteenth-century women faced when moving through the public realm. The streets were regarded as part of the public sphere of men. If a woman went out to a park, or shopping, or traveled to a concert or library, it was expected that she travel with a friend or appropriate male escort (Fines, 1990, pp. 17–18). In such conditions it is not clear how a woman could manage a rushed morning commute into work.

Women and the Changing Work Force

And yet, there they are; literally hundreds of women in the photograph, filling the picture from edge to edge. They are seated at their desks, and they are typing. This is evidence that in spite of rigid and segregated nineteenth-century gender ideas, great changes were underway.

One reason for these shifts was the typewriter machine itself.[8] It was said to physically resemble a sewing machine, and required nimble finger dexterity to operate, similar to that mastered by young women while learning to play the piano. Furthermore, by industrializing the production of business correspondence, the typewriter allowed letter writing to be split between an author who wrote and a machine that printed. In that divide, men might maintain the privileged position of

author, while women could be hired as stenographer/typists to take their dictation and type the final copies. Within this divided structure of author and typist, the presumed docility and incurious nature of women—previously thought so undesirable in the rough and manly world of business—was transmuted into a positive corporate virtue.

A second reason why women entered the clerical workforce in large numbers at this time was a severe and sustained clerical labor shortage due to changing industrial needs. In the decades from 1870 to 1930, the number of clerical workers employed in the United States essentially doubled every ten years—from 77,000 to nearly 4,000,000. This represented an ever-increasingly percentage of all workers; in 1870, approximately one worker of every 160 was a clerical worker; by 1930 one of every 12 workers was a clerk (Davis, p. 178). By definition, the job required literacy, fluent English, math skills, and a respectable office demeanor. To the ideas of the day, this ruled out most of the recent immigrants, the uneducated, the laboring classes, and freed African Americans. One logical alternative was to permit women to join the clerical workforce. In 1870, only 2 percent of clerical workers were women. By 1930, approximately 50 percent of all clerical workers in the United States were women. And of the typists in 1930, 95 percent were women (Davis, pp. 178–9).

Tremendous forces were aligning in the late nineteenth century to shake gender assumptions about the nature of clerical work. When Nimmons designed a large

---

[8] Jane Addams (1912, p.74) declared alarm at the possibility, recounting how "Often an unattached country girl who has come to live in a city, has gradually fallen into a vicious life from the sheer lack of social restraint."

floor-plate for Sears, he did not design an empty room in a spatial void. The interior of that room was already the locus of complex and contested ideas about the relationship between work and gender: Who was allowed to participate in economic public life? Who could walk on the public streets? How was literacy distributed among the middle classes? How was sexual attraction regulated and channeled? How would rapid technological change alter existing social relationships and gender assumptions?

The interior of the Sears, Roebuck & Co. order entry department was gendered and social before it was even built.

Things Not Seen

"For the private person, living space becomes for the first time antithetical to the place of work. The former is constituted by the interior; the office is its complement."
—Walter Benjamin (1969)

Walter Benjamin reminds us that interior spaces do not exist one at a time. They are not isolated nor neatly contained within the boundaries of their four perimeter walls. Rather, interior spaces are embedded within larger systems of spatial organization; they are components of larger, multifaceted spatial paradigms. Consider all

Fig 4.4 Dearborn & Randolph street traffic jam.
Photo credit: © Chicago History Museum

of the structures and contexts, invisible to the camera lens, that brought this moment into being: a massive continent-scaled web of railroad lines to deliver Sears merchandise, tenement buildings, streetcars, even the brutal racial segregation of post-fire Chicago. The office comes to be an office only in relationship to the sidewalk, the street, the courthouse, the ghetto, and the dance hall. Like every interior space, it is made possible only in relationship to all of those spaces that it is not.

Technological Space

"Full lighting and the eye of a supervisor capture better than darkness, which ultimately protected. Visibility is a trap. It is an important mechanism, for it automatizes and dis-individualizes power. . . . It does so not for power itself, nor for the immediate salvation of a threatened society: its aim is to strengthen the social forces—to increase production, to develop the economy, spread education, raise the level of public morality; to increase and multiply."

—Michel Foucault, (1977)

The Sears Order Entry Department was a technological space. The work that women performed there, and the environment in which they labored, were fundamentally structured and permeated by machines. Look again at Figure 4.1. Consider first the workers. Each is seated before a typing machine. The operator's task involved the pressing of metal buttons on the surface of the typing machine, in rigidly defined sequences. Her supervisors would keep

TRANSCRIBING FROM THE PHONOGRAPH.

Figure 4.5 Transcribing from Edison's perfected phonograph.
Photo credit: © CORBIS

careful track of productivity by recording and graphing her keystrokes per minute. The human operator and her machine were an inseparable ensemble, so closely linked that in the early decades of the machine's use, both were called by the same name— "typewriter" (Kittler, 1999, p.191).

Two workers per desk sat facing each other upon an identical factory-made chair. These desks were designed to facilitate the movement of paper. Each was kept deliberately clear; in addition to the typewriters, only letter files and copy-stands were permitted on the surface. Whereas previous generations of clerks managed their own storage in the cubbies of their workspaces, the Sears typists were strictly prohibited from removing any piece of paper from the visible workflow. It was imperative that there be no place for papers to pause or become lost. Careful inventories would have regulated which tools and supplies were permitted to be stored in the desk drawers provided, and the managers would conduct periodic inspections to ensure compliance.[9]

Seated in a carefully designed position before her machine, the labor of each typist would be overseen by the manager. Nothing in the room was permitted to block the view of the overseer; visual control from the back of the room was absolute. Every typist understood that she could be observed at any given moment. Conversely, the typists were never in a position to observe the manager; their seats faced uniformly forward. Eyes locked on their papers and machines, the rows of typists resemble rows of pupils in a schoolroom. In Foucault's sense, the typists were always the objects of the manager's controlling gaze; the ones looked upon. Never were they the subjects who could look.

The gridded layout of desks was almost certainly the design of a manager (it is certain that it would have been a man) who would no doubt have read the numerous office planning manuals published in that era. He would have mastered the principles of "scientific management" developed by Frederick Winslow Taylor from his studies of manual laborers on the factory floor.[10]

Like Taylor, he would have attempted the quantification of each clerical work-task (in time, materials, and money) and then proposed the design of assembly-line-like systems. The work of each typist would have been measured by mechanical counters and clocks, and to improve speed, typists would have been instructed in the latest techniques of nonvisual "touch-typing" (Schlereth, 1992, p. 160).

Every single worker, task, and item of furniture and equipment in the room would have been studied—timed, weighed, photographed, measured, counted, graphed—and optimized.

Then, as if building an engine, the scientific manager would have connected each element to the next, creating a predictable and quantifiable mechanical system. In theory, nothing was left to habit or chance. Everything would be rationalized, optimized, controlled, and made visible.

We are accustomed to thinking of modern architecture as being shaped by technology. The revolutionary consequences of the steel (and concrete) frame, the elevator, electricity, HVAC, and indoor plumbing are well known and widely accepted. But the example of the Sears Order Entry Department challenges us to think more broadly about the ramifications of technological change. With the clarity of its extreme example before us, we are reminded that the spatial implications of industrial technologies are not limited to architectural elements. Typewriter keys are a spatial technology. Industrially manufactured chairs are spatial technologies, as is the file cabinet. Even the railroad lines that

---

[9] Standards and practices for the early scientific office managers were described in manuals such as Galloway (1919), Leffingwell (1917), Parsons (1909), and Schulze (1913).

[10] The most comprehensive biography of Taylor is Kanigel (1997). Taylor's most important work was published late in his life, long after his ideas had won wide acceptance (Taylor, 1911).

shipped Sears' orders across the continent were interior spatial technologies.

Which is to say that the history of interior space of the last 150 years is inseparable from the lived experiences of technological modernity—experiences shaped by the ongoing convergence of space, machinery, machine-made objects, and the human body (Sparke, 2008).

A Magical Mirror

"History is a magical mirror. Who peers into it sees his own image in the shape of events and developments."
—Sigfried Giedion (1948, p. 2)

The mystery of looking into the past is also an invitation to look into the present; the photograph is also a mirror. While we sometimes imagine ourselves as living on a knife's edge of technological change, destabilized by a seeming avalanche of modernization, the mirror of the Sears photograph reminds us that the avalanche has been with us for generations. The Chicago world in which those typists lived was as shaken by technological modernization as

is our own. They are unsettling confirmations not of our uniqueness, but rather of a paradoxical continuity-of-discontinuities across the generations.[11]

Opening our eyes to the lost spaces of the past is no mere exercise in good taste, erudition, or refinement. It is a theoretical tool to pry open the hidden possibilities of the present. Looking into the photograph, we are reminded that the world was once a radically different place. Our contemporary present becomes recast as provocative and strange; how volatile, how malleable, our moment suddenly appears against the sweep of historical possibility. If young farm girls from Iowa and Minnesota could end up seated in rows by the hundreds, operating "discursive machine guns" (Kittler, 1999, p. 191) in a paperwork factory on the west side of Chicago, what kind of world might we designers imagine for our own young gardeners, video game hackers, or Bollywood dancers?

---

[11] For an extended and thought-provoking discussion of the cultural ramifications of technological modernization, see Marshall Berman (1982).

Discussion Questions

1. Discuss the main themes of this article. What concepts emerge from reading Ronn Daniel's ideas?
   a. Typology
   b. Gender
   c. Spaces of the past
   d. Looking through the mirror
   e. Reconciling society with architecture, activity with gender and space

2. How is Daniel constructing meaning in the way he is studying the Victorian-era office workers? The architecture? The interior space and its use? Why is this valuable to understand?

3. Daniel writes, "Looking into the photograph, we are reminded that the world was once a radically different place. Our contemporary present

becomes recast as provocative and strange; how volatile, how *malleable,* our moment suddenly appears against the sweep of historical possibility." Unpack this concept in more detail. What does he mean?

4. Find a historic image of a well-known building that you have studied, but perhaps only seen the exterior. Find the interior photos and place it in its actual historic context: the era, political or economic times, the place, and its society.

a. How do you perceive the past and how you live now?

b. What impact does space and history have on whether you are a man or a woman? In your hometown or on another continent? Discuss the impact of culture and gender on how we make design meanings. What are these specifically in terms of gender? Culture? History? Whose history?

References

Addams, J. (1912). *A New Conscience and an Ancient Evil.* New York: The MacMillan Company.

Anderson, G. (1976). *Victorian Clerks.* Manchester, UK: Manchester University Press.

Barthes, R. (1982). *Camera Lucida: Reflections on Photography* (R. Howard, Trans.). New York: Hill and Wang. (Original work published in 1980).

Benjamin, W. (1969). Paris: Capital of the Nineteenth Century. In H. Arendt (Ed.), *Illuminations.* New York: Doubleday.

Berman, M. (1982). Introduction: Modernity—Yesterday, Today, and Tomorrow. In *All That Is Solid Melts into Air: The Experience of Modernity.* (pp. 15–36). New York: Penguin Books.

Bjelopera, J. P. (2005). *City of Clerks: Office and Sales Workers in Philadelphia, 1870–1920.* Urbana, IL: University of Illinois Press.

Bruegmann, R. (1997). *The Architects and the City: Holabird and Roche of Chicago, 1890–1918.* Chicago: University of Chicago Press.

Chandler, A. (1988). The Organization of Manufacturing and Transportation. In T.K. McCraw (Ed.), *The Essential Alfred Chandler: Essays Toward a Historical Theory of Big Business* (pp. 218). Boston: Harvard Business School Press.

Chandler, A. (1977). *The Visible Hand: The Managerial Revolution in American Business.* Cambridge, MA: Belknap Press.

Condit, C. (1964). *The Chicago School of Architecture.* Chicago: University of Chicago Press.

Current, R. (1954). *The Typewriter and the Men Who Made It.* Urbana, IL: University of Illinois Press.

Davies, M. (1982). *Woman's Place is at the Typewriter: Office Work and Office*

Workers, 1870–1930. Philadelphia: Temple University Press.

Dickens, C. (1839). *The Life and Adventures of Nicholas Nickleby*. London: Chapman & Hall.

Evans, R. (1997). Rites of Retreat and the Rites of Exclusion: Notes Towards the Definition of a Wall. In *Translations from Drawing to Building and Other Essays*. Cambridge, MA: MIT Press.

Fines, L. (1990). *The Souls of the Skyscraper: Female Clerical Workers in Chicago, 1870–1930*. Philadelphia: Temple University Press.

Folland, A. K. (1994). *Engendering Business: Men and Women in the Corporate Office, 1870–1930*. Baltimore: The Johns Hopkins University Press.

Foucault, M. (1997). Of Other Spaces: Utopias and Heterotopias. In N. Leach (Ed.), *Rethinking Architecture: A Reader in Cultural Theory*. London: Routledge.

Foucault, M. (1977). *Panopticism. In Discipline and Punish: The Birth of the Prison* (A. Sheridan, Trans.). New York: Vintage Books, 195–228.

Galloway, L. (1919). *Office Management: Its Principles and Practice, Covering Organization, Arrangement, and Operation with Special Consideration of the Employment, Training, and Payment of Office Workers*. New York: The Ronald Press Company.

Gatter, L. S. (1982). *The Office: An Analysis of the Evolution of a Workplace*. Master's Thesis, Massachusetts Institute of Technology.

Giedion, S. (1948). *Mechanization Takes Command: a Contribution to Anonymous History*. Oxford, UK: Oxford University Press.

Hill. G. (1901). Office Building. In R. Sturgis (Ed.), *A Dictionary of Architecture and Building: Biographical, Historical and Descriptive, Vol. 3*. New York: The MacMillan Company.

Kanigel, R. (1997). *The One Best Way: Frederick Winslow Taylor and the Enigma of Efficiency*. New York: Viking.

Kittler, F. (1999*). Gramophone, Film, Typewriter* (G. Winthrop-Young & M. Wutz, Trans.). Stanford, CA: Stanford University Press.

Landau S. B., & Condit, C. (1995). *Rise of the New York Skyscraper, 1865–1913*. New Haven, CT: Yale University Press.

Leffingwell, W. H. (1917). *Scientific Office Management: A Report on the Results of the Applications of the Taylor System of Scientific Management to Offices Supplemented with a Discussion of How to Obtain the Most Important of These Results*. Chicago/New York: A. W. Shaw Company.

Melville, H. (1853, November and December). *Bartleby: A Story of Wall Street* (pp. 546–550; pp. 609–616) Putnam's.

Mills, C. W. (1951). *White Collar: The American Middle Class*. New York: Oxford University Press.

Orbell, J. (1991). The Development of Office Technology. In A. Turton (Ed.), *Managing Business Archives* (pp. 60–83). Oxford: British Archives Council.

Parsons, C. C. (1909). *Business Administration: The Principles of Business Organization and System, and the Actual Methods of Business Operation and Management.* Chicago: The System Company.

Pevsner, N. (1976).Warehouses and Office Buildings. In *A History of Building Types.* Princeton, NJ: Princeton University Press.

Poe, E.A. (1840, December). Man of the Crowd. *Burton's Gentleman's Magazine.*

Rowe, C. (1976). Chicago Frame. In *Mathematics of the Ideal Villa and Other Essays.* Boston: MIT Press.

Schlereth, T. (1992). The World and Workers of the Paper Empire. In *Cultural History and Material Culture: Everyday Life, Landscapes, Museums.* Charlottesville: University Press of Virginia.

Schulze, W. (1913). *The American Office: Its Organization, Management and Records.* New York, Key Publishing Company.

Sears, Roebuck, & Co. (1908). Plate 23-Rear. *50 Stereoscopic Views of the Great Plant of Sears, Roebuck and Co.* Retrieved August 2, 2010, from http://www.flickr.com/photos/wroush/sets/72157623441381709/with/4144595045/

Sparke, P. (2008). *The Modern Interior.* London: Reaktion Books.

Taylor, F.W. (1911). *The Principles of Scientific Management.* New York: Harper and Brothers Publishers.

The Early Office Museum. (n.d.). Retrieved July 2010 from http://www.officemuseum.com.

Willis, C. (1995). *Form Follows Finance: Skyscrapers and Skylines in New York and Chicago.* New York: Princeton Architectural Press.

Yates, J. (1989). *Control Through Communication: The Rise of System in American Management.* Baltimore: The Johns Hopkins University Press.

SUMMARY

If we consider what the theories propose and then the provocation, we see divergent ideas about historic contexts of space. We might think about space as history, space as ornament or absence of ornament, or space as promoting gender divisions in a specific historic era. We understand spaces and their meanings through the lens of history and how historic contexts enrich our understanding of spaces today. While we turn to different theoretical constructs about spatial experiences in Chapters 5 and 6, the context of history remains a component of how spaces are understood as a backdrop to how we understand cultural theory, gender, and other issues that emerge as we continue enriching our understanding of the theories and concepts that explore spatial experiences at various time periods.

SUGGESTED READINGS

Rose, G. (2001). Visual Methodologies. London: Sage.

Hodder, I. (1994). Interpretation of Documents and Visual Culture. In N. Denzin & Y. Lincoln (Eds.). Handbook of Qualitative Research. Thousands Oaks, CA: Sage.

OVERVIEW QUESTIONS FOR DISCUSSION

1. What perspective of history is understood in this chapter?

2. How are ideas about artefacts and ornament framed within contexts of spaces by Turpin and Attiwill?

    a. How are they similar?
    b. How different?

3. What is Turpin saying about Modernism and the rejection of ornament?

4. Compare Turpin's ideas and the concepts of "ornament as social qualifier" and "ornament as social equalizer" to how Mendoza unpacks Modernism as an "equalizer" in Brazil in the Provocation in Chapter 6. Examine these concepts of "equalizer" and the impact of space on how political and social meaning occurred in different historic periods.

5. Discuss Tucker's presentation of Borden and Rendell's nine epistemological frameworks for architectural history: theory as objects of study, new architectures, framing questions, critical history, interdisciplinary debates, disclosing methodology, self-reflexivity, re-engagement with theory, and praxis.

    a. What are their specific characteristics?
    b. How are they explicated in a theory, historic, or design problem?

6. How would you frame the context of the example presented by Daniel within the context of the frameworks as Lisa Tucker lists them when she refers to Borden and Rendell?

7. What are the meanings of history when Daniel speaks of the mysteries that are deep in the visual images?

    a. Why is this important when learning about meanings of spaces?

CHAPTER 5
Alternative Spaces of Experience

users, ephemeral interiors, immaterial contexts, lived experiences, location, place-making, meanings of objects/things in diverse spaces, voices, interior linings as storytellers, theatrical contexts, theatrical space, inside-outside, internal experiences, external experiences, linings, spatial rationality, space as a user's logic, patterns, pattern-making, technological spaces, prototyping experiences

AFTER READING THIS CHAPTER, YOU WILL BE ABLE TO:

- Interpret how users understand and perceive spaces from their perspective.
- Distinguish concepts about users and how they might understand and perceive spaces from their perspective.
- Theorize about "spaces of experience."
- Ask questions about how we attribute different meanings to different types of experiences.
- Assess why a space may not only be a "container."
- Distinguish space as an experience of linings—what are the voices uncovered?
- Judge how the interior space is inherently ephemeral and what this means in the context of experiences within diverse spaces.
- Characterize what it means to prototype lived experience.

INTRODUCTION

What is our actual, lived experience as we move in and around diverse spaces and places? Who is the user? Whether we appropriate, transform, or move in diverse spaces, we engage spaces as places of experience: living, working, for recreation, for comfort. All spaces, no matter what the context, are appropriated by people and for their personal and subjective experiences. As we physically move about our environment spaces and places, we are informed by those spaces; however, the experience of the spaces occurs through inner senses.

This chapter investigates alternative spaces of experience in the context of the material as immaterial, the real as perception, the ephemeral as the theatrical or poetic, and what it means to change our perspective of a given space or place, object, or environment at any point in time as we experience it. This means understanding the idea of user, of the person who experiences space in all of its various contexts. As a teacher, I always tell my students we cannot know how a person experiencing the spaces we design thinks or perceives, as we cannot know the inside of their mind. Ornament, object, and artefact and the spaces that they inhabit—all of these exist for people to appropriate (use) them perceptually, psychologically, or physically. These users are people, you and I, and these perceptions are informed in many ways.

Recently in a paper about living in outer space, I wrote:

> People's experiences are shaping inhabited spaces regardless of their location . . . [People's] responses begin with visual perception and subjective internal responses that we have within our heads, and each of us responds independently of the next person, depending on our cognitive self. As individual human beings, we have as much intelligence as we have ways of understanding and learning. We develop meanings of both what we learn cognitively and subsequently how we react within our environment with others and with the objects that surround us.

These are, in very general terms, elements of a phenomenological perspective (Poldma, 2011, pp. 3–4). The phenomenological experience of space is a subjective one, wherein people have lived experiences in real time and in all of the senses (Vaikla-Poldma 2003; Poldma 2011). Phenomenological experience understands spaces in multiple ways and allows us to think of places as space experienced, and not necessarily in the physical way we see a place filled with objects, a container.

Maurice Merleau-Ponty, philosopher (1945/1958), suggests that perception always is affected by both past and present concepts every person has of self, of the spaces they have inhabited, and of the objects and experiences they already possess (pp. 315–329). Each experience is lived in the complete understanding of other contexts that influence our lived experience. Merleau-Ponty challenges the perspective of philosopher Emmanuel Kant by suggesting that:

> Kant tried to draw a strict demarcation line between space as the form of external experiences and the things given within that experience. (p. 283)

Conversely, Merleau-Ponty suggests that this is impossible:

> Space is not the setting (real or logical) in which things are arranged, but the means whereby the position of things becomes possible. This means that . . . I do not reflect,

but rather live among things and vaguely regard space at one moment as the setting for things, at another as their common attribute or else I do reflect: catching space at its source, and now think . . . [space as living] only through the medium of a subject who traces out and sustains them; and pass from spatialized to spatializing space. . . . with geometrical space having interchangeable dimensions. (p. 284)

Merleau-Ponty suggests that space has far more nonphysical qualities than we have been led to understand, and he goes on to challenge physical ideas of space as separate entities, defined by boundaries like top and bottom or of space as a container (pp. 284–288).

With these ideas in mind, in this chapter we begin with a theoretical perspective from Rabah Bousbaci, who considers the user in the context of changing and dynamic spaces. Bousbaci suggests that space, and our experience of it, changes with each and every individual, context, and the way we move through it. Whether it is in the poetic expression of place and self or the examination of philosophical theory, users are human beings who use spaces subjectively, however they perceive and grasp them, in other words, following Bousbaci's logic of the user.

DJ Huppatz in "The Spaces of Interiors: Staging Fantasies" explores how the interior is inherently ephemeral and theorizes about the changing nature of the ephemeral. Huppatz challenges historic views of interior spaces as "coherent stable objects of study" and the lack of critical theorizing about interior spaces in and of themselves. Huppatz proposes that first and foremost interior spaces are "places of habitation" by exploring these ideas in the context of retailer Ralph Lauren's flagship store in New York. He brings together historic perspectives of designs in the 1980s with spatial concepts of desire and theatrical context in lived experiences of spaces.

In "Lining Stories: Conversations with Inside Trades," Julieanna Preston provokes with her consideration of the spaces of linings as places of experiences. The collection of stories provokes understanding of everyday objects and their resistance to the "hierarchical division between concrete reality, that is, the here and now, and philosophic inquiry, or the poetic constitution of things."

Finally, we examine Merleau-Ponty's ideas in the C. Thomas Mitchell's Dialogues and Perspectives entitled "Prototyping Lived Experiences." Here we apply these ideas to specific contexts of buildings, spaces, and places through the eyes of lived experiences. Mitchell explores historic ideas of aesthetic form, about ideas of top and bottom and how lived experiences are not always consistent with the aesthetic concepts of buildings as architects and designers perceive these. Mitchell's dialogue considers how environments are more than geometric compositions, how spaces become places of experiences lived out in daily life, and how technology and its mediation are constantly affecting spatial contexts by adding different dimensions in ways never before experienced.

REFERENCES

Merleau-Ponty, M. (1945/1958). *Phenomenology of Perception.* London: Routledge.

Poldma, T. (2010). Transforming Interior Spaces: Enriching Subjective Experiences Through Design Research. *Journal of Research Practice, 6(2),*12.

Vaikla-Poldma, T. (2003). *An Investigation of Learning and Teaching Processes in an Interior Design Class: An Interpretive and Contextual Inquiry.* Unpublished doctoral thesis. McGill University, Montreal, Québec, Canada.

Since the accession of design knowledge to the ranks of modern university departments, the built environment, which represents one of the main areas of study of this knowledge, has endured a huge fragmentation according to the analytical model of modern inquiry. It too finds itself fragmented into several disciplinary fields, most often erected into competing silos: product design, graphic design, interior design, architectural design, urban design, landscape design, and so on. This parceling of logic in itself can be quite beneficial to the extent that it ensures a certain depth of thinking when the time comes to consider objects of limited and very specific knowledge. Nonetheless, in its most basic and essential aspects, there is one object of knowledge that continues to elude the understanding and reasoning of all these disciplinary silos. It continues to stand as an obstacle and challenge to all the leakages of what Henri Raymond (1984) calls "spatial rationality." We refer, of course, to the occupant, the individual who is commonly called the *user* of the built world:

> The occupant . . . remains at the heart of architecture: as a negative, refusing to dwell in theory, and as obstinacy, attaching himself obstinately to housing models that architectural reason has

condemned. But he is also at the heart of the problem of spatial rationality: Should we plan without the occupant? How should we plan with him? . . . In all of this, the occupant's situation and skill can play a major role; we may be permitted to think that this is one of the future adventures of reason. (pp. 252–253)

The User's Obstinacy and Refusal to Dwell in Theory

For the purposes of this essay, consider a very ordinary urban occurrence: An individual, a city dweller, strolls along Sainte-Catherine Street in Montréal, Canada, on a sunny autumn afternoon and, every so often, stops in front of a store window to examine and admire the objects displayed. Two questions, existential at the very least, challenge design disciplines. First, in which disciplinary or professional boundaries does this person find himself? Is it in the product designer's, the graphic designer's, the interior designer's, the architect's, the urban designer's, or the landscape architect's? Each of these professionals would seem to have a right to claim that this person is truly within his field of expertise: Each would say, "He's my user." But does the person in front of the store window really care about knowing which disciplinary field he finds himself in, or at what moment he crosses over from one to the other? Yet, at that very moment, that actual experience or slice of life that the person in our example is undergoing in front of the store window is not fragmented into various experiences. The person is not telling himself, *I'm living an architectural experience, now suddenly I'm going through a manufactured object experience, and now I'm off on an urban experience,* and so on.

These same questions can be asked in the same way for many other situations: a person seated at a table on a bistro terrace, or in an office at the top of a highrise in New York City or Singapore with an inverted view of the city; a driver of a car or a city bus who manoeuvres through the streets of the city every day; a person waiting for the bus in a bus shelter; or a glazier working to repair part of the stained glass in a church, or perhaps even to repair the outside of a shop window on Sainte-Catherine Street in Montréal. In fact, these very ordinary urban occurrences in which our city dweller, or *Homo Urbanus* (Paquot, 1990), engages constitute a comprehensive or a total situation, according to the meaning of the concept advanced by Maurice Merleau-Ponty in his famous phenomenology of the body (Merleau-Ponty, 1962). The experience that this city dweller lives is not fragmented at all; conversely, it is integral and whole. In an editorial on an issue of the journal *Urbanisme* devoted specifically to the theme of the user, Thierry Paquot readily points out and drives

home this whole and total condition: He explains that the user "is first and foremost a human being, a mortal who exists, there, and tries to enable the plurality of his ego to express itself without accepting to have his personality parcelled out and broken down into tiny fragments. The user remains whole and refuses to divide himself up and play an infinite number of roles. This unity confers on him his identity and enables him, at all times and in all places, to be a user of the world" (Paquot, 1999, p. 51).

If our user's life experience is a total one, what idea have all these design disciplines come to respectively about this person who still lays no claim to any disciplinary field? Do they have or share a common conception of the user's human condition? (Arendt, 1958) Or instead do they hold different but complementary views? I would venture to say here that the user constitutes a phenomenon that, in essence, escapes disciplinary logic: The user is a transdisciplinary phenomenon, crossing all these disciplines without any one of them being able to claim complete right of ownership to understanding and acquiring all the issues that might flow out of each of the professional design practices. This complexity, which characterizes the phenomenon of the user, is the true difficulty and presents an obstacle and a challenge to understanding among our disciplines. Based on this, it might appear that a setback exists for the design disciplines, but in reality, this is an opportunity to be seized. First and foremost, it is a chance for our disciplines to cultivate a certain spirit of modesty toward what we know: The object of thought is, by principle, always superior to the thought process that attempts to understand it, to grasp or even to manipulate it. As well, design disciplines might find there a common issue to unite them when the time comes to assign themes to the disciplinary and professional specialties unique to each of them; our achievements and professional work are aimed at the same user whose life experience is not divided. Given this, the theme of the user could be used in true arbitration fashion to clarify boundary disputes among our disciplines.

The Lesson of Prévert's Glazier

How should we now consider and approach the notion of our common user? Are there specific concepts or visions that can help us in this endeavour? In fact, when it comes to much of the essential dimensions that make up the user's human condition, there are major gaps in our disciplinary design knowledge that researchers need to address on a priority basis. For example, I cite the primordial phenomenon of the body. Setting aside the knowledge that biology, ergonomics, psychology, anthropology, physics, and geometry all offer on this subject, what knowledge and visions have we developed about our user's body, his spatiality, and the various situations he encounters, among others? What common ground can the product designer, the graphic designer, the interior designer, the architect, the urban designer, and the landscape designer find to address the issue of the body?

In this section, I would like to explore the possibilities offered by a concept so common that we use it regularly, even spontaneously and automatically, in our everyday conversations and professional language as designers: the concept of *solution*. I will attempt to expand my ideas on the subject by using some supporting texts borrowed from three authors in particular: poet Jacques Prévert and architectural theorists Robert Prost and Philippe Boudon. Design professionals often express their ideas, and the results of their projects, in terms of solutions: design solution, architectural solution, urban planning solution, simple solution to a complex situation, inspired solution, and the like. But when we engage in a little phenomenology of this concept in the framework of our disciplines, we soon realize that what seems to one professional like a final solution in a design process may be nothing more than an initial solution to another professional. A chair, a bench, a lighting fixture, or an electrical appliance that is the final solution in the industrial design process may simply be initial solution elements in the interior design process, landscape architecture, or urban design. An atmosphere or existing interior space can be the starting point for a craftsperson's or a product designer's proposal (for instance, made-to-measure furniture). In the same way, the plans and guidelines for an urban project may provide the initial conceptual backdrop to the work of the architect. What constitutes the end point for one person becomes the starting point for another's work. The eye that Prévert's glazier casts on the world illustrates this phenomenon clearly and perceptively. What sociologists dryly call the social division of labor is in fact a basic characteristic of the human condition, one that famed poet Jacques Prévert renders admirably in his poem "Chanson du vitrier":

How beautiful is
What you can see
Through the sand through the glass
Through the window panes
Here look for example
At how beautiful
This tree feller is
There in the distance
Chopping down a tree
To make boards
For the furniture maker
Who must fashion them into a large bed
For the young flower girl
Who is marrying
The lamplighter
Who lights the streetlamps every night
So that the shoemaker can see clearly
To repair the shoes of the shoeshine boy
Who polishes the shoes of the grinder
Who sharpens the scissors of the hairdresser
Who cuts the hair of the bird seller
Who gives his birds to everyone
So that everyone may be in good spirits.
(1963)

But what then becomes of the user in this tangled web of solutions that are final for some and starting points for others? In reality, the user has a vital role to play because he or she is the one who brings closure to all the design processes: The user is the equivalent of Mr. or Ms. Everyone in Prévert's poem. Once all the designers have delivered their final solutions, everything in the user's world becomes a starting point, an initial solution for experiences and life projects. They become part of the user's overall experience, his or her life experience, and the user imbues them with his or her own meanings.

I borrowed the concept of initial and final solutions from Robert Prost's thoughts, particularly his thesis on architectural works as "works in progress": "We want to draw attention to the possibility of considering architectural phenomena as works in progress and not merely works that find status and complete and definitive legitimacy only at the moment of their creation, like works of art" (Prost 1991, p. 40). Robert Prost's reading of the problem posed by architectural design (Prost, 1992) attempts to group together the four main players in an architectural project: the client, the architect, the builder, and the occupant. Each appears as a player acting completely in his or her own area of skill: the client formulates the goals and uses of the project; the architect proposes architectural solutions; the contractor turns the architectural solutions into reality; and the occupant appropriates and transforms the architectural work. The notion of the work—that is, the architectural solution for Prost—appears to be at the heart of the process: "Rather than looking at architectural solutions from the standpoint of one question (What are they made of?) I will introduce three additional questions: What ends/uses do they fulfill?

How are they made? And, finally, how do they transform themselves?" (Prost 1992, p. 13). The first two questions query the design process. The work, or built architectural solution, appears in a nodal position, constituting the end of the design and realization process and, at the same time, marking the beginning of another process, that of appropriation and transformation through social practices (whence the notion of a work in progress). The work, which the architect considers to be the final solution, acquires the status of an initial solution for the occupant, a sort of infrastructure that provides support to his projects and initiatives regarding his dwelling. In other words, it is "free of its designers and status as the final solution and open to the social practices and status of the initial solution" (Prost 1992, p.133).

The user is the one who brings closure to the overall process. Once the solution (or solutions) is delivered, it becomes an open work: open to the user's life experience, his or her appropriation and transformation projects. This concept of *open work*, formulated by Umberto Eco and taken here in its architectural sense, is borrowed from Philippe Boudon (1969). Boudon's study of those living in a residential neighborhood designed and completed in 1926 by Le Corbusier at Pessac, near Bordeaux in France, shows the scope of transformations introduced into the work of a famous thinker of the Modern Movement by the occupants. Henri Lefebvre, who penned the preface to Boudon's book, underscores this act of acquisition: "And what did the occupants do?

Instead of incorporating themselves into this receptacle and adapting to it impassively, they occupied it actively to a certain extent. They showed what it means to inhabit a place: in one activity. They worked on, changed and added to what they were given. What did they add? What they needed. Philippe Boudon shows the significance of the differences they made. They introduced qualities. They built a differentiated social space" (Lefebvre, 1969). It is in this sense that one of the proposals Boudon made in the study was the conclusion that architecture is an open work, in other words, open to the occupant's initiatives and corrections: "Based on an occupant's own expression, architecture can be considered an infrastructure upon which the occupant's free expression can evolve both qualitatively (combinations) and quantitatively (surfaces) within fairly broad boundaries" (Boudon, 1969, p. 106).

We have seen that the user's logic extends far beyond the disciplinary logic in which we are involved. To end on a poetic note, I gladly offer Prévert's "Cancre" as a fitting comparison to the user:

He says no with his head
But yes with his heart
He says yes to what he likes
He says no to the teacher
He stands
He is questioned
And all the problems are posed
Suddenly he is overcome with uncontrollable laughter
And he erases everything
The numbers and the words

The dates and the names
The sentences and the traps
And in spite of the teacher's threats
And the jeers of the prodigal students

With chalk of all colours
On the blackboard of misfortune
He draws the face of happiness. (Prévert, 1972)

Discussion Questions

1. Bousbaci proposes a theoretical concept of the "user."
   a. Who is this user? What is his or her experience of the life-world?
   b. How does this user experience differ from that of the architect, designer, or businessperson?

2. How can we examine the idea of "user" and the meanings that they construct?

3. Unpack the concepts of Prevert's poem in light of Bousbaci's ideas. What is the initial and final solution? Why is Bousbaci referring to design solutions?

4. Discuss the ideas that Bousbaci concludes with in the essay.

References

Arendt, H. (1958). *The Human Condition.* Chicago: The University of Chicago Press.

Boudon, P. (1969). *Pessac de Le Corbusier.* Paris: Dunod.

Lefebvre, H. (1969). Preface. In Philipe Boudon, *Pessac de Le Corbusier.* Paris: Dunod.

Merleau-Ponty, M. (1962). *Phenomenology of Perception.* New York: Routledge.

Paquot, T. (1999, July/August). Editorial. *Urbanisme , 307,* 51.

Paquot T. (1990). *Homo urbanus: essai sur l'urbanisation du monde et des mœurs.* Paris: Éditions du Félin.

Prévert, J. (1963). Chanson du vitrier. In *Histoires.* Paris: Gallimard.

Prévert, J. (1972). Le cancre. In *Paroles.* Paris: Gallimard.

Prost, R. (1991). L'architecture et la question de l'éthique. *Informel* 4(2), 40.

Prost, R. (1992). *Conception architecturale: une investigation méthodologique.* Paris: L'Harmattan.

Raymond, H. (1984). *L'architecture, les aventures de la raison.* Paris: CCI.

The interior is a fluid and often disputed territory claimed by architects, interior designers, and decorators. In his provocative essay, "Curtain Wars: Architects, Decorators, and the 20th-Century Domestic Interior," Joel Sanders traces the twentieth-century battle for the interior by professionals from interior decoration, interior design, and architecture, concluding with the idea that these once rigid boundaries seem to have collapsed in the early twenty-first century (Sanders 2002). As the disciplinary boundaries have collapsed, the way we conceptualize the interior has also changed. While a common-sense definition of the interior as a contained or enclosed space seems straightforward, the interior is more elusive than this initial definition suggests.

Defining and Placing Interiors in the Historic Context of Contemporary Space and Time

I want to begin this paper with three propositions that might challenge this preliminary definition. First, the interior is inherently ephemeral, as people are constantly moving objects around in interior spaces, changing the way the space is configured and thus how it operates. Second,

the interior is in a constant state of flux due to its inhabitation by humans—that is, the interior is in some respect inseparable from the people who inhabit it. Finally, our initial definition of the interior is further destabilized by the current saturation of media culture and digital technologies, which affects our understanding of the interior in two ways—in the way physical spaces are reproduced and circulate as either two-dimensional photographic or virtual (digital) images, or in the way our use of mobile digital devices change our perception of space.

Beyond the Architectural Container

To date, the few available historical surveys of the interior have treated it as a subset of architecture, whereby enclosed spaces designed by well-known architects, interior designers, decorators, or design firms are analyzed as coherent, stable objects for study. For example, this sense of the interior as a contained architectural space is emphasized by design historian John Pile in the introduction to his pioneering book *A History of Interior Design*: "interior design is inextricably linked to architecture and can only be studied within an architectural context" (Pile, 2005, p. 11).

Pile's narrative of exemplary architectural containers—from the caves at Lascaux to Frank Gehry's Walt Disney Concert Hall—is accompanied by images of furniture and objects typically found within them.

More recently, Susan Yelavich, in the introduction to her book *Contemporary World Interiors*, highlights the lack of critical attention given to interior design compared to architecture or other design disciplines. She writes: "discussions of the interior have been prejudiced by its perception as a container of ephemera" (Yelavich, 2007, p 1). The book itself comprises a survey of exemplary contemporary interior spaces organized according to loose typologies: The House, The Loft, The Office, and so on. Most of these spaces were designed by well-known designers, architects, or design firms, and Yelavich makes no distinction between disciplines. This suggests that we may be beyond the point where the interior is considered simply a subset of architecture, and that the boundaries between disciplines in the twenty-first century are more fluid than in the last century.

Although organized differently from Pile's book, Yelavich's range of contemporary spaces are illustrated via images of empty architectural containers largely devoid of people. While there is some attempt in both books to provide a little social context, many of the important social questions (who uses these spaces? when? why? how do they affect their inhabitants? how do they relate to their socioeconomic context?) remain unanswered. Given the interior's inherently unstable condition

noted above, it is worth extracting the interior from this particular architectural context—less for the sake of disputing disciplinary territories and more in order to expand our understanding of the interior as something other than a static decorated architectural container.

If we are to think about the interior as more than an architectural container, we must first acknowledge that it is also a space of human habitation. In his book *A Philosophy of Interior Design*, Stanley Abercrombie argues that while architectural histories tend to focus on the façades of buildings (the exterior), to understand the containers within (the interior) requires a different experience: "We do not merely pass them on the street; we inhabit them. When we enter a building, we cease being merely its observer; we become its content" (Abercrombie, 1990, p. 3). Importantly, Abercrombie defines the interior as inseparable from the people who inhabit it, so an interior history that simply catalogues and analyzes empty architectural containers seems inadequate.

Despite Abercrombie's point about inhabitation, a brief flip through any recent book or magazine on interior design (or architecture, for that matter) will reveal scant evidence of human habitation. In photographs of contemporary interiors, the absence of people (and their ephemera) is remarkable. If we follow Abercrombie's idea, the interior is not an empty, architectural container, but a space that is always marked by human habitation. Even when a house is empty, someone has left a pair of dirty socks on the floor or dishes in the sink; even when the office is empty, someone has left a coffee mug or a stack of papers on the desk. The interior is always contaminated by traces of human presence, traces that are usually absent in the photographic representation of interior spaces.

In the twenty-first century, our understanding of the interior is predominantly a visual one. This is no doubt compounded by a media culture in which the first time we see an interior space it is often as a glossy color photograph in a magazine, book, or brochure, or an image on a website. This mediation of the interior by a flat, two-dimensional image gives us a limited understanding of the space. For design historian and theorist Suzie Attiwill, this flattening of three-dimensional space into a two-dimensional image suppresses the interior's temporal aspect: "Interior design histories have . . . ignored temporality in the design of interiors through a focus on objects and built space as static form" (Attiwill, 2004, p. 6). Given that our history of interiors is largely based on two-dimensional images, our interaction with the temporal aspect of the interior is lost. What is also lost is the range of sensory phenomena beyond the visual—the sounds and smells (or lack thereof), the touch and weight of materials. By including these additional aspects of the interior—the temporal and the phenomenological—into an interior history, we can start to understand how the interior is more than simply an architectural container.

Histories of the interior thus far tend toward a mummification of spaces as empty containers, their ephemera frozen as in a museum's period room. Even when we consider contemporary interiors in books, magazines, or websites, we will note that our media culture of the spectacle privileges visual perception, suppressing the rich phenomenological experience when we interact with a space. The fixity of photographs tends to reinforce the idea of the interior as an ideal or pure space comprising a series of abstract forms, lines, color, and objects such as furniture and fixtures. It may well be easier to admire a pure empty container, and such spaces uncontaminated by inhabitation are certainly easier to catalogue, classify (according to style or function), and analyze as data.

Finally, beyond an architectural container filled with ephemera, the interior is also a dynamic space. It is dynamic in at least four senses: in the sense of people flowing in and out; in its interactions with the surrounding context; in its interactions with media culture (the circulation of images); and in its interactions with new technologies (which includes the virtual realm from closed caption television [CCTV] cameras to cell phones or mobile listening devices that alter our perception of space). These dynamic aspects of the interior suggest that issues such as how we interact with and experience spaces seem more vital than simply cataloguing styles or functions of architectural containers. In this way, we may begin to consider how the interior affects psychological states or plays a role in shaping individual or collective identities through projections of lifestyles, class, gender, or social values.

Ralph Lauren/Naomi Leff's Rhinelander Mansion

If the contemporary interior is no longer simply an architectural container, but a kind of stage set for experiencing narratives of identity and lifestyle, then there is no better place to explore these issues further than Rhinelander Mansion. Prominently positioned on Madison Avenue, the Polo/Ralph Lauren flagship store is both emblematic of New York's Second Gilded Age and a definitive example of concepts that are important for understanding the contemporary interior (at least in an American context). Rhinelander Mansion is also an unlikely example to begin a discussion about the contemporary interior beyond the architectural container for several reasons: first, it is easy to dismiss the project as mere decoration (versus an architectural definition of design); second, the design is aesthetically historical and lacks obvious high-tech symbols of progress that might mark it as contemporary; and third, the Ralph Lauren brand and the store's populist appeal are probably unappealing for most academics and critics (that is, it is not avant-garde in any conventional sense).

However, Rhinelander Mansion certainly deserves to be included in any discussion of exemplary contemporary interiors for another set of reasons: first, its longevity. The store has survived with the same design for over 20 years, which, given the size, location (in one of the most expensive neighborhoods in the world), and the high-turnover nature of retail interiors, is impressive in itself. Second, Rhinelander Mansion integrates interior design with set design (drawing upon both theater and cinema) to a new level, creating a distinctive experience for its inhabitants. Third, the broader synthesis of the interior with Lauren's advertising and branding makes the space a physical manifestation of the Ralph Lauren mythologies: the Mansion is a space that realizes collective dreams. Beyond the conventional understanding of the interior as a contained architectural space, these reasons suggest a broader psychological, sociological, and anthropological understanding of the contemporary interior. To begin with, I will introduce the Mansion itself, next examine Lauren's development of the mythologies that inform the design, then sketch out the role of the designer, Naomi Leff, and finally, tie these aspects together.

Rhinelander Mansion

Designed by Naomi Leff and completed in 1986, Rhinelander Mansion is the pinnacle of the Ralph Lauren image-world. While in the first Gilded Age, nouveau riche Americans modeled their lifestyles on European aristocrats, in the second, Lauren returned to this collective aspiration with his fashion collections and advertising campaigns, until finally making the dream manifest with his flagship store. Gertrude Rhinelander Waldo originally commissioned the five-story Rhinelander Mansion in 1898. Occupying a corner block, the limestone townhouse was inspired by the chateaux of the Loire Valley, although its eclectic mix of European Renaissance and Gothic forms and elaborately carved ornamentation situate it squarely in the New York Beaux Arts tradition. The location, the external aesthetic, and the direct historical reference to the earlier Gilded Age were all-important to Lauren, who purchased the property in 1984. Even before the interior design process had begun, the site itself had pedigree. While the exterior is suitably impressive, inside, the experience begins.

Upon entering, I was first struck by the huge bouquet of flowers on a heavy wooden table. Then a Lauren-attired man offered me a glass of water on a silver tray: I was clearly playing the role of the master of the manor returning home, my attendant servants discreetly hovering in the background. This aristocratic fantasy was completed by the warm mahogany wall paneling and the monumental staircase, accentuated by hand-carved balustrades and lined with gilt-framed portraits that lay ahead. The immediate impression was less a retail store and more the parlor of an English country house or gentleman's club—every detail underlined the ideals of tradition, wealth and stability. Above the entrance hung a huge Waterford chandelier on the intricately carved plaster ceiling, and to the right a sideboard featuring Art Deco glass panels of polo players. The adjacent rooms were filled with props—polo mallets, riding accessories, gilt-framed paintings, worn brown luggage, large overstuffed leather armchairs, old photographs, and walking sticks—as much as with clothes racks of Lauren ties and sweaters.

The Mansion looks lived-in, the antique carpets worn but not shabby, the luggage well traveled, the patina of history coating every detail. Though grand, the scale of the store is residential, and the experience of inhabiting the Lauren image-world seems more important than retail sales, with the clothes themselves integrated seamlessly into the installation. Menswear features amongst the props on the ground floor, and continues upstairs below lower ceilings but similarly intricate plasterwork and amongst a similar array of props. Polo is a recurring theme, with mallets, balls, and helmets hung on the walls and placed on shelves and on the floor, but other gentleman's pursuits are referenced through oars or a cricket bat. On the third floor, the palette is lighter for the women's wear collection, while the fourth floor contains model rooms displaying the latest Ralph Lauren Living collections. These are changed regularly, but on the occasions I have visited, I have seen a Western collection and a Jamaican collection, both of which included a model bedroom set featuring Lauren designs. While the first two floors and the grand staircase are certainly the most spectacular spaces of the Mansion, the attention to detail throughout the store is consistent and comprehensive, the design enveloping the inhabitant in a complete environment.

Ralph Lauren: Lifestyle Living

At this point, it is worth briefly reviewing Ralph Lauren's development of his lifestyle marketing, as it both informs and complements the Mansion's design. Lauren was born in the Bronx as Ralph Lifshitz in

1939 to Russian Jewish immigrant parents. After graduating high school, he began selling suits at Brooks Brothers, a stockist of Ivy League menswear. In 1967 he began designing neckties and named his brand *Polo*. Polo evoked a certain European style: masculine, sporty but simultaneously aristocratic and elite. Lauren's ties were more than just ties: through clever advertising and branding, they quickly became status symbols that sold at twice the price of ordinary ties. "In 1970," writes fashion critic Teri Agins, "Lauren convinced Bloomingdale's to put all his ties, suits, dress shirts, and raincoats together in his own special little boutique. Lauren designed this outpost to feel like a gentleman's club, with mahogany paneling and brass fixtures" (Agins, 1999, 87). From almost the beginning of his branding empire, Lauren's clothing was intimately linked to a physical stage set that could reinforce certain lifestyle aspirations, namely, the aura of tradition for nouveaux riches who have none.

From humble neckties, Lauren's collections expanded in the 1970s until he settled on themed collections based on a set of archetypal figures—sportswear for gentlemen athletes who played tennis or polo and went rowing or yachting; blazers, ties, and school crests for the Ivy League college graduate; and the nonchalant elegance of his English aristocratic collections. Lauren soon branched out into women's wear, then further themes with his cowboy collection in 1978, and in the early 1980s, an American folk and a safari collection. Circumventing the Parisian haute couture guild system, Lauren developed his themed collections for a mass market from the very beginning. The themes themselves were particularly nostalgic—historical references lent them an aura of authenticity and honesty—and particularly American, with the emphasis on individuals, nonconformists, and outsiders such as the cowboy, the aristocrat, the gentleman amateur, and the adventurer on safari. And if Lauren's image-world was both nostalgic and patriotic, it was not derived from any shared remembering but rather from a cinematic remembering, the imagery derived from *Brideshead Revisited*, *The Great Gatsby*, *High Noon*, or Merchant Ivory films rather than from real historical events or figures.

While Lauren's thematic visions became more complete and expansive through the 1970s and 1980s, an important turning point came in 1979 when Lauren and photographer Bruce Weber began collaborating on an innovative style of fashion advertising. Rather than single model shoots in studio settings, Weber created long spreads for magazines, up to 20 pages, with little or no text, shooting non-models or non-actors in appropriate locations. Weber's cinematic lifestyle imaging was described by Lauren thus:

The advertising campaigns became the movies in print. It wasn't about seeing a man or woman posing against an anonymous backdrop, but seeing him or her in a life doing something you could relate to or dream about. When you see a good movie, old or new, you become a part of it; you have a dream. What I wanted to do with my ads was what I did with my collections—make people dream and aspire. Bruce understood. (Lauren 2007: 134)

For mass market America of the 1980s, Lauren and Weber's cinematic images of an authentic life, lived as an individual with wealth to enjoy leisure time, must have struck a chord, because Lauren's business grew into a multimillion-dollar empire. (Lauren himself became a billionaire, at least on paper, when the company went public in 1997.) The promise was social status through consuming a shirt or a sweater, inclusion as an actor in a fantasy lifestyle, an escape from the contemporary world of work or the banality of suburban living. Lauren himself starred in his own advertisements, a living embodiment of the self-creation myth, inhabiting his own fantasy world of the American West on his Colorado ranch or in his colonial bungalow in Jamaica: the boy from the Bronx self-made through style. While the cinematic advertising campaigns provided the initial imaging, for Lauren, the image-world ultimately needed a physical environment to fulfill the dream.

Naomi Leff

The designer for Lauren's flagship Manhattan store was Naomi Leff, whose background is worth sketching briefly in order to understand the Mansion from the designer's perspective. In an interesting coincidence, only a year before Lauren, Leff was also born in the Bronx. She graduated from SUNY at Cortland in 1960 with a degree in education and sociology before entering the master's program in sociology (a background that may well have contributed to her particular understanding of interior design). In 1966, Leff began studies at the New York School of Interior Design and in 1973 studied interior design at Brooklyn's Pratt Institute. She worked for an architectural firm, John Carl Warnecke and Associates, from 1973 to 1975, and then began working at Bloomingdale's under the legendary designer Barbara D'Arcy. Perhaps not coincidently, Lauren began at Bloomingdale's in the 1960s, during which time the store "rode the wave of a youth rebellion, a sexual revolution, and a revolution of rising incomes and aspirations" (Zukin, 2004, pp. 128–129). D'Arcy's contribution to Bloomingdale's new lifestyle marketing was the development of a series of model rooms in the late 1960s and early 1970s. More than simply furniture displays, these were complete environments or installations that contributed to Bloomingdale's renowned "retail as theater" approach.

Leff began her own firm in 1980, and her first big break came in 1982 when she was commissioned to design a showroom for Ralph Lauren Home. Situated within the JP Stevens building on 6th Avenue, and possibly modeled on Bloomingdale's earlier model rooms, Leff created a scene from a log cabin ideal of America, presenting Lauren's homewares in a context dripping with nostalgia for the pioneering West. This first Lauren commission led to numerous subsequent commissions from him, including the Rhinelander Mansion and other Polo Ralph Lauren stores in Beverley Hills and Philadelphia, as well as international stores and Lauren's private Double RL Ranch in Colorado. While Rhinelander Mansion remains Leff's best-known work, she also designed private homes for celebrities Tom Cruise and Nicole Kidman, Steven Spielberg, and David Geffen. Leff's design of the A/X Armani Exchange in Soho in 1992 and development of Armani's brand belie the idea of a signature style but instead underscore Leff's understanding of the relationship between design and lifestyle marketing.

As a designer, Leff had an appreciation for quality craftsmanship, a keen eye for detail, and, as Steven Spielberg commented, "one of the best color senses of anyone I've met. She'd make a fine cinematographer" (Stephens, 1994, p 164). And cinematic may well be the best way to describe her approach to the Rhinelander Mansion project. When Lauren signed the deal on the property in 1984, the building was completely dilapidated with much of the interior beyond repair. Leff described it as an "archaeological" project: "Only one ceiling was in good condition. The rest of the building would have to be recreated from a splinter of mahogany paneling here, a scrap of carved plaster there" (Kornbluth, 1986, p. 140). It was less a renovation project and more of a re-creation project, with Leff employing master wood carvers, plasterers, and carpenters to create the ceilings, mahogany staircase, and paneling largely from scratch. At the same time, an army of buyers spread out over Europe and the United States buying antiques—consis-

tent period or authenticity did not necessarily matter, so long as the props looked authentic. With a committed client with an appreciation for detail and deep pockets, this was a dream commission for any designer. While the original budget was $5 million, Lauren finally admitted to a blowout to $14 million, although his staff estimated the Mansion cost over $35 million (Gross, 2003, p. 249).

The Mythological Interior

With the Rhinelander Mansion, Leff and Lauren created a profoundly mythological space. In it, objects (whether for sale or not) function like props that contribute symbolic meaning, each polo mallet or sweater entangled within threads of the overarching narratives. In contrast, an earlier generation of modernist designers strived to create neutral spaces filled with functional objects devoid of such symbolic meanings or theatrical effects. Florence Knoll's corporate interiors of 1960s, for example, were based on highly controlled, rational systems and utilized high-tech materials. The irrational Mansion also challenges other modernist ideals, such as the division between real and fake: some of its props are real antiques, such as the Art Deco glass panels taken from the Polo Lounge of New York's Westbury Hotel, while others are contemporary reproductions, such as the staircase, modeled after the one in London's Connaught Hotel. Consistent historical or geographical truths are also challenged, as Leff's assortment of antiques, furniture, and props hail from various historical periods and places (although all are ultimately consistent with Lauren's brand). Clearly, the divisions between the real and the copy do not matter in this simulacrum of an aristocratic lifestyle.

In historical terms, we could locate the Mansion within the broader discussion of 1980s architectural postmodernism. Thus, we could situate Leff's design alongside, for example, Hans Hollein's theatrical interiors, the reinstatement of historical and symbolic forms in both the writings and the work of Robert Venturi and Denise Scott Brown, or the historicism of Robert Graves' architecture and furniture design. But it is only when we shift focus away from a definition of interior design as the creation of architectural containers to the creation of spaces that shape identities and express the aspirations of particular individuals or social groups that we can begin to understand the significance and complexity of a space like Rhinelander Mansion. In this sense, Leff's design is perhaps better situated within the tradition of interior decorators, a line extending back through Dorothy Draper to Elsie de Wolfe, designers who also understood how the interior might shape its inhabitants' identity and how cultural values are embedded within interior spaces.

Interior design, as both Lauren and Leff well understood, is as much about stimulating desire as it is about creating functional spaces. Tapping into the fantasies of middle-class Americans required an anthropological or sociological understanding of mythologies already existing in popular consciousness. These mythologies—the refined aristocratic lifestyle, the rugged cowboy lifestyle—were absorbed by middle America through means such as Hollywood cinema, then reinforced by Lauren and Weber's advertising campaigns, and finally found a physical embodiment in the Mansion. The cinematic approach to the retail experience of Leff and Lauren was explained by sales staff who described being trained as actors: "This isn't retail, it's theater," Charles Fagan, who started out selling sweaters and ended up managing the store, told a journalist. "We present our clothes in lifestyle. They're all little movies. At the mansion, you get lost in different worlds" (Gross, 2003, p. 251). Just as the staff feel like actors, so too the customers—acting within Leff's set in their own variations of Lauren's mythological movies. Beyond marking a particular time in late-twentieth-century interior design, the Mansion's longevity suggests that both this cinematic experience and the collective fantasies it manifests are far from historical, and Leff and Lauren's exemplary artifice sets the stage for a renewed understanding of the contemporary interior.

Discussion Questions

1. Unpack Huppatz's idea of "space as container" and the ways that space has been "flattened" by contemporary history and theory until very recently.

2. Huppatz suggests "beyond an architectural container filled with ephemera, the interior is also a dynamic space." Analyze the four senses of "dynamic space" Huppatz describes:
   a. In the sense of people flowing in and out
   b. In its interactions with the surrounding context
   c. In its interactions with media culture (the circulation of images)
   d. In its interactions with new technologies
      How do these affect our understandings of space and our experiences of it?

   (These include the virtual realm from CCTV cameras to cell phones or mobile listening devices that alter our perception of space.)
   e. How is our perception of space becoming altered?

3. Why is the Ralph Lauren Mansion interesting in the context of the theoretical ideas presented?
   a. How do we unpack space in the context of "staging fantasies"?
   b. How is the Lauren/Leff Rhinelander Mansion emblematic of a way of understanding space and finding meaning in "self"?
   c. Space as identity?

References

Abercrombie, S. (1990). *A Philosophy of Interior Design.* New York: Harper & Row.

Agins, T. (1999). *The End of Fashion: The Mass Marketing of the Clothing Business.* New York: William Morrow and Company.

Albrecht, Donald. (2008). *Naomi Leff: Interior Design.* Exhibition catalogue. Pratt Institute, New York.

Attiwill, Suzie. 2004. Towards an Interior History. *IDEA.* Brisbane, Australia: QUT Publishing,

Cohen, E. L., & Allard, F. (1987, June). Polo Ralph Lauren, New York: Naomi Leff and Associates Renovates the Rhinelander Mansion for the Flagship Store. *Interior Design, 58.*

Geran, M. (1984, February). Ralph Lauren Comes Home: A Collection of Decorative Furnishings as Seen in the J.P. Stevens Showrooms Designed by Naomi Leff and Associates. *Interior Design, 55.*

Gross, M. (2003). *Genuine Authentic: The Real Life of Ralph Lauren.* New York: HarperCollins.

Kornbluth, J. (1986, October). Polo/Ralph Lauren: Refashioning New York's Rhinelander Mansion. *Architectural Digest, 43*(10).

Lauren, R. (2007). *Ralph Lauren.* New York: Rizzoli.

McDowell, C. (2002). *Ralph Lauren: The Man, The Vision, The Style.* London: Cassell Illustrated.

Pile, J. (2005). *A History of Interior Design* (2nd ed.). Hoboken, NJ: John Wiley & Sons.

Sanders, J. (2002, Winter/Spring). Curtain Wars: Architects, Decorators, and the 20th-Century Domestic Interior. *Harvard Design Magazine, 16.*

Simpson, J. (1995, August). AD at the Smithsonian: Our Master Class with Four Top Designers in Washington, D.C. *Architectural Digest, 52*(8), pp.42–44.

Stephens, S. (1994, November). Architecture: Gwathmey Siegel, Steven Spielberg's Guesthouse in East Hampton. *Architectural Digest, 51*(11), pp.158–167.

Theroux, P. (2002, November). Ralph Lauren: The Designer's Sprawling Double RL Ranch in Colorado. *Architectural Digest, 59*(11), pp. 250–263.

Williams, K. (2008). *Naomi Leff: Interior Design.* New York: The Monacelli Press.

Yelavich, S. (2007). *Contemporary World Interiors.* London: Phaidon.

Zukin, S. (2004). *Point of Purchase: How Shopping Changed American Culture.* New York: Routledge.

This collection of stories dwells on everyday objects and their capacity to resist hierarchical division between concrete reality, that is, the here and now, and philosophic inquiry, or the poetic constitution of things. Steeped in anonymity and monotony, qualities at the very heart of the everyday objects and interior environments featured in these stories resist being heroic, novel, and spectacular—traits often associated with consumptive products and processes of modernity. In the face of its presumed insignificance, Lefebvre insists, "the everyday is enduring and solid, humble and 'taken for granted'; it is the ethics underlying routine and the aesthetics of familiar surroundings."[1]

It is on this basis that I have explored the linings of everyday objects. One degree further removed from sight, linings are the insides of objects and, therefore, even more susceptible to disregard. Not simply the back side of the outside, they represent an additional fold in the surface of the seamlessness of daily life. Linings are a supplementary feature, often serving to protect, give comfort, or further enhance

the occupation of things within things. Consider that which is readily at hand in your immediate surroundings. The jacket that you hung up behind the door dons a slippery inner face with a flashy paisley pattern that is obscured only when your body fills its volume. Your feet are kept warm, dry, and smelly by a sheep's sacrificial coat. That satchel you lug to and from work each day organizes your pencils, pens, USB stick, and bus pass in the creases of polypropylene and nylon such that they do not escape or comingle. Your grandmother's silver cutlery lies in state in a flat pine box amongst valleys of iridescent satin. The thin white cotton pants' pocket pressed against your upper thigh belies your thriftiness as much as it harbors the few coins you saved in the purchase. Such linings endow the inner cavities of external forms with extended performativity. They keep secret their purpose to equip an intimate, and for the most part, small-scale inhabitable pocket of space.

Conceiving of such linings as interior surfaces is a metaphoric trope that I employed in the reconstruction of everyday objects into sculptural works and their immersion into the context of common interior rooms. These works probe the limits of this analogy, and at the same time, they investigate the potential

---

[1] Henri Lefebvre. (1971). *Everyday Life in the Modern World*. Trans. by Sacha Rabinovitch. London: Allen Lane, 24–25.

of objects and materials to exert vitality in relation to their making processes.[2] The text, images, and objects are bound together as spatial narratives situated at the confluence of the banal and the wondrous. They reform conceptions of furnishing reliant on an architectural container to enclose a void with the aid of the floor, walls, and ceiling.[3] They resist the temptation to reduce an interior lining to simply a surface treatment, a mere backdrop to movable fittings and furniture charged with the pursuit of comfort, taste, and fashion. The notion of an interior lining at play in these works migrates amongst various voices, time frames, and bodies such that the emphasis is directed not toward what each story means, "but what it does and incites to do. What it does: the charge of affect it contains and transmits. What it incites to do: the metamorphose of this potential energy into other things—other texts, but also paintings, photographs, film sequences, political actions, decisions, erotic inspirations, acts of insubordination, economic initiatives, etc."[4] These stories assert interior linings as microcosmic ecologies that reinforce the elusive, political, and persistent nature of the everyday.

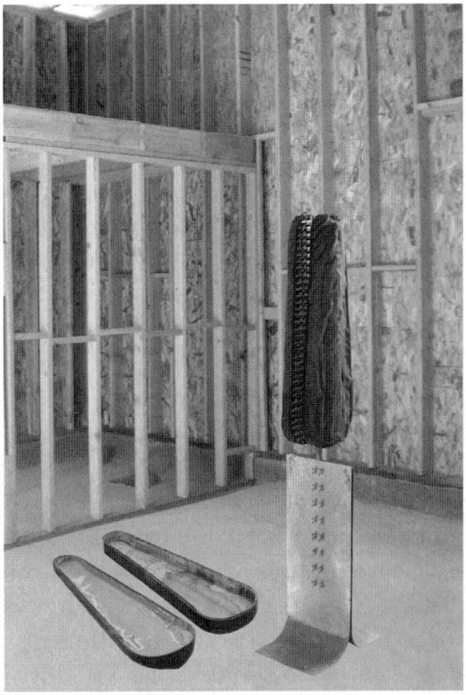

Figure 5.1 The Joiner
Photo credit: Courtesy of Julieanna Preston

The Joiner

I am lured to things made of wood.

At first glance
I feel the tree's felling, falling, sawing.

I see where this thing lived in the trunk, the seasons it has sipped, the geography of its provenance: a sacrificed bundle of phylum trafficking chlorophyll.[5]

---

[2] Jane Bennett. (2010). *Vibrant Matter: The Political Ecology of Things*. Durham and London: Duke University Press.

[3] Imma Forina. (2010). *Many Voices, One Story: Interiors Through Italian Eyes*, an unpublished manuscript, 7.

[4] Francis Lyotard. (1984). *Driftworks*. New York: Semiotext(e), 9–10.

[5] George Hersey. (1995). *The Lost Meaning of Classical Architecture*. London, England: MIT Press, 11–45.

My body struggles involuntarily to locate the postures of the object's crafting.
Digits fidget. Visceral mapping of the making process.

Like this case. Pinched it from a bin. Thought I could rebuild it.

The case is pretty basic. White pine, probably not from New Zealand, soft, close, uniform grain, even texture, lightweight, very few markings. Doesn't tend to warp.

See the way the strip has been wrapped around a jig to make the curved profile! Probably steamed and clamped. Look at the tip of the lid where three surfaces meet! Remarkable constructed geometry! I get the same joy from raising a stud wall plumb and true.

It collapsed to two halves the moment I opened the clasp.

An interior tumbled out in despair of its stripped down existence. Sad blue stain. Felt that wanted to be velvet. Velvet that yearned to possess a body, mediate a suspended life or summon a dream state.[6]

I assembled a skeletal mannequin of square stock Rimu:
a clove hitch on one spar and a

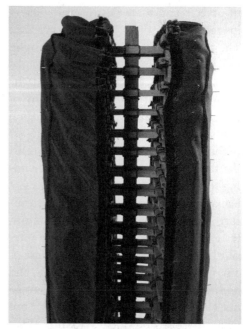

Figure 5.2 The Joiner (small)
Photo credit: Courtesy of Julieanna Preston

minimum of four complete turns around both members followed by two frapping turns between the vertical and the horizontal spar to tighten the lashing and finishing tying off the
running end to the opposite spar
with another clove hitch
to finish the square lashing.[7]

A body leapt out of the timber form work as
An inverted cladding is added to repair the cleavage that ruptured her wholeness though it maintains her two-ness.
Guarded internal softness.

---

[6] Freyja Hartzell. (2009). "The Velvet Touch: Fashion, Furniture and the Fabric of the Interior" in *Fashion Theory*, 13(1), 51.

[7] Knots, Splices, Attachments, and Ladders, 2–24. Accessed August 1. 2010, from www.webstile.com.ch.

Figure 5.3 The Finisher
Photo credit: Courtesy of Julieanna Preston

She sways back and forth announcing her presence and the potential harm of her sharp ends.
Fit as a fiddle.[8]

The Finisher

They were on the footpath.
Four of the same, violin cases left out in the weather. A bit of an odd find, a section of the orchestra huddled outside the performance hall.

---

[8] Edwin A. Abbott. (1998). *Flatland: A Romance of Many Dimensions.* New York: Penguin Books.

The sign said free so I took one.
Sad to break up the set but I was already carrying a heavy load that day. I don't even play the violin. The shape of the case was simply compelling. Besides, there was nothing inside that case, nothing but empty space and a few patches of tattered paper lining. Light and flimsy, merely a shell, a hull, it rattled with a barren purpose to protect. So I filled it. The case swallowed the plaster. Only a wee bit leaked from the edges where the handmade bent timber form was imperfectly matched. Dry wood grain now slightly swollen. The plaster defeated the hollow interior's semblance of function.

The space of a violin not living in there was quiet. Muted. Stifled. Choked. What could you possibly put in it now? It lay dormant for weeks, its faces splayed open, sunning, sweating, in the window sill while I finished the walls of this house. Day in, day out, tape, spackle, sand, wipe, tape, spackle, sand, wipe. These walls insist upon the perpendicular, the planar, the smooth and the seamless. I labour upon them obsessively. The light, unforgiving. The echo, disconcerting. I am resting now, taking a break while the last skim coat dries. Bored with the flatness. Listen, what is that sucking sound? The walls and my skin competing for moisture? Spatula aside, I hear something within the casting, something buried in the dense mass of the case, a murmur. Too crude, too coarse, too cold, the spoon, skews, fluted and veining gouge tools are no longer useful. My caresses are finding the limit of your shadow-filled body amongst the granules

Figure 5.4 The Dresser
Photo credit: Courtesy of Julieanna Preston

of white hydrated calcium. Bringing you to the interior surface.[9]

The Dresser

Tent, pitched.
Netting, draped.
Carpet, laid.
Tables, propped.
Chairs, shrouded.
Lights, hung.

---

[9] J. G. Ballard. (2009). "The Sound Sweep" in *The Complete Stories of J. G. Ballard*. New York: W. W. Norton & Company 106–136.

Set out cutlery.
Marshal caterers.
Arrange flowers.
Muster quartet.
Usher in guests.[10]

An interior atmosphere materializes at the hands of the dresser who keeps the exterior at bay with techniques of cloaking, masking, veiling, and wrapping. A magician of textile techniques, hers is an art of arranging space played out in the duration of a social event, book-ended by meticulous planning. Lists upon lists. Tricks of the trade.

As the evening commences, she retreats to the margins of the production.

---

[10] See Georges Perec. (1999). *Species of Spaces and Other Places.* Trans. by John Sturrock. London: Penguin Group for inspiration on poetic list making.

Figure 5.5 The Dresser (small)
Photo credit: Courtesy of Julieanna Preston

A perennial wall flower. Vegetal rinceau.
A prop no more prominent than one of the
potted plants.
At the service of . . . subservient to . . . the
dresser is herself, decoration.

She watches the event unfold,
undetected amongst
the raucous symphony of
clatters and chatters.

In the wake of the event's consumption,
she emerges from its porous lining into a
composition reordered.

Stale air.
Stained cloths.
Furnishings in disarray.

Drawing the four corners of the room together, the dresser binds and hauls the bundled interior away to be laundered in time for the next event in eight hours.[11]

Note: Thank you to Paul Hiller (Photographic Technician), Richard Bernard Jr. (President of Pilgrim Interiors Inc.), Ryan Price (Fairtrade), Melissa Kirmse, and Tina Payne (Weddings by Tina) for their contributions of assistance and/or base interior images used in the construction of the images published here. My appreciation goes to Wendy Neale and David Carleton for technical advice during the crafting of the sculptural objects.

All images by Julieanna Preston © 2010

[11] Bernard Cache. (1994). "Vegetable Rinceau: Ornament and the Vegetable Rinceau." *Wiederhall*, n.17, 20–25.

5.4 Prototyping Lived Experiences

C. Thomas Mitchell

The question "what is good design?" is a frequent topic in the design community, but one that rarely leads to satisfying answers. One reason for this is that the definition of "design success" varies widely, depending on who is being asked. For designers, formal beauty and material innovation are most highly prized, as a glance at architecture and design magazines reveals. For those who interact with design, however, effectiveness in use is generally most important. In other words, for designers static aesthetic criteria predominate, as embodied in Goethe's definition of architecture as "frozen music" (Goethe), whereas for users their dynamic experience is most significant. This divergence of opinion over such a fundamental issue underlies much of the public's dissatisfaction with the designs ostensibly produced on their behalf. There are specific technical reasons why this discordance developed, and many examples of it are to be found, but there are also encouraging new developments in a range of fields that focus more on prototyping lived experience than simply modeling static form and hoping for the best.

Seeing the Building from the Top Down: A Matter of Experience not Perspective

The discordance between architects' aesthetic focus and the experiential concerns of those who interact with design is emphasized in the presentation of architecture in books and magazines. Other than the occasional throwaway line, "this was done for the benefit of users," the emphasis is firmly on the aesthetic, with people rarely seen in the images presented.

This awareness came into focus for me in architecture school when asked to line up walls in plan—an aesthetic criteria—though this visual relationship would only be seen from an aerial view of the building if the roof had blown off! Making this change would affect the experience of those using the resultant rooms by changing their proportion and volume—but this experiential consequence was not considered.

Understanding Experiences versus Practices

There is a lack of correspondence of traditional design methods, the most common of which design methods pioneer John Chris Jones terms by "design-by-drawing" with the lived experiences that design planned in this way gives rise to. Jones notes in his seminal book *Design Methods:*

> The method of designing by making scale drawings will be familiar to many readers . . . The essential difference between this, the normal method of evolving the shapes of machine-made things, and the earlier method of craft evolution, is that trial-and-error is separated from production by using a scale drawing in place of the product as the medium for experiment and change. (Jones, 1970, p. 20)

The consequence of separating planning from making in this way is that—unlike in craft evolution, where a trial-and-error process was used to evolve objects— designs are not truly tested until they are placed in the world.

As long ago as 1964, Christopher Alexander addressed the consequences of this issue in his landmark book *Notes on the Synthesis of Form,* noting that

> we do not know how to express the criteria for success in terms of any symbolic description of form. In other words, given a new design, there is often no mechanical way of telling, purely from the drawings that describe it, whether or not it meets the requirements. (Alexander, 1964, pp. 74–75)

Addressing a similar theme more recently, Alexander explains:

> If you think about a typical development that would be done today, the place where it starts is with the drawing. And we've assumed that if it's a good drawing then the thing is going to be okay. That's simply a mistake. Life cannot be produced from a drawing; life can only be produced from a process. (Alexander, 1990a)

In other words, the methods being used by architects and designers match their criteria for aesthetic success, but very likely will not lead to experiential success in terms of lived experience.

Issues of Beauty and Perspective in Architectural Spaces

Robert Hughes (1991) nicely summed up the perspective of spaces as understood by modernist architects in his book *The Shock of the New:*

> The central image of the new architecture was not the single building. It was the Utopian town plan, and the planners of the time saw their paper cities with the detachment granted the possessors of the bird's-eye view—very high up, very abstract, and thus nearer to God. (Hughes, 1991, p. 184)

Often one finds that the concept of a building can only be appreciated from an aerial view. The most commonly presented view of Walter Gropius' design for the Dessau Bauhaus is from above, showing the interrelationship of the volumes of the three wings.

Figure 5.6 Aerial view of Walter Gropius' Dessau Bauhaus building
Photo credit: © akg-images/Peter Weiss

From ground level, or in the building, it would be impossible to appreciate the key animating idea of the design. See Figure 5.6.

One consequence of being more elevated and nearer to God in this sense is that the architect is less grounded and further away from the realities of those who interact with their designs.

The reliance on Platonism is particularly apparent in the work of Ludwig Mies van der Rohe as present in his final commission, the New National Gallery in Berlin, which was completed in 1968.

In a monograph on this building shown in Figure 5.7 Maritz Vandenberg (1998) explains:

Mies proposed that for temporary exhibitions a noble space, five times the height of a man, would be formed by an extensive slab floating high above a podium. The volume between roof and podium would be completely transparent, with the urban space flowing straight through the interior with only minimal

Figure 5.7 Exterior view of Mies van der Rohe's New National Gallery in Berlin
Photo credit: Courtesy of Jeffrey Howe

modifications. The interior would be almost completely unobstructed, allowing a free arrangement of artworks and display panels to suit any particular occasion. (Vandenberg, 1998, p. 5)

Though Vandenberg in the last line states that the interior would allow free arrangement, in fact, it was found that in this, as in other of Mies' later works,

. . . practical considerations are repeatedly subordinated to his single-minded

Figure 5.8 Interior view of Mies van der Rohe's New National Gallery in Berlin
Photo credit: Courtesy of Jeffrey Howe

quest for ideal, abstract form, thus rending him guilty of the very "formalism" he had attacked in his polemics of the 1920s. (Vandenberg, 1998, p. 19)

As we can glean, the architect's expression of form overrides the experiences of the user in the context of the building designed. I propose that here we hit on a central issue of designs done in more formalist modes—the belief that architecture is an art form in and of itself, attention to functional requirements and the lived experience of those who interact with it being optional.

Architecture as Art versus Craft

From my perspective, it is manifestly clear that architecture is not just an art form. Noted folklorist Henry Glassie (1982) has drawn an important distinction between the idea of architecture as an art and the idea of architecture as a craft by differentiating between the roles of an artifact:

If a pleasure-giving function predominates, the artifact is called art; if a practical function predominates, it is called craft. (Glassie, 1982, p. 126)

No one would deny the importance of the "pleasure-giving" function of architecture as an artifact (think of Vitruvius's dictum of "Firmness, Commodity, *and* Delight). However, when the practical function is purposely neglected then, as Charles Jencks says of Mies' architecture, it is "half-baked" (Jencks, 1973, p. 108). In essence, then, in the New National Gallery we lack spaces that are fit for the purpose of the building.

Contemporary Experiences of Buildings as Places of Living

Frustration is a common experience of those who interact with new buildings. For example, some years after his seminal publication in 1964, in a letter to the editor of *Progressive Architecture*, Christopher Alexander writes:

> Few people genuinely like what architects do today or what they have done in the last decades. Yet many people go along for the ride because they are afraid of being thought to have "bad taste" or afraid to seem ignorant of the niceties of "Architecture" with a capital A . . . Like the sinister tailors in *The Emperor's New Clothes*, they use the ordinary person's fear of seeming ignorant as a weapon to maintain a monopoly of the profession's status quo. (Alexander, 1990b, p. 11)

The fundamental problem, according to Alexander, is that we—all of us, designers and not—have, in this era of specialization, lost our intuition about what make a space *living* or *whole* (c.f. Alexander 1977, 1979). In the video *Places for the Soul: The Architecture of Christopher Alexander*, he views an area of downtown Oakland, California, and comments on a variety of modernist buildings:

> There's lots of that . . . which is very very big, very undifferentiated, very alienating. I think most people know that there's something wrong with it, don't really like it. (Alexander, 1990a)

He notes additionally of a more recent, postmodern, development.

> The difficulty is that the whole thing is still imprisoned in the idea of images and surface things which are utterly insincere and, in a way, make you feel like death almost more than that . . . [modernist building] . . . does. (Alexander, 1990a)

Reflecting on what has been lost, Alexander explains:

> For thousands of years the architecture that was made in a traditional society was essentially connected with our feelings—my feeling, your feeling—what was built arose out of that feeling and was intended to strengthen a person in their feeling. [The] places in history that one admires now which have a sort of incredible roundness and comfort, whether it's at the sort of extreme high end, like some sort of great palace or cathedral, or whether it's at the extreme low end like it could be a little shack or something, they all share a lack of their own self importance because they're concentrating on what life is, not what they are, so to speak. (Alexander, 1990a)

Summarizing his critique of contemporary architecture—modern and postmodern, Alexander says:

> The point is that the architects who are working today are so embarrassed by all of this, along with everyone else, that in order to show that they're good architects they've got to make it so it alienates you. And that's what's up there—the absolute intent to destroy emotion. (Alexander, 1990a)

Alexander's response to the failure of contemporary architecture of all movements to adequately address feeling, emotion, and the lived experience is set out in a remarkable series of books; the philosophy is contained in *The Timeless Way of Building,* and the application of this, a comprehensive design method, is first set out in *A Pattern Language.*

Case Study: Patterns of Architecture and Christopher Alexander

Alexander and his work, particularly the actual quality of his buildings, are somewhat controversial. For the purposes of this article, what is important is his articulation that design should recognize from the outset the relationship between the "patterns of events," which encompass what happens in the space and what it means to people, and the "patterns of space," which support those events. Alexander argues that if considerations about how space is used and what it means to people are overlooked at the outset, the result is a disconnector friction between users and designed environments that is so prevalent today. To overcome people's frustration and dissatisfaction with the built environment, new methods are needed that address the interrelationship of experience and form from the beginning of the design process.

The patterns that Alexander and his team articulated were based on their observation of successful—living and whole—built environments from around the world. Each pattern addresses both spatial relationships and the ways in which they support experience and use. In Figures 5.9 through 5.11, two patterns from the book *A Pattern Language* are shown in conjunction with a design created in dependence upon the patterns. In Figure 5.9, the generic "Roof Vault" pattern is shown; Figure 5.10 is a representation of the pattern "Courtyards That Live," showing a generic spatial relationship and the activities that are supported by it. Figure 5.11 shows a model for the Mountain View Civic Center in California, the design of which was guided by the Courtyards Which Live pattern.

Emerging Approaches in the Design Professions—Prototyping Alternative Spaces of Experience

Within the profession, a number of approaches have been tried that attempt to more directly model user interaction and experience. In addition to the pattern language, scale models (cf. Mitchell, 1992) and full-scale mock-ups (Brown, 2009) have also been used to allow preconstruction interaction with a design, but these are time-consuming and are fairly rarely used.

Technology has also been used to increase the scope of designers' activities—video walkthroughs can give a sense of aspects of a building, but they can only be created once key decisions have been made. AutoCAD has achieved deep penetration in the profession but is primarily a drawing and documentation tool. One particularly promising technology that has the potential to anticipate lived experience is Building Information Modeling (BIM),

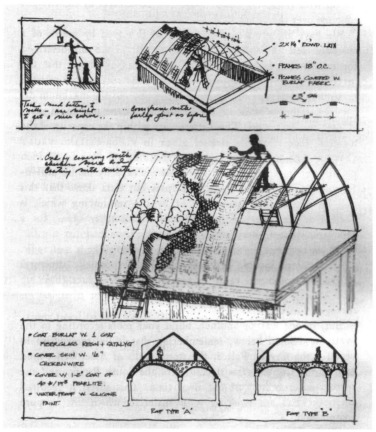

Figure 5.9 Alexander's patterns: Roof vaults
Photo credit: © Christopher Alexander, A Pattern Language, p. 1041

though currently this is primarily being used to bolster existing, object-oriented professional practices rather than to challenge and extend them.

The current state of play with regard to the use of digital technology in the design professions was nicely summarized in an article titled "From Blueprint to Database" in *The Economist*. The author writes:

The advent of powerful computers has enabled architects to produce stunning images of new buildings and other structures. No proposal for a big project is complete without a photorealistic rendering of how the *final* [my italics] design will look, or even a virtual walk through. Perhaps surprisingly, however, those fancy graphics tend to be

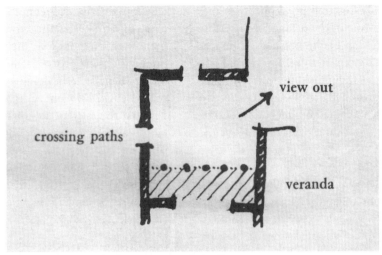

Figure 5.10 Alexander's patterns: Courtyards that live
Photo credit: © Christopher Alexander, A Pattern Language, p. 564

Figure 5.11 Alexander's patterns: MTVcourtyard
Photo credit: © Christopher Alexander, A Pattern Language, p. 564

used only for conceptual purposes and play no role in the detailed design and construction of the finished structure. For the most part, this is still carried out with old-fashioned two-dimensional elevation and plan drawings, created by hand or using computer-aided design (CAD) software. (From Blueprint, 2008)

With the advent of BIM, there is potential for fundamental change in the way design professionals work. This technology is being rapidly adopted since it became available after the purchase of Revit by Autodesk in 2002 and as has been noted:

> The widespread acceptance of BIM is amazing. The 2008 McGraw-Hill "SmartMarket Report on Building Information Modeling" noted that of industry research participants, architects were using BIM most. At that time, 43 percent of surveyed architects were heavy users, with 54 percent expecting to be heavy users by 2009. (Mow and Naylor, 2010)

These methods transform how we understand spaces in the context of the physical, as the new technology of BIM provides a single building model. From this all views and information is derived, and as noted in *Mastering Revit Architecture 2009:*

> Building information modeling is a revolutionary approach to the design, analysis, and documentation of buildings that takes full advantage of modern-day computational technology. At its core, BIM manages the flow of information throughout the lifecycle of a building-design process, allowing you to experience the building before it is built. Using BIM from early conceptual design through construction documentation and into construction administration and beyond, it's possible to better predict, plan, and execute the complex task of creating architecture to meet today's demanding requirements. (Krygiel, et al., 2008, p. 12)

While it is true that such physical models may be possible through the use of BIM, it is equally true that technology such as BIM and future products have the potential to model the experiential qualities of space as well. The example of BIM shows us that dynamic computer-aided virtual 3D enables the interactive collaboration of all relevant technical specialists on a single building model, and, in this context more significantly, it offers the potential for clients and users to participate in the design process from its outset. Thus, they are no longer limited to commenting on what a designer has already done; they can help shape the outcome of design from the beginning.

Methods for Prototyping Lived Experience—The Case Study of IDEO

Design consultancy IDEO has worked with numerous clients globally, developing design/research approaches that prototype the quality of lived experience. IDEO CEO Tim Brown says his firm produces "experience blueprints" to model people's interactions with designed phenomena. In his book *Change by Design*, Brown explains:

> Just as a product begins with an engineering blueprint and a building begins with an architectural blueprint, an *experience blueprint* provides the framework for working out the details of a human interaction . . . The difference is that unlike the plans for an office building or a table lamp, an experience blueprint also describes the *emotive* elements. It captures how people travel through an experience in time. Rather than trying to choreograph that journey, however, its function is to identify the most meaningful points and turn them into opportunities. (Brown, 2009)

One of the key methods IDEO uses to develop experience blueprints is the use of physical prototypes. These are created to foster interaction—and are produced early and often in the design process. Brown explains, "Prototyping at work is giving form to an idea, allowing us to learn from it, evaluate it against others, and improve upon it" (Brown, 2009). Brown addresses the use of prototypes for environmental design in one of IDEO's projects:

> Traditionally, one of the problems with architectural design is that full-scale prototyping is virtually impossible because it is just too expensive. Instead, an imaginative team of "space designers" rented an old warehouse in a dicey part of San Francisco's Bayview district, where they built a full-scale mock-up of the entrance lobby and a typical guest suite of foam core. Their mock-up was not intended to showcase the aesthetic qualities of the space. Rather, it served as a stage on which designers, the client team, a group of hotel owner-operators, and even customers could act out different service experiences and explore in real space and real time what felt right. All the visitors were encouraged to add Post-its to the prototype and to suggest changes. This process yielded a host of innovations that included personalized guidebooks with local information tailored to repeat clients . . .
>
> This full-scale space for acting out whatever occurred to them gave the design team a rich set of ideas for further testing. Moreover, they had a much better sense of how good the ideas were. No amount of survey work or virtual simulation would have achieved the same result. (Brown, 2009)

Thus, instead of having to put a traditional design—in these terms an "untested prototype"—into the world, Brown and his team were able to model the future behavior that would take place in the space and refine the design in advance to support the interactions they observed and that would be taking place in the real space in the future.

Converging Concepts: The Case Study of Steelcase

Finally, a framework for modeling experience has been developed by contract furniture company Steelcase (which, in fact, owns IDEO). The stages Steelcase sets out emphasize an iterative process in which lived experience is prototyped and tested before final design decisions are made. In discussing Steelcase's methodology Brown says:

> Steelcase works outward from the perspective of human-centered design thinking.
>
> One unit within the company, Workplace Futures, operates as a sort of internal think tank to explore areas ranging from higher education to information technology. Workplace Futures includes anthropologists, industrial designers, and business strategists who conduct observations in the field to gain insights into the problems of Steelcase's actual and potential clients. They develop scenarios to help them anticipate the future needs of university researchers, IT workers, or hotel managers; build prototypes to help them visualize solutions; and create compelling stories describing potential opportunities. (Brown, 2009)

Within Steelcase, the Applied Research and Consulting (ARC) group uses a four-stage process for human-centered design: Ask, Observe, Experience, Realize, as follows:

Ask: We ask, probe, and listen. We seek to clearly understand the current situations and future potential. Tools include surveys, interviews, and data collection.

Observe: First-hand observations, photo journals, video ethnography, shadowing, and other techniques create a detailed picture of the organization, user relationships, and behaviors.

Experience: Here we engage users in various experiences, from mapping present situations to envisioning the future. These events spur a shared perspective, provide deeper insights into the issues, and form the basis for user buy-in.

Realize: Users help develop solutions (co-design), then evaluate these new concepts via models or full scale environments. Such pilots validate concepts, reduce risk, and accelerate acceptance of new ideas. (Steelcase, n.d.)

The ARC group processes then go on to develop various tools to investigate how people will react in different types of experiences. Key to this is the use of physical prototypes to test "in situ" interactions. Rigorous evaluation is conducted to determine what does and does not work—experientially. And, as noted, there are many advantages of such an approach. The process of collaboration itself will increase buy-in from those who will use the new space. The design will be refined to suit its purpose, and problems can be identified and addressed *before* construction takes place. This will ultimately save time and money and result in a more effective environment.

Conclusion

Contemporary design methods, such as design-by-drawing (whether by hand or computer), are becoming increasingly inadequate as a means of modeling positive and actual, lived experiences in diverse spaces. A good drawing doesn't necessarily lead to a good building. There has been an overemphasis on the formal and aesthetic, and a concomitant failure to meaningfully consider the lived experience of a space, the result of which is the frustration and dissatisfaction so often expressed by the users of new buildings when they actually appropriate them by using them daily.

Digital technologies, such as AutoCAD, have primarily been used to extend existing design methods, not to challenge them. Likewise, Building Information Modeling (BIM) has thus far largely been slotted into existing professional practices, but it has the potential to be a very disruptive technology. Innovative design consultancies, like IDEO, and companies like Steelcase have already developed design/research approaches that use lived experience as the basis for design decision making. IDEO develops "experience blueprints" to capture the emotive elements of design experience. The iterative use of physical prototypes to model people's interactions is key to both IDEO's work and that of Steelcase's Applied Research and Consulting group.

What is currently taking place is a fundamental shift in the motivations, goals, and methods of design. This change has the potential to democratize design decision making, produce more responsive environments, and so overcome the alienation felt when interacting with designs that are insensitive to the lived experience of their end users.

Discussion Questions

1. Discuss the issues raised by Mitchell about how buildings were conceptualized as idyllic.

2. What were the ways that design methods created spaces?

3. Why were these problematic for users in the past and still problematic in the present, according to Mitchell?

4. Examine the ways that design thinking has been hampered by current design methods as explored by Mitchell.

5. How does the user's lived experience need to be explored in designing spaces using technology?

6. What methods and techniques so companies such as Steelcase and IDEO employ?

7. How do these methods account for an aesthetics of user experiences?

References

Alexander, C. (1964). *Notes on the Synthesis of Form.* Cambridge, MA: Harvard University Press.

Alexander, C., et al. (1977). *A Pattern Language: Towns, Buildings, Construction.* New York: Oxford University Press.

Alexander, C. (1979). *The Timeless Way of Building.* New York: Oxford University Press.

Alexander, C. (1990a). Quoted in *Places for the Soul: The Architecture of Christopher Alexander* [videorecording]. Produced and directed by Ruth Landy; written by Ruth Landy & Stephen Most. Berkeley, CA: University of California Extension Media Center. Transcribed by the author.

Alexander, C. (1990b, April). Letter to the Editor. *Progressive Architecture, 71,* 11.

ARC: Applied Research & Consulting by Steelcase. (n.d.). Workplace Piloting. PDF Retrieved June 14, 2010, from www.steelcase.com/en/services/applied-research-and-consulting/pages/services.aspx.

Blake, P. (1977). *Form Follows Fiasco: Why Modern Architecture Hasn't Worked.* Boston: Little, Brown.

Brand, S. (1994). *How Buildings Learn: What Happens After They're Built.* New York: Viking.

Brown, Tim. (2009). *Change by Design: How Design Thinking Transforms Organizations and Inspires Innovation.* [Kindle 2 version]. New York: HarperCollins e-books.

From Blueprint to Database. (2008, June 5). *The Economist.* Retrieved June 3, 2010, from www.economist.com.

Glassie, Henry. (1982). Folk Art. In T. Schlereth (Ed.). *Material Culture Studies in America* (pp. 124–140). Nashville, TN: Association for State and Local History.

Glynn, Simon. (2009). *Neue Nationalgalerie, Berlin by Mies van der Rohe 1968.* Retrieved June 19, 2010, from http://www.galinsky.com/buildings/neue_nationalgalerie/index.html.

Goethe, Johann Wolfgang von. (1839). 1749–1832. *Conversations with Goethe in the Last Years of His Life.* Johann Peter Eckerman. M. Fuller (Trans.). Boston: Hilliard, Gray, and Company.

Hughes, R. (1991). *Shock of the New.* (Revised ed.). New York: Knopf.

Jencks, C. (1973). *Modern Movements in Architecture.* Garden City, NY: Anchor Books.

Jencks, C. (1977). *The Language of Post-Modern Architecture.* New York: Rizzoli.

Jones, J. C. (1970). *Design Methods: Seeds of Human Futures.* Chichester, UK: John Wiley & Sons.

Krygiel, E., Demchak, G., & Dzambazova, T. (2008). *Mastering Revit Architecture 2009.* Indianapolis, IN: Sybex/Wiley.

Mitchell, C. (1992). *Redefining Designing: From Form to Experience.* New York: Van Nostrand Reinhold.

Mow, A., & Naylor, K. (2010, May 3). Navigating the Legal Landscape of BIM. *Design Intelligence.* Retrieved June 24, 2010, from www.di.net/articles/archive/navigating_legal_landscape/_bim/.

Steelcase. (n.d.). *Unique Approach/Applied Research and Consulting/Services/Steelcase.* Retrieved June 14, 2010, from www.steelcase.com/en/services/applied-research-and-consulting/

pages/uniqueapproach.aspx.

Tigerman, Stanley. (1986). Mies van der Rohe: A Moral Modernist Model. *Perspecta, 22,* Paradigms of Architecture, 112–135.

Vandenberg, M. (1998). *New National Gallery, Berlin: Ludwig Mies van der Rohe.* London: Phaidon Press.

Wolfe, T. (1981). *From Bauhaus to Our House.* New York: Farrar Straus and Giroux.

SUMMARY

Spaces are evolving into domains of understanding that challenge physical concepts as the sole means by which we experience spaces. As we move from physical space to spatialized space, we cannot ignore the ways that spaces are appropriated and changed, how we might experience them subjectively yet deliberately, and how each one of us assigns meanings based on our specific contexts and experiences. We perceive spaces as places of engagement, as sources of understanding about ourselves as users, as hidden linings, and as theatrical domains. These new meanings engage us in ways that begin to consider the user as a person engaged with the environment from their perspective. When we move into the next chapter, we will begin to apply these concepts to more specific ways that we live at home and in different spaces we appropriate.

SUGGESTED READINGS

Alexander, C. (1964). *Notes on the Synthesis of Form.* Cambridge, MA: Harvard University Press.

Brown, Tim. (2009). *Change by Design: How Design Thinking Transforms Organizations and Inspires Innovation* [Kindle 2 version]. New York: HarperCollins e-books.

Merleau-Ponty, M. (1945; 1958). *Phenomenology of Perception.* London: Routledge.

Wolfe, T. (1981). *From Bauhaus to Our House.* New York: Farrar Straus Giroux.

OVERVIEW QUESTIONS FOR DISCUSSION

1. What perspectives about users and space are understood in this chapter? Explore Preston and Mitchell's ideas about spaces as places of experience.

2. What is a sense of space as an experience of place? How do we move from one experience to another and what do we uncover? What is critical design?

3. How do we make meanings and interpret these to be able to understand spaces of lived experiences?

4. How do we attribute meanings to the sights, sounds, and senses that we experience when moving in the city, approaching a building for the first time, or gleaning the stories of things that an object might reveal? Compare and contrast the ways that Preston portrays objects as places of storytelling, by contrast with Mitchell and how our tools of expression prototype lived experiences.

5. What are the new and emerging ways that we prototype lived experience and why would we be interested in examining this further critically? How?

6. What are Bousbaci and Huppatz telling us about users and how spaces are experienced? How is this different than the topics that we examined in Chapter 4?

7. How is the idea of ephemeral spaces explored in the context of the Ralph Lauren flagship store? What is seen, not seen, real, not real? How is this theatrical yet not theatre?

8. How are Bousbaci's and Preston's perspectives about user experience the same? Different? What are they saying about the perspectives of the user in each instance?

9. How are technology and history woven around C. Thomas Mitchell's and Huppatz's ideas of spaces as noncontainers?

10. What are subjective experiences when we move in and through spaces?

CHAPTER 6
Spaces of Everyday Life, Self, and Social Constructions

Significant space, house, habitat, home, dwelling, gender, social status, spatial arrangements, living well, escapism, semiology, cultural and visual content analysis, politically social spaces, social space construction, theatrical space construction, cultural space construction, public and private spaces, political spaces, proxemics

AFTER READING THIS CHAPTER, YOU WILL BE ABLE TO:

- Glean ideas about social spaces, spaces of living, and how spaces become places of social constructions.

- Differentiate philosophical approaches to spaces of living.

- Consider what constitutes a significant space.

- Distinguish concepts of "living well" versus "home as defining a sense of self."

- Understand spaces of living and the social constructions of space and place.

- Identify characteristics of house as home, dwelling as home, and house as habitat.

- Consider cultural contexts to issues of dwelling, gender, and space.

- Understand how identity frames spaces as places of dwelling.

INTRODUCTION

Spaces we live in formulate our experiences. We attribute meaning to the things and spaces that surround us. Our sense of self, the way we engage in our daily life, depends on our surroundings, our home, our place of work, and the places we hold dear. Spaces of living impact our sense of self, what we do, and the ways that we define ourselves in society, and in turn they provide us with meanings alongside a host of multiple perceptions and reactions. How might spaces of the everyday be understood from the perspectives of domestic life? How do living spaces reflect social constructions that affect our sense of self and who we are in the world?

While spaces are created with visual and aesthetic properties in mind, they are ultimately meant for people to experience. People appropriate spaces they occupy and change them to suit their purposes. People attach value to the things that they have, while values are also imposed by society and are complicated by the fracturing of contemporary society. This is further complicated by the ways spaces are framed that determine social status as much as well-being. What values we hold as a society also affect both our capacity to make choices and our social place in the world, and often inadvertently frame our design decision making. All these factors affect the spaces we inhabit, the ways we design these spaces, and the underlying values that shape spatial constructions we then experience.

We place great value on culture, politics, and social norms and customs while we are also caught up in changing values. Among the underlying values that shape a society are social customs, voices of diverse people, or cultural customs. Although dwellings vary greatly as spaces depending on the societal values, economic location, and a host of factors that drive how we live, dwellings also are places where people often look to others to help them achieve meaning.

Christian Norberg-Shultz has suggested that home represents

> the very nature of human existence. It gives man a place to be, a place in which to stay and spend time in safety and comfort. (Rengel, 2003, pp. 51–52)

And while our aspirations are to achieve these goals, for many in our world, their places and spaces of living are far from this ideal. More often the values we set in terms of our dwelling places are tied to the acquisition of material goods, while for others this is a distant reality as they eke out an existence on the fringe (Poldma, 2008). Furthermore, this problem of value-setting creates a need for some to actualize values through the designs of lived spaces at the expense of the meaning of home and house. In a philosophical sense, the meanings of house and home have been subjugated:

> We look for meaning in our dwellings, and some hire architects and designers to actualize their values spatially. . . . and many do not know how to do so. The meanings of home and house have become lost in the quest to dwell, and the quest for dwelling has become lost in the acquisition of more goods and cultural symbols of that same house and home in a given society. (Poldma, 2008)

These issues will be examined in this chapter from the perspectives of dwelling and gender as social or philosophical spaces. Two theoretical papers examine meanings of house and home. Virginie LaSalle takes a philosophical perspective about how the concept of "living well" intersects with notions of design spaces by providing spaces that form places of habitation that symbolize beauty and material wealth. She examines the sense of home as a habitat, and how an individual's experience of inhabiting is more than the physical and material visual attributes we assign. She explores Bachelard and Serfaty-Garzon's ideas of intimate spaces. She further juxtaposes the symbolic views of home with the philosophies of Heidegger and Lévinas, who examine the dichotomy of the environment/spaces of living as a concept versus the daily experiences of the inhabitants. LaSalle is promoting the concept of a "significant space" that bridges the forms and substance with the meanings of those who live and perceive the space as a dynamic place.

Hanna Mendoza and Matthew Dudzik provide a provocation that contrasts living well with realities in a cultural context. Mendoza and Dudzik examine how home becomes a culturally defined place of identity, and how economics and cultural contexts change not only concepts of house and home but also determine territoriality and sense of self in social stratification. Using Brazil as the setting, Mendoza and Dudzik examine the impact of globalization and economic values juxtaposed against the realities of dichotomies, where we look for meaning in our dwellings, and some hire architects and designers to actualize their values spatially. ownership and control of personal space has become battle between the marginalized and empowered in Brazilian society. Notions of tribalism, nostalgia, and escapism are explored in these contexts, as is how spaces become frameworks for changing territorial and personal experiences.

The second part of the chapter examines the socially constructed nature of gendered spaces. Theoretical constructs of gender and spaces are defined as I examine both gender and physical spaces as determinants in how social relations are played out. Tracing two seminal texts, fundamental ideas about space and gender are defined by Shirley Ardener, who unfolds concepts of social spaces, while Daphne Spain examines what constitutes gendered spaces. The paper then elaborates on views about culturally determined rules in terms of space and gender.

Finally, the Dialogues and Perspectives closes the chapter with an examination of gender and social relations set in an examination of a woman photographer's framing of spaces at the turn of the century. Susan Close presents the context of gendered space within the framework of the photographic interiors of Lady Clementina Hawarden, from the perspective of cultural theory and gendered spaces. The ensuing dialogue examines issues of boundary, making it a historic context while also introducing a research methodology that uses cultural analysis as the framework for the methodology of reading the images. This semiotic approach in research that uses found images (as in photography) analyzes the interior spaces as a means of comparing and contrasting social space, theatrical construction of space, and gendered space and in the context of social status.

REFERENCES

Poldma, T. (2008). Dwelling Futures and Lived Experience: Transforming Interior Space. *Design Philosophy Papers*, http://www.desphilosophy.com/dpp/dpp_journal/paper2/body.html.

Rengel, R. (2003). *Shaping Interior Space.* New York: Fairchild Publications.

What help is it, to solve philosophical problems, if [one] cannot settle the chief, most important thing—how to live a good and happy life? "Live well!" is the supreme philosophical commandment.

—Ludwig Wittgenstein
(excerpt from Shusterman, 1997)

In the above quote, Wittgenstein is suggesting that one's will to contribute to good living should guide the design of the philosophical approach. If the thinker considers the goal of a good and healthy existence as predominant, it is because this existence underlies aspirations residing in everyone. For professionals in the disciplines of design, the will to contribute to this good living of our peers is a consideration that always inspires and is echoed in our spatial conceptions. The same applies to the design of interior space, notably when it comes to thinking and to shaping people's habitations, a proven material symbol of good and happy living in North American culture. The concept of home is often used as an archetypal refuge for dwellers in their intimacy and their way of being.

As designers of the interior inhabited space, we must ask ourselves what this intention—to live a good and happy life—means intrinsically and to strive to endow the space with solutions that, if adequate, will contribute to satisfying of this fundamental need. In a succinct look at the phenomenon of habitation, let us introduce the perceptions of thinkers to diverse disciplinary orientations for which the reflections guide the process of designing the residence.

The Senses of Habitation

This will to develop the sense of home as habitat and to find the design approach has resided within thinkers and designers for a long time; the reiteration and expansion of reflections clearly confirm the importance still attributed to the habitation today. For example, the versatility of the habitation's forms, which vary greatly with a number of criteria—including the functions of the space, needs, the living and cultural habits of the inhabitants, and the geographical situation. If reflection on the habitat's constructed frame ultimately concerns design professionals, then the theories that guide their actions are frequently the fruit of thinkers from diverse disciplines; the writings of philosophers, anthropologists, sociologists, and psychologists participate in the founding of the design approach. A good part of this situation can be explained by the great complexity of the phenomenon of habitation, which firmly establishes itself to encompass a multitude of factors to be considered. Among the host of sources existing today, Gaston Bachelard, Perla Serfaty-Garzon, Martin Heidegger, and Emmanuel Lévinas are invaluable references for their study of the phenomenon of habitation.

In his phenomenological work, *The Poetics of Space* (1957), Gaston Bachelard examines the being's invariable essence of inhabiting, while analyzing the poetics of habitation, perceived as an image of intimacy through its most authentic object that is the home. According to Bachelard, the home, in its unity and complexity, represents the material sense of the human experience and the materialization of its poetics. It is man's concrete anchoring, his primary world, and it characterizes him in his fundamental dimension of habitation:

> We should therefore have to say how we inhabit our vital space, in accord with all the dialectics of life, how we take root, day after day, in a "corner of the world." [. . .] For our house is our corner of the world. [. . .], it is our first universe. (1957)

Bachelard's analysis of the poetics of habitation considers two predominant phases of analysis for this living space. First, the home is approached as an analysis instrument of the soul. Then the home is regarded more as an object to be developed, a collection of symbols for phenomenological material analysis. This second phase of analysis deals with the material and symbolic properties of the home. Through

formal observation of his object, the philosopher expands on the poetic images that are found—such as the fireside, the space conducive to reverie—which make the habitation significant and bring it to the status of home for the resident.

With her interest in the various senses of habitation, sociologist and environmental psychologist Perla Serfaty-Garzon(notably in the 1999 work *Psychologie de la maison* and 2003's *Chez soi. Les territoires de l'intimité*) observes the semantic richness of the various terms used to denote habitation—residence, house, home, hearth, etc.—in connection with their manifestations constructed over time. According to Serfaty-Garzon, this archetypal inhabited space merits the appellation home; for it is the anchoring point that provides life with spatial rooting. Inhabiting means living in a historical perspective, in symbiosis with a space and the people who share it.

Thus, Serfaty-Garzon considers the phenomenon of habitation in a historical and sociological perspective. In her understanding, the emergence of the sphere of private life that led to the design of intimacy in occidental societies would be related to the specialization of spaces and would have brought about a sacralization of the dwelling. The appropriation envisaged by Serfaty-Garzon as an active component of home (2003, p. 102) includes a moral, psychological, and affective sense. She suggests that the material character and ways that we personalize the space are in part identified by a cultural model and then adjusted by our own particular individual expression that affirms our identity and how we construct oneself through our inhabited space (p. 92).

The symbolic analysis of the home's premises, as perceived by Serfaty-Garzon in a Bachelardian spirit, leads her to examine the hidden areas, such as the cellar and the attic—territories of the unconscious—through their own symbolism, but also through a constituent analysis that considers the verticality of the construction filled with dreamlike meaning in the experience of home (pp. 182–183). Related to the states of the person's soul, these spatial qualities fill the home's premises with meaning. They allude to an apparent irrationality (1999, p. 83) associated with the secret of what is concealed to foreign observation, corresponding to an inner self (1999, p. 86). Serfaty-Garzon suggests that the rooms of the home thus encompass meanings, essential to the respect of the living space's boundaries that are more or less permeable. Thus, the entrance would represent the area that civilizes intrusion; as a midway, it can call for or invite the passage to the interior space, or it can stop a movement. The entrance is the true in-between area: it is neither inside nor outside (2003, pp. 143–145). The living room is defined in modernity by the home's archetypal space for socializing. It is the home's foreground, the spatial conveyance of the inhabitant's construction and social consolidation process (2003, p. 162).

Among the written sources that examine the phenomenon of man's inhabitation, the text "Building, Dwelling, Thinking" (Essays and Conferences, 1954) by Martin Heidegger is a choice reference.

Through a semantic study of the German word *bauen,* Heidegger discusses the existential dimension of inhabiting, and through an analysis of the relationships of meaning, developing the significations of building. This etymological work leads the thinker to build the action of inhabiting as a fundamental feature of the human condition. Heidegger's judgment of the context, which to him is contemporary, underlies a flaw between meaning and the taking of shape, as he observes dwelling. He claims that dwellings can be well understood, can facilitate practical living, can be affordable, and can be open to the air, light, and sun, but he questions whether they can actually guarantee in and of themselves that dwelling takes place (p. 171).

Heidegger guides us toward this all-too-frequent dichotomy that can be observed between the environment in a conceptual state, the dwelling as a constructed environment, and, ultimately, the daily experiences lived by the inhabitants of the designed space. This observation is also made by architect and theorist Juhani Pallasmaa, who deplores the recurring impertinence of responses lavished by designers to subtle, emotional, and diffused aspects of the home (1992).

One of the theories that philosopher Emmanuel Lévinas develops in his work *Totality and Infinity: An Essay on Exteriority* (1971) incites one to think about the habitation and to see it anew as more than a space expected to meet the relative needs of habitation. On the premise of reasoning intrinsically relating the need, the act of satisfying this need—through what he calls contents of life—and the pleasure occasioned by the satisfying of the need or by the contents of life, Lévinas presents his idea of a joy essential to human existence:

> Even if the content of life ensures my life, the means is immediately sought as an end, and the pursuit of this end becomes an end in its turn. Thus things are always more than the strictly necessary; they make up the grace of life. (. . .) Qua object the object seen occupies life; but the vision of the object makes for the "joy" of life. (1971, p. 114)

Applied to the person's habitation space, this approach calls for a projection of the habitat that goes far beyond strictly functional considerations to which the construction must provide and refers to a qualification of the interior premises that supports and promulgates the pleasure of inhabiting, the joy of dwelling. Further, when Lévinas discusses the dwelling and the habitation, he sees it first as a tool, but insists on its privileged purpose:

> The home would serve for habitation as the hammer for the driving in of a nail or the pen for writing. For it does indeed belong to the gear consisting of things necessary for the life of man. It serves to shelter him from the inclemencies of the weather, to hide him from enemies or the importunate. And yet, within the system of finalities in which human life maintains itself the home occupies a privileged place. (1971, p. 162)

For Lévinas, this distinction of the home among other tools comes from its dimension as the beginning of human activity. Thus, the home would provide the retreat and intimacy the person needs in this archetypal private domain to be able to engage in subsequent social activities with others.

Designing Significant Living Spaces

Such theories undoubtedly foster reflection in a good number of designers who focus on the habitation qualities of the living spaces that they imagine. One question remains: How does one concretely interpret these notions so that within the designed space, these features and qualities can participate in the experience of the habitation space and enrich the occupants' living? Based on the work of selected theorists—Edward T. Hall, Juhani Pallasmaa, and Maurice Merleau-Ponty—let us expand on the means by which, as thinkers of inhabited architecture, we can move from these inspiring theories to the design of significant spaces that promote good living through habitation.

In their analysis of the person's holistic experience, and notably from their spatial and habitation experience, a number of thinkers tend toward an initial perceptual understanding of the phenomenon. In *The Hidden Dimension* (1966), Edward T. Hall adopts an anthropological approach oriented toward man's sensory perception; he asserts that man—"as with all other members of the animal kingdom—is until the end and irrevocably a prisoner of his biological organism" (p. 8). The originality of his approach involves his supposition that what is the human's own is the experiencing of his culture, which conditions him in his relationships with the world. Hall states that we attach ourselves to this type of profound, general, non-verbalized experience that all the members of a single culture share and communicate without knowing, and that constitutes the backdrop in relation to which all the other events are situated (p. 8).

In this sense, the central theme of his study focuses on the cultural dimension of human habitation, which, undeniably, is crucial in the design of habitation spaces. Hall states that as the perceptive view varies with the cultural identity, experience must not be placed in a state of stable reference. The sensory device—extended in its organism by the new dimension proper to man, the cultural dimension—and the way man uses it are, in Hall's view, the tools that enable man to build himself a world. The anthropologist thus asserts the importance of reeducating designers of human environments that must consider man as an interlocutor of his living space, and model this space with constant concern for the needs envisaged as specific cultural products—Hall assigns the neologism **proxemics**—of occupants. The design thus cannot be developed without in-depth knowledge of the cultural context that the constructed and developed environment belongs to, and a keen sensitivity to the consequences of the residents' living experience.

Architect Juhani Pallasmaa has also studied the importance of the person's sensory perception in the architected environment. Through various essays, of which the most famous is likely *The Eyes of the Skin: Architecture and the Senses* (1995), Pallasmaa expresses his particular concerns about hegemonic vision in occidental architecture to the detriment of the other senses, thus leading to the disappearance of sensory and sensual qualities in arts and architecture. The tactile dimension of the environment and the sensory experience of the body influence our understanding of the world, as well as the habitation we make out of it. Pallasmaa claims that through our bodies we are at the center of the world; not as central observers of an environment, or as spectators, but as a place of reference, memory, imagination, and integration in the world (p. 11). Consequently, he asserts that the architectural experience should provide more than visual communication; it should question the person's haptic (that is, relating to touch) interest through the sensual qualities involved. He identifies the natural materials—such as stone, brick, and wood—as communicating effectively with the person, as these materials express a certain wear that tells of their life—their age, marks left from wear and the passage of time, and their history (p. 31). Pallasmaa advocates a building approach aspiring to re-sensualize architecture through a heightened sense of its materiality, its haptics, its texture, its weight, the density of its space, and the materialization of light (p. 37).

Finally, as a summary of these reflections, Maurice Merleau-Ponty (notably in the 1945 work *Phénoménologie de la perception*) highlights the consideration of the person's subjectivity in the experience of his senses and his human habitat in the world. He reminds us that the needs to be satisfied by the home and its interior space are not so much about considering the design's strictly physical attributes—such as the finishes of surfaces and the aesthetics—as they are about overall communication with the senses and the space's necessary potential for flexibility. In his view, the experience of space cannot be reduced to a list of perception criteria—senses, culture, etc.—as it is an experience through which the multitude of possible contributions comes together and combines in a living experience proper to each person. It is a process both temporal and spatial, created and justified through lived experiences that interior design must encompass, as a backdrop for the person's activities.

Variances and Constancies in Habitation

Although certain justified *a priori* elements seem to remain intact in the space's design process, we notice that the constructed manifestations of the authentic habitation vary as an echo of the complexity of the factors involved during the design process. In the practice of interior design—or interior architecture—designing the space frequently means developing an existing space with form, material, and objects in the creation of spatial solutions. It is also important to understand that people adapt the space in their own manner, a fundamental aspect that must be considered during the project's design. Our success as professionals of inhabited space depends on our ability to discern what facilitates—in the person's real and lived experiences—the adapting of the space that is his or her own and his or her pleasure to be there. Finally, it appears to us that the use of spatial devices emerges in the inhabited space, and that these components appear to be on the path to effectively satisfying certain manifest needs of these residents. To name only one of them, note the passage from a temporal spatiality (one room for one activity) to a spatial temporality (a multifunctional space) that demonstrates a patent potential to be modeled with the passing time, the moment of the day, the week, or the year.

Discussion Questions

1. Virginie LaSalle describes Bachelard's concept of home as "unity and complexity, repository material sense of human experience and materialized in its poetics."
   a. What does this mean?
   b. How is home a "collection of symbols"?

2. How does Serfaty-Garzon understand home as an anchor point?

3. What is Heidegger's idea of home as dwelling?

4. What is the significance of lived space as home, as dwelling?

References

Bachelard, G. (1957). *La poétique de l'espace.* Paris: Éditions Quadridge/Puf., English version: *The Poetics of Space. 1964.* M. Jolas, Trans. New York: Orion Press.

Hall, E. T. (1971). *La dimension cachée.* Paris: Éditions du Seuil. Original American edition: *The Hidden Dimension.* (1966). New York: Anchor Books.

Heidegger, M.,(1954). "Bâtirhabiterpenser" from *Essais et conférences.* Paris: Gallimard, pp. 170–193.

LaSalle, V. (2007). *Alvar Aalto et l'expression de l'humanisme dans l'espace habité.* Master's thesis submitted to the Faculté des études-supérieures of the Université de Montréal to obtain a master's degree in applied sciences in design with an option in history and theory (unpublished).

Lévinas, E., (1971). "Section II :Intériorité et économie" *from Totalité et infini.* Essai sur l'extériorité. Paris: Biblioessais, Le Livre de Poche, pp. 111–200. English language version: *Totality and Infinity: An Essay on Exteriority.* A. Lingis (Ttrans). Pittsburgh: Duquesne University Press, 1969.

Merleau-Ponty, M. (1945). *Phénoménologie de la perception.* Paris: Gallimard,.

Pallasmaa, J. (1992). Identity, Intimacy, and Domicile: Notes on the Phenomenology of Home. *The Concept of Home: An Interdiciplinary View.* Symposium presented at Trondheim University, Norway, from August 21–23..

Poldma, T., "Dwelling Futures and Lived Experiences: transforming interior spaces," in *Design Philosophy Paper.* No 2, 2008.

Serfaty-Garzon, P. (2003). *Chez soi: Les territoires de l'intimité.* Paris: Éditions Armand Colin.

Serfaty-Garzon, P. (1999.) *Psychologie de la maison: Une archéologie de l'intimité.* Montréal: Éditions du Méridien & Éditions Cursus Universitaire.

Shusterman, R., *Practicing Philosophy: Pragmatism and the Philosophical Life.* New York: Routledge, 1997.

Note: This text is taken in part from an article by LaSalle, V. and Poldma, T. (2009). "Les sens de l'habitation en design d'intérieur," *Revue ARQ Architecture-Québec,* No. 146, February, 2 pages.

Space, in design terms, has usually been studied primarily in terms of the physical, situated in the perception of *Man and His World* (Hall, 1969). Specifically, and for most of the twentieth century, theories about interior space have centered on either physical or psychological perceptions, heavily influenced by Jungian and Freudian psychology and concepts surrounding abstract perceptions of space (Malnar and Vodvarka, 1992; Rodemann, 1999).

Social and gendered spaces frame how people exist. Consider how spaces frame voices and how design intersects boundaries of value making in diverse types of environments:

From the moment of birth, spaces shape who we are and how we function as males and females. The social constructions of space and place, at least in part, create the social roles and relations that govern how we live, work and play. I believe that there is a relationship between gender and space, and that social constructions affect this Relationship. (Poldma, 1999, p.1)

Until recently, sociological studies of space have been limited in interiors and are usually appropriated from other disciplines such as geography, sociology, or anthropol-ogy (Ardener, 1981; Spain, 1992; Vaikla-Poldma, 1999). In this paper we will look at perspectives on spaces and gender, and how these are socially constructed, in response to the work of Shirley Ardener, Daphne Spain, and others. In particular, Ardener and Spain, from the perspectives of sociology and geography, respectively, each considers how social relations are constructed through the spaces that vehicle them.

When we create spaces, the different professionals involved are rarely aware of the impact their designs make on social relations. Homes are defined for assumed uses rather than the varied actual, lived experiences: single women, cultural variables, families, and diverse family social arrangements such as parents living with children or similar situations outside what has been thought of as the traditional family unit. Both Ardener and Spain evolve arguments about how physical space perpetuates values of the culture that occupies it.

Spatially Perpetuated Relations Between Men and Women

Daphne Spain (1992) cites examples of the interrelationship of "spatial and social processes, that space is constructed by social behavior at a given time" (p. 6). Spain provides numerous examples of space as social and physical, and looks at how space reproduces power relations in both industrial and nonindustrial societies, as historic precedence and as contemporary phenomena in perpetuating social relations at work, at home and in school. Spain discusses Max Weber's view of knowledge differences in men and women as spatially perpetuated:

> [S]patial difference reinforced knowledge differences between men and women . . . Weber recognized explicitly this relationship between spatial segregation and gender stratification. His study of non-industrial societies identified men's houses as repositories of power from which women were excluded . . . men gathered there for religious ceremonies and initiation rites and made major decisions affecting the village. Women were barred from participation—and thereby barred from training . . . for leadership positions. (p. 19)

Most social theory does not link gender difference to space and its design; in fact, space as designed entity or framework for human interrelations is often not considered. Spain and others maintain that the social segregation of space blocks access to knowledge and power through institutions such as the family, school, and the workplace, and this may be due to (but is not limited to) issues of gender (Thomas, 1986; Ruddock, 1994; Spain 1992; Vaikla-Poldma, 1999). For example, historically in the construction of buildings, buildings have embodied social values; those who create the interior spaces in these buildings wield power in that they can manipulate space to political, cultural, and/or social advantage.

As space and time dimensions mutate and change with new technologies and immersive dimensions, these concepts become ever more complex. As more immaterial spatial experiences become heightened, the new definitions of what constitutes space as a nonphysical entity are shifting these more traditional concepts of spatial manipulation for political or social ends. Before we can explore these new dimensions, we turn to the recent past for ideas about social languages and gender stances.

Space as a Form of Communication and Coded Language

An alternative way to look at space is as the social means of communication and coded language. As long as 30 years ago, Shirley Ardener (1981) presented space as a place of social boundaries and communication codes, suggesting that social boundaries are created in its design. She states that:

> Much of social life is given shape, and that when dimension or location are introduced we assert a correspondence between the so-called "real" physical world and its "social reality" . . . There is, of course, an interaction such that appreciation of the physical world is in turn dependent on social perceptions of it. . . . Societies have generated

their own rules, culturally determined, for making boundaries on the ground, and have divided the social into spheres, levels and territories with invisible fences and platforms. (pp. 11–12).

Ardener continues by arguing that space forms social boundaries that serve as reinforcing social rules:

[T]he categories that we make in order to codify and confront the worlds we create and how we cope with some of the problems that arise from the existence of these boundaries . . . a restricted area, like a night club . . . has a set of rules to determine how its boundary shall be crossed and who shall occupy that space . . . The notion (boundary) has been seized and applied to the meaning of concepts, and to the classification into groups. . . . The appreciation of the physical world is in turn dependent upon social perceptions of it. (p. 11)

This would explain the relative popularity of one place/one moment, then its subsequent eclipse or rejection the next (what is trendy at a given time). Social perceptions drive uses as much as physical aspects of spaces, and often underlying values shape these perceptions.

Social Maps, Boundaries, Territories, and Power Relations

Ardener chronicles an extensive study of women and space in both Western and non-Western cultures, concluding that women's space in many instances is mini-malized, and is made invisible in many others. Concepts of space overlap with concepts of power, of private versus public, and particularly the sexual division of space in some cultures. Research in other disciplines such as geography and art (Ardener, 1981; Irigaray in Ross, 1994; Spain, 1992) support these ideas. Not only do we create social relations within spaces, we also react and act in part according to how a space is presented to us. Ardener says that this "reflects social organization . . . behavior and space are mutually dependent" (p. 12). She believes that social maps for men differ than those for women, and that resultant spaces are boundaries that keep in certain groups and keep others out. Ardener proposes a mutually dependent concept of space with communication codes and how

we might visualize a semiotic system that depended, in the absence of speech, [on] . . . the relevant position of each participant to another in a gathering, and to items in a fixed environment . . . spaces define people in it. (p. 12)

In another example, West and Zimmerman (1997) suggest that the physical setting helps to construct social difference, when they state, "The physical features of social setting provide one obvious resource for the expression of our essential differences" (p. 137). Space thus becomes an agent of transforming the people and defining their activities, becoming the physical embodiment of the social setting, mutually interdependent with sex, and thus perpetuating gender difference.

Space as Social and Political Value Construction

Spain (1992) , in her book *Gendered Spaces*, establishes the socially and mutually dependent relationship between sex, gender, and space and how this relationship creates power relations. She states that:

> Spatial arrangements between the sexes are socially created, and when they provide access to valued knowledge for men while reducing access to that knowledge for women, the organization of space may perpetuate status difference . . . To quote geographer Doreen Massey, "It is not just that the spatial is socially constructed; the social is spatially constructed too."(pp. 3–4)

Spaces impose on us and create the social constructions that govern social and power relations between men and women.

Others propose that power relations are manifested in concepts of culture and power as well. For example, Bourdieu and Passeron (1990), in their treatise *Reproduction in Education, Society, and Culture*, propose a theory of dominant culture, where a combination of the dominant class, pedagogic work, and values taught to legitimize dominant classes is perpetuated by and supported by spatial design. Institutions of home, school, and workplace reinforce value constructions, while historically spatial institutions in both nonindustrial and industrial societies create divisions of labor and that these influence space and its occupants (Spain, 1992; Bourdieu & Passeron, 1990). Space segregates gender and tasks,

reinforcing prevailing male privilege in most of these societies.

Toward Space, Body, Gender, and Social Identity

More recently, Jos Boys (1998), in the article "Beyond Maps and Metaphors: Re-thinking the Relationships Between Architecture and Gender," proposes a politics of space and difference, citing feminist architectural discourse as evolving away from the current dualistic debates about space and gender, toward a different discourse altogether. Boys has studied various feminist authors who have positioned postmodern debates about architecture as dualistic in nature, countering arguments about the nature of public/private, man/woman, home/work, and so on (Soja & Hooper, 1993; Boys in Ainley, 1998). She proposes an alternative way of understanding human relationships in terms of spaces, such as social identity:

> The relationships between body, social identity, space, and representation across such previous diverse disciplines as philosophy, linguistics, cultural studies, geography, sociology and anthropology (Harvey, 1989; Soja 1989; Jameson, 1991; Wilson 1991; Rose 1993; Keith and Pile 1993; Lash and Urry 1994; Massey 1994; Grosz 1995) . . . the rethinking of the space theory itself thus searches for new categories of position beyond man/woman, home/work, and so on. (p. 204)

Boys suggests a relocation and rethinking between space and identity occurs, both as social and physical entities, in considering feminist viewpoints. She asks the question "How might we build alternative structures for explaining the connections between material landscapes and social structures?" (p. 205)

Social Constructions of Space and Place

The design of space and the multiple contexts that are associated with space and its forms are guided by the social constructions that are required within the spaces, and further by the impact upon the space that vehicle these social constructs (Poldma, 1999). These contexts include actions played out by various subjective human relations, which may guide a design process that is also situated in ethical, social, or gender-associated contexts. From the moment of birth, spaces shape who we are and how we function as males and females. The social constructions of space and place, at least in part, create the social roles and relations that govern how we live, work, and play (Spain, 1992; Vaikla-Poldma, 1999).

So we see that spaces have an influence on social relationships, and they also create the social constructions that govern social and political relations between men and women. Not only do these value constructions influence how we see and design space, they also contribute to the reproduction of the values through the spaces that assist in their evolution (Spain, 1992; Vaikla-Poldma, 1999). What we do inside our homes, offices, and public spaces is grounded in social, political, and personal

relationships that we create to navigate in our everyday world. We are not always aware of what these relationships are, nor do we always want to know.

Politics, Social Norms, and Spatial Structures

In terms of a geographic context, for example, Daphne Spain considers our gender constructions to be a direct result of the spatial environments that we create, and that these are often political acts as much as design decisions. As Spain (1992) states:

> The spatial structure of buildings embodies knowledge of social relations, or the taken for granted rules that govern relations of individuals to each other, and to society . . . Thus, dwellings reflect ideals and realities about relationships between women and men within the family and in society. The space outside the home becomes the arena in which social relations are produced, while the space inside the home becomes that in which social relations are reproduced. (p. 7)

Framed within broader philosophical and social-psychological contexts, these taken-for-granted rules require scrutiny and discussion.

Feminism, Postmodernism, and Social Constructions of Space

Feminism and postmodernism have had a major impact on not only how we live but also in the increased awareness about fundamental values and how we understand knowledge construction. For over 30 years feminists have argued for change in the ways in which we disseminate knowledge; we accept absolutes and thus the status quo (hooks, 1984; Irigaray in Ross, 1994; Grosz, 1995; Rothschild, 1999). Specifically, they have voiced concern and critical debate about art, aesthetics, and architecture as determinants of the spatial environment (Grosz, 1995; Irigaray in Ross, 1994), which often fails to take into account the ways that women navigate the environment in which they live. Feminists also have a deep concern for aspects of the spatial and the social, as psychological and personal states as well as physical states (Ainley, 1998; Grosz, 1995).

Elizabeth Grosz (1995) has been influential in providing insights into issues of space and how women are perceived within diverse types of spaces. In terms of space, Grosz positions women's lack of voice as a physical non-presence. In her book, *Space, Time, and Perversion*, she states:

> The organization and management of space—the organization of architecture and regional planning, among others—has very serious political, social and cultural impact, and in a sense cannot be but of concern for feminists. . . . [Irigaray's] concerns are directed towards the establishment of a viable space and time for women to inhabit as women. The ways in which space has been historically conceived have always functioned to either contain women or to obliterate them. (p. 120)

Space and its organization as "containing or obliterating women" is a strong statement about the ways that architectural and interior/exterior spaces are political and social tools of meaning.

Feminism: Context, Types, and Roots

Feminist literature has an influence on art history, on social issues, on how we study art, architecture, and design, and on the subsequent ways we see and understand spaces. Feminist critical theories can be a part of how we position ways of understanding the world and specifically understanding designed spaces, as these exist in history and as perceived in today's contemporary society.

Feminism evolved in the 1970s and into the 1980s primarily as an anti-aesthetic reaction against the values that underpin society social institutions: the home, school, and the workplace. In looking at the values that underpin what we teach, feminists and others suggest that many of these values are Eurocentric, and are embedded in educational, social, and political systems (Code, 1991; hooks, 1984; Grosz, 1995; Field Belenky et al., 1997). Eurocentrism is a core value attitude defined by Stam and Shohat (1994) as:

> [A] single paradigmic perspective in which Europe is seen as the unique source of meaning, "reality" to the rest of the world's shadow ... seeing the world from a single privileged point, attributing to the West an almost Provincial sense of historical destiny. (p. 296)

The feminist view of Eurocentrically structured phenomena is that it systematically excludes women from its center. More recent epistemological theory is ground in traditional roots of the philosophies of Socrates, Plato, and Aristotle (hooks, 1984; Code, 1991; Grosz, 1995; Field Belenky et al., 1997). This philosophy does not take into account multiple vantage points, be they female, cultural, or multiracial (hooks, 1984; Code, 1991; Field Belenky et al., 1997). For example, in her book *Women's Ways of Knowing*, Lorraine Code (1991) dissects the relationship of reason and knowledge and the link with power and gender:

> Throughout the history of western philosophy there is a demonstrable alignment between the ideals of "autonomous reason" and ideals of masculinity. That alignment suppresses and even denigrates values and attributes long associated with the "feminine" at the same time and in the same way it devalues epistemic dependence in the name of the cognitive self-reliance. Both philosophical discourse and the everyday ideology that bears its mark take universal, essential . . . concepts of masculinity and femininity for granted. . . . Yet the ideals of masculinity that align with the ideals of reason derive . . . from the experiences of men that construct the dominant theories of both. . . . It is commonplace of western philosophy . . . that women are irrational creatures . . . utterly lacking in reason. (p. 117)

Thus, feminism defines the root of its discourse as the issue of subjectivity and identity. bell hooks (1984) describes how the feminist movement began as a militant reaction and was reactionary in nature, springing out of white upper class America (p. 33). hooks says that this movement was "generally reactionary . . . [the fact that feminists] argued that all men are the enemies of all women . . . did not strengthen public understanding of the significance of authentic feminist movement" (p. 33). hooks saw the issue as sexual oppression of either gender, not necessarily oppression only against a particular class of women. hooks advocated an authentic feminist movement to end all oppression, be it racial, social, or sexual.

Woman as Subject and Issues of Body and Space in Aesthetic Values and Feminist Theories

Feminists such as hooks and others foresee an end to this type of oppression. Sexual oppression does not allow woman as subject or identity to exist. Woman as gender is relegated to second place or virtually nonexistent as self. For example, in discussing aesthetics, Ross (1994) and Cooper (1992) present two primary ways that the traditional art canon has affected voice in aesthetics. First, Ross cites that "the masculine has been passed off as universal, neutral" (p. 565). Second, Cooper cites Irigaray, who states that "aesthetic values are essential and universal and thus self-evidently reflected in a broad and stable canon of great works of art" (1992, p. 59).

And this leads to the idealization of form and beauty, as philosophers contend that "aesthetic values arise out of formal and structural complexity peculiar to works of high art and one of which of these modes is form—beauty is the supreme idealization of form" (Cooper, 1994, p. 58). The example of the value placed on aesthetic categories in architecture is situated in this thinking, including the symbolic reverence of beauty in certain types of form.

Irigaray, in her paper "The Speculum of the Other Woman," theorizes that this idealization of woman creates "a disappearance of woman as subject" (Irigaray in Ross, 1994, p. 578). According to Irigaray the subjective self in women is thus denied. She argues that in "taking over all [social] spaces, they effectively have placed women in a "tomb"(pp. 121–122). Grosz (1995) defends Irigaray's stance as not only that of subject denial, but also of denial of the female body in space (pp. 26–28). Grosz does a substantial critical analysis of the Irigaray position, for example, in presenting Irigaray's position on the concept of dwelling:

> The containment of women within a dwelling that they did not build, . . . it becomes a space of duty, of endless and infinitely repeatable chores that have no social value or recognition, the space of the affirmation and replenishment of others . . . (p. 122)

This description of woman's perception of dwelling is in contrast to other examples, such as Gaston Bachelard's ideal of the house as a repository of memories, or even Heidegger's concept of location in dwelling, as we noted earlier in LaSalle's ideas of "habitat as home." Thus, space as dwelling has numerous connotations. It is social and experienced differently by women and men. News reports of women doing double duty at work and at home, and the actual experiences of women constantly on the run are indicative of this social reality. Single parents, fractured relationships, and other social issues are other common benchmarks of our changing society, and these are further evolving through social, political, and technological movements.

Toward an Inclusive Epistemology of Voices from Diverse Spaces of Identity

Code (1991) and Field Belenky, Goldberger, and Tarule (1997) suggest alternative ways of understanding knowledge production, suggesting that female knowledge differs from male but that the two can coexist. Code and Field Belenky et al. construct theories that expand female ways of knowing as a gender-based means of identity. They advocate the recognition of female voice as fundamental to epistemology, yet they do not fall into the epistemological divide of militant feminists. Rather, their interest is recognition of voice and experience as central to an epistemology of constructed knowledge, as opposed to separate knowledges of man and woman. They explore different knowledges (Field Belenky et al., 1997) and the importance of subjective knowledge. Code (1991) suggests that this involves transforming current epistemological theory, rather than rejecting it altogether:

> Many feminists, by contrast, respond by calling for a more generous, more honest epistemology that takes into account the range of capabilities, discursive positions, attitudes and interests that contribute to the construction of knowledge. (p. 158)

In recent years, feminist critical theory has shifted emphasis, and this is most evident in art. Although the emergence of feminist artists and their work is too extensive to mention here, it is important to note the shift to a more pluralistic feminism within feminine thinking in art (Chadwick, 1996, p. 379). In *Women, Art, and Society*, Whitney Chadwick (1996) states that the emphasis is shifting toward arguments situated in uncovering the feminine within the masculine:

> Feminist critics remain sensitive to the dangers of confusing tokenism with equal representation, or the momentary embrace of selective feminist strategies with the ongoing subordination of art by and about women to what is, in the words of Griselda Pollack, "falsely claimed to be gender free Art of men." . . . Although recent critical debates within the mainstream have often focused on deconstructive art practices, many women artists continue their commitment to political activism and to evolving images, materials, and processes that address concerns central

to women's experiences and to their personal, sexual and cultural identities. (p. 380)

Chadwick points out that women artists are exploring cultural, personal, and social issues while using postmodernist strategies in terms of mass media and popular culture. Art in the 1980s moved into realms such as AIDS and gay awareness, and cultural realizations such as racial and sexual orientation. As Chadwick goes on to argue:

> [F]eminism in the 1980s conceptualized both race and sexual orientation as major components of identity politics under the influence of the rise of Queer Theory (a body of writings that often presented sexual orientation as a way of talking about gender) and post structuralism, with its emphasis on difference rather than universalizing tendencies as the basis of politics. (p. 386)

Furthermore, art has become a narrative for the meanings about society for both sexes, and a means to "use multiple personae and voices . . . fusing fact and fiction . . . to deconstruct patriarchally based cultural forms" (p. 415). Thus, women's art situates itself within the larger art world as both feminist and as a means to effect social change.

Possibilities for Understanding Meanings in Design

Grosz, Irigaray, and others offer potential critical means to situate the relationship of the body, space, and gender in terms of psychological, social, and physical spaces of exploration. As Grosz (1995) states:

> Among the more interesting writings on (philosophical notions of) space and spatiality are Irigaray's, whose works, perhaps less known in architectural theory, have had considerable impact on Anglo-American feminist theory and philosophy, and through them, on the ways in which space, time, subjectivity, and corporeality are currently considered. (p. 120)

Thus, concepts such as time and space can be thought about in terms of the ways that women think and act in environments, and how the activities they engage in are affecting the ways of adapting to the world around them.

Discussion Questions

1. Discuss the various themes of this chapter.
   a. What are the social, gender, and political values underlying how we construct meaning?

2. Discuss and elaborate issues
   a. Surrounding how we construct our sense of identity.
   b. About how spaces are intimate places of self and identity.

3. What is the nature of the underlying values that form gender social constructions of space?
   a. How are these perpetuated?
   b. How are these broken down and changing?

References

Ainley, R. (Ed.). (1998). *New Frontiers of Space, Bodies, and Gender*. London: Routledge.

Anderson, G. L. (1994). The Cultural Politics of Qualitative Research in Education: Confirming and Contesting the Canon. *Educational Theory*, 44(2), 225–237.

Ardener, S. (Ed.). (1981). *Women and Space: Ground Rules and Social Maps*. New York: St. Martin's Press.

Bourdieu, P., & Passeron, J-C. (1990). *Reproduction in Education, Society, and Culture* (2nd ed.). London: Sage Publications.

Boys, J. (1998), "Beyond Maps and Metaphors: Re-thinking the Relationships Between Architecture and Gender." In Rosa Ainley (Ed.), *New Frontiers Space, Bodies, and Gender* Oxford, UK: Routledge.

Field Belenky, M., McVicker Clinchy, B., Rule Goldberger, N., & Mattuck Tarule, J. (1997). *Women's Ways of Knowing: The Development of Self, Voice, and Mind.* New York: Basic Books.

Chadwick, W. (1996). *Women, Art, and Society.* London: Thames and Hudson Ltd.

Chafetz, J. (1997). Feminist Theory and Sociology: Underutilized Contributions for Mainstream Theory. *Annual Review of Sociology, 23,* 97–120.

Code, L. (1991). *What Can She Know?* Ithaca, NY: Cornell University Press.

England, P. (1993). *Theory on Gender/Feminism on Theory* (pp. 3–24). New York: Aldine de Gruyter.

Field Belenky, M., McVicker Clinchy, B., Rule Goldberger, N., & Mattuck Tarule, J. (1997).

Women's Ways of Knowing: The Development of Self, Voice, and Mind. New York: Basic Books.

Grosz, E. (1995). S*pace, Time, and Perversion: Essays on the Politics of Bodies.* London: Routledge.

hooks, b. (1984). Educating Women: A Feminist Agenda. In *Feminist Theory: From Margin to Centre* (pp. 107–115). Boston, MA: South End Press.

hooks, b. (1984). The Significance of the Feminist Movement. In *Feminist Theory: From Margin to Centre* (pp. 33–41). Boston, MA: South End Press.

Irigaray, L. (1994). The Speculum of the Other. In S. D. Ross (Ed.), *Art and Its Significance: An Anthology of Aesthetic Theory.* Albany, NY: State University of New York Press.

Jaynes, J. (1976). *The Origins of Consciousness in the Breakdown of the Bicameral Mind.* Boston: Houghton Mifflin Company.

Kaukas, L. (2000). Learning from Others: What Recent Postmodern Theory Has to Offer Interior Design. *International Design Education Council Annual Conference.* Chicago: Interior Design Education Council.

Mohanty, C. (1992). Feminist Encounters: Locating the Politics of Experience. In M. Barret & H. Phillips (Eds.), *Destabilizing Theory: Contemporary Feminist Debates* (pp. 74–93). Stanford, CT: Stanford University Press.

Malnar, J. M., and Vodvarka, F. (1992). *The Interior Dimension: A Theoretical Approach to Enclosed Space.* New York: Van Nostrand Reinhold.

Pallasmaa, J. (1990). *The Eyes of the Skin; Architecture of the Senses.* London: Academy Editions.

Rudduck, J. (1994). *Developing a Gender Policy in Secondary Schools.* Pennsylvania: Open University Press.

Spain, D. (1992). *Gendered Spaces.* Chapel Hill, NC: The University of North Carolina Press.

Udry, J.R. (1994). The Nature of Gender. *Demography, 31,* 561–73.

Vaikla-Poldma, T. (1999). *Gender, Design, and Education: The Politics of Voice.* McGill University, Montreal: Author.

West, C., and Zimmermann, D. H. (1997). Doing Gender. *Gender and Society, 1*(2) 125–51.

Note: Parts of this paper were originally published as a master's thesis by Tiiu Poldma, entitled *Gender, Design, and Education: The Politics of Voice*, McGill University, 1999, and the unpublished doctoral thesis entitled *An Investigation of Learning and Teaching Processes in an Interior Design Class: An Interpretive and Contextual Inquiry*, McGill University, 2003.

Brazilian society has a markedly bifurcated class system, and the economic and social distances between the small number of citizens of wealth and the large number of those living in devastating poverty is widening rapidly. Brazil continues to have a disparity of income greater than any other Latin American country, with 22 percent of its population living below the poverty line.[1] As the differentiation rises and the number of underprivileged grows, there is a simultaneous rise in fear felt by those who have regarding the desires and envy of those who don't have. Perceptions of the dangers presented by the poor and the marginalized continue to exist even while unorganized street crime has actually decreased.

The paradox of globalization occurs in the moment of conflict between the rapid, transnational flow of goods and services and the increasingly strict mobility regime that operates to keep individuals located and rooted. Despite the possibilities for narrowing the differences between rich and poor nations, globalization offers very limited possibilities for erasing the differentiation between rich and poor people. In conjunction with ongoing development, there are also processes of underdevelopment. Rather than adhering to a strict center/periphery distribution, the distance between the two groups can now be measured in meters.

While the cosmocrats of society are indeed able to detach themselves to a degree and be part of the flow of networked interactions, the vast majority of the world's inhabitants have no such opportunities.[2] Instead, what we see is an increasingly strict control over movement and decreasing opportunities for meaningful participation in social interaction and mobility by those perceived as marginal or dangerous. This paradigm of suspicion operates to decrease the possibilities for humanizing contact among disparate groups and reinforces the stranger anxiety present at each momentary threshold between worlds. In a self-reinforcing cycle, the "radical anxiety that plagues those who inhabit the lightning-fast network resolves itself in paranoid reaction formations that

[1] United Nations Development Programme, "Statistical Update 2008/2009—Country Fact Sheets— Brazil," *Human Development Reports*, 2008, http://hdrstats.undp.org/en/2008/countries/country_fact_sheets/cty_fs_BRA.html.

[2] Ronen Shamir, "Without Borders? Notes on Globalization as a Mobility Regime," *Sociological Theory* 23, no. 2 (2005): 197– 217.

make productive self-other relations more or less impossible."[3]

Globalization has weakened claims by nation-states to be sole sources of authority and protection. In the case of Brazil, any new weakness need not have been great given the profound mistrust that exists between Brazilians and the criminal justice system, most clearly represented in the public mind by the police. Individuals have assumed the burdens of self-protection through private responses to urban insecurity.[4] These responses include not only hiring private security guards or maintaining personal firearms but also investment in protective architecture and defensible design. Brazilians spend $4.5 billion annually on private security, creating one of the most prosperous market sectors in the entire economy.[5]

This escapism and retreat "reflects deep social anxieties operating as systems of protection and social filtration which confer or deny access on the basis of ownership and affluence."[6] As issues of social welfare and collective good fall out of view by those with the power to address them, so too does the sense of their urgency.

Globalization, however, is not a singular cause but rather exists within the context of the concurrent discursive framework for identity and personal value. Brazilian land policy has both reflected and created a culture of land ownership in relation to a republican ethos of citizenship.[7] In Brazil those governing were interested in pursuing economic liberalism but in a culture that recognizes ownership and territorial dominion as markers of civic rights and engagement. The patronizing relationship that arose in conjunction with this ideology is one in which:

[I]t is only insofar as an individual's personality (or free will) is embodied in things that it becomes capable of being recognized as such by others. In this way, property owners recognize each other as persons struggling through the same processes of self-realization. They respect others' property rights because they want the same respect in return. As a result of such mutual recognition and respect, they regard each other as equals. Thus . . . a person's sense of both universal equality and intersubjective distinction develops through property.[8]

Ownership and control of personal space has become a central point for the conflict between the empowered and the marginalized in São Paulo. This struggle

---

[3] Mark Featherstone, "The State of the Network: Radical Anxiety, Real Paranoia and Quantum Culture," *Journal for Cultural Research* 12, no. 2 (2008): 181.

[4] Paul Chevigny, "The Populism of Fear: Politics of Crime in the Americas," *Punishment and Society* 5, no. 1 (2003): 77– 96.

[5] Shamir, "Without Borders? Notes on Globalization as a Mobility Regime."

[6] Rowland Atkinson and Sarah Blandy, "Panic Rooms: The Rise of Defensive Homeownership," *Housing Studies* 22, no. 4 (2007): 445.

[7] James Holston, *Insurgent Citizenship: Disjunctions of Democracy and Modernity in Brazil* (Princeton: Princeton University Press, 2008).

[8] Ibid., 114.

for possession and dominance over domestic territory provides the context in which those with little are perceived as constituting a dangerous underclass, susceptible to radical ideas as a result of immature civic development.

The result of this historical path is a society in which social and spatial injustices are inexorably interrelated. In a country in which 1.7 percent of the population owns 50 percent of all arable land and with one of the greatest gaps between the rich and the poor in the world, feelings of insecurity on the part of the wealthy have become a part of nearly every decision and interaction. The anxieties felt manifest themselves in conscious decisions about security and in choices made with regard to the representation of identity through the focus placed on the secure interior environment.

The public nature of architectural and urban space has made them obvious locations for the study of designed responses to issues of security.[9] However, behind the gates and walls of the fortified urban enclaves created for the elite are interiors expressive of dominant emotive institutions that operate to legitimate spatial practices of exclusion and differentiation at the scale of the individual. Societal and cultural norms are not abandoned at the thresholds between public and private spaces. Instead, residential interiors in cultures of insecurity are particularly important, as they physically manifest the creation of a national identity in the face of "transnational flows of both people and ideas [that have] blurred the sense of separation between 'insiders' and 'outsiders.'"[10]

Social life is fundamentally recursive, and as human beings create interaction patterns based on past patterns, the entrenched structures of social discord become rigidly institutionalized.[11] The failure to engage in public spaces and the unscripted interactions with difference that occur in those spaces fuels the fear-fantasies of the elite, leading to further withdrawal in a self-perpetuating cycle of increasing segregation and hostility.

Interiors are not only responses to the world as it is perceived, but active components in its creation and expression, as "environment-making is an open-ended and speculative process for projecting possibilities of how we might live."[12]

[9] See: Edward Blakely, *Fortress America: Gated Communities in the United States* (Washington, DC and Cambridge, MA: Brookings Institution Press and The Lincoln Institute of Land Policy, 1999); Mike Davis, *City of Quartz: Excavating the Future in Los Angeles* (New York: Verso, 1990); Nan Ellin, ed., *The Architecture of Fear* (New York: Princeton Architectural Press, 1997); Steven Flusty, "Building Paranoia," in *The Architecture of Fear* (New York: Princeton Architectural Press, 1997), 46–59; P. Harrison and Alan Mabin, "Security and Space: Managing the Contradictions of Access Restriction in Johannesburg," *Environment and Planning B: Planning and Design* 33, no. 1 (2006): 3–20; Setha M. Low, *Behind the Gates: Life, Security, and the Pursuit of Happiness in Fortress America* (New York: Routledge, 2004); Bryan S. Turner, "The Enclave Society: Towards a Sociology of Immobility," *European Journal of Social Theory* 10, no. 2 (2007): 287–303.

[10] Christopher Clapham, "The Challenge to the State in a Globalized World," *Development and Change* 33, no. 5 (2002): 791.

[11] Anthony Giddens, "Problems of Action and Structure," in *The Giddens Reader*, ed. Phillip Cassells (Standford, CA: Stanford University Press, 1993), 88–175.

[12] Cathy Smith, "Spaces of Architectural Overcoming," *IDEA Journal* 2, no. 1 (2005): 51.

Home is a place where the myth of self is created and serves as a "major fixed reference point for the structuring of reality" and provides its inhabitants with a sense of "security from the outrages of the outside world."[13] The myths of taste that are enacted in these fortified residences operate as an aesthetic regime that enforces social differentiation based on belonging. Further, the aesthetics and ideals of interior space are not just reflections of personal taste or fashion but rather comprise a *habitus* of design through which the organizing principles, naturalized assumptions, and rituals and habits of societal interactions are both created and expressed.

Nostalgia, Retribalization, and Escapism

São Paulo is a city with explicit borders and clearly marked spaces created as a process for distinguishing those who are part of cosmopolitan globalization from those who are excluded from participation. The exclusion practiced is not the government-mandated segregation of the past, and the spatial distance between the two types of spaces often can be measured in centimeters. In the homes that served as the sites of analysis for this exploration, the mechanisms of retribalization, nostalgia, and escapism were used to attempt to mitigate the fears felt by the wealthy in connection to the circumstances of contemporary urban life. Escape and defense reflexes led to attempts to control encounters through the elimination of contact with the unexpected. The aesthetics, spatial relationships, and security measures instituted in these spaces, intentionally or subconsciously, either responded to fear or were created to compensate for the disruptions to identity caused by those direct responses. In addition, the aesthetics and layout of the spaces act to enforce the social control of taste as an identifier of belonging, through definitions of the mores and the behaviors deemed appropriate for those who belong.

Retribalization

The simultaneous collapse and expansion of the global and the local has acted to destabilize the traditional boundaries of the nation-state, shifting the negotiations of national identity to networked connections rather than proximity of location. The reduction of the perceived primacy of the nation-state that "permitted and encouraged the development of an idea of nationalism, which both served to distinguish the legitimate territory and population of one state from those of its neighbors,"[14] has led the elite to engage in the struggle to (re)define the essence of Brazilianess and to look for alternative methods by which to institutionalize that identity.

Vernacular design and the idiosyncrasy of the local are embraced to forge

---

[13] J. Douglas Porteous, "Home: The Territorial Core," *Geographical Review* 66, no. 4 (1976): 386.

[14] Clapham, Christopher. "The Challenge to the State in a Globalized World." *Development and Change* 33, no. 5 (2002): 777.

connections and stake claims of mutual belonging between particular spaces and identity. There exists in the (re)embrace of Brazilian Modernism both assertions of independence from European design and of the equality of Brazilian products, ideals, and aesthetics to those produced on the continent. Retribalization operates to reassert cultural distinctions in response to perceptions of globalized homogenization.[15] The paradox of Brazilian identity lies in the push against European cultural neo-colonization, creating a desperate desire for distinction both from European hegemony and Latino absorption. Upper-class Brazilians act to co-opt markers of the local as part of their cultural aesthetics, leaving indigenous Brazilians coming from the north or living in the periphery to be reclassified as invaders and outsiders.

Materials act to indicate status directly through the money that is necessary to purchase them but also indirectly through their nature—polished, reflective, and high maintenance—as signs of the availability of disposable income to pay someone to take the care necessary to keep them up. The susceptibility to smudging or disarrangement also serves to regulate the behaviors of those who occupy the spaces. The materiality of the interior supports and encourages indications of group belonging through appropriate performances of behaviors. The hard, polished materials not only indicate the ways in which they can be touched but

also the amount of noise that can be made. The primacy of cultural expression over the physical is expressed in these interiors; disguised as good taste and constructed in implicit reference to the existence of bad taste. Along with the connected references to morality, taste acts to reinforce shared identity through distinction and claims of superiority.

Nostalgia

Nostalgic design focuses on creating connections across time through the idealization of the past and the insertion of self into the history of location. In escapism, rather than (re)imagining cultural or temporal connections to place, design turns away from connecting and retreats.

The loss of the legitimacy of Modernism's grand narrative fractured the stability of value and taste as universal and fundamental. The communicative potential of a primary aesthetic regime was replaced with a chorus in which many still struggled to see their way through incorrect taste to the true voice of design. The disturbance of this narrative leaves those whose knowledge and experience had stood for the entirety longing for a return to a time that venerated their values as worth striving to reach. The shift from modern to postmodern has meant an acknowledgement of the values of mass media, consumer society, and infinite reproduction. A resulting fascination with the authentic and the original on the part of wealthy residents restores the sense of connection with familiar systems of class distinction.

---

[15] Nan Ellin, "Thresholds of Fear: Embracing the Urban Shadow," *Urban Studies* 38, no. 5–6 (2001): 869–883.

Unlike in the United States or Europe, Modernism in Brazil is not only for the elite; modern architecture and popular architecture in Brazil are much more closely connected. What is reflected in this type of interior, however, is nostalgia for the historical moment when Modernism was introduced and began to flourish in Brazil. The 1950s in Brazil was "a unique moment in the development of the nation's self-image, due not only to the success of the nation's modern architecture abroad but also to the pervading optimism, relative political and economic stability, and acceleration of national modernization."[16] In other words, the atmosphere was pregnant with optimism and modernism, the two becoming part of a metonymic network in which the Golden Years can be re-presented through interiors expressive of that time.

Postmodernism is also associated with "a melting away of fundamental borders and divisions, in particular the old division between the culture of the educated classes and that of the masses." In its place, a "new subjectivity was emerging, centered in the gradual loss of any sense of history, any hope for the future, and any memory of the past, all scattered by a feeling of the 'eternal present' that became a diminution of human feeling and a lack of any deep awareness."[17]

Escapism

Residential space is particularly fitting as a site for the creation of uncontested identities because of the nature of interiority as an indicator of belonging and the conceptualization of the domestic as a place for respite from the troubled world.[18] The individual rights and responsibilities enshrined in the neoliberal doctrine have transferred to an intensification of both the fear of violation of home space and the desire to peremptorily remove the possibility of occurrence even at the cost of human rights. There is a marked increase in "defensive homeownership [that] therefore appears not only as the aspiration of homeowners for safety but also as a result of a complex interrelationship between political, media and ideological systems that have generated strong impressions of risk and victimization."[19]

Residents escape the exterior world through a simple denial of its existence. The most obvious mechanism of such a denial is the construction of a wall that obscures and erases the space beyond. A second level of escape is provided in the active resistance to the organization and aesthetics of the public street. Not only does São Paulo contain vast numbers of *favelas* in which construction has been piecemeal and highly individualized, but Brazil also

---

[16] Fernando Luiz Lara, *The Rise of Popular Modernist Architecture in Brazil* (Gainesville: University Press of Florida, 2008), 6.

[17] Tania Pellegrini and Laurence Hallewell, "Brazilian Fiction and the Postmodern Horizon: Rejection or Incorporation," *Latin American Perspectives* 33, no. 4, Race and Equality in Brazil: Cultural and Political Dimensions (2006): 110.

[18] Setha M. Low, "Fortification of Residential Neighbourhoods and the New Emotions of Home," *Housing, Theory & Society* 25, no. 1 (March 2008): 47–65.

[19] Atkinson, Rowland, and Sarah Blandy. "Panic Rooms: The Rise of Defensive Homeownership." *Housing Studies* 22, no. 4 (2007): 443.

has a very active and primary street life. The broken lines, volumetric variety, and multitude of colors of the exterior world is denied upon entering the interiors which either enforce spatial regularity or diffuse irregularity through exquisitely crafted, precisely planned transgression.

The possibility for absolute cleanliness, with all of its moral implications, is longed for as an antidote to the dirt and garbage of the world beyond their gates. The public spaces of streets had already been defined by modernists as locations of disease and criminality; in contrast, the home can then become secure from intrusion of such unseemliness but also a signifier of the advanced, cosmopolitan, developed city its occupants wish for São Paulo to become.[20] The home embodies the metaphors of Brazil as modernity, as development, as prosperity, as the future. Those metaphors enacted in the dwelling are intended to extend outward into and over the city such that the plan of the home becomes the plan of the nation.

The cleanliness and order of the interiors evidenced in the photographs is not one that was artificially constructed in anticipation of the camera but is only a degree or two different from the order that is maintained as part of the experience of day-to-day interactions with the home. As dirt is conflated with disorder and disorder begets

danger, safety is reinstated through an exaggerated attendance to order and control.[21] The removal of impurities is a culturally unifying ritual. Exaggeration of distances of differences contributes to clarity of reorganization that distinguishes these private interiors from the disorder of public space that has been stained or sullied through the introduction of dangerous ambiguity.

Finally, the very basic mechanism of escape—the wall—succumbs to the double escape of denial of its existence through nature or naturalization. Some walls were completely planted over, to give the impression of looking to the edge of a forest rather than at the boundary of a safe zone. In others instances, the gaze is turned away from the wall toward the connection between the interior of the home and the interior of the exterior wall, telling a story of openness and connection.

Escapism does not necessarily imply only a turning away from the outside world, but also an escape from the realities of the interior world created in response to that exterior one. The feeling of entrapment repeatedly expressed by wealthy residents of São Paulo leads to interiors that express exteriority, albeit in a safe, orderly, and controlled manner. The streetscape, with its potential for discomfort and anxiety, is represented inside perimeter walls. The difference is not only in the texture and aesthetic of the artificial streetscape, but also in the

---

[20] Justin Read, "Obverse Colonization: São Paulo, Global Urbanization, and the Poetics of the Latin American City," *Journal of Latin American Cultural Studies* 15, no. 3 (2006): 281–300.

[21] Mary Douglas, *Purity and Danger: An Analysis of the Concepts of Pollution and Taboo* (London: Routledge, 1966).

frame that is placed around it. Rather than the open visual frame that makes reference to an unknown beyond, these interiorscapes offer a sense of security by removing the possibility of something lurking or waiting beyond the viewer's realm of vision.

(a)

(b)

Figure 6.1 The Dichotomy of Home in Sao Paolo, Brazil.
Photo credit: Courtesy of Matthew R. Dudzik.

Figure 6.2 Highly reflective surfaces, large expanses of glass, and light colors create high-maintenance spaces that exist as clean rooms in contrast to the dirt and disorder of the world outside.
Photo credit: Courtesy of Matthew R. Dudzik.

Figure 6.3 Interiorized exterior surrounded by a high protective wall in center city Sao Paolo.
Photo credit: Courtesy of Matthew R. Dudzik.

Discussion Questions

1. Describe and detail the numerous concepts and ideas Mendoza unfolds:
   a. Paradigm of suspicion and the global economy.
   b. Class systems and the sense of home under siege.
   c. Cultural issues of tribalism.
   d. Modernism and postmodernism as agents of change in Brazil.

2. Discuss the meaning of *home*.
   a. What is the ideal home for you?
   b. How do you reconcile your ideal sense of home with what Mendoza is suggesting here?
   c. How does home represent a refuge, a place to escape?
   d. What is escapism and how is this manifested in the home of the communities that Mendoza describes?

3. What is retribalization?
   a. How is your neighborhood a place where retribalization occurs?

4. Why is Brazil different from where you live? What are similarities?

5. What is your idea of space as place as a female? As a male?

6. Where you live—what is the space culturally? What does this mean to you?

7. How is culture a determinant of how we understand and make meanings of spaces?

8. How does Mendoza reveal things about living in Brazil that you were not aware of? Aware of?

9. Document your reflections and thoughts in a series of free writing memos about
   a. Where and how you live.
   b. How Mendoza describes concepts of home.

10. What does this mean in terms of designing spaces for living?

11. Write an analytic memo that summarizes these thoughts and reflections.

References

Atkinson, R., & Blandy, S. (2007). Panic Rooms: The Rise of Defensive Home-ownership. *Housing Studies, 22*(4), 443–458.

Blakely, E. (1999). *Fortress America: Gated Communities in the United States.* Washington, DC/Cambridge, MA: Brookings Institution Press/The Lincoln Institute of Land Policy.

Chevigny, P. (2003). The Populism of Fear: Politics of Crime in the Americas. *Punishment and Society 5*(1), 77–96.

Clapham, C. (2002). The Challenge to the State in a Globalized World. *Development and Change, 33*(5), 775–795.

Davis, M. (1990). *City of Quartz: Excavating the Future in Los Angeles.* New York: Verso,

Douglas, M. (1966). *Purity and Danger: An Analysis of the Concepts of Pollution and Taboo.* London: Routledge,.

Ellin, N, Ed. 1997. *The Architecture of Fear.* New York, NY: Princeton Architectural Press,.

Ellin, N. (2001). Thresholds of Fear: Embracing the Urban Shadow. *Urban Studies, 38*(5), 869–883.

Featherstone, M. (2008). The State of the Network: Radical Anxiety, Real Paranoia, and Quantum Culture. *Journal for Cultural Research, 12*(2), 181–203.

Flusty, S. (1997). Building Paranoia. In *The Architecture of Fear* (pp. 46–59). New York: Princeton Architectural Press.

Giddens, Anthony. Problems of Action and Structure. In Phillip Cassells (Ed.), *The Giddens Reader* (pp. 88–175). Standford, CA: Stanford University Press, 1993.

Harrison, P., and Mabin, A. (2006). Security and Space: Managing the Contradictions of Access Restriction in Johannesburg. *Environment and Planning B: Planning and Design, 33*(1), 3–20.

Holston, J. 2008. *Insurgent Citizenship: Disjunctions of Democracy and Modernity in Brazil.* Princeton, NJ: Princeton University Press,

Korff, Rudiger. (2001). Globalisation and Communal Identities in the Plural Society of Malaysia. *Singapore Journal of Tropical Geography, 22*(3), 270–283.

Lara, F. L. (2008). *The Rise of Popular Modernist Architecture in Brazil.* Gainesville: University Press of Florida.

Low, Setha M. (2004). *Behind the Gates: Life, Security, and the Pursuit of Happiness in Fortress America.* New York: Routledge,.

Low, Setha M. (2008, March). Fortification of Residential Neighbourhoods and the New Emotions of Home. *Housing, Theory & Society, 25*(1), 47–65.

Pellegrini, T., & Hallewell, L. (2006, July). Brazilian Fiction and the Postmodern Horizon: Rejection or Incorporation. *Latin American Perspectives, 33*(4). Race and Equality in Brazil: Cultural and Political Dimensions, 106–121.

Porteous, J. D. (1976). Home: The Territorial Core. *Geographical Review, 66*(4), 383–390.

Read, J. (2006). Obverse Colonization: São Paulo, Global Urbanization and the Poetics of the Latin American City. *Journal of Latin American Cultural Studies, 15*(3), pp. 281–300.

Shamir, R. (2005). Without Borders? Notes on Globalization as a Mobility Regime. *Sociological Theory, 23*(2), 197–217.

Smith, C. (2005). Spaces of Architectural Overcoming. *IDEA Journal, 2*(1), 51–59.

Turner, B. S. The Enclave Society: Towards a Sociology of Immobility. *European Journal of Social Theory, 10*(2), 287–303.

United Nations Development Programme. (2008). Statistical Udate 2008/2009–Country Fact Sheets–Brazil. *Human Development Reports,* http://hdrstats.undp.org/en/2008/countries/country_fact_sheets/cty_fs_BRA.html.

6.4 Gendered Space and the Photographic Interiors of a Victorian Lady

Susan Close

Interior design education has evolved significantly in the past decade and has become increasingly more interdisciplinary, with educators now studying issues and ideas drawn from cultural studies, the humanities, and social sciences. This is evident as significant international design conferences now consider questions of history and theory in the disciplinary evolution of interior design, as issues that previously existed on the boundaries are explored from an interdisciplinary perspective from within. For example, identity concepts such as gendered space are now being examined in relation to the study of the interior (Sparke, 2008; Rice, 2008).

Gendered space refers to a physical or virtual space associated with a particular gender. One such study is Daphne Spain's (1992) research on women's social status in association with spatial arrangements in the home, workplace, or school since the mid-nineteenth century. In this essay, I consider gendered space in interiors as seen in photographic interiors made by the noted Victorian photographer, Lady Clementina Hawarden (1822–1865). I have selected Lady Hawarden, as she is one of the earliest significant examples of women photographers who made interiors related to gendered space. Her domestic interiors feature images of her adult female children and reflect the private sphere of Victorian women.

While publications and research on Hawarden does exist (Haworth-Booth & Dodier, 1999; Mavor, 1999), this study is significant because it considers that her work from another perspective informed the study of design culture. It builds on current biographical and art historical research to consider Hawarden's work as a reflection of issues such as the place of women in the private and public spheres. To date, photographic practice related to design culture has had only limited attention.

This study differs, as it considers the images of Hawarden as readable texts that are examined as research and that reveal aspects of visual narratives about their maker and the interiors that she and her family inhabited. These photographs carry social history that becomes revealed in the analysis.

There is also a gap in the study of gendered space related to women photographers. A recent literature review indicated that little analysis has been done in this area. Although a number of studies have dealt with gender issues and space, they are primarily from an architectural point of view (e.g., Colomina, 1996; Ainley, 1998; Adams & Tancred, 2000) and do not include photography in their analysis.

Theoretically, this essay situates the interiors of Hawarden as visual narratives that can be read as texts using a methodology drawn from cultural analysis (Bal, 2002). Currently there is no established canon of design theory that can be directly applied to the study of photography. Like art and architectural theory, most design theory is drawn from interdisciplinary sources that include concepts such as the private and public spheres. Research for the theoretical framework that informs this study includes cultural and critical theorists such as Mieke Bal and design theorists such as William J. Mitchell. A number of issues are considered in terms of gendered space, including the concepts of framing and mise-en-scène apparent in Hawarden's photographs within their gender, cultural, and historic contexts.

Using the research methodology of close reading from a visual, cultural analytic perspective , I examine the visual narrative in four representative images from Hawarden's oeuvre. Specifically, I consider two research questions: 1. Does the photographic work of Hawarden examine space from a gendered perspective? 2. What is the visual narrative in Hawarden's photographs as related to interior design studies? Before we undertake this research and analysis of her images, it is necessary to briefly provide some context about their production.

Historical Context: Aristocratic Amateur

Lady Hawarden was one of a number of Victorian photographers that curator Mark Haworth-Booth (1984) has described as "aristocratic amateurs." Haworth-Booth places her in the company of contemporaries such as Julia Margaret Cameron (1815–1879) and Lewis Carroll (1832–1898). Hawarden was born to a wealthy family in Glasgow in 1822. In 1845 she married the fourth Viscount Hawarden (Haworth-Booth, 1984, p. 120). Twenty years later, she was dead at age 42 from a sudden bout of pneumonia, having borne 10 children and made over 800 photographs (Armstrong, 2000, p. 110). Despite the fact that Hawarden had only practiced photography during her last years, she was celebrated as a distinguished amateur photographer in her own time. A number of prestigious photographic awards from the Photographic Society of London attest to her competence as a photographer, a level of recognition seldom paid to a woman at this time (Lawson, 1997, p. 5). Women photographers were primarily seen as family archivists, not as artists who participated in public displays of their work. Like watercolor and china painting, photography was condoned as suitable pastime for women.

A significant factor contributing to the acceptance of photography as an appropriate, womanly pursuit was the interest in the medium shown by the most influential woman of the age, Queen Victoria, who came to the throne in 1838, just a few months before the public introduction of photography. Victoria was not just a collector, however. She was an enthusiastic amateur image-maker and even had the royal photographer, Roger Fenton, set up a darkroom for her in Windsor Castle (Hall, Dodds. and Triggs, 1993, p. 13). While this royal approval of the medium sparked the interest of many women, only those very few who also had some independence of position and means could afford to explore the creative potentials of the medium. Hawarden was one of those lucky few. She began by making conventional documentary stereographs of views and family but quickly moved on to concentrate on her more intriguing interiors series.

A variety of publications about Hawarden and her work do exist (e.g., Haworth-Booth, 1999; Smith, 1998; Mavor, 1999; & Armstrong, 2000), notable among them are Virginia Dodier's comprehensive study, "Clementina, Lady Hawarden: Studies from Life, 1857–1864" and Lindsay Smith's "The Politics of Focus: Women, Child, and Nineteenth-Century Photography." Dodier provides in-depth analysis of the photographer's work, public exhibitions, and election to the Photographic Society and places it in context to the Victorian genres that the photographer shared with her contemporaries (Codell, 2001, p. 482). Smith argues that Hawarden's images reflect private, womanly space, retreats where women have the opportunity for contemplation (1998, p. 39). Hawarden's photographs have been shown in several contemporary photographic exhibitions in the United Kingdom (Lawson 1997; Haworth-Booth 1999), yet despite all this exposure, there is still an aura of enigma about her images that continues to attract attention. The photographer herself facilitates this by refusing to title her work, instead referring to her images as "photographic studies" (Dodier, 1999, p. 44).

Reading Hawarden's Photographic Studies

The act of reading the image is the final act of a collaboration in which the photographer creates the image and the viewer decodes it (Bal, 2004; Mitchell, 2005). To read a photograph, one accepts that an image can be considered as a visual text. The image must be examined closely and a detailed analysis made of the information or signs it contains. Then it can be considered in relationship to related concepts and theory. It is widely accepted that this reading of photographic images is informed by semiotics, the study of the use and social function of signs, both linguistic and visual (Silverman 1983). Photography is of specific interest to semiologists because of its indexical nature. Semiotics allows for the consideration of texts resulting from combinations of signs that yield meaning. My readings of Hawarden's images employ concept-based semiotic analysis. The selection of these photographs brings to the fore several repeating photographic studies that she made that feature the concepts of framing and mise-en-scène. Hawarden frequently used mirrors and window corners to establish frames and boundaries between the private and the public spheres in her images. There is a kind of boundary-making in the process of making or framing photographs. For the photographer, this carefully orchestrated manner of image-making has become ritualized. As

Figure 6.4 Clementina Maude, about 1857–1864, Albumin print from wet collodion-on-glass negative
Photo credit: © Victora and Albert Museum

Mieke Bal explains, "[t]he act of framing produces an event " (Bal, 2002, p. 135).

Hawarden also employed a theatrical construction of space known as mise-en-scène in many of her interiors. This concept, borrowed from theatre, is defined as "the arrangement of actors, props, and scenery on a stage in a theatrical production or the environment or setting in which something takes place" (Bal, 2002, p. 96). I argue these two concepts are key components in the representation of gendered space in Hawarden's photography.

This first image introduces the viewer to an intimate space resembling an upper-class woman's private retreat or boudoir that Hawarden preferred to use as her photographic studio. This photograph, as well as most of Hawarden's other interiors featuring her daughters, was made at the family home in South Kensington, Lon-

don, which has since been demolished. Hawarden, an aristocratic Victorian, was well aware that upper-class women were expected to function primarily within the private sphere, and so she conducted her photographic practice there or at the family estate in Ireland. As art historian, Griselda Pollack has observed:

> It has been argued that to maintain one's respectability, closely identified with femininity, meant not exposing oneself in public. The public space was officially the realm of and for men; for women to enter it entailed unforeseen risks. (Pollack 2000: 163)

This photograph exemplifies the theatrical nature of Hawarden's image-making. Clementina Maude, Hawarden's second oldest daughter, poses for her mother's camera in fancy dress. The billowing white dress illuminated by sunlight is in keeping with the Victorian's idealization of women as "angels of the house" (Massey1994: 193). Her exaggerated pose is dramatic and somewhat unnatural; for example, her hand is pressed to her throat and her head is leaning back against the wall.

While it is difficult to know what the exact narrative was that the photographer and her subject collaborated on, this enigmatic pose implies that the young woman is lost in thought. She looks neither at the camera nor out the nearby window but instead appears introspective. This type of photographic study that features a pose with a young woman alone in a secluded interior is repeated often throughout

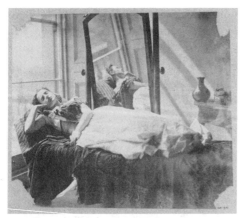

Figure 6.5 *Study from Life,* c. 1863–64, Albumin print from wet collodion-on-glass negative
Photo credit: © Victora and Albert Museum

Hawarden's work. These images portray well-dressed and obviously wealthy young women who appear trapped within a private domestic space. Consistently in these photographs, the subject is backed against a wall and appears lost in a private meditation while confined in the interior and framed by the camera.

Here Clementina Maude appears as a reclining figure—she has raided a costume box and struck a pose that is reminiscent of the odalisque. This image, like the previous one, is a window-corner study featuring mise-en-scène that also recalls the feminine boudoir. W. J. Mitchell argues that in the creation of mise-en-scène, it is not merely the objects gathered but also the "spatial relationships among them [that] can assume significance" (2005: 5). The location has been carefully selected for several reasons. First, the corner is used to give a sense of three-dimensional space to the otherwise flat photographic print, and

second, window light is be exploited to create shadow that emphasizes form and creates ambiance.

It is noteworthy that Hawarden created a version of Virginia Woolf's "room of one's own" by turning an empty interior in her home into her studio. She was not merely using an existing space but constructing a stage set where she was both the director and cultural producer of images where gender is performed through the use of props, costume, and décor, all signifying that Hawarden's studio is a somewhat clandestine, feminine space. For example, the space is tightly packed with furnishings blocking the door. There appears to be no visible way out of the interior. The subject closes her eyes and contemplates her fate, allowing herself to be surveyed by the camera's gaze.

The corner window in the photograph acts as a boundary between the private gendered space of the boudoir and public space of the exterior of the house. It is fundamental to her practice as a photographer that Hawarden preferred to make her images in such private gendered spaces as the boudoir. Here the reclining pose signifies intimacy in a category of seductive fantasy that was a popular theme of the Pictorialists and Pre-Raphaelites. Art historian Carol Armstrong alludes to the possibilities present in the frame:

Uncaptioned, this photograph evokes a promiscuous number of stories, characters and stock figures: from vaguely orientalist odalisques to Sleeping Beauty to Juliet, Desdemona and

Ophelia. Again, the pose and its associations link it to a host of earlier and later nineteenth-century Pictorialists images, from Henry Peach Robinson's Sleep . . . to Lewis Carroll's . . . series of Victorian Lolitas." (p. 116).

Hawarden's perspective on this is complicated by the fact she is a woman who posed her daughters as her subjects. From a revisionist point of view, her photographs appear to be precursors of some of Cindy Sherman's early work, the Untitled Film Stills. Sherman's visual narratives feature a deconstruction of the objectification of women by making images with herself as the protagonist. Hawarden's daughter becomes a stand-in for the photographer

Figure 6.6 Clementina Maude, about 1862–3, Albumin print from wet collodion-on-glass negative
Photo credit: © Victora and Albert Museum

and the visual narrative constructed is heavily coded in terms of her own experience of the domestic interior and its relationship to women.

A final image of Clementina Maude is theatrical in its use of light and emotional in its content. It is a dramatic representation of her reaction to the containment and the often claustrophobic confinement to domestic sphere of Victorian women. Armstrong suggests that the exaggerated gesture of the image evokes states of hysteria, rage, or despair (2000: 117). The sense of rather frenzied escape from the cloistered interior is amplified by the fact that the corners of the photograph are ripped, having been torn from a family album. This is an image of rebellion that contrasts with the quiet contemplative compliance demonstrated in the previous images.

The space depicted in this study is flattened significantly; this is achieved through the placement of the camera lens parallel to the background wall. Here the young woman appears like a specimen pinned to a card in a Victorian butterfly collection. Blatant objectification of women as decorative objects was typical of the period, yet Hawarden's image transcends this. The heroine of this visual narrative is not merely compliant. Seen in profile, she is struggling to pull back a swag of drapery to access the window beyond. This gesture is more spontaneous than other images; the camera captures a discrete and decisive moment.

Hawarden's use of light is one of her greatest strengths as a photographer. She is able to animate and illuminate both her female subjects and her interior spaces through her skilled handling of light. The shadow of the drapery and the ample skirt of the dress integrate to form an illuminated structure that mimics the wings of a butterfly. As the window drapery is pulled back from the window, a shower of light baths the figure and the interior. There is no door visible in the image; the implication is that the path out of this domestic space is literally through the window. Metaphorically, the butterfly is drawn to the light to escape outside and away.

Conclusion

In summary, a close reading of the three images selected confirms that Hawarden did examine space from a gendered perspective. She offers the viewer a look into her own studio where she constructs visual narratives about the concealed, familial interiors she inhabited. Her perspective was both privileged and gendered. The interiors she created with a camera speak of her own personal experience as a Victorian woman.

The visual narratives in Hawarden's photographs are complex. Major themes that thread through her imagery include contemplation, privacy, self-reflection, and containment. Her studio walls act as both barriers to and from the outside world. Views through windows often only hint at a larger world outside the domestic sphere. Lighting, props, costumes, and furnishings are all arranged in a theatrical manner where the performance of gender is played out.

Despite a considerable passage of time, these images continue to fascinate viewers. They clearly exist at an intersection of document and fantasy, alluding both to social history and play-acting, drawing us in to look into the private, contained world of a privileged Victorian woman. While they allow us only a limited access into this world, being photographs, we have more than a quick glance into this seductive gendered space.

This study is additionally significant because it considers Hawarden's work from another perspective informed by the study of design culture. It builds on current biographical and art historical research to consider Hawarden's images as a reflection of issues such as the place of women in the private and public spheres. In the broader context, it adds an important dimension to this research by examining Hawarden's images as artifacts that reveal attitudes and practices related to gendered space in Victorian Britain.

Discussion Questions

1. What is a gendered space? Examine this concept in relation to Close's examination of photographs and what she finds in them.

2. What is the close reading method of research? How might this be useful in design research when this is about historic perspectives?

3. Using the Close references, select a series of pictures of women in your life that you have in photograph form and in interior settings or in social situations. What are they doing? How are they in the frame of the photograph? What do you see? Document what you see in the form of memos and annotations alongside the photos.

Use this method of examining visual documents, and refer to Gillian Rose and the method of content analysis. What are the photographs saying in terms of the historic period, the context of the activity within the photo? The gender-personalities within the photo?

References

Adams, A., & Tancred, P. (2000). *Designing Women: Gender and the Architectural Profession.* Toronto: University of Toronto Press.

Ainley, R. (1998). *New Frontiers of Space, Bodies and Gender.* London: Routledge.

Armstrong, C. (2000). *From Clementina to Kasebier: The Photographic Attainment of "Lady Amateur."* October, V91: 101–139.

Bal, M. (2004). Light Writing: Portraiture in a Post-Traumatic Age. Ed. Dawne McCance *Mosaic, 37,*(4), 1–19.

Bal, M. (2002). *Travelling Concepts in the Humanities: A Rough Guide.* Toronto: University of Toronto Press.

Codell, Julie F. (2001). Review of *Becoming: The Photographs of Clementina, Viscountess Hawarden* and of *Clementina: Studies from Life, 1857–1864, Biography, 24*(2) 482–483.

Colomina, B. (1996). *Sexuality and Space.* New York: Princeton Architectural Press.

Dodier, Virginia. (1999). *Clementina, Lady Hawarden: Studies from Life, 1857–1864.* New York: Aperture.

Hall, R., Dodds, G., & Triggs, S. (1993). *The World of William Notman: The Nineteenth Century Through a Master Lens.* Toronto: McClelland and Stewart.

Haworth-Booth, Mark, ed. (1984). *The Golden Age of British Photography, 1839–1900.* Millerton, New York: Aperture.

Haworth-Booth, M., & Dodier, V. (1999). *Lady Clementina Hawarden, Studies from Life, 1857–64,* London: V & A Productions.

Lawson, J. (1997). *Women in White: Photographs by Clementina, Lady Hawarden.* Edinburgh: Scottish National Portrait Gallery.

Massey, D. (1994). *Space, Place, and Gender.* Minneapolis, MN: University of Minnesota.

Mavor, C. (1999). *Becoming: The Photographs of Clementina, Viscountess Hawarden.* Durham, NC: Duke University Press.

Mitchell, W. J. (2005). *Placing Words: Symbols, Space, and the City.* Cambridge, MA/London: The MIT Press.

Mitchell, W. J. T. (2005). *What Do Pictures Want? The Lives and Loves of Images.* Chicago/London: University of Chicago Press.

Pollock, G. (2000). Excerpts from "Modernity and the Spaces of Femininity." J. Rendell, B. Penner, & I. Borden. *Gender, Space, Architecture: An Interdisciplinary Introduction.* (pp. 154–167). London: Routledge.

Rice, C. (2007). *The Emergence of the Interior: Architecture, Modernity, Domesticity.* London: Routledge.

Silverman, K. (1983). *The Subject of Semiotics.* New York: Oxford Press

Smith, Lindsay. (1998). *The Politics of Focus: Women, Children and Nineteenth-Century Photography.* Manchester, UK/New York: University of Manchester.

Spain, Daphne. (1992). *Gendered Space.* Chapel Hill, NC: The University of North Carolina Press.

Sparke, Penny. 2008. *The Modern Interior.* London: Reaktion.

SUMMARY

Culture and social rules frame our underlying values, and they also formulate interactions that are perpetuated in society through the spaces that vehicle them. As we have seen, explorations of these issues are framed in issues of space, social relations, and political and aesthetic choices (Poldma 1999; 2003). Ideas are proposed about socially constructed spaces, how spaces define social relations in cultural contexts, and how both gender and physical spaces are determinants in how social relations are played out.

Gendered and culturally contextualized spaces have been examined, as have theoretical concepts that examine these issues. Philosophical and pragmatic issues raised include how gender or cultural identity frames spatial awareness and how these very human factors all affect the reading of interior spaces as they are created and used. While culturally determined rules create interactions that are perpetuated in society through the spaces that vehicle them (Poldma 1999; 2003), who we are and how we engage our personal sense of how we appropriate spaces is meaningful when understood with these lenses.

SUGGESTED READINGS

Ardener, S. (Ed.). (1981). *Women and Space: Ground Rules and Social Maps.* New York: St. Martin's Press.

Heidegger, M. (1971). *Poetry, Language, Thought.* New York: HarperCollins.

Poldma, T.(2008). Dwelling Futures and Lived Experience: Transforming Interior Space. *Design Philosophy Papers,* http;//www.desphilosophy.com/dpp/dpp_journal/paper2/body.html; 8 pages.

Rothschild, J. (1999). *Design and Feminism: Re-Visioning Spaces, Places and Everyday Things.* Piscataway, NJ: Rutgers University Press.

Spain, D. (1992). *Gendered Spaces.* Chapel Hill, NC: The University of North Carolina Press.

OVERVIEW QUESTIONS FOR DISCUSSION

Compare Close's cultural study of women in the domestic home with Daniel's study of women in the workplace in Chapter 4.

1. How are spaces framed culturally? As social spaces? As gender places?

2. Compare the notions of gender and dwelling in each article. What is understood by these terms?

3. What spaces are framed by gender and social status in today's society?

4. What cultural values are implicitly understood as values in society in this historic context? How have these values changed in our society today?

5. Would spaces today show these types of values? How?

6. Examine Shirley Ardener's ideas about social spaces and Daphne Spain's perspective on gendered spaces. What does it mean if spaces are conceived for one group as opposed to another? What political issues are uncovered in this type of value-setting? What values are put into play?

7. Discuss the cultural visual analysis approach in research. What is visual analysis?

   a. How are the research questions framed?
   b. What is uncovered in this type of research?
   c. How is the research transparent and thus provides rigor?

CHAPTER 7
Transformative Spaces, Bodies, Movement, and Aesthetic Meaning

body perception, movement, form-giving spaces, photographic perception, dance, movement, spatial interaction, visual dynamics, meaning of dance through movement-space-time, visual dynamics, weaving, aesthetic meaning-making, artful spatial experience, dialogue, meaning-making, intentional change, transformative spaces, design thinking, conversation, communication, aesthetic communication, space-time, conversational meaning-making

AFTER READING THIS CHAPTER, YOU WILL BE ABLE TO:

- Attribute meanings to body-space-experience relationships.

- Consider how "space-time" collapses as the body navigates space and the impact this has on dynamic relationships with space.

- Examine how bodies, technologies, and art intersect with materials and spaces.

- Determine bodily relations in dialogue with transformation.

- Identify different types of thinking and the concept of "discontinuous change" as catalysts to changing how we design now and into the future.

- Discover why meaning making using dialogue is aesthetic and how this might be a fundamental way to transform design spaces.

INTRODUCTION

Our bodily relationships in space with people, with art or other media, and intersections with technology are increasingly creating the mediated environments that we experience. Whether it is engaging in a direct manner with art, using technology to enhance well-being, or dialoguing with others during the design process, each is a form of body-space relationship. We are moving into new territories of space, design, and meanings when we use our bodies and senses. As we move dynamically in space, we experience new sensations and interactions as intersubjective experiences.

The body-object-space relationship is bounded by the experiences of the five senses interacting with space, place, ephemeral elements, and material/immaterial exchanges as much as by physical elements. Yet all are bound by our lived experience in real time. This perspective accounts for the intersubjective and real, lived experiences we have. Magda Wesolkowska and I noted this in terms of a phenomenological approach in relation to space and aesthetics:

> A phenomenological approach situates the user as the originator of the spatial experience, and the human experience as grounded in actual lived experience within the context of the lived event that the person experiences in real time. This experience is grounded in turn in the idea that aesthetic experiences guide the spatial elements that then form the backdrop to human activity. This is the inverse of much of previous theory and notions of space and time as separate elements. (Poldma & Wesolkowska, 2005)

Our actions and reactions guide the ways that we experience spaces. As such, we are no longer recipients of a space or design as much as we are engaged in space through dynamic personal and bodily interactions with movement/time/space, and with the various aesthetic experiences we have personally and with others.

This chapter will explore emerging concepts about the body-space continuum in terms of aesthetics, art, and both personal and social experiences. Explored within these contexts are the ideas that we interact with space and with the designs, and make meaning of both design processes and products. To be able to both experience spatial environments and engage in generating them as designers, we must consider the dynamic interrelationships that people have, using various forms of art, dialogue, and making meaning with the people with whom we create the experiences.

Increasingly, researchers are investigating the relationship between bodies and different forms of spaces. Art, photography, design, and technology all intersect with bodies in creative scholarship as emerging researchers tackle subjects such as the body in space and how spaces are interacting with people in innovative ways. For example, we might explore the city and run into urban art-spaces, installations that engage the body-space experience of urban dwellers in real time, dynamic experiences. This type of "theory in action" (Gosselin & Coguiec, 2006) has as its purpose understanding how spectators become engaged in aesthetic experience that transforms how they see and experience the urban world that surrounds them (Guay et al., 2010).

In this chapter we will explore personal and social examples of engagement of body-space dynamic relations. Examples of mediums allowing for free bodily expression and engagement with spaces and design processes include dance, photography, and dialogue/visual communication between people. First, Nancy Blossom considers how time-space dimensions are actualized through architecture, music, and dance, and suggests how these might be put into practice. Using the work of Peter Collingwood as the catalyst, she explores how technology and art intersect in exploring spaces of architecture and design.

As a provocation Marie-Josèphe Vallée, an artist-architect-designer, explores body-space relationships put into practice with art through the use of photography. Her artwork "Cine-torsion" forms a basis for theorizing on the social condition of body-space relationships and the interactions with the technology of chronophotography.

The Dialogues and Perspectives then examines how aesthetic social engagement plays out in a designer-client relationship through the medium of dialogue. The idea of aesthetic meaning-making is explored as a theoretical idea as well as how meaning-making happens through the medium of conversation in exchanges between various participants in design decision making and in real-time, direct experiences in practice. These forms of engagement transform processes into solutions through the meaning-making that occurs and using both visual and aesthetic tools of design thinking. The process of engagement of the design and the ways that the dialogue occurs are fundamental to understanding both the desired project realization and the framework for how people collaborate.

REFERENCES

Ainley, R. (1998). *New Frontiers of Space, Body, and Gender*. London: Routledge.

Bolter, J. D., & Grusin, R. (1999). *Remediation*. Cambridge, MA: MIT Press.

Davies, C. (2004). Virtual Space. *Space: In Science, Art, and Society*. F. Penz, G. Radick, & R. Howell, (Eds.). Cambridge, UK: Cambridge University Press, 69–104, illus.

Dholakia, N., & Zwick, D. (2003). *Mobile Technologies and Boundaryless Spaces: Lavish Lifestyles, Seductive Meanderings, or Creative Empowerment?* HOIT Proceedings.

Dewey, J. (1934/1994). Art as Experience. In S. D. Ross, *Art and Its Significance: An Anthology of Aesthetic Theory*. Albany, NY: State University of New York Press.

Gosselin, P., & Le Coguiec, É. (2006). *La recherche creation: Pour une comprehension de la recherche en pratique artistique*. Québec: Presses de l'Université du Québec.

Guay, L-M., Vallée, M-J., & Poldma, T. (2010). Body Aesthetics Enveloped in Space and Time: Art, Experience, Urban Environment. Unpublished paper submitted to SSHRC, Montreal.

Hagberg, G. L. (1995). *Art as Language: Wittgenstein, Meaning, and Aesthetic Theory*. Ithaca, NY: Cornell University Press.

Heidegger, M. (1971). *Poetry, Language, Thought*. New York: Perennial Classics/HarperCollins.

Merleau-Ponty, M. (1945/1958*). Phenomenology of Perception*. London: Routledge.

Poldma, T. (2009). *Taking Up Space: Exploring the Design Process*. New York: Fairchild Publications.

Poldma, T., & Wesolkowska, M. (2005) *Globalisation and Changing Conceptions of Time-Space: A Paradigm Shift for Interior Design?* (pp. 54–61)

Using the innovative works of Peter Collingwood, master weaver, as impetus, this paper aims to reveal the synergistic properties of movement in space-time shared by the three disciplines of architecture, dance, and textile design. As a means of situating the context, there are systematic affinities between architecture and dance that are evident in the theoretical constructs of the twentieth century. Likewise, affinities in basic structural systems identified by nineteenth-century building theorists are apparent between architecture and textiles. Less obvious but more intriguing is the systematic relationship between architecture, dance, and textile arts explored in the articulation of interior spaces, the choreography of modern dance, and the manipulations of fibers.

In order to understand or experience the true nature of space, one must project (or move) through it. It is in this context that the simultaneous yet independent theories on movement, space, and time in the fields of modern architecture and dance evolved, but not before the groundwork was laid through the experimentation and innovation of Cubism. The manipulation of planes became an essential ingredient of the Cubists' work. Interpenetration of planes became the form-giving principles of the new space.

Time Experiential Arts

Giedion summarizes the changes in attitude about architecture that emerged from the development of twentieth-century theory in the terms of space conception, the organization of forms in space (Giedion, 1967). Certainly the preoccupation of the early Modernists was with the manipulation of space.

Le Corbusier, with his elemental structural system, Le Domino, reduced necessary building structure to a grid of freestanding columns supporting three slabs that were joined by a stair. Space was no longer the by-product of construction but an element to be manipulated freely (Le Corbusier, 1931). Frank Lloyd Wright

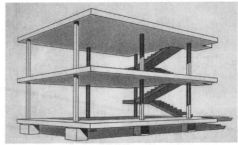

Figure 7.1 Le Corbusier's musings about structure as demonstrated in his sketches of Mansion Domino suggested that interior spaces could be freed of cumbersome internal structures. We take this for granted today, but it gave early twentieth-century designers a new perspective on the experience of space and time in a building.
Photo credit: © 2013 Artists Rights Society (ARS), New York/AGAGP-Paris/F.L.C.

found the core of his work in the interior spaces of a building. In the sanctuary of the Unity Temple in Oak Park, Illinois, he discovered the importance of the interior space, claiming it was the first time the interior space began to come through as the reality of the building. Wright understood that the reality of the building did not consist in the walls and the roof, the exterior profile, but in the space within (Malnar & Vodvarka, 1992).

Concepts of Time-Space

It was through technology that the full exploitation of space as an element of composition could be explored. Mies van der Rohe, Buckminster Fuller, Konrad Wachsmann, and others believed that advanced technologies offered opportunities for new ways of understanding architecture. Reflecting on their works and others, Giedion described modern architecture as a time experiential art. The **space-time** conception of the twentieth century—that is, the acknowledgment that the character of space changes with the point from which it is viewed, focused architectural experimentation on the way volumes are placed in space and relate to one another. Universally, modern architects considered both the separation and interpenetration of interior and exterior space. As they created this new definition of architecture, the emphasis of composition shifted from the development of the planar surface of the façade to the articulation of the interior spaces. And the articulation of interior spaces is entirely dependent upon the manipulation of planes. To fully experi-

ence an architectural composition, one must project or move through the interior space. This movement is measured by time. A successful composition thus exploits the sequential placement of spaces to bring meaning to the whole (Giedion, 1967).

Meaning of Dance Through Movement-Space-Time

The works of modern choreographers reflect a similar exploration of the meaning of dance through movement, space, and time. Choreographer Doris Humphrey described dance as an art in which design has two aspects: time and space. This more complex design concept ranges from a simple transition of one movement to another, which forms a relationship in time and thus has shape, to the lengthier phrase-shape, a series of movements that evolve into an overall structure for the dance and can be compared to form in architecture. Humphrey's concepts are similar to the Modernists, as they explored the articulation of interior space by structure and form of buildings. Humphrey explained that every movement made by a human being has a design in space and a relationship to other objects in both time and space (Humphrey & Pollack, 1987).

Choreographer Alwin Nikolais believed movement was the essence of modern dance and that space was the element that gave motion its emotional expression. Nikolais described space as a three-dimensional canvas that allows relationships to be established in dance. Through action, the dancer creates linear boundaries or volumes of space. Nikolais posited that adding the presence of one

Figure 7.2 Doris Humphrey dancing. She understood the movement of her leg, from the floor to her side, as a time and space relationship. It takes seconds for the leg to rise and as it does, a plane is traced in space.

Phot credit: © Bettmann/CORBIS

or more dancers serves to add structure to the composition, as in the parallel or intersecting planes of a building. The motion of bodies in relation one to another serves to articulate the space that is the essence of the dance (Brown, 1979).

Figure 7.3 A dance choreographed by Alwin Nikolais demonstrated Nicolais' understanding of space as a canvas that creates relationships in dance. Each dancer is framed within a plane; each plane is positioned in relation to another.

Photo credit: Julie Lemberger/CORBIS

Figure 7.4 Von Laban has sketched the pathway that a dancer will trace on the floor throughout the execution of a dance. In his hand he holds a three dimensional model of the planes a dancer penetrates through the movement arms and legs as they dance.

Photo credit: © Universitaetsbibliothek Leipzig

Rudolf von Laban devised a method of identifying the pathways and forms of human movement described by Nikolais through modeling the kinesphere in accordance with the forms of crystalline structure. With this technique the spatial organization of body movement can be described or articulated in planes. Laban contends that space is a hidden feature of movement and movement is a visible aspect of space. He described dance as an architecture that is created by human movements and is made up of pathways tracing shapes of space. The living building of trace-forms that a moving body creates is bound to certain spatial relationships.

Such relationships exist between the single parts of the sequence, and can be understood through the passage of time, the seconds it takes the dancer to execute the parts of the sequence. The dancer is moving in time creating a transitory illusion, an image of a specified space, shaping our awareness (Laban and Ullmann, 1966).

Arnheim brings to closure the formulation of the concept of time experiential arts with the term **visual dynamics**. The term describes the visual perceptual translation of static art forms such as painting, sculpture, and architecture into time. In the case of architecture, Arnheim points out that one's image of a building is a result of one's spontaneous integration of multiple visual projections into a total perceptual image (Arnheim, 1971, 1977).

Weaving a Time Experiential Art: The Work of Peter Collingwood

The act of weaving is in itself an expression of movement and time. The shuttle carries fiber back and forth in succession along the paths of warp stretched tightly on the loom. If there is space in the composition, it is illusionary space. If there are planes that intersect or overlap, it is in the relationship that Cubism explored in the two-dimensional plane. There is no pathway to be traced using Laban's choreutics, no penetration of space as with Wright's planes, no perception of movement, no measure of time. That is, unless the weaving is the work of Peter Collingwood. Here is a weaver who has advanced his craft to naturally translate a static two-dimensional discipline into a time experiential art. Collingwood's work demonstrates the realization of movement in space and time through material, technique, and process. These compositions involve a complex manipulation of lines and planes to define space and create a sense of movement.

Collingwood was an inventor at heart. Throughout his career he pushed the basic technology of hand weaving beyond tradition. Like his architectural contemporaries, Collingwood pushed materials and technology to discover the full exploitation of his discipline.

Collingwood seldom speaks of art when he speaks of his own work (Collingwood and Theophilus, 1998b). Nevertheless the result is art. And space is a key element of the compositions. The essence of this space is its many-sidedness and the

infinite potential for relations within it. It is within these compositions that the common system of movement, time, and space is realized. Collingwood accomplished this through the precise manipulation of warp threads in the macrogauzes. "That the warp threads run parallel to each other from one end of a textile to the other is part of the definition of weaving, but in macrogauze the warp no longer carries this restriction. Stripes of warp can move sideways, cross each other, twist, coalesce, separate and even enter and leave the weave in the form of weft" (Collingwood and Theophilus, 1998a). Collingwood explored the rich geometry of weaving and ultimately escaped the static right angles of the craft.

Collingwood used black and white linen to exploit the graphic qualities of the

Figure 7.5 Peter Collingwood used black and white linen to explore the potential of three dimensions in weaving. In this photograph the warps of his compositon move side to side creating a strong sense of movement.
Photo credit: Courtesy of Carla X. Gladstone

works. The shifting warps shape the composition, and movement is perceived in the oblique lacing of the threads. The result is a dramatic play of positive and negative space. Collingwood eventually reduced structure in the weavings, creating greater freedom and movement in the composition. Reducing the weft (the threads which cross the warp) to a minimum resulted in more work of transparency in the macrogauze. Transparency suggests the interpenetration of planes resulting in the form-giving principles of space (as in Cubism). As the experimentation progressed, Collingwood discovered ways to manipulate the warp further using wefts reinforced by fine stainless steel rods at the widest point of the composition to allow for repeated oblique warp movements (Collingwood and Theophilus, 1998b). The result is carefully tensioned warps that move together, intersecting forward and back as they interlace. The tensioned threads articulate planes that in turn define space and set movement, space, and time relationships into play.

In his most monumental piece installed in Kiryu, Japan, in 1997, Collingwood achieved the themes of the twentieth-century arts: the abstraction of form from light, space, time, mass, perspective, and material. In his macrogauzes the common language of modern art, architecture, and dance is confirmed. As in dance, the single fiber is not important; it is the choreography of the many fibers that form the image of intersecting planes, articulating space in sequential order as the planes of a building articulate its interior spaces.

Conclusion

Meanings of space-time transform through how material, form, and space intersect with bodily movements. With dance and weaving, the material and body forms a dynamic interaction with space. Space is the essential element of the creation, the eye moves in and out as a dancer, the viewer perceives motion and time in the work. Space thus moves beyond the space-time relations of architecture and toward material and ephemeral meanings perceived and experienced.

Discussion Questions

1. How does Blossom describe the choreographer Alwin Nikolais's approach to dance in space?
   a. Describe the ways that spaces and dance intersect.

2. How is this way of collapsing space and time in materiality exploited by Peter Collingwood?
   a. How is technology a catalyst to full exploitation of space and design?
   b. How do Mies van der Rohe and Buckminster Fuller explore this?

3. Who are modern architects and designers exploiting design and space through technological means?
   a. Find and discuss other examples of interest in your community, in the world around you.

4. How, as Blossom suggests, is space the essential element of the creation in the work of Collingwood?

References

Arnheim, R. (1971). *Visual Thinking* (pp. 274–293), Berkeley: University of California Press.

Arnheim, R. (1977). *The Dynamics of Architectural Form* (pp. 9–31). Berkeley: University of California Press.

Brown, J. M., Ed. (1979). *The Vision of Modern Dance* (pp. 111–119). Boston: Princeton Book Company.

Collingwood, P., with Theophilus, L.. (1998). In Conversation. In *Peter Collingwood, Master Weaver* (pp. 5–27). Exhibition Catalog, Colchester, UK: Firstsite.

Collingwood, P., with L. Theophilus. (1998). In Conversation. *Peter Collingwood, Master Weaver*. Video. Signals Production.

Giedion, S. (1967). *Space, Time, and Architecture* (pp. 429–615). Boston: Harvard University Press.

Humphrey, D., & Pollack, B., Eds. (1987). *The Art of Making Dances* (pp. 45–49). Princeton, NJ: Princeton Book Company.

Le Corbusier. (1986). *Toward a New Architecture* (pp. 225–267). Mineola, NY: Dover Publications.

Malnar, J. M., & Vodvarka, F. (1992). *The Interior Dimension: A Theoretical Approach to Enclosed Space* (p. 41). New York: Van Nostrand Reinhold.

Margetts, M. A. (1998). A Craftsman's Web. In *Peter Collingwood, Master Weaver* (pp. 29–31). Exhibition Catalog, Colchester, UK: Firstsite.

The body moving in space constitutes our perception of the world. I create dialectical images that question the status of representation in contemporary art and photography as registers of reality. As an artist, I explore through installations how photography and space interact with the body in motion to enhance our perception of reality. One of the goals of the artworks that I create is to deconstruct key concepts of modern motion.

Ciné-torsion draws energy from the history of photography, diverting images into another spatial and social dimension. To fully appreciate the aesthetic experience and social assertion underlying the work, one needs to step back in time to the sources of inspiration.

Historical Context

Close to 40 years after its enshrinement, the photographic device developed long ago by Daguerre now seems to be much more of a prototype containing the indispensable seeds of progress. Numerous technical improvements to the original photographic process considerably changed how photography is used, infusing it with a second life in the hands of scientists. In the 1880s, the advent of bromine silver gel ushered in the world of instant photography. Scientists became adept at extracting the most benefit from this new discovery by exploring new avenues that were just waiting to be revealed. French physiologist Étienne-Jules Marey (1830–1904) and in his wake, Anglo-American Eadweard Muybridge (1830–1904) developed the sequential photography of motion or chronophotography. If the methods used by the photographer (Muybridge) and the scientist (Marey) differed from a purely technical standpoint, the result nevertheless was essentially the same: through a succession of images taken at regular intervals, they succeeded in deconstructing the movement of photographed subjects. The aura of objectivity surrounding photography was set aside to scrutinize, freeze, and analyze human and animal motion. Acts of everyday life, such as walking and running, or the movements of a galloping horse were captured on silver plates. By placing the frames side by side, the slowed actions of the subject now amazingly appeared in a specific context that no human eye could have detected otherwise. By stopping time and motion, these two fathers of chronophotography succeeded in making the invisible visible. Their surprising achievements, revolutionary for the time, became an aid of great precision to artists. In the daguerreotype, Delacroix saw a way to "record reality more objectively and more rapidly than with the human eye and hand" (Vigneau, 1963, p. 59). With chronophotography, artists such as Rodin, Eakins, and Degas were finally able to unravel the mystery of motion. It has been said that the artist Meissonier changed some of his historical scenes after studying a still plate on which a series of images showed that at certain times a galloping horse has all its feet off the ground simultaneously.

Since the late fifteenth century, numerous artists have tried more or less successfully to reproduce motion using technical means as diverse as they are varied. Results were rather unsatisfactory. Because the artist's canvas represents a still scene and not a succession of images, movement could only be hinted at (and not produced) by actions, attitudes, or the presumed locomotion of the body. Chronophotography, on the other hand, introduced elements that were indispensable to decoding and suggesting motion more accurately than simply as a sensation. The influence of chronophotography on the history of twentieth-century art was unprecedented, ushering in the birth of the Seventh Art. The list of artists who were inspired by Marey's scientific experiments or Muybridge's frames is a long one; however, we can cite a few names here: Duchamp, Carrà, Marinetti, Balla, Boccioni, Calder, Agam, Soto, Tomasello, and Tinguely, among others, to help the reader better understand the contribution of chronophotography in the quest to make the speed of motion visible. As a contemporary artist, I am also interested in chronophotography, as witnessed in the *Ciné-torsion* installation that I will present next.

Ciné-torsion

Ciné-torsion draws its inspiration directly from the photographic work of Eadweard Muybridge. I was inspired by two series of photographs of eight frames each, taken from the side and back, of a nude man running. This series of images is from the book *The Human Figure in Motion*, published in 1887. To achieve his results, Muybridge developed a technique that was intrinsically different from the photographic "gun" designed by Marey. This new technique used a series of 12, 20, or 24 cameras arranged in a straight line at approximately 15-cm intervals; the shutters of the cameras were triggered to release successively. The subject began running in front of a black background divided by white lines into a grid pattern to suggest a pseudo-scientific process. In this experiment, motion was not deconstructed in order to synthesize it, but staged to provide some academic poses around a subject or theme of motion. It took more than eight images to understand the mechanics of the runner; in fact, some 30 to 40 images were needed to produce fluid motion, which is one of the reasons Muybridge's photographic frames were not always enthusiastically received. Oftentimes they provoked a certain amazement, laughter, and even scepticism.

Muybridge and Altering Perception

Chronophotography enjoys a singular relationship with reality. There is a disconcerting realism between the image produced and its subject, but it still remains an image. If the goal of the technical process is to document reality, it does not automatically confer objectivity on photography. Precisely because of its technical parameters, chronophotography interprets reality by altering our perception. The viewing angles, physical limitations of the framing, distortions caused by various lenses, and paper on which the images are reproduced are all criteria that imply a subjective disassembling of reality. The runner is not represented as we see him but rather as Muybridge shows him to us. In the words of photography expert Jean-Dominique Lajoux: "The Muybridge genre and style are exclusive, of great aesthetic quality. Each image has its own charm and together they form a magnificent abstract image made up of 12, 24 or more small rectangles of each photograph. Muybridge was a photographer, a great photographer. Marey was a physiologist, a great researcher. Therein lies the essential difference" (Lajoux 1996, p. 101).

The Installation

I appropriated Muybridge's chronophotographs as a starting point for the installation's design and reinterpreted them in a modern context. My technique involved transferring the nude man's body onto white tulle, a fabric normally used for bridal veils. Muybridge's runner was moved from the support of a rigid still frame to a soft and airy one. I also inverted the chronophotography codes, changing the black background on all the sequences to a pure white

background. Using a photographic transfer technique, I inlaid six carefully chosen images of the runner, in a different pose each time, on three huge pieces of tulle. Once the fabric was printed, the images were covered (above and below) by an additional layer of pristine tulle. The entire assembly was then attached to rigid curved supports and suspended from the ceiling like a mobile. The grain of the photographs, which had been altered by the transfer technique, was magnified once again by the effect of the tulle as it captured the rays of natural light. Once completed, the installation occupied a space of 45 cubic metres (2 m x 9 m x 2.5 m) and could be viewed both from the inside and outside.

As previously mentioned, photography as an illusion of reality is merely a semblance of what is visible. Yet photography always bears witness to the existence of something real; without this, there would be no image. The theoretical term for this is the *referent in photography*. Theorist Roland Barthes explained this clearly: "By 'photographic referent' I do not mean what is *arbitrarily* real as referenced by an image or sign but what is *necessarily* real as placed in front of the camera lens; without the latter, there would be no photography" (Barthes 1980, p. 120). *Ciné-torsion* creates the illusion of the photographic image having lost its referent, allowing the body to be seen only at certain times partially restored to its whole. Here and there, through the use of photographic transfer, a leg or a hand almost disappears, frayed, damaged, and torn. This fragmented body, which owes much to the legacy of Greco-Roman statuary, ends by becoming an autonomous work in itself, an expression of ideal beauty in its classical form. This fragmentation—on the one hand inherent in the technique and on the other hand voluntary—allows the body to be reframed on sheer fabric, displaying it to the viewer in an unaccustomed way. The nude man now becomes his own object of artistic questioning. Here is a source of inspiration as I created the work (artist narrative language):

As an artist, I was inspired by the index value of the photographic transfers in Ciné-torsion. These images can signify either a trace of reality or an aspect of reality that differs from its original context. In the latter case, the image has a symbolic value, signifying the upheaval of the human condition. The frame in which the subject evolves has changed from celluloid to tulle. The runner is provided with a new spatial reality by means of the soft-focus effect, light and the contrast between the shades of grey of his body and the white background that supports him. Tulle is essentially a light, airy fabric. Its sheer quality enabled me to highlight the runner in black and grey contrast, seemingly tearing the white veil. Through the gentle play of overlapping fabric, bit-by-bit the image of the runner emerges and appears from out of the maze of folds. The transparent tulle opens and reveals the figure on each side, multiplying the views of the nude runner. As a metaphor for the bridal veil, the tulle is stained with multiple printed images of the human form distorted in the moving folds of the tulle. The runner ceases to be a scientific subject and becomes an anonymous man without any pretension.

Not only am I creating a different form of perception of space, I also am inspired as an artist to use the materials to explore new immaterial spaces with the photography and the material of the tulle. In chronophotography, one becomes aware of the ephemeral character of time, a measurable unit at the origin of motion. Through the mechanics of the photographic process, the camera is able to stop time and freeze the subject captured by the lens, permanently etched in silver salts. This perspective is tempered throughout Ciné-torsion. The mechanical action of ambient air or the passing of a visitor, subtle as it may be, produces a gentle movement within the installation, imbuing life into the runners who are caught in a defined no man's land from which escape is impossible. All the pieces of fabric assembled together form a structure that sequentially represents the human body in motion. The effect is reminiscent of the zoopraxiscope, invented by Muybridge in 1879, which projected images from glass discs as they rotated at a certain speed to create the impression of motion. This projection device is considered to be the first modern cinematographic viewer. Ciné-torsion can be viewed as a singular operative point, midway between photography and cinema, with the goal of creating a new reality.

Playing on Dimensions and Spatial Perceptions

The strategy behind *Ciné-torsion* was to place 2-D images in a 3-D space. By inserting photographic transfers into a specific location during the Florence Biennale, those viewing the installation were summoned to an overall re-reading of the images. More importantly, they found themselves integrated into the installation, moving from a passive role to an active one. Viewers had the option of looking at each image individually or taking a more global view and, unbeknownst to them, becoming an integral part of the work. To quote Marcel Duchamp, "spectators are canvases."

Duchamp has been a major source of inspiration to me, especially Eliot Elisofon's image of *Marcel Duchamp Descending a Staircase*, which appeared in the January 1, 1952, issue of *Life* magazine. The photograph echoes Duchamp's famous painting *Nude Descending a Staircase* (1912). The work of art is a direct continuation of the chronophotographic experiments of Marey, deconstructing the phenomenon of motion on canvas and imbuing the easily identifiable human silhouette with a sense of movement. In the painting, the body is reduced to several poses that describe its trajectory, while at the same time creating the impression of suspended time and of automatic movements. The scientific images of Marey instilled a new awareness in Duchamp, paving the way to the use of abstract vocabulary to represent the human form. Since the 1970s, Marey's chronophotographs have not only

become a source of inspiration but also an integral part of Yugoslav artist Vladimir Veličković's work, whose artistic concerns I share. The artist delves Muybridge's *Human Figure in Motion* to find the images necessary to complete his work. In an article on Veličković, Marc Aufraise explains the artist's purpose in pursuing his pictorial research: "By inserting Muybridge's photographs into his work, Veličković discovers new accents, i.e. new words to express his doubts about the validity of a process of charting the progression of humankind and representing human nature" (Aufrèse, year unknown). *Ciné-torsion* falls within this same continuum.

Figure 7.6 Ciné-torsion installation, photographic transfers in acrylic on tulle
Photo credit: Courtesy of M-J Vallée

Figure 7.7 Ciné-torsion View 2
Photo credit: Courtesy of M-J Vallée

Conclusion

The *Ciné-torsion* installation seeks to prove that the body is an artistic impression of the social order and that diverting photographic images causes the rerouting of our society's values. The nude man becomes the reflection of postmodern man, a subject of reflection, and one that merits that we stop to think about him. This new man exposed in his nakedness possesses all the ascribed qualities of an Adam symbolizing the first man in the history of humanity. Trapped in the folds of this sheer labyrinth, he runs incessantly, enclosed in a box, in a space. But to where is he running? Through the process of repetition on overlapping tulle, the silhouette appears to become lost in infinity. To the extent that man's destiny is interwoven

Figure 7.8 Ciné-torsion View 3
Photo credit: Courtesy of M-J Vallée

intimately with that of woman, one might wonder about his intentions: Is he running away or is he running to find Eve? What roles and place does man occupy in twenty-first-century society? How can he give of himself differently than his great grandfather? What are his new reference points? All these questions form the starting point for more in-depth reflection about the deconstruction of the male identity, its complexity, and its new reality.

Discussion Questions

1. How does Vallée explore the mystery of motion in space, the use of chronophotography, and space itself to explore the issue of body in space?
   a. How do photography and science intersect with the past to evoke new concepts for the present and future?
   b. How do the representation of the images and the figures in movement create spatiality?

2. What is the "photographic referent" in the theory of Roland Barthes?
   a. How does Vallée use this theory to create an illusion in an artistic expression?
   b. What is this process used and what new spatial realities emerge?

3. What is the resultant proof that the "body is an artistic expression of the social order and that diverting photographic images causes the rerouting of our society's values"?
   a. How is this cause for reflection?
   b. How do we understand the theoretical premise and the application into the installation?

4. Why is this work more than just an art installation?

5. What is it saying about theorizing and reflecting upon the social human condition?

References

Abel, O. (2005). *Le mariage a-t-il encore unavenir?* Collection "Le temps d'une question," Bayard, Paris.

Aufraise, M. *L'homme en mouvement ou l'utilisation de quelques photographies chez Vladimir Veličković*, http://keny-wan.free.fr/pdf/marc-aufraise.pdf

Aufraise, M. Colloque. Retrieved January 30, 2011, http://kenywan.free.fr/pdf/marc-aufraise.pdf

Barthes, Roland. (1980). *La chambreclaire Note sur la photographie.* Éditions de l'Étoile, Gallimard, Le Seuil, Paris.

Braun, M. (2001, November). Muybridge le magnifique. *Études photographiques.* Retrieved January 23, 2011, from http://etudesphotographiques.revues.org/index262.html.

Marey/Muybridge pionniers du cinéma. Recontres Beaune/Stanford. Conference proceedings 19 may 1995 Palais des Congrès, Beaune. Conseil Régional de Bourgogne, Ville de Beaune & Stanford, CA, 1996. Retrieved from http://www.beaune.fr/spip.php?article232.

Salomon, C. (Ed). (2008). M. Sicard, et al. *Marey, penser le movement.* Paris: Harmattan.

O'Reilly, Sally. (2010). *Le corps dans l'art contemporain.* London: Thames & Hudson.

Rouillé, André. (1989). *La Photographie en France: Texts et controverses, une anthologie, 1816–1871.* Paris: Macula.

Vigneau, André. *(1963). Une brève histoire de l'art de Niepce à nosjours.* Paris: Éditions Robert Laffont.

Introduction

Sociologist Sherry Turkle recently wrote an article in *The New York Times* titled "The Flight from Conversation." Turkle has studied the impact of mobile technologies and plug-ins extensively for the past 15 years, and suggests that these various technologies are changing how we communicate and ". . . they change not only what we do, but who we are" (Turkle, 2012). She adds:

> We are tempted to think that our little "sips" of online connection add up to a big gulp of real conversation. But they don't. E-mail, Twitter, Facebook, all of these have their places—in politics, commerce, romance and friendship. But no matter how valuable, they do not substitute for conversation.

Conversation is a vital component of how meanings are made, processes are understood, and knowledge is gleaned for diverse spaces. Listening to the needs of the people who will be the recipients of a concept, design, practice, or project is fundamental during the process. For example, when design thinking is used to explore issues, activities such as dialogue between two people are real, lived experiences that transform systematically concepts and ideas into the realities of projects or spaces and that functions in the context for which it was conceived (Poldma, 2003; Zahedi et al., 2012, Poldma 2012 in process).

Dialogue, as a form of communication, is a direct engagement of stakeholders, users, and those interested in the design/space. When dialogue is used alongside design thinking during this communication process, this is a form of making meaning that infuses bodily relations, conversations, design thinking, and the transformation of ideas. First introduced in my doctoral thesis (Vaikla-Poldma, 2003), this concept of **conversational meaning-making** integrates design thinking, aesthetic means, and situational issues as a catalyst to transforming ideas into realities, within diverse types of spaces—physical, informational, knowledge, and others (Vaikla-Poldma, 2003; Poldma, 2010; Poldma, 2012 in press; Zahedi & Poldma, 2011). It is through the experience of communication, of working over ideas through both conversation and visual means that the aesthetic/functional and client meanings become clearer, thus creating meaning and moving the project or situation toward a finished product, solution, or ideal situation made real (Nelson & Stolterman, 2003). This may be a one-to-one situation between designers and client, a designer and user, or a collective process with multiple stakeholders, depending on the actors and contexts of the particular situation.

Theoretical Context

If we begin with the foundations of design thinking, three issues come to light. First, design thinking is a very broad concept that has at its root the design process, a process that guides problem solving in particular situations. This process embraces change, where change is transformative and leads to a different type of future. Second, the design process, when considered in context and with ethical notions of care and service to both clients and users (Nelson & Stolterman, 2003), affects outcomes. Third, when design thinking is used to engage various actors, including stakeholders and users, alongside consultants, experts, and other specialists, this requires dialogue in one form or another. Dialogue and conversation "in situ," meaning together and in live situations, allows both designers and stakeholders to determine the level of engagement of each participant in any process. This in turn determines the roles of the various stakeholders, their level of engagement, the structure of the process itself, as well as the values that will underpin the ways solution spaces are conceived. During this engagement, core values and needs are often defined through communication between the actors or stakeholders, and these interrelations are not confined to a singular purpose; they change with the context and within the context no matter what the situation at hand.

Dialogue, within this context, integrates meaning-making in an aesthetic way as it engages people and issues through design thinking. This occurs when people actively engage in discussing design problems and issues, linking design systematically through the integration of functional issues with aesthetic concepts, and making decisions that then are implemented. Dialogue happens with design thinking in diverse contexts, with both verbal and visual aids. Conversation and dialogue clarify meanings, identify contexts, and reveal the values important to diverse actors in the processes of decision making, whether this is for design purposes, research purposes, or other reasons. Quite often words might be accompanied by visual aids, such as computer models, diagrams, and/or visual sketches done during the conversations, and the communication of the idea is manifested through the dialogue that occurs in the act of designing. For example, designers often use drawings or schematic sketches to document what clients say, what stakeholders discuss, and what situations call for, all to help resolve the problem and develop solutions within the dynamic of the particular issue or problem.

The Design Process as a Process of Doing, Inquiry, and Action with Intention

The design process uses design thinking to move intention toward solution. Nelson and Stolterman speak of a "design culture" purely from the context of creativity and how the limitation of thinking design exists only as creative also limits us in understanding the value of design thinking as more. Design thinking is, at its foundations, both a creative process and an act of inquiry that infuses thinking and doing, inquiry and action (Nelson & Stolterman, 2003, pp. 4–5). We need design thinking to infuse action with different ways of seeing potential futures, and doing so requires the concept of *intention* (Nelson & Stolterman, 2003; Jones & Van Patter, 2009; Vaikla-Poldma 2003). With intention comes reflection and action (Schön, 2003) and considerations of solutions based on research, inquiry, action, and intention.

Design Thinking and Meaning-Making as a Systematic Process

Design thinking is a form of "meaning-making" that has as its root an aesthetic end. If we consider designing to be a process or a system (Nelson & Stolterman, 2003), then we make meaning through the ways that we use design to move forward ideas from vague concepts to realizable realities. Nelson and Stolterman define meaning-making in the context of systems thinking:

> Meaning making is essentially the creation of relationships of understanding, specifically between that which is experienced and the one who experiences. These relationships form a belief system, inclusive of the real, true and ideal, that informs actions, reflection and imagination in specific situations. (Nelson & Stolterman, 2003, p. 80)

When the designer and client, user, and/or stakeholder engage in systematic dialogue, and when this dialogue systematically builds something within the structure of the experience itself, then the process of communicating includes action, reflection, and imagination using design thinking processes. This engagement of people in this type of process provides meanings within specific contexts that help move forward business strategies, design, and the making of things within different spaces. Often this is in situated, lived experiences such as collaborative groups, meetings, and situations where people get together to make decisions.

Voices in Design Thinking and Processes

Communication through dialogue thus becomes a form of giving voice to various participants whether this is in research inquiry, design as inquiry, or design as a place of problem resolution. Dialogue informs decision making and provides systematic formulations of ideas through designing, and moving decision making toward what is possible. This in turn allows decision making to move toward realizable goals, whether in design or in business or in collaborative work (Zahedi & Poldma, 2012). This use of dialogue and conversations as ways of making meaning may be utilized for early design concept development, for design decision making and for inquiry when cooperative forms are used to construct the reality of the particular situation with clients, users, or other stakeholders.

The Systematic Nature of Dialogue with Design Thinking

The construction of this particular reality has both tacit and systematic qualities. People get together and dialogue occurs to move a design issue or situation from one state toward another using controlled and intentional actions on the part of the designer (Nelson & Stolterman, 2003). In the context of interior design projects and problems, for example, this is usually done by phasing the work, through the customary design phases such as information gathering, preliminary design brief and program development, preliminary design ideas, design concept development, and design implementation via contract documents (Poldma, 1999; Vaikla-Poldma, 2003; Nelson & Stolterman, 2003). When designers work together with clients and various stakeholders, they do so systematically, each time meeting to review the design project in different stages, and each time the project evolves with different actors at different stages of the process. They develop an active communication that uses dialogue and conversation, assisted by visual modeling or aids of some form or another, that are used in a transformative manner engaging stakeholders in decision making.

Dialogue as an Aesthetic Value: Facilitating Change Through Transformation

The designers' role in decision making is to be both attentive and active in solving problems and creating change through transformation. Discussion helps to generate understanding of the intentions and all stakeholders are active in the decision-making process. Intention is explicated and then is supported by communication, and the entire process becomes an aesthetic value of the design space created. For example, within a project context for the built environment, designers and architects often meet clients, other colleagues, consultants, and specialists, with pen in hand or virtual visual means at the ready, to converse and document the decisions made. It is through the experience of communication and working over visual ideas together in real-time situations using conversation that the aesthetic meaning of the project or subject in its specific context becomes clearer. Each time the designer moves from one phase of the design process to the next, visual tools may change, but the verbal communication that occurs is a vital integrative component of the way that meaning is constructed.

Making Meaning Through Dialogue and Artistic Intention: A Pragmatic Case Study

We will now examine a case study examining how this process occurs in real-world situations. The following figures explore the retail concept for a space: the renovation of a retail space that moved from one space to another and, in the process, upgraded its brand image. This space was conceived and built based on a series of conversations supported by drawings done in situ, that is, during the discussions between the designer and the client. While initial discussions to work out the brief happened between designer and clients exclusively, they quickly moved into meetings with contractors and engineers as needed in various stages of the project, through a series of concept drawings, then plans, and then meetings.

Each time the designer and client met, vague ideas at the outset became crystallized into a design, each time filtering out the ideas toward a concept that responds to the client's aesthetic, functional, and economic concerns. Once the ideas were set down, the designer developed a concept, working through the ideas directly with the client at every step of the way. This type of designing happens through these conversations and resultant drawings that are created, first as a result of the communications between designer and client, and next the designer and consultants and/or contractors along with the client.

The following series of images are examples of visual results of conversations and multiple iterations of ideas that have been explored by the designer and client together. After a first and very thorough examination of precedents for what the client desires, the designer and client work together in developing rough preliminary ideas (Figure 7.9), then filtering down to specific materials and details of design elements within the space (Figures 7.10 and 7.11), and finally rendering the various drawings that communicate to both the client and the contractors involved the means to transform the space into a built reality (Figure 7.12).

These conversations with the client then continue through each phase of the project, from design to economic decision making, and to the construction and realization of the project. The materials and plans reflect branding, allow for expression of client needs and vision, deal with various technical and functional issues, and become transformed into a retail space that serves its purpose.

The example of the retail store is a relatively simple one. When large-scale projects

Figure 7.9 Rough preliminary designs are created through a variety of inspiratons and ideas.
Photo credit: Courtesy of Tiiu Poldma

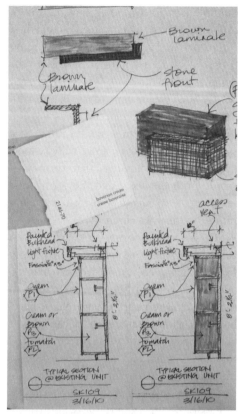

Figure 7.10 Preliminary concepts for the store concept
Photo credit: Courtesy of Tiiu Poldma

Figure 7.11 Final materials for the space
Photo credit: Courtesy of Tiiu Poldma

are done, the conversation and meaning-making becomes infinitely more complex. Knowledge is constructed with stakeholders, users, and actors who contribute to the problem solving at hand, and this becomes very complex when multiple stakeholders are together or when large projects are at stake. Larger-scale projects require meetings among clients, engineers, contractors, project managers, and architects regularly, to move a design concept from the planning stage into the development and construction stage, working in concert with various people in the management and decision-making process, and always with concerns about investment decisions.

Discussion : About Reflection in Action and Theory-Building

In the case study retail space the meetings and decision making happened through the medium of talk and sketch, model and dialogue, both happening simultaneously. In this medium, the artistic form of visual drawing was the linking catalyst between the dialogue and the ideas and was also a way to document the experiences that transformed the design blockage toward the generated ideas. Nelson & Stolterman

Figure 7.12 The final space is built from bringing the concept and details together

Photo credit: Tiiu Poldma, Courtesy of Kim Mackenzie

systems, including all images and symbols, gives us access to information. . . . Language . . . is also a source of social values. (2002, pp. 3–4)

When communicating with dialogue, we use language to explicit meaning. Access to new knowledge happens in the context of the designer flushing out what the client needs, wants, desires, and requires. The designer interprets languages and vast amounts of information, and creates "that which does not yet exist" (Nelson & Stolterman, 2003). The designer tries to understand what he or she hears, empathizing with the user while listening to the client. The designer also tries to vision the space in ways that capture the meanings of the words and language interpreted. In addition, the designer comes back with conceptual ideas and tries to represent, through the verbal discussion and visual forms, the intent of the client as expressed through the intention of the designer. This goes back and forth through iterations (design process) until vague ideas (Figure 7.9) become clearer and grounded first in a final design concept and finally in the built or realized final form/reality (Figure 7.12).

These are the elements of meaning-making. Designing facilitates an orchestration of intent with making meanings using languages of both words and visuals. The meaning-making that occurs happens due to the very nature of the design activity and the "working through" of ideas in real time as subjective and systematic experiences. The mixing together of visual drawings with dialogue provides the means for communication of ideas that become transformed into what the client wants

suggest that these types of dialogue "are essential to the process of making design images concrete realities" (pp. 174). It is in the "thinking and doing" of the bodily experiences together that create a co-construction of the aesthetic experience that ensues (Nelson & Stolterman, 2003; Vaikla-Poldma, 2003). In terms of language, Catherine Belsey suggests that

Language, understood in the broad sense of the term to include all signifying and needs. Communication tools are used to help to convey the dialogue of working through the ideas. As I have noted recently:

> Experiences, dialogue and aesthetic conversational meaning-making give life to the concept. Meaning is achieved through the conversation and direct visual contact with the ideas being generated, through whatever visual means are provided or available. (Poldma, 2012, in process).

However, in this implementation phase we are also dealing with conflicting views, goals, and stakes of each and every stakeholder. Motivations are many, and as Nelson and Stolterman conclude, often groups' processes and dynamics must align with the intentions again for the process to bring the design to fruition (pp. 148–149). They suggest:

> The alignment of function and intention is necessary for the design process as well. The condition of alignment integrates the intentional behaviour of all the individual participants. (p. 149)

It is through dialogue and conversation, in part, where these intentions can be made clear.

Conclusion

Conversation and dialogue, when used integrating both narrative and visual means, allow us to make meaning about design questions and issues. When we use design thinking to express together what is needed in the transformation of ideas into reality, we engage in dialogue to do so. Design is about solving problems for intimate human use and human interaction that is everyday life, captured within the design made, the spaces lived, or the diverse places and spaces experienced (Poldma, 2003).

This type of meaning-making uncovers tacit knowledge, legitimizes the client needs and goals, and captures design intent explicitly through verbal and visual tools. Direct experiences that use conversation through dialogue and meaning-making as their root transform designs and make them work in the context for which they are intended.

Discussion Questions

1. How do designers and clients create meaningful decision making through conversation?

2. What is aesthetic meaning-making?
   a. How is this achieved with people in the action of designing?

   b. How is this a component of design thinking that integrates innovative thinking?

3. What are the spaces of conversation and communication that occur when design thinking is used?

References

Belsey, C. (2002). *Poststructuralism: A Very Short Introduction.* Oxford, UK: Oxford University Press.

Dewey, J. (1934/1992). Art as Experience. In S.D. Ross (Ed.), *Art and Its Significance: An Anthology of Aesthetic Theory* (3rd ed., pp. 204–221). Albany, NY: SUNY.

Friedman, K. (1997). Design Science and Design Education. In T. McGrory (Ed.), *Helsinki: University of Art and Design* (pp. 54-72). Helsinki, Finland: UIAH.

Gorman, C.R. (2004). Why Designers Should Study Foreign Languages. *Design Issues, 20*(1), pp. 40–47.

Laczko, I., Hendricks, J., Hardenbrook, M., & Robinson, J. (2002). Self-Centred , Irreverent, Artsy-Fartsy Inquiry: Girl Talk About Narrative Research. *Arts & Learning Research Journal, 18*(1), pp. 132–155.

Nelson, H., & Stolterman, E. (2003). *The Design Way: Intentional Change in an Unpredictable World.* Englewood Cliffs, NJ: Educational Technology Publications.

Poldma, T. (2012, in press). The Working Interior. In N. Blossom & J. A, Thompson (Eds.), *The Handbook of Interior Design.* Hoboken, NJ: John Wiley & Sons.

Poldma, T. (1999). *Gender, Design, and Education: The Politics of Voice.* Unpublished master's thesis. McGill University, Montreal, Québec, Canada.

Poldma, T. (2010). Aesthetic Meaning-Making as Design Thinking: Communicating within the Design Process. IDEC International Conference, Atlanta, GA.

Schön, D. (2003). *The Reflective Practitioner: How Professionals Think in Action.* New York, NY: Basic Books

Turkle, S. (2012, April 12). The Flight from Conversation. *New York Times.*

Vaikla-Poldma, T. (2003). An Investigation of Learning and Teaching Processes in an Interior Design Class: An Interpretive and Contextual Inquiry. Unpublished doctoral dissertation. McGill University, Montreal, Québec, Canada.

Weigand, J. (2006, winter). Defining Ourselves. *Perspective.* IIDA.

Zahedi, M., & Poldma, T. (2011). Defining Goals Through Collaboration Using Design Thinking: Building Consensus Among Designer-User-Client Stakeholders. IASDR International conférence, Delft, The Netherlands.

Zahedi, M., Poldma, T., Baha, E., & Haats, T. (2012). Design Thinking and Aesthetic Meaning-Making: Interlaced Means to Engage in Collaborative Knowledge-Building. Paper submitted to the NordDesign, August 22–24, 2012, Aalborg, Denmark.

Note: Parts of this text were first published in the author's doctoral thesis, and presented at the IDEC 2010 conference in Atlanta, GA. Some of the concepts are also developed in the book *The Handbook of Interior Design*, edited by J. A. Thompson and N. Blossom (2012).

SUMMARY

Aesthetic forms of expression in spaces manifest themselves as bodily experiences artistically, aesthetically, and socially through experience. Each form has its particular context in the personal and the social: in dance and textile designs we understand intersections of spaces with movement and pattern, while in the body movements captured in photography there is an interweaving of body, space, fabric, and image. These are body relationships in dynamic interactions with form or with others. In a similar vein, the actual design thinking done with people in dialogue with one another requires bodily relationships in the form of conversation that intersects with visual forms that may include everything from poring over an idea written on a napkin over a meal to artist renderings to virtually modeled ideas to actual built scenarios.

As we move into the next two chapters, we will explore some of these techniques and ideas, and how spaces are redefined in light of how we engage stakeholders, infuse design thinking in new practices, and understand the broader meanings that these new ways of working generate in business and in everyday life. Aesthetic meanings are moving from art, dance, and mediated forms toward collaborative spaces, dialogue spaces, and alternate places.

SUGGESTED READINGS

Ainley, R. (1998). *New Frontiers of Space, Bodies, and Gender.* London: Routledge.

Dewey, J. Art as Experience (1934/1994). In S. D. Ross, (Ed.). *Art and Its Significance: An Anthology of Aesthetic Theory.* New York: SUNY.

Grosz, E. (1995). *Space, Time, and Perversion: Essays on the Politics of Bodies.* New York: Routledge.

Guay, L. M., Vallée, M-J., & Poldma, T. (2010 *Body Aesthetics Enveloped in Space and Time: Art, Experience, Urban Environment.*

Langer, S. (1953/1994). *Feeling and Form.* In S. D. Ross (Ed.). *Art and Its Significance: An Anthology of Aesthetic Theory.* New York: SUNY.

Tuan, Yi-Fu. (1977). *Space and Place: The Perspective of Experience.* Minneapolis, MN: University of Minnesota Press,

OVERVIEW QUESTIONS FOR DISCUSSION

1. Consider how dance and photography change the lens of the viewer when in different types of spaces. One way to glean how movements and bodies react in spaces is to get

a camera and, with a partner, go to a specific place and photograph it from different angles. If possible, make sure that the camera lens is a 28–35 mm (interior-wide angle).

- Photograph the space from all angles.
- Take long-view shots, short-view shots of images with and without your partner.
- Take detail views and long views of the same element.
- Find the focal point of the place and create images in both detail and with a wide view.
- Take a video of the same spot and as you walk through it with the partner in the video and then without.

When you have printed the images, compare them to the video that you have taken. How are the scenes similar and different? How is the space understood relative to the person? Examine the perspectives and views and what you discover as a team.

2. Read Sherry Turkle's article about "The Flight from Conversation" in light of the discussion in the Dialogues and Perspectives. What is your personal experience with plug-in devices? How is conversation used when designing? How would you go about having a conversation with a client to work through design ideas?

3. What perspectives about users and space are understood in this chapter?

4. What is a sense of space as an experience of place? How do we move from one experience to another and what do we uncover?

5. How do we make meanings and interpret these to be able to understand spaces of lived experiences?

6. How does the body intersect with space
   a. In dance?
   b. In movement with textiles?
   c. As an interweaving of time and space?
   d. As a body in interaction with ephemeral spaces?

7. How do body movements change in relation to time and space? Examine Blossom's ideas about dance and weaving as time experiential arts and the intersections with space in architecture. What is an experiential way of weaving? Why is this an important concept for spaces of intersection? Examine Blossom's idea of experience in space and how one might "move through it" as she suggests.

8. What is salient in the artists' experience in shaping the Ciné-torsion?

9. How do people make meaning using design tools and design thinking as catalysts? Why is dialogue so vital in this process?

CHAPTER 8
Changing Conceptualizations of the Real World

cultural spaces in the workplace, fourth-order design, design management, visual sensemaking, design innovation, design effectiveness, employee well-being, heightened aesthetic awareness in business, business culture, change management, creative behavioral work flow, symbolic design thinking, users and clients, symbolic thinking drivers

AFTER READING THIS CHAPTER, YOU WILL BE ABLE TO:

- Discriminate between cultural spaces in the workplace and design thinking as a catalyst for business decision making.
- Assess design thinking as a corporate strategy.
- Evaluate how design thinking and design effectiveness might create a new kind of design space.
- Examine the contexts of design thinking in terms of visual sensemaking.
- Interpret how design thinking and business strategic thinking are merging.
- Appraise the perspectives of designers, businesspeople, and design managers as various stakeholders in work environment space creation and operation.
- Distinguish the means by which corporate spaces effect change and what knowledge spaces offer for corporate effectiveness. What spaces are needed for these new purposes?

INTRODUCTION

As we begin to frame the design spaces available to those who work to effect changes, it becomes clear that meanings in design/spaces have become transformed by new ways of working and living in the real world. Two concepts that begin to emerge are the increased service-oriented nature of design work and the means by which design thinking transforms effectiveness in business and in business management strategies. Not only are design practices for interior spaces changing, but also the way business considers design thinking has evolved and is continuously evolving.

We will explore these concepts in this chapter next, first by situating design process as a service-oriented process and then by examining what stances currently guide design thinking in the contexts of practices. Using the situation of office design of work environments, we will examine business use of design thinking, how designers understand these directions, and what perspective clients and users offer in response.

The Meaning of Design Process as a Service-Oriented Process

In their seminal book *The Design Way*, Harold Nelson and Erik Stolterman speak of the designer-client relationship as a service relationship. This relationship is not one of servitude, but rather one of the designer serving the needs of the client in resolving the problem or situation at hand (2003, pp. 47–48). As Nelson and Stolterman state:

> A service relationship is a distinct, complex and systematic relationship, with a particular focus on responsibility, accountability and intention. Designed products, whether concrete or conceptual, only have value and meaning, because of this intentional service relationship. Therefore, it is through the presence of a service relationship that intentional change, and the consequences of intentional change, can come to have meaning and give to individual collective lives. To a designer, a service relationship is a basic teleological cause of design. (2003, pp. 48–49)

Nelson and Stolterman go on to nuance this meaning in two ways:

> There is a subtle distinction between designs that are done *with* clients and designs that are done *at* clients, like customers or consumers. . . . It is important at this juncture, to make an important distinction between "finding meaning" in things that happen, and "making meaning" by causing things to happen. The former is reactive and adaptive, while the latter is proactive and intentional. To be in service is to be proactive. This means that the designer cannot wait around for things to happen, as wished for by the client. Clients may not know what is concretely desired in the beginning. They are only aware that something is pressing for expression. . . . The designer must help bring to the surface a clearer articulation of a client's desiderata as a positive, proactive impulse. (p. 49)

Ultimately it is the designer's role to articulate uncertainty and change in a manner that allows clients or users to make meaning in their terms. In this sense, designers often help clients make meaning through the different creative design tools that they have available. When designing spaces for the work environment, this aspect of design thinking and doing becomes magnified when working with one or more actors in a particular design context, and when applied to business needs and strategies in the very real and pragmatic context of the corporate world.

Cultural Contexts and Spaces of Business Management Thinking in the Real World

We will introduce two concepts related to these ideas:

1. Cultural contexts of the world of work and emerging cultural spaces (Stevenor Dale)
2. Fourth-order design (Richard Buchanan) and how design thinking emerges as a strategic and sensemaking tool (VanPatter and Jones)

Design thinking is a strategic tool for transformation, and, increasingly, business schools are harnessing design thinking as part of strategies for innovation. Richard Buchanan presents a series of articles based on the idea that design is a catalyst for organizational change. Buchanan suggests that over the past 15 years business schools have begun to

> . . . investigate design—often under the term "innovation"—and its role in management and organizational change. . . . For designers who have begun to explore the impact of their work on organizations. . . . as well as the impact of organizations on their work, the trend and the conference are important. They further elevate the idea that organizations are products, as well as the idea that . . . organization can be designed by intelligent aforethought and appropriate action. (2008, p. 2)

Buchanan suggests that strategic design thinking in organizations might be used in both for-profit and nonprofit organizations, and that design thinking is a tool for management and change (pp. 6–7). Buchanan names this **fourth-order design**, which embraces new ways of designing yet does not abandon the more traditional forms of design thus:

> The articles selected . . . are examples of "fourth-order" design . . . the design of organizations, environments, and systems that serve the diverse purposes of human beings. They represent different approaches to the problem of organizational change, and they all employ an expanded concept of human interaction, that is elevated from individual interactions to collective interaction in complex environments. . . . [T]hey also demonstrate that the new, expanded forms of design practice do not abandon the traditional concerns of form-giving and making that have defined design in the past. . . . [T]he concept of form . . . has grown more supple and complex, embracing the social and environmental context of design. (p. 9)

Using design thinking as a transformational tool for business requires understanding the nature of design thinking and design wisdom as a place for adding value and innovation to business decision making (Nelson & Stolterman 2003; Poldma 2009).

Using the concept of knowledge acquisition in business, Ash Amin and Patrick Cohendet suggest this to be a form of "relational space." In their book *Architectures of Knowledge* (2004) they identify the Japanese concept proposed by Nonaka and Konno (1998) of how this type of sharing of services considers the "shared space of emerging relationships [and] is a foundation in knowledge creation" (Amin & Cohendet 2004, p. 94). Using their idea of an "alternative ontology of spatial awareness . . . towards the sociology of knowledge practices" as these might be understood in the corporate world, Amin and Cohendet suggest that this spatial awareness moves from people to spaces to knowledge-building in corporate organizations (pp. 92–95), and is also manifested in the designed spaces that are created to house these knowledge spaces.

Design Wisdom as a Catalyst for Change

To further elaborate on this idea and how this is understood as design wisdom, Harold Nelson and Erik Stolterman (2003) speak of design thinking as this catalyst and use the idea of design wisdom as this agent of change that is part of what is used to add value and innovation to organizational practices. They suggest that design when understood as design wisdom is an agent of change: "[D]esign wisdom . . . provides an escape from [the] limited state of affairs."(p. 20) They suggest that

> Change is difference; Change of difference is process; Change of process is evolution: Change of evolution is design. . . . [and] the only cultures that successfully move through major changes, or crises, are those that engage in change in a manner that is consistent with design wisdom and leads to transformational change. (pp. 20–21)

The approach for transformational change suggested by Nelson and Stolterman makes change as a means of innovation, and this is explicit when it comes to cultures such as the work environment and their designs.

With these concepts in mind, we will examine perspectives from the pragmatic spaces of the real world as design thinking merges with business and innovation strategies. First, Janice Stevenor Dale examines the cultural contexts of workspaces and what emergent issues are salient in change management and the integration of business needs with designed spaces. Using specific and diverse case studies from North America and Asia, Stevenor Dale draws specific links between the everyday objects and things within spaces and the broader workplace cultures within which decision making is made, by proposing concepts such as **creative/behavioral work flow** and **symbolic design thinking**.

We then turn to a provocation by GK VanPatter and Peter Jones, who propose a fourth dimensional space called **visual sensemaking**. In this reissue of the first published interview for Humantific in the *NextD Journal* in 2009, VanPatter and Jones discuss how sensemaking and changing paradigms of design thinking are changing emerging ways of design integration into business management practice.

Finally, the Dialogues and Perspectives examines perspectives of designers and businesspeople "on the ground" in the real-world spaces using the example of corporate design. In conversation with Florian Weiß, Donna Cummings, and Michael Arnold, we glean different views of the practices of the every day and what real-world contexts add to the dynamics of corporate spaces both of design and of knowledge construction in pragmatic spaces of the world of work.

REFERENCES

Amin, A., & Cohendet, P. (2004). *Architectures of Knowledge: Firms, Capabilities, Communities.* Oxford: Oxford University Press.

Buchanan, R. (2008, Winter). Introduction: Design and Organizational Change. *Design Issues, 24*(1), 2–9.

Margolin, V., & Buchanan, R. (1999). *The Idea of Design.* Cambridge, MA: MIT Press.

Nelson, H., & Stolterman, E. (2003). *The Design Way: Intentional Change in an Unpredictable World.* Englewood Cliffs, NJ: Technology Publications.

VanPatter, G. K., & Jones, P. 2009. *NextD Journal.* Special Issue, *Understanding Design 1.0, 2.0, 3.0, 4.0.*

8.1 Cultural Contexts and Coded Cultural Forms
in the Workplace: Changing Paradigms?

Janice Stevenor Dale

Shifting forces are reshaping America. There is a return to limited access to capital and cash for improvements, and a slow return to self-investment. While invention and innovation is critical, we explore the evolution of the design texture of business itself.

Consumers of office space are evolving from simply utilizing spaces in a highly utilitarian way into commissioning spaces that inspire. The visual impact of the office is valued by employees, as it represents the visual definition of the firm for which they work, a motivation for coming to work each day, the way the employee feels at the place of business, and the way the employee feels about his or her place of business. Serving the purposes of the business itself, it attracts new employees and functions as described, as a way of retaining existing employees. Smaller-scale elements within the space, like the transitional details between walls and ceilings, thresholds, or options on seating, seating sizes, and workstation accessories, allow the employee to feel tailored within the space and to give them the freedom to personalize their own space.

As a global culture, we have evolved from the primitive forms of shelter in tents or cabins, into more sophisticated housing. So, too, is the office evolving. The object of this essay is to call attention to the increasing interest on the part of the client and his or her business on the higher aesthetic nature of the space in which they choose to work and the benefits that the aesthetic brings to the business. A comparison is drawn between clients in two geographically diverse major cities and how their business culture and geography affect the value they place upon the interior design.

Culture + Behaviors = Design

This exploration of cultural identity is not advertising in any sense, and as such does not constitute branding, but simply the design aesthetic culturally appropriate for each organization and its current business goals. For example, the design for Bank Negara Indonesia, a newly established bank in Los Angeles, involved a series of undulating low-height walls, which were reminiscent of a Dutch Colonial architectural landscape. Alternately, consider the funky backlit corrugated plastic panels highlighting the reception area contrasted with toon-town furniture selections that captures the character of a cartoon art software development firm in Los Angeles. Or, further consider the use of an Asian concept with moon gates interpreted into a door and sidelights solution at private offices influenced by the head of the Los Angeles branch of AIG, who had worked extensively in Hong Kong. Or even the presence of blue three-dimensional ceiling systems symbolizing air moving through the ceiling plane at a Boeing corporate headquarters space. Each design concept was inspired by cultural identity found by inquisitive designers, described by the businesses and creatively expressed by our design firm.

Translating client businesses, corporate culture, cultural heritage, and personalities into a spatial expression requires the full understanding and analysis of large organizational behaviors and characteristics to achieve the idealized collaboration of human connections. Design thinking toward change management requires the study of the logical/rational/technical work process and the creative/behavioral work flow (Rock, J.). Design translates that multivariate culture from its abstract characterizations through a **symbolic design thinking** process resulting in a three-dimensional expression. Spatial redefinition provides for the manipulation of people, workflow, and the environment, which all contribute to the summative corporate organization and its behavior. The success of those future interactions is paramount to having the space achieve the desired results to meet the business goals, be they efficiency, interaction, innovation, or other defined business improvements.

The designer's role is to produce contributions to the body of knowledge from innovative design solutions that derive from a client-driven project language coupled with their business goals. This is what leads to new design innovations from which further research can be documented.

While some projects utilize design history, there is no historical reference necessary for design innovation. The In-types project holds that the physical context of a project begins with a few linguistic indicators that center the design. While clients express the business goals, often the designer is the lyricist that characterizes the aesthetic goals of the project. These indicators, such as *light, clean, open* are normally quite vague and lacking in real direction beyond the potential value scale of the finishes. These indicators must accompany a physical massing of the project in order to meet functional goals. In the strategic planning phase, the designer is responsible for shaping that translation.

For example, on the Morrison & Foerster project, during the programming phase of design, the client clearly articulated a need for a large number of conference rooms in varying sizes. In their then-current facility, the conference rooms were located at the perimeter of the space, primarily in building corners due to window configurations and the desired avoidance of partner relationships with certain corners of the building. But the dispersed nature of the conference rooms presented distinct operational disadvantages. The client envisioned that the needed ten conference rooms serving a 125,000-square-foot office space would best be co-located on a single floor.

Grouping the conference spaces on a single floor would exceed allowable occupancy levels, generating the need to add a third vertical exit from the conference floor. Given that the project was to be located on the 35th floor of the building, this was impossible, not to mention unaffordable. Equally driven by client request and code requirements, the design solution evolved. A series of conference rooms in a crescendo of sizes was balanced on two floors and both sides of a two-story atrium, providing for an interconnecting stair between the 35th and 36th floors.

The client signed a lease prior to the construction of the building and was one of the first tenants in this major high-rise in downtown Los Angeles. The steel frame of the building was under construction while the interior design of the tenant improvements were designed. Meeting with the base building architect, SOM, we learned that The Gas Company Tower was designed with the symbol of a flame as part of its architectural shape. But unconventionally, the flame was not used vertically on the height of the high-rise, but formed the shape of the plan on the upper stories of the building cap. With a philosophical practice of a cooperative relationship between building architecture and interior design, we began exploring the idea of the curve of the flame, as it shaped potential massing schemes within the law firm's five-floor space. A design solution was arrived at that featured a slightly curving atrium with interconnecting stair that serves as an essential connection, visually and functionally to the two conference centers located at the southern portion of the rectangular space. The curve provides a graceful transition between varying depths of conference rooms and mirrors the curve of the architectural building indentation.

The further design development of the democratic-natured space rendered the cleanest element to be stainless steel. Due to the curvilinear reference, exploration began with an Art Nouveau sinuous curve for handrail and stair rail designs. We chose bar stock, a thin highly polished stainless steel bar. This decision led us to select a Miesian aesthetic for the reception furnishings, given their incorporation of bar stock in the chair design. Upon further evaluation of the Miesian aesthetic, we were inspired by the purity of the Barcelona Pavilion, believing it represented the democratic ideal, and began to explore detailing with a similarly clean aesthetic.

At the time of the project, the law firm was deeply involved in a nationally visible lawsuit that involved the rights of women employees from a Fortune 500 company. The overtones, while not often discussed during project meetings, were clearly expressed by the client as an appreciation of equal rights in the workplace and had a psychological impact toward an open and straightforward design solution.

The space was completely open. Contrasting many typical high-rise environments, and before the security concerns of 9/11, there was no rated tenant corridor. The rated corridor traditionally provides additional security to some degree, fire protection, and transition space, and it allows for future downsizing of the further division of tenant space on that particular floor. Full floor users can meet

Figure 8.1 Nova Delevelopment graphics message "conquer the world" in the interactive conference zone featuring backlit translucent elements.
Photo credit: Paul Bielenberg, © J S D A Inc.

code without it, arranging exiting in other ways. But the corridor also wastes space that would only need to be replicated within the tenant space. Eliminating it was a conscious choice, and one that redirected project costs and boosted overall efficiency toward the triple net lease. Once the elevator, controlled by card key reader, arrives at the designated main floor of the space, one steps out onto the open floor. The design directs the path of the visitor to the reception atrium. Exposing the exterior curtain wall was part of the aesthetic at each quadrant of the space, connecting every employee to natural daylight.

In the Chicago marketplace, where climate is clearly defined and people are more aware of the amount of time that they spend within interior environments, a heightened need for interior design exists. A client producing high-grade chemicals to multiple markets practices at the top of its profession. With its reputation as a blue-chip company, and because it had learned from fellow businesses in the Chicago area that good design is good business, it sought the best design firm to re-outfit its new corporate headquarters with leading-edge design solutions. This 500,000-square-foot company appointed its director of administration to hire an architect and an interior designer. As the floor plan concept was being developed, the company realized how the interior requirements of the space might have an impact on the overall building design. Although the company was not open to reshaping the exterior of the three-stepped building blocks, it recognized the importance of the design firm studying the functional needs of the interior and to adjust interior circulation, workflow, departmental relationships, and mullion dimension to align with interior workstation standards.

The design firm began with a thorough study of the business functions, standards, goals, and cultural influences on the project. Our first concern was for the length of the circulation through each 90,000-square-foot single level, the equivalent of four or five conventional floor plans. We designed a colonnade that had a defined beginning and end at each of the 30,000-square-foot "pods." Through block planning for executive offices and corporate cafeteria, sections of the building were designated. Budget was prioritized in those spaces, and less in the more practical open office. There was less shaping of the interior space, as systems furniture was the norm throughout the mass of the office plan, and the company's culture was more utilitarian. At that time, interior design was less aggressive in its ability to sculpt the interior space in corporate environments. Design had not evolved to push the limits of creativity, at least not at the scale of this project.

Contrasting the two projects, the Chicago building design was not completed by noted architects, as was the major high-rise in Los Angeles. While the Chicago firm sought the top interior design talent, the choice was less for style than for the purposes of efficiency and business benefit. In the Los Angeles marketplace, the aesthetic was of equal importance to the function of the interior. Historically, the work of Frank Lloyd Wright influenced consumers toward the value of the interior in Chicago; while the Case Study houses introducing mid-century modernism solidified the import of design in Los Angeles.

In today's practice of interior design, leaders of projects realize that in large-scale organizational relocations, the complex problems require a team of experts from multiple disciplines in order to properly solve the problem. This approach involves integrative thinking where each respective team member is invited to participate in and contribute best practices and research (VanPatter & Pastor). Projects that seek innovation have learned how to recognize and respect conventional solutions yet push beyond those toward inventing new solutions that clearly disrupt convention. The team's collective ability enables greater thinking across organizational and societal contexts. In this way, design innovation is an essential element and strategic asset in business transformation.

Branded interior design can be transformative. Interior designer Eva Maddox has been largely responsible for the emergence of branded interior environments, where advertising firms employ the evolution of super-graphics as a design device to heighten interest and brand spaces. In theses branded environments, culture can be created from the form and graphical expression, where little existed prior. The strong, bold character of the space commands attention, attracting interest and excitement in the space. It is effective in marketing the firm and attracting employees and prospective clients. It can be transformative if strategically used by the right end user.

Some organizations have a cultural orientation that defines judgment as the highest form of value, while others prize innovation. Is decision making or creating more ideas most important to the firm? Often, differences exist in working and thinking, and design must create spaces that enhance social interactions to stimulate innovation. In the NOVA Development space, referencing the software firm described earlier, has an employee "oasis" at its center. It is defined with palm trees, cool colors and game tables—a gathering place for an afternoon coffee or ice cream encounter and for the germination of new ideas among colleagues. Cultural orientation aside, the opportunity to convey business identity to and by employees and customers is one of the primary reasons for workplace relocations and renovations (Morgan & Anthony). The relationship between the business identity expressed by the coded design and the spatial form, the phenomenon (the business workspace, tools, social structure, and abstract conceptual idea) is critically important to its cognitive visual success through a convergence of perceptions.

The future is tempered by behavioral-environmental cultural norms, highly influenced by economics and politics as well as religious beliefs. Design syntax must respond to social and political stress, where companies struggle with employment risk and low productivity enduring periods of boom and bust cycles (Pomeroy). Traditional cultural tensions continue to perpetuate schisms of unease, distrust, and inability to elicit effective collaboration among varying groups of people in the workplace. Human interaction is elevated to matters of faith tested, and a new spiritualism increases as Christian denominations are challenged. The largest human demographic, the baby boomers, will face eldercare issues as America becomes diversified, and by contrast, there will be job shortages. Contrasts abound.

Sustainability may be the largest social factor that, ever too slowly, attempts to address climate change and its affect on the global population and its societies, presenting new challenges to present cultures and benevolent adopters/rescuers. Will new museums or online resources spring forth to capture lost lands and cultural artifacts? Will new energy solutions with sustainable power resources be readily accepted, making transitions smooth? Will open-source education empower the underserved while funding decreases to support the institutions of the past? Our alternative life in social media redefines us and our activities. It influences our thinking and changes our face-to-face human interaction.

Responding to these driving forces is an overarching demand for great, tectonic design innovation. Business culture is evolving from space utilization to spatial inspiration. Leading designers are adept at expressing a unique cultural message, to brand the client's imagery or align with the greater sustainability movement. Increasingly in America and beyond, clients seek a higher aesthetic space in which to work, influenced by geographical climate and their emotional response to their interior environment. In sophisticated centers of business, large businesses place great priority on design, now reinterpreted for economic conditions. The abstract coded nature of space is evidence of the significance of the cultural symbology, both reflecting and causing idealized human and business interaction. Design syntax is a direct reflection of the context of business, carefully balancing behavioral-socio-political goals. Not the least of any of the **symbolic thinking drivers** is technology, which makes life more interesting each day. The challenges for design fluency and its cultural context during this time of global upheaval are daunting.

Discussion Questions

1. What is "design thinking toward change management"? We explored these ideas in Chapters 6 and 7. How do we weave cultural identity into the office environment through design-business as change "management"?

2. What is the cultural shift going on that Stevenor Dale is describing?

3. How is Stevenor Dale, as a professional designer, articulating the changes she is seeing in the ways that we perceive workspaces and workplaces?

References

Rock, J. (n.d.) Retrieved September 20, 2010, from http://www.linkedin.com/groupItem?view=&srchtype=discussedNews&gid=37821&item=28791962&type=member&trk=EML_anet_qa_ttle-0St79xs2RVr6JBpnsJt7dBpSBA.

Van Patter, G. K., & Pastor, E. (2002–2011, in process). Design Thinking Made Visible Project. Humantific. Available at http://issuu.com/humantific/docs/humantificthinkingmadevisible . Retrieved June 2, 2010.

Morgan, A., & Anthony, S. (2008). Creating a High-Performance Workplace: A Review of Issues and Opportunities. *Journal of Corporate Real Estate*, 10(1): 27–39.

Pomery, B. Retrieved September 20, 2010, from http://www.linkedin.com/groupItem?view+&srchtype+discussedNews&gid+145854&item+28007192&type+member&trk+EML_anet_qa_ttle-cnhOon0JumNFomgJt7dBpSBA.

Provocation

8.2 NextDesign Geographies:
Understanding Design 1, 2, 3, 4:
The Rise of Visual SenseMaking*
GK VanPatter interviewed by Peter Jones PhD

Peter Jones: GK, as you know, the interaction design community is comprised of user experience and interaction designers, human-centered researchers, academic researchers, and other design professionals. However, I have never seen anything like your theory of change in design practice described in these pages. Let us assume that most readers may not have encountered Design 3 or 4 (D3, D4)—may I ask you to start with an overview of your perspective of the historical changes happening around the design professions?

GK VanPatter: We have many friends in the interaction design community, and I am delighted to do this. In reference to an overview of historical changes in design practice, I will back up and suggest an overview of an overview for this compressed format. Let me start by saying, that what we do at NextD is not create theories, but rather provide synthesis of what we see occurring all around us. The dots are there. We just connect them.

When Elizabeth Pastor and I launched NextD as an experiment in 2002, we did not know exactly what we were looking at

in the marketplace and in academia, but we had general concerns about the state of design leadership—that it was falling behind, and was badly out of sync with the real world that we were familiar with at that time. We knew from our practice that "design" was, for numerous reasons, changing rapidly and significantly—but we did not see much evidence of this in graduate design education. Quite frankly, much of American design education did not seem to understand the massive continuous change occurring outside of design. We were not the owners of this problem, but we thought it might be useful to lend a hand, since we both come from design backgrounds.

The term "design" is so loaded, so we initially considered proceeding with this rethinking exercise under a different terminology banner. For ten years, Humantific has gone to market as an innovation enabling company, not a design company. For us, going back—or sideways, so to speak—to rethink design, was somewhat of a counterintuitive exercise. For a number of reasons, we felt that pitching in to help would be useful to a community that is near and dear to us, and one that we will always be part of.

In 2002, it appeared that leaders of both design education and the professional design associations were missing in action regarding the rethinking of design—so we jumped in. It is important to understand that NextD was created as a sensemaking and changemaking experiment, not a design promotion initiative. Upon launch, we described the traditional model of design leadership as a burning platform. Not everyone appreciated that view.

From the outset, we focused on how we might utilize sensemaking to convey, in specific terms, what was changing and why change was needed. To do this, we undertook sensemaking conversations with many thoughtful people from inside and outside of design.

With a ReRethinking Design orientation, NextD Journal began creating authentic views into the conditions of design, and also illuminated new paths for designers.

Along the way in that journey, we learned a tremendous amount about the design community, interconnected communities and the various forces in play in the marketplace: what was changing, and what was not. Being a seasoned professional yourself, I think you must know that not all of what was encountered was pleasant. To be frank, the competitive marketplace that now includes design education, design practice and professional design associations can be brutal. In NextD Journal conversations, we saw some thought leaders questioning whether there was a design community at all. Encountering this community context reminded us that this kind of changemaking work is not for the faint of heart.

After several years of sharing in-depth thought leadership conversations, NextD created several sensemaking frameworks—including DesignGeographies, which was launched at the national AIGA conference in 2005. We recognized at that time, that it is impossible to have a meaningful conversation about the changing nature of design today without some kind of sensemaking framework. With many well-meaning government leaders around the world trying to determine how to make use of their design communities in the face of globalization, we wanted to provide a few simple dialogue tools.

Inside the NextD Geographies story is the NextD Complexity Ladder of D1, D2, D3, D4. It is a post-discipline view that is process, not content, focused. As a field of knowledge, design is an amorphous time warp that exists across several time zones, or paradigms, simultaneously. Some are old, rather static paradigms, while others are transforming and/or just emerging. Unlike in traditional science, the various paradigms of design do not necessarily replace each other as they emerge. As activity zones, the paradigms within design (D1, D2, D3, D4) exist in parallel. These operational states of design exist simultaneously. There are often competing and conflicting interests between the zones, which tends to generate a lot of heat in the marketplace.

Early on, we determined that the best way to explain the degree of change occurring inside and outside of design was to focus on how the scales of challenges facing organizations—facing Earth—are changing.

In our conference and workshop talks, we attempt to place the change in everyday work context. We point out that if one was

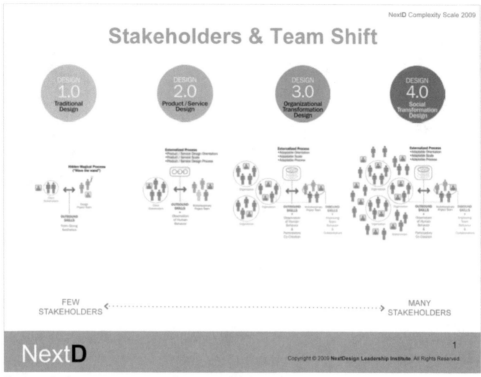

Figure 8.2 Design 1.0, 2.0, 3.0, 4.0 Transformational Shifts

trained to tackle poster sized, framed challenges, it is likely that new skills and tools will be required to tackle highly complex, fuzzy challenges, like organizational transformation or world peace.

We point out that globalization, i.e., the off-shoring, shrinking and commoditization of once thriving North American design markets, is driving a strategic space race. The reality is that design educated designers now have to compete for design and/or innovation leadership roles. To say this another way, the question of who frames the challenges in the strategic space

upstream from briefs has become a hugely competitive aspect of the market. It is a relatively simple message.

The truth is, when we started presenting the NextD Complexity Ladder at conferences in 2005, it was controversial. At the time the two most high profile graduate schools in this country were busy selling product design (D2) as the future of design. In addition, the then high-flying new business press was closely aligned with the product-centric D2 view, busily encouraging designers to be gleeful about chasing the next

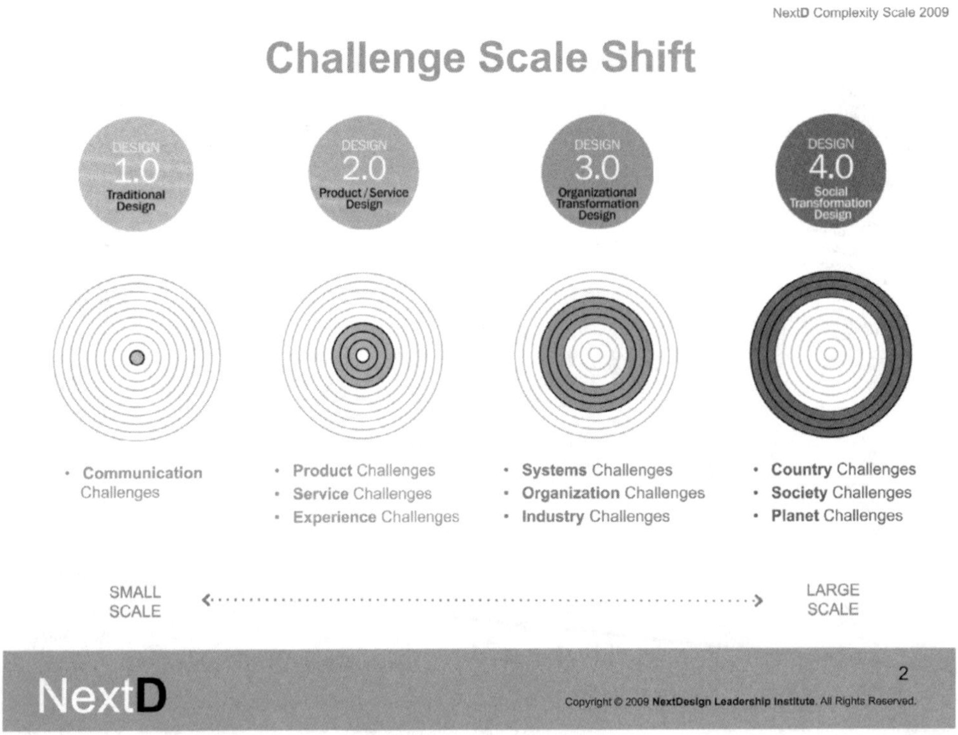

Challenge Scale Shift

| DESIGN 1.0 Traditional Design | DESIGN 2.0 Product/Service Design | DESIGN 3.0 Organizational Transformation Design | DESIGN 4.0 Social Transformation Design |

- Communication Challenges

- **Product** Challenges
- **Service** Challenges
- **Experience** Challenges

- **Systems** Challenges
- **Organization** Challenges
- **Industry** Challenges

- **Country** Challenges
- **Society** Challenges
- **Planet** Challenges

SMALL SCALE ⟨··⟩ LARGE SCALE

NextD

2

Figure 8.3 Challenge Scale Shift and Complexity Scale

iPod. In presenting the existence of an emerging Design 3 [and] 4 community in 2005, we were already pointing out that many of the challenges facing organizations—facing our communities—cannot be solved by creating more products, services, or related experiences, however human-centered they might be. In making that case, we were far out in front of the graduate design schools and professional design associations, regarding the tricky work of significantly re-envisioning design. The difficult truth is that product creation (D2) is often a solution to a problem that 21st century humans do not have.

Although our perspective made NextD controversial in some local design community circles, it also generated high interest among global readers not smitten with the American product-centric perspective. When it comes to design, the wheels of change are often moving faster outside the United States. NextD has always been focused in the global design community.

Today, the synchronization of tools and skills to problem scale is a quest underway in most disciplines around the world. No graduate school, and few practices, can escape that reckoning.

PJ: You and I have spoken at some length about the different orientations to the collaborative design skill we call "sensemaking"—a critical emerging skill, and fairly recent perspective in the design field. Historically, design has been dominated by the model of "individual designer engaged in branding-related differencing." How could experience designers start to incorporate sensemaking into the context of large product/service design projects?

GKVP: These are difficult questions to properly address in this compressed format. Of all the issues in the mix around the changing nature of design today, the rise and transformation of sensemaking is, from our perspective, among the most important elements of the story.

At Humantific, we distinguish between making the strange familiar and making the familiar strange. As a scholar, you might recognize this two-part terminology, as it can be found in William JJ Gordon's original 1950s–60s era *Synectics* work.[2] Anyone who has studied the history of the applied creativity movement will know that Gordon was among the 20th century pioneers of this knowledge domain. He was interested in developing new creative methods and the development of deliberate creative capacity in humans. In the context of your question, it is important to recognize that Gordon was working on and modeling such issues long before the later generation sensemaking pioneers arrived in the 1970s, 80s and 90s. We saw in Gordon's work a methodological orientation seed

that remains central to our approach to sensemaking today.

At Humantific, we call making the strange familiar, "sensemaking," and making the familiar strange, "strangemaking." For those who have never heard the term "strangemaking," at the scale of products and services, it's about differencing, i.e., how to make one bottle of water, cell phone, soda or car different from another. The entire branding industry is focused on differencing—on what we call strangemaking—and so, too, are huge chunks of the design community, and much of design education. How to do differencing is a huge aspect of what young people learn about in traditional design schools. As a mental process, sensemaking is very different from strangemaking. You are asking your brain to do very different things. This is part of what we have been trying to get the graduate design schools to understand, as shifting from one to the other will require some re-tooling, re-skilling. Like Gordon, we recognize both dimensions as an interconnected, continuous cycle linked to innovation. We have built our somewhat oddball, hybrid Humantific practice on the exploration and examination of the interconnections between sensemaking and strangemaking. For more than fifteen years, Elizabeth and I have been working at the intersection between the two, so at this point we understand well how they are connected.

In 1998, I wrote my first paper on differences and similarities between organizational sensemaking, the understanding [of] business and innovation-enabling, while working for Richard Saul Wurman. We were working on a large innovation ecology project in intervention mode, and we had to figure out how to explain what we were proposing and doing to organizational leaders who had been reading Karl Weick.

In that era, there was significant emphasis on the human capacity to process what Wurman described, in his now famous 1989 book, *Information Anxiety*, as "a tsunami of data crashing on our shores."[5] At that time, very intelligent people from information science, organizational psychology, cognitive science, knowledge management and many other fields were working on various aspects of information processing in humans and in organizations, without always having views into each other's work. Part of my job at that time was to synthesize and explain how the various streams might be interconnected. How did Wurman connect to Weick, etc. was among the many questions that our clients had at that time. I had to explain it to them.

Coming from very different backgrounds, Dervin, Weick, and Wurman were focused, in one way or another, in the direction of human information processing. Most of those streams were underway in the context of academic study and research. In contrast, Wurman and the understanding business folks were among the first to make sensemaking into a form of practice. Still today, these areas of study and work remain largely blind to each other, unless you are deliberately looking across these streams. From our Humantific perspective, they inform each other.

Since those early years, much has changed in the world—and certainly in practice. We have built steadily on those early foundations. To compress a lot of learning and complexity here it took us many years to figure this out: What organizations (and humans in general) are trying to do in the 21st century is not just process mountains of data, but make sense of complex, fuzzy situations of all kinds—often before any data exists. Today, data visualization and information processing are only a small aspect of the sensemaking that is already operationalized in next-generation, design-oriented practices. We have known for 15 years that data visualization alone will not get the job done if the job is to enable changemaking.

It also took us a long time to figure out (and be able to explain) the correlation between the rise of complexity facing planet Earth and the parallel interest, in more robust forms, of sensemaking. In retrospect, it is quite obvious. The good news is that the proportion of sensemaking to changemaking shifts as challenges grow in complexity. In the context of highly complex, fuzzy messes, there is most often a need to do significant sensemaking before changemaking begins. If we are working on a tiny problem, this is not likely the case. In its various forms, sensemaking now plays a key role in the fuzzy front end of most significant innovation and change initiatives, both in organizations and in society. This shift has significant implications for future design education.

In our Complexity Navigation Program, business executives learn a five-dimensional model of sensemaking that

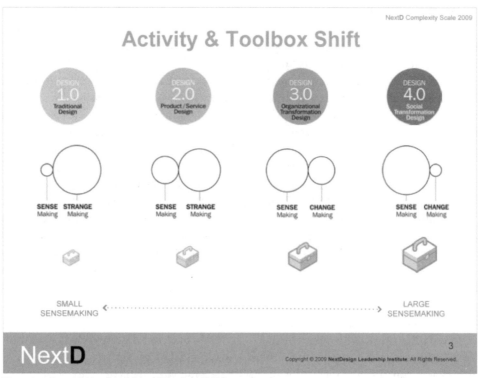

Figure 8.4 SenseMaking "Activity and Toolbox Shift"

includes how to make sense of the opportunity/problem space, the humans in the space, the information in the space, the problem owners and the project team. As you point out in your question, the activity of co-creation is at the center of a lot of sensemaking today. Often we are creating cognitive scaffolds that accelerate and enable collective sensemaking. To do this requires a much different kind of approach, and a different toolbox than those in use in traditional design-oriented practices.

I don't think it is any secret that our design education institutions have, for decades, been teaching what amounts to a huge emphasis on strangemaking. The branding business is all about strangemaking, as one toothbrush, bottle of water, or website is made to be different from another as a form of value. Strangemaking is about differencing. For a long time, there has been a public perception that differencing is the value-add that design brings to the party. Today, the design industries contain zillions of people focused on differencing services. It is a huge business that sustains many companies.

We always felt a little odd at design conferences, as we were designers in the sensemaking business. Much to our surprise, as complexity continues to rise, the outside has become the inside. Today, sensemaking (inclusive of design research, strategic co-creation and visual sensemaking) is at the center of the revolution, within design thinking, innovation, transformation— whatever you choose to call it. It is the change inside the change.

Regarding the other part of your question, about what UX practitioners can do: In these economic times, with so much web-related work already off-shore, the question is not how to do the same thing better, but instead how to help their companies address difficult challenges and become more adaptable to change.

We have worked with several experience design focused groups to help them rethink their mission and their value in the context of what their organizations now face. They are essentially working on this challenge: How might they become more strategically useful to their companies? If you put your adaptability hat on, the good news is that the sensing and sensemaking aspects of UX can be updated and repurposed. If you look closely at the present leading firms in the shrinking and commoditizing UX space, this is what they are trying to do. Many are working hard on getting themselves into the strategic space. Some seem to have no clue what that really means, in terms of skills and tools, but there is no question that this is where they are headed. For those who choose to do the same thing better (or differently), new

forms of sensemaking add significant value to the front end of any innovation effort, including those focused on user experience design.

PJ: As I know your work, I'm aware that you have been extending the model to include Design 4.0, which may be a nascent weak signal on the horizon for most practitioners. How might we become aware of the need for D4 thinking in our design and organizational contexts? Simply put, what does this mean to most of us?

GKVP: When we were at the EXPOSED conference, held at Arizona State University School of Design, we presented "NextD Geographies / Understanding Futures that Have Already Arrived." It was the first time we have presented Design 4 / Social Transformation Design.

I do like your descriptive term "nascent weak signal on the horizon." I think that is a generally true depiction; however, we are seeing a lot more action in the D4 activity space than what might have been imagined only a year ago. Anyone on Facebook will know that there are already dozens of social innovation related initiatives being launched every month on that platform. With invitations to join various groups overflowing, soon there will be social innovation initiative fatigue, no doubt.

What we are likely seeing is the first post-9/11, post-Inconvenient Truth, post-World Changing cycle of social innovation initiatives move through the social network system, complete with a lot of energy, enthusiasms and probably a certain amount of naiveté regarding many of these highly complex social challenges that face occupants of planet earth. The social networking platforms are making it easy to launch and get started. Apart from the excessive exuberance around social innovation, what is actually going on seems a little messier and more complicated, as life tends to be. At NextD, we try to look at what the activity occurring under the banner of social innovation actually is—from a methods perspective. Although no perfect lens exists, the NextD complexity scale helps us in this regard.

So far, much of what is going on seems to be what we call "Cross-Overs." In the Design 4 activity space, we see multitudes of branded and unbranded approaches that can be grouped into five basic categories:

- The Algorithm Group
  Network-based up or down voting & data patterns analysis.
- The Science of Dialogue Design Group
  Technology-enabled, transformation-focused dialogue.
- The Transformation by Design Group
  Hybrid toolbox applied to social change.
- The Problem Solving Group
  Creative problem solving applied to social change.
- The Cross-Over Group
  Design 1.0 & Design 2.0 methods applied to social change.

The groups vary in terms of size and focus. From what we see, the Algorithm Group is working on various network platforms focused primarily in the direction of "decision-making". How might they harness the power of the demo-cratic collective? This is what this group seems to be interested in presently. Of course the web works best for up or down judging—a giant judging table. Presently in Algorithm Group literature, there is much less focus on where the ideas are going to come from. Wouldn't it be interesting to see the change patterns around how the public feels about Obama today, next year, and four years from now? These are issues of interest to this group—or group of groups, as there are many different streams involved. The tricky part is that while global society has never had such technologies, we already know that there is a lot more to transformation than judging. How do we get to social transformation from collective judging? The tremendous amount of unstudied terrain here will keep graduate students and practitioners busy for years to come.

The Science of Dialogue Design Group, Transformation by Design Group and The Problem Solving Group are more action, intervention, or design-enabling focused and seek, in several different ways, to engage multiple constituents upstream from briefs without any preconceived notions of what the problems and solutions might be. They seek to enable collective and individual ideation, judging, decision-making and change-related action. This is quite different from just focusing on judgment. Without getting into describing the various toolboxes, some are digital, some are analogue and some are combined. The emphasis among these groups tends to be on process, rather than content. There is considerable energy around this group today, as it is being transformed with new hybrid tools and practices.

As far as we know, no one has yet gathered any scientific numbers on these activities, but we are guessing that the Cross-Over Group is probably the largest growing—and rapidly, as many young generation designers actively seek meaningful work and engage with their existing skills and toolsets.

There seems to be a lot of young generation designers not wanting to just chase the next gadget creation in Chicago or Hong Kong. Instead, many want to somehow engage with their mindset and toolset in more socially meaningful work in Africa and other countries in need. Inevitably embedded in "Cross-Over" social innovation initiatives are the methods from D1 and/or D2, where high degrees of co-creation, framing and sensemaking have historically not been front and center. In many "Cross-Overs," designers are working in a social context, but what they are really doing is still D1 or D2 work.

In "Cross-Overs," one can see the assumption being made that exporting D1 and D2 is what we need to do to help in Africa, etc. With the best of intentions, there is often the engrained predisposition that products and services are the solutions needed. Although this might often be the case, in some situations and in some countries it might not be. Most often in complex D3 and D4 work, arriving with pre-framed challenge or solution assumptions up front is a problematic recipe.

There are many ways to undertake "Cross-Overs." Last year, Humantific's Understanding Lab was involved in *The Measure of America*, the first human development report focused on a developed country. This was, essentially, a social sensemaking initiative at the scale of a country— the USA. We were engaged to make the research understandable and engaging, as part of a broader social changemaking initiative that is still underway. The book is designed as a simple-to-digest, sensemaking acceleration tool that government leaders and others now use to clearly spell out the need for social change in this country. In that kind of project, we focus on fact-finding illumination and problem reframing, rather than driving specific solutions.

Generally in D3 and D4, there is more need for open challenge framing—more need for deep, local, human-centered sensemaking. The design community seems to be in the midst of a Cross-Over wave. In all the enthusiasm, few seem to be asking if this approach is really working, but we have no doubt that such questions will arise as the various initiatives unfold. It is still very early in that cycle. The lessons and realizations will, in time, be emergent!

It does seem unlikely that simply exporting D1 and D2 to developing countries will, in itself, solve world hunger, world peace and the multitude of other wicked problems facing our collective selves.

Presently, there are considerably fewer design-oriented folks operating in the fuzzy front end of social transformation design, where challenges are co-created and framed far upstream from briefs. I know that you have been involved in the "Dialogue Design" arena for some years, so you probably see this yourself.

D3 and D4 work tends to involve multiple constituents, and quite different challenge types. Upstream from where D1 and D2 jump off, these challenges are fuzzier, more complex and involve many constituents—so a different toolbox is needed.

Most designers know a lot more about the D1 and D2 activity spaces, so, for many, the D3 and D4 spaces are much more experimental. What does it mean to take human-centered tools into organizational and social transformation situations? No one really knows the complete answer to these ongoing questions. These are questions being worked on every day in practice. This is part of why what makes this terrain of D3 and D4 is rapidly becoming so interesting to many.

To a significant degree, D3 and D4 still represent relatively undiscovered countries for many with design backgrounds, but that, too, is rapidly changing, as globalization takes hold and drives change in the design community. Ten years from now, I think many more will be engaged in the D3 and D4 activity spaces, with more knowledge and better tools. Certainly, many smart people are hard at work on this around the world.

PJ: Considering the models you've disclosed, can you further illuminate how designers, inspired by the possibilities of transformation design and sustainable design, might adopt these distinctions and put them to work in real practice situations?

GKVP: The NextD message is quite simple: The changes underway, outside of design, are due to the very real forces of globalization that exist in the marketplace. It is not rocket science to point out that, as the market changes, many design-oriented firms are proactively adapting to change. Some design markets are shrinking, while others are emerging. What is going on around Design 3 and 4 is not someone's cool idea. It is change, in response to change. Those in the various design communities can draw their own conclusions regarding how (or if) they see that change, how (or if) they want to change, and at what speed. Change outside of design is occurring, whether everyone likes it or not.

From the NextD perspective, design (and design thinking) is moving from:

- Tactical to Strategic & Tactical
- Defined Briefs as Starting Points to Fuzzy Situations as Starting Points
- Tiny SenseMaking to Huge Sense-Making
- Trends Tracking to Complexity Navigation
- Aesthetic Focused to Human-Centered
- Vertical Content Expertise to Adaptable Process Expertise
- Intertribal Communication to Cross-Disciplinary Communication
- Creating to Co-Creating & Creating
- Thinking & Doing to Thinking, Doing & Enabling
- Deliberate Exclusion to Deliberate Inclusion
- Cool Object Creating to Innovative Culture Building
- Design as Subservience to Design as Leadership

Discussion Questions

1. What is meant by Design 1, 2, 3, and 4?
   a. What are the characteristics of the Activity and Toolbox schema?
   b. How is designing shifting according to GK VanPatter?

2. What is the nature of sensemaking?
   a. How is sensemaking creating new meanings using design thinking?
   b. What is co-creation?

3. What is the nature of the Design 4 Activity Space?
   a. What are the five groups GK Van-Patter outlines, and how are these developing spaces of change in terms of
      i. Social change?
      ii. Decision making?

4. Why are these concepts so vital for us to understand when trying to make design meanings and when understanding changing spaces of design?

References

Dervin, Brenda. (1992). From the Mind's Eye of the User: The Sense-Making Qualitative, Quantitative Methodology. In J. D. Glazier & R.R. Powell (Eds.), *Qualitative Research in Information Management* (pp. 61–84). Englewood, CO: Libraries Unlimited.

Gordon, William JJ. (1961). *Synectics: The Development of Creative Capacity*. London: Collier Books.

Weick, Karl E. (1995), *Sensemaking in Organizations*, Thousand Oaks, CA: Sage Publications.

Weick, Karl E. (1988). Enacted Sensemaking in Crisis Situations. *Journal of Management Studies.*

Wurman, Richard Saul. (1989). *Information Anxiety*. New York: Bantam Doubleday.

In this Dialogues and Perspectives we examine the ways that people in practice engage in design spaces of the corporate work environment. Donna Cummings offers perspectives on how the corporate spaces integrate design thinking with corporate strategies, while Florian Weiß provides ideas about design effectiveness. Finally, Michael Arnold provides a summary perspective of the recipient from a corporate perspective of those who received the design spaces provided both as service and as product.

Perspective I: An Interview with Donna Cummings

Donna Cummings, Interior designer, co-principal of Marshall Cummings & Associates

Tiiu Poldma: Let me pose the following questions about the future of the business of design:

- What is forward thinking and innovation in the business world and how does design offer tools for innovative practices?
- What are the complexities inherent in corporate design?
- What is, in your mind, the future of space and different ways of under-standing space, whether it is through interdisciplinary approaches or the role of research?
- What are your thoughts about designing for and with people as users or clients and what are their preoccupations and the reasons they hired you?

Donna Cummings: In thinking about your questions, I would say that forward thinking today means different things than it did back when I first started with my partner, Marian [Marshall].

Corporate clients saw our industry as space planners and interior architects. Clients wanted a pleasant place to work that showcased their corporate values. The offices reflected their organizational charts and allocated space and amenities accordingly. During our design investigative phase of projects, we learned a great deal about how businesses functioned and we began questioning our clients and challenging them to think about use of space from a more functional relationship aspect. As MC matured, we were hired for our creative design solutions to the current business challenges. Design had expanded beyond the physical and now encompassed the sharing and building of Knowledge.

In regard to the corporate design world, lately I have been reading published articles on projects and what strikes me is that many years later, things seemed not to have changed a great deal, and in fact our clients at Marshall Cummings (MC) must have been way ahead of the game, as others are now just talking about issues such as hoteling, remote working, etc.

Regarding the value of design thinking in business thinking, we had always started design projects by questioning and chairing focus groups with the CEO and other business unit heads to gather and assess their business goals, their culture, and how physical space could support and help improve their success. We insisted on project goals that could be directly linked to the business goals in order to judge the decision making as the project developed and the success in the end. We quickly found that many times the companies' business plans and brand were very much in the minds of the executives, and when you got down in the ranks, no one knew what you were talking about. So part of the process was to push the information down and excite the folks, and look for support and ideas from within. Some companies who were reinventing themselves would come armed with reports from business consultants without an active implementation plan or possibly a plan but no idea of the time, training, and money/technology needed to make it succeed. The value that we could demonstrate was usually one of improved communication, support of work processes, integration of corporate culture and visual branding, multiple uses of space, and sometimes space saving. What we wanted to add was an environment and work tools that would enable creative business thinking and therefore grow the business, not just reduce costs.

Some business schools are trying to tie design thinking into business thinking, such as the University of Toronto Rotman School of Business and Roger Martin's idea of design thinking as a combination of new ideas (intuitive thinking), and current activities (analytical thinking), combining to produce what might be. This is what Marshall Cummings has been doing for the last 10 or 15 years, in a very practical way. We have combined our knowledge and experience with research and analysis of clients' working habits to develop new ways of working. Our value as interior designers often combines the two activities. We can produce spaces that encourage this thinking in others to some degree, but there are many other factors involved that we have little influence over as designers.

Interdisciplinary Teams

Which takes us to your question on the complexities inherent in this type of work. This leads to the need for interdisciplinary teams encompassing the client and many representatives within their business models, the architect with emphasis on sustainable thinking, and the techies who can make possible the sharing of many spatial ideas, through communication and knowledge. We can expand the list to include the industrial psychologist, the planner/brander/colorist/furniture/finishes expert/project manager and coordinator/interior designer, engineers, contractors, and suppliers. This type of collaboration takes time

Figure 8.5 Flexible "touch down" work areas for international management consultants returning to home base.
Photo Courtesy: Donna Cummings

and money, and success is rarely achieved unless the team is willing to be innovative, nonterritorial, and guided by a highly skilled facilitator.

I also keep thinking about the educational challenges that face future designers. If students and staff do not have time for all the design disciplines and academics, how can they learn business thinking? Post-grad studies may be an answer, or possibly design becomes the post-grad learning after a design business degree.

Technology is driving our culture and how we interact with people and spaces

in ways as never before. Technology is an enabler in Knowledge sharing. We need to explore possibilities to make this interaction more understood and positive. Part of this could be counterbalance to technology, areas where you check your tech toys at the door.

As Dean Matsumoto says, design is changing. Dean worked for MC for over 25 years and is a principal at Kasian Architects. Dean was our *futurist* at MC and was always one step ahead in planning ideas. I asked Dean why it seems projects have not progressed, and he commented that many of our earlier clients who explored non-dedicated work space, work anywhere attitudes—for example, the office as a home base for sharing knowledge—were very progressive in their approach, [and were] often management consultants and accounting firms.

Culture and technology have aligned as users demand these same requirements of their working spaces. New generations of workers are more technologically savvy; aware that they can work anywhere they want. Clients now have wireless networks, with the bandwidth and integrated business systems to make this possible. At the same time, this generation recognizes they have much to learn from Boomers and some of them still like the idea of entitlement and status. Is a dedicated workspace the new emblematic corner office?

Dean and I talked about the mixed success of interdisciplinary teams at MC where we had an industrial psychologist on our staff. Achieving client understanding of the different scopes of involvement and the competency of the team members is still the challenge. Many professional scopes are similar, and it is difficult for the client to see the integration and not the overlap, as well as sharing of fees and responsibility. Often a project manager becomes the leader and the integrated thinking can get bogged down in left-brain management.

Flexibility has always been a key word used to describe many clients' goals. This type of thinking requires maximum flexibility, as the resulting space must be able to morph and change as the ideas expand. Cultural and local issues affecting design are another whole topic of their own,

including the tech effect, the respect for many cultural and religious differences, three generations in the workplace, being green. There is a lot to think about!

Perspective II: Measuring Design Effectiveness

Florian Weiß, PARK Advanced Design Institute

With shrinking design budgets due to the financial situation in many companies, design managers, like most professions, are trying to explain themselves and justify their value. Occasionally, efforts made in this cause appear too obsessive. Terms like *key performance indicators, critical success factors,* and *performance management systems* are becoming part of the lingo of design managers. However, the more recent trend to try to measure design effectiveness sets a near-impossible task, at just the wrong moment. Many of the current attempts focus on short-term results by only defining CSFs and KPIs for the next quarterly meeting with the boss; others try to prove the effect of design in the limits of one design project (e.g., measure perceived quality in craftsmanship clinics or identify the design effect in brand equity). Ironically many neglect (conscious or unconscious) the importance of setting up a quality management program. Are they too busy with justifying their results? More and more design managers have turned to crunching numbers. Sometimes they do this to reassure themselves; sometimes they do it to look professional; more often, we hope, they do it for substantive reasons.

It's fine to keep watch on a few very vivid measures of design effectiveness. But to be governed by a search for the quantitative impacts of design is a mistake. In design, it's particularly hard to measure both inputs and outputs. Even at its most successful, design is only part of a wider budgetary mix of technology and marketing, and on the output side. There the effect of design is computed on revenues, profit margins, and even stock market performance. Statisticians make little allowance for the time lag between studio drawing and first-year sales.

Designers and design managers may have felt the need for numbers when they were in the corporate wilderness. But apart from the inherent difficulty of producing those numbers, they should focus on design effectiveness. While design effectiveness is focusing on doing the right things, design efficiency is focusing on doing the things right. The downside of high design efficiency is that it comes at a price we probably don't want to pay—low effectiveness. Good design management cannot look at design efficiency and design effectiveness in isolation, but has to seek a good balance between both aspects. Design management must evaluate the degree to which design effectiveness and efficiency matter in a particular situation and ensure results with the right proportion for the particular situation.

As a design management consultancy, we talk to practicing design managers in international companies every day, Here are some of their comments on this:

- "Finally! At a time when we are trying to let go from over-engineered planning and risk assessment, liberating design, from wasting time trying to prove its effectiveness, is both liberating and necessary. Proving our effectiveness was always a demonstration and a re-enforcement of our insecurity."
- "I believe it is true that design has been more accepted into the mainstream of business culture, and that its potential as a business driver is more understood now than it has ever been. Nowadays, even the international business press has become a proponent of design as a contributor to business success. The design industry no longer needs to feverishly generate doubtful statistics as a matter of survival. Design is recognized—it has a place in the world."
- "I would wish that design effectivity was of no importance, but today there is a general tendency to think that only things we are able to measure have a value. If, therefore, we had some good, simple tools to measure design effectiveness with, it would be much easier to sell the message that good design is good business. Finance directors do not wish us to be bean counters, but to many of them it is still hard to understand what design actually is about."
- "We do not need to measure design as long as the design efforts within a given context (like a company) are doubtlessly successful. However, when they are not, then you need to get better. Better performance is what? Something somewhere between measuring/

estimating/sensing that design has done a better job. Or you might be asked to reduce your resources (people, etc.) in order to perform the same mediocre job as before with less strain on the financial system. How do you react? You justify. You explain. You develop and propose actions to improve performance. Your vocabulary will be close to measuring your own performance—just like anyone else in a corporate environment."

- "You can't measure design effectiveness as you could measure the impact of an advertising campaign on the sales. But I am convinced that if you abandon the effort to identify what should be measured, you can enter in an illusion land where you will forget to fix the aims of design."

- "[While] it might be true that design is more and more recognized for its added value to the success of companies by senior management, it's certainly not the case on most lower levels in the organizations. Where top management start to think in terms of value, operational level still tend to think in terms of costs. We therefore might consider to sell our services more often on a value base, e.g., on an hourly compensation base."

Wouldn't It Be Better to Strike a Midway Position?

Design is part of mainstream corporate culture nowadays. That means that designers and their managers are asked

to account, numerically, for what they're doing. This is fine—in costs and budget allocations, design managers need to run a tight ship. What we don't need to worry about is measuring design effectiveness, which is a rather different matter. Such an endeavor is time-consuming and much more subjective than its pretensions to objectivity allow. It's hard to isolate the effect of design from other effects. For instance, we help companies to follow activities to maximize the value of design. On top of this there is (in most companies) no need to measure the value of design.

- Efficient and effective design process: Making design a quality program (related to requirements of ISO 9001) with clear roles, responsibilities, timings, and deliverables.

- Setting clear objectives and strategies for design management: Defining, monitoring, and communicating KPIs and CSFs for design management, which are linked to the corporate strategy.

- Training and establishing leading practice: Implement design management training and define the leading practice for a particular situation.

- Establish a structure for effective design: Building design management capabilities and clear interfaces to other disciplines

- Ensure quality of external design partners: Select and review external design partners and ensure high quality.

- Creating an understanding for design in purchase and HR departments: Educating relevant decision makers (e.g., in human resource and procurement) to understand the value of design and provide decision-making tools that are not only cost-based.

- Communicating visions and successes: Visualizing a vision, running lighthouse projects, and communicating successes explain the value of design without the need to measure it.

Perspective III: A Client Perspective as a User

Michael Arnold, CA, President, Dyne Holdings

What is valuable when a designer is involved on a project depends a lot on how they are involved. When the interior designer or architect puts on a business hat, this adds a dimension of reality to the project, and in my mind, this adds to the creative process, as both are vital to the overall success of the built project, whether it is a new building for office lease or a hotel for visitors or businesspeople. However, imposing creative ideas or intentions, rather than using it as means to bring together function, aesthetic, and also business need, is not productive for the bottom line of the project. The project designed outside of the context of economic realities surrounding the project, using only the creative process, is useless.

The designers' role is to pull everything together. First, images or sketches show ideas to reflect business and practical responses. These ideas help the building and its spaces realize its full potential in terms of business needs, revenue for future rental of unoccupied spaces, and the overall look of the building as a statement of corporate representation. For example, the financial office building that we just completed has been built to show a future tenant a level of service, access, and representation of financial stability and contemporary design to support the tenant needs. The interior had to be built to reflect a certain corporate image for a corporate tenant, show this to a certain quality, yet also at a reasonable budget.

From my perspective, the designer acts as the catalyst and the glue that holds it all together during the development/construction/leasing period. When we look at our initial plans to build or at existing buildings, we create spaces. The life span of buildings depends on how people use and respect them after they have been appropriately designed. They, in turn, give back to the people that use them, and who use all their senses when in/around the building. The positive interaction of the senses of these people leads to a more positive lifestyle, and this in turn directly relates to much higher levels of productivity in our workplaces.

The designer has the training to understand how all the design elements come together and to help people use their senses when they come into the space. The trained designer knows what is needed to achieve the end results. I then turn the building into rented space. We, as investors, then have a much higher valued property to lease out, resulting in greater investment returns. This in turn makes the design input highly valuable.

Discussion Questions

1. What are the new ways of thinking and what are business goals according to Cummings?
   a. How are cultural and local issues changing the tone of business strategies and objectives?
   b. What are Cummings and Matsumoto saying in terms of innovative and forward thinking ways of reconceptualizing spaces as designers?

2. How do Donna Cummings and Florian Weiss view the roles of the designer and design manager in the real world of corporate work?

3. How is design an effective tool for business from Weiß's perspective?
   a. What are design effectiveness principles and how are these values for the client and user?

4. What is the business view of the designer from Arnold's perspective?
   a. How is this similar or different from Cummings' and Weiß's perspectives?
   b. How does the designer offer (a) value, (b) design effectiveness, for the client from Arnold's perspective?

SUMMARY

This chapter brings to light emergent perspectives from designers, clients, and businesspeople to provide perspective on the ways things are in the real world using the example of corporate design. Both Stevenor Dale's ideas about changing cultures and VanPatter and Jones' ideas about sensemaking culminate with the ideas proposed by Richard Buchanan, and how these shifts affect clients and businesspeople and the way designs are produced and moved into the realities of the workplace environments. New cultural spaces intersect with design spaces as meanings become vital to corporate success.

We now turn to an examination of these ideas with the contexts of technological spaces and what this means as design thinking and creativity are explored from the context of technological change.

SUGGESTED READINGS

Gertner, J. (2012). True Innovation. *New York Times* reprints. Retrieved from http://www.nytimes.com/2012/02/26/opinion/sunday/innovation-and-the bell labs-miracle.html.

Kao, J. (1996). *Jamming: The Art and Discipline of Business Creativity.* New York: Harper-Collins.

LeGault, M. (2006). *Think! Why Crucial Decisions Can't Be Made in the Blink of an Eye.* New York: Threshold Editions.

OVERVIEW QUESTIONS FOR DISCUSSION

Consider both the essay by C. T. Mitchell in Chapter 9 and the interview in this chapter between GK VanPatter and Peter Jones. Reflect on the following questions in groups in the classroom:

1. What is a wicked design problem as proposed by Richard Buchanan and originally defined by Horst Rittel?

2. What is the nature of design in 1.0 compared to 3.0 or 4.0 in VanPatter and Jones' discussion?
   a. What are the differences?
   b. How is what VanPatter and Jones discuss manifested in the way that Mitchell suggests business is using design process for strategic decision making?

3. Explore the nuances of the perspectives of each author. What is salient in the discussion about design thinking, design wisdom, and corporate strategies?

4. How does Stevenor Dale explore cultural contexts of corporate offices? How does she bring together issues of the business culture with specific aspects of designed interior spaces?

5. How does Cummings reflect on how designers think about corporate design strategies?

6. What is design effectiveness according to Florian Weiß? What is this necessary to understand in terms of responding to client needs?

7. What are client needs according to Michael Arnold?

8. What new knowledge spaces become evident when examined through the lenses of the different authors? What knowledge positions does each hold in his or her respective positions as a designer, a businessperson, or a corporate client?

PART III
Provocations about Spatial Meanings and Future Design and Spaces

CHAPTER 9
Pragmatic and Collaborative Spaces in Practice and Research

design thinking, design logic, democratic aesthetic, designerly ways of knowing, critical design, pragmatism, pragmatic experience, wicked problems, critical design ethnography, critical pragmatism, third-space discourse, pragmatic aesthetic experience, researcher stance, designer intention, community practices, knowledge making, (critical) pragmatism, meaning construction, cooperative inquiry, participatory action research, collaborative research, communities of practice, vision

AFTER READING THIS CHAPTER, YOU WILL BE ABLE TO:

- Determine how design thinking can be mediated by critical design, pragmatism, and collaborative approaches.

- Understand what constitutes critical design.

- Distinguish the characteristics of pragmatic experience.

- Explore how critical design constructs meaning in diverse spaces.

- Determine the ways that research informs practices through collaborative and cooperative research modes.

- Understand communities of practice and their role in transformational change.

INTRODUCTION

In this chapter, we explore critical design, design thinking. and emerging critical pragmatic spaces as understood in practice, as explored in research, and as new spaces of research/practice. As the complexity of design problems and situations becomes the norm, pragmatic and critical design thinking approaches become vital to understand and explore. These are new spaces of exploration.

We have explored thus far how design thinking is at the root of how we consider design/spaces when we are trying to move a particular solution through transformational change, or when a vision is not-yet-existing (Nelson & Stolterman, 2003). Design thinking, when critically informed and pragmatically situated, consciously integrates perspectives of holistic thinking about problems and situations, where contexts and research provide grounding, and proposals are situated within collaborative and cooperative contexts. Whether it is a lone designer transforming spaces through projects or where multiple stakeholders get together to create communities of practice, when this is approached with consideration for the experiences and views of those for whom the designing occurs, then each is striving to effect change through transformative design thinking processes (Buchanan, 2000; Nelson & Stolterman, 2003).

Process and Complexity in Design Situations

If we consider design in general to be a complex activity that requires flexibility and problem-solving ability, then creating experiences in diverse spaces using design thinking requires added multifaceted considerations. Whether in virtual or real spaces, the complexity of the design requires the issues and problems of design itself be situated within real contexts, such as the experience of the user in the environment within which the product or service will be used or the design experienced. This dynamic cannot be situated as separate from the more intimate aspects of human experience, including senses and affective responses (Pallasmaa, 1990). Objects and spaces are interacting simultaneously with human perceptions of those objects and spaces at any given moment, and are also in movement through time. Space and time interact, and both are in changing dimensions that increasingly are mediated by human collective actions.

These processes require two fundamental concepts to be productive and useful: (1) considering designing through design thinking as a holistic approach; and (2) considering how critical design is informed by research, context, and pragmatic thinking in both research-based and project-/practice-based situations.

A Holistic Approach to Designing

A holistic approach to designing considers resituating the nature of the design problem in the context of the people, the spaces, of the business or of the community, as well as being built around knowledge, form, and intention, depending on the needs and requirements as determined by all the players, actors, stakeholders, and voices of the people involved. In part, designing consists of a complex series of overlapping situations, not fixed in time and space, where designers intervene (Rengel, 2003; Buchanan, 2000). For example, in a learning situation, students need to explore a design problem by first examining the whole problem and understanding the contexts and the issues. In another type of situation such as a collaborative community situation, all interested participants require a holistic view of the situation or problem beforehand, with all contexts understood and multiple voices heard. Research and critical considerations play a vital role in these initial stages. Design thinking then provides context for the engaged participants through a critical consideration of the issues at hand.

Design Thinking as Beyond the Design Problem

Early considerations of design thinking placed emphasis on the design problem. On a very basic level William Pena (1977) provides an example in his seminal book, *Problem-seeking*:

> The designer should look at the whole problem before starting to solve any of its parts. If the designer does not have a clear understanding of the whole problem, how can he come up with a comprehensive solution? (Pena, 1977, p. 29)

Pena's assumption of the whole problem is fundamental to understanding the complexity of the design task (Pena, 1977; Pena et al., 2001). Furthermore, problem solving presupposes a realistic and viable end product or environment arrived at through the designer intention alone. Further, there is the presumption that "problem solving" will define solutions to spaces in a close, controlled manner.

And yet, as we have already explored, objects and spaces are rarely in a static relationship with users. Situations of everyday complex problems become a sort of moving target. For example, while interior space might be conceived for a particular purpose with a specific intention of a designer, people will appropriate and find their own meanings, and ultimately may use space in ways that the designer may not anticipate (Rengel, 2003; Poldma, 2009). For spaces to fully represent what people need or desire, and also be the product of the designer intent, they must be conceived both with the understanding of what has gone before and with what might be possible but has not yet happened—perspectives the designer offers through the means of design thinking but that are framed broadly from a holistic perspective.

Critical Design as Informed by Research, Context, and Pragmatic Thinking

In real-life situations we experience space and places of the everyday (Rothschold, 1999; Steeves, 2006). To be able to change these everyday situations in spaces, we need to contextualize the meanings that are honest to those who experience them, no matter what the context. Design thinking can act as a place for developing new types of spaces, be these situational or physical, virtual or real, and also by engaging pragmatic ways of knowing within a collaborative and contemporary context that includes the meanings of those involved and their particular concerns.

Diverse perspectives from theory, academia, practice and end-user frame discussions in the following chapters. In Chapter 9 these critical design spaces are explored as the means of engaging design thinking from both research and practice contexts. First, Gavin Melles and Luke Feast investigate contemporary ways that design thinking and critical approaches inform contexts of spaces and their meanings. They examine the nature of design thinking, wicked problems and critical design, and how designing is informed by particular worldviews. They propose a philosophically pragmatist approach of critical design and critical ethnography, built on John Dewey's ideas about pragmatic experience and actualized in collaborative and co-design situations, and situated in contemporary thinking.

A Provocation by Michael Joannidis considers what we actually do as designers within the context of driving innovation forward through design thinking grounded in context and understanding the problem at hand. Joannidis suggests that from the perspective of the design practitioner, it is not enough to apply design as a method; rather, design thinking encompasses passion, dedication, and logical, systematic thinking processes applied with a view to what has come before. Joannidis argues that to be innovative and to provide the best possible concept, designers must use research to inform design thinking and that this is something students need to understand from the outset. He provokes us to consider why informed design thinking is critical in engaging curiosity to transform space when designing, and what constitutes research from a practical perspective.

Finally the Dialogues and Perspective presents a case study considering all of the contexts of a context-research situated project that involves both researchers and participants with stakeholders in collaborative research. Eva Kehayia, Bonnie Swaine, and Tiiu Poldma describe what happens when researchers get together with corporate business, and with users of all ages and stages in the public domain of the commercial shopping mall. In this case study context, several layers of design thinking and research approaches are used to move a community from one state to a new, transformed situation. The urban public space of a commercial mall becomes a "Living Lab" used to understand issues of access for people with disabilities. In this project, collaborative and individual research approaches come together to study the issues, establish a baseline evaluation of the issues/spaces, and create communities of practice (CoP) that evolve to explore people's experiences as disabled persons in the public environment of a mall. Research methods include exploratory work in quantitative, qualitative, and mixed methods research, while communities of practices are supported by action research and interpretive approaches. This is an example of what transpires when research-informed practice aligns with corporate needs, community needs, and lived experiences of the people who live in the environment every day.

REFERENCES

Buchanan, R. (2000). Wicked Problems in Design Thinking. In V. Margolin & R. Buchanan (Eds.), *The Idea of Design: A Design Issues Reader* (pp. 3–20). Cambridge, MA: MIT Press.

Dewey, J. (1994). Art as Experience. In S. D. Ross, *Art and Its Significance: An Anthology of Aesthetic Theory* (pp. 203–220). Albany, NY: SUNY.

Nelson, H., & Stolterman, E. (2003). *The Design Way: Intentional Change in an Unpredictable World.* Englewood Cliffs, NJ: Technology Publications.

Pallasmaa, J. (1990). *The Eyes of the Skin.* London: Academy Editions.

Pena, W. (1977). *Problem-Seeking: An Architectural Programming Planner.* Houston, TX: CBI Publishing.

Pena, W. M., S. A. Parshall, & HOK Group (2001). Problem-Seeking: An Architectural Programming Planner (4th ed.). New York: John Wiley & Sons.

Poldma, T. (2009). *Taking Up Space: Exploring the Design Process.* New York: Fairchild Publications.

Rothschild, J. (1999). *Design and Feminism: Re-Visioning Spaces, Places and Everyday Things.* Piscataway, NJ: Rutgers University Press.

Steeves, H. P. (2006). The Things Themselves: Phenomenology and the Return to the Everyday. Albany, NY: SUNY.

As the twenty-first century unfolds, we find ourselves in a world characterized by rapid innovations, expanding technologies, and an increasingly voracious consumer culture—all situated within unstable economic, political, social, and ecological conditions. In this changing world, design has expanded its agenda to engage with spaces far more diverse than those of its industrial origins. Design thinking has become one of the leading responses of design fields to the expanded agenda of design practice into areas of management, organizational systems, and other fields and territories. To date, such versions of design thinking have been remarkably good at pointing to the entrepreneurial advantage of such practices while only peripherally considering the social, ethical, and ideological dimensions of design practice. Two critical design strategies have developed that capture the need for attention to the ideological dimensions of designing—critical design and critical design ethnography. Neither conventional design thinking focus nor critical design seem fully adapted to addressing the Janus-face of most design solutions as potentially liberating or constraining. Combining critical design and the pragmatism underlying design thinking into a pragmatist-inspired critical pluralism, which architecture has already begun to

flag as the way forward, seems best adapted to acknowledging the material, experiential, ethical, and aesthetic of the design of spaces in the twenty-first century.

Introduction

This paper offers a personal perspective on the ways in which aspects of design thinking and critical design are found in the critical pragmatism or pluralism that is currently being promoted within material (and virtual) architecture as an answer to the third space discourse Grosz (2001) wants to see develop between architecture and philosophy. There are many ways in which philosophy and (interior) architecture might converse and sustain each other. What is offered here concerns what the authors see as a movement in architecture toward critical pragmatism and pluralism with potential, but as yet unexplored, consequences for interior design.

Design Thinking

The idea that design constitutes a different mode of thinking or logic to that of science and the humanities is not new (see Cross 2006). For engineering design, Dym et al. (2005) offers a recent definition: "Design thinking reflects the complex processes of inquiry and learning that designers perform in a systems context, making decisions as they proceed, often working collaboratively on teams in a social process, and 'speaking' several languages with each other (and to themselves)" (p. 104). This definition highlights the human and systemic complexities of developing solutions to design questions. In addition to the study of the practices of working designers, design thinking also refers to the *open* problem-solving process decision makers, including designers, use to solve real-world wicked problems (Rittel & Weber, 1973). Referring to the increasing variety of "places of invention" where design is applied within and beyond traditional design practices, Buchanan (1992) claims this expansion of design into other spaces is "possible is in part due to the fact the fields themselves lack a specific subject matter . . . Design problems are 'indeterminate' and 'wicked' because design has no special subject matter of its own apart from what a designer conceives it to be." In his account of design thinking, Owen (2007) suggests that the combined effect of design thinking and science thinking for problem solving with designerly aims is better than either alone, "Either is valuable, but together they bring the best of sceptical inquiry into balance with imaginative application. Both are well served by creative thinking. In preparation for a wider consideration of design thinking, therefore, it is time to look at the general characteristics of the creative thinker" (p. 22).

Buchanan (1992) notes similarities between John Dewey's pragmatism as described in *Art & Experience* in particular and design thinking. Dewey's focus on experience and his democratic aesthetic—that is, on the desirability of solutions to educational, social, and other problems—offer parallels to design work. Design thinking has a logic (*technologia*) with potential applications to different fields. This logic favors the use of visual and material thinking: "Argument in design thinking moves toward the concrete interplay and interconnection of signs, things, actions and thoughts" (p. 20). In his consideration of organizations as design, Romme (2003), for example, notes that design is concerned with systems that do not yet exist and the key question is "will it work" not "is it true"—in other words, it considers questions about fit for future purpose with potential for experimentation. This orientation to a future aesthetic is surely fundamental to much design thinking and practice, along with Dewey's focus on the significance of experience, itself a development of William James's (1907) pragmatist account.

One of the leading exponents of design thinking is Tim Brown at IDEO. Tim Brown (2008) suggests that a shift to designerly thinking in product innovation has come about through designers taking on innovation as upstream innovators with a focus on physical products and systems and services: "Rather than asking designers to make an already developed idea more attractive to consumers, companies are asking them to create ideas that better meet consumers' needs and desires" (p. 2). Citing a range of past and present examples, Brown illustrates design thinking as a three-stage process of inspiration, ideation, and implementation. Effectively, then, the shift to design thinking in other fields can be seen as a by-product of the expansion of the innovation process to include the ecology or system of the product(s) being imagined.

Claims have been made that design thinking in this pragmatic sense is radically changing or improving practices in other fields. Thus, the Mayo Clinic joins design thinking to improve health-care delivery by engaging with patients and other stakeholders (Duncan & Breslin, 2009). Elsewhere, applications of design thinking to strategy and management (Dunne & Martin, 2006), and operations and organizational studies (Romme, 2003) also show the potential of applying designerly tools and strategies to wicked design problems. These solutions and applications suggest that we have made some progress in defining what designerly ways of knowing are as the distinctive disciplinary logic of design fields (Cross 2001).

One could be forgiven for thinking that design thinking has little to do with the resolution of social and community questions, as it has predominantly surfaced in management and business settings as a new enterprise solution. However, nothing in the nature of design thinking as practice and model excludes its application to such issues. Indeed, Brown, in one of his more recent publications (Brown & Wyatt 2010), notes that although there has been an emphasis to date on design thinking in entrepreneurial profit contexts, the same practices can deliver for not-for-profits addressing social and community issues in under-resourced and developing world contexts. Such a move is not synonymous with critical design but does suggest that design thinking may not be trapped exclusively in an entrepreneurial web. In addition, that, as Buchanan (1992) has signaled, design thinking has pragmatic Deweyan roots suggests that the bridge or the path to a compromise with critical design is not impossible.

Critical Design

In design teaching and learning, including interior design, the use of critical thinking in terms of using good analytic skills has precedents apparent in teaching of critical thinking in the latter sense (Eidson 1986; Sanchez, Height, & Gainen 1995). This same sense connects critical thinking in design to the ideology critique of critical theory—specifically, the Frankfurt School and beyond (e.g., Held 1980), technology design (Coyne 1995), and other disciplinary designed spaces. The kinds of spaces that critical design inquiry can inform include much more than the traditional spaces of architecture.

A specific focus in this essay is critical design (e.g., Dunne 2006) as an approach demanding that the social, ideological, and other considerations also inform design. These ideological accounts originally emerged with the rise to prominence of postmodern thought and writing in architecture and design, and are resurfacing as significant at the outset of a new century characterized by pressing social, environmental, and other concerns. This is not the place to rehearse the rise of critical theory in pre- and post-war Germany and its migration to other continents and fields of application. Its Marxist origins and the history of its chief protagonists—Adorno, Horkheimer, Marcuse, etc.—have been reviewed elsewhere (Held, 1980; Antonio, 1983). Suffice it here to say that broadly speaking critical theory approaches society and its practices as characterized by injustice and ideological forces. The term **critical design** has been popularized by Dunne and Raby, and Dunne employed the term in his book *Hertzian Tales* (Dunne & Raby, 1999) to name an approach to design that created products that helped question current social assumptions.

The critical design approach is underpinned by the belief that design is not neutral but informed by particular worldviews; the focus is particularly on the effects of the introduction of new technologies in our lives (Dunne & Raby, 1999). A design is not just a tool but also form of communication that embodies particular political and moral meanings. For example, the idea of product design as merely developing efficiently functioning tools is misleading because mass production and distribution is dependent upon the large, dominant systems of finance and power needed to support industrial capitalism. This dependence on existing power structures means, "at its worst, product design simply reinforces global capitalist values. It helps to create and maintain desire for new products, ensures obsolescence,

encourages dissatisfaction with what we have and merely translates brand value into objects" (Dunne & Raby, 2001, p. 59). Dunne and Raby argue that design should be more socially responsible and become more independent. Design must develop an intellectual stance of its own otherwise the design profession is destined to lose all intellectual credibility and be viewed simply as an agent of capitalism. A parallel design activity is needed that questions and challenges current expectations, and explores a subversive role for design as a form of social critique.

Such an approach to design that seeks to criticize global capitalist values, Dunne and Raby (2001, p. 60) argue, must also shift from an aesthetic of production to an aesthetic of experience. Rather than seeking to extend the technical medium of design, critical design aims to create a dialogue between users and objects that pushes the limits of the cultural values that underpin lived experience. Critical design presents alternatives to how things are now and critiques the prevailing situation. Through mixing fiction and reality, critical design aims to create proposals that challenge dominant cultural values and industry's technological agenda. As Dunne and Raby (Dunne & Raby, 2001, p. 58) state,

> Critical design is related to haute couture, concept cars, design propaganda, and visions of the future, but its purpose is not to present the dreams of industry, attract new business, anticipate new trends or test the market. Its purpose is to stimulate discussion and

debate amongst designers, industry and the public about the aesthetic quality of our electronically mediated existence.

It is this opposition between design that merely reflects the current situation and design that seeks to change the situation, which makes critical design critical. Truly critical design is a praxis that combines reflection and action on the world in order to transform it. It is not merely cerebral, nor action for action's sake. It invites participants to open themselves to new ways of understanding and take effective action for change. This concern with combining social critique and practical action closely associates critical design with approaches to social change situated within the broad philosophical tradition of critical theory and the Frankfurt School.

Critical Design Ethnography

Less speculative and more empirical in its engagement with communities is critical design ethnography, an approach that combines participatory action research, critical ethnography, and design practice. The goal of critical design ethnography is to empower communities and facilitate social change. This change agenda distinguishes critical design ethnography from traditional ethnographic research methods that primarily seek to understand the conditions of a community. Critical design ethnography intends to support the transformation of a community through collaboratively developing a designed intervention with the community members (Barab et al., 2004, p. 255). The

critical aspect of critical design ethnography aims to empower community participants to become activists through critically reflecting on their social positions.

The Value of Codesign and Context

As a codesigner, the researcher is in the complicated position of being located both outside the context as a participant observer and inside the context as a change agent. Critical design ethnography carries with it the double danger that the researcher both imposes outsider values and assumptions through taking a critical stance and also reifies this critique into a designed artefact. When researchers explicitly advocate a changes agenda, they are not simply writing about the culture of a community, and ongoing participation and collaboration raises issues of voice, ownership, and intentionality (Barab et al., 2004, p. 256). The researcher's social position, history, and political stance influences the conduct and communication of the research as well as what resultant actions are taken. The researcher may become confronted with situations where there are multiple competing perspectives or where participants' and the researcher's views are at odds. To avoid imposing a hegemonic influence, the researcher must tailor his or her design work to local contexts through aiming to structure users' participation through offering opportunities through which users can come together, interact, and come to understand their world (Barab et al., 2004, p. 258).

Building trust and shared commitment with community participants is essential to critical design ethnography. This requires that the participants are open to collaborating with the researcher, and the researcher being honest about his or her intentions as well as being open to changing those goals while remaining committed to the project (Barab et al., 2004, p. 261). Developing and maintaining a collaborative dialogue is supported through continually presenting interpretations of field data to the community to test how the researcher's interpretations resonate with the participants' perspectives. Allowing all participants a legitimate voice is essential so that the researcher does not undermine local knowledge, people, and power that could potentially contribute to producing mistrust and undesirable outcomes. Developing such a rapport with a community takes time, commitment, and trust.

Thus, both critical design and critical design ethnography encourage social and individual critique of design while differing in the participatory content of the method. Both practices offer potential to interior design to provoke critique of technology and other market and commercial forces dictating design solutions. However, neither practice comes close to exploring the aesthetics and experience of meaning making in spaces the way critical pragmatism does. Here, the lessons for the discipline of interior design come principally but not exclusively from architecture.

Why Critical Pragmatism for Design, Architecture, and Interiors?

It is certainly not only architecture and design that have noticed pragmatism's appeal and legacy. One undisputed terrain for critical pragmatism is interaction design and human computer interaction (HCI; see especially Coyne 1995), where experience, and knowledge making and finding through this process bring designer and user and society together in a common interface. For example, in HCI disciplines, and as Ghaoui (2006) points out, this type of pragmatism is in fact a combination of critical design and pragmatism in that there is an eye for the ideological dimensions of technology and experience (see especially Feenberg 1990). But HCI is not the only designed space where new or critical pragmatism can offer a perspective that combines critical reflection with the need to also come up with practical aesthetically and socially desirable futures. Thus, Wicks and Freeman (1998) see the reinvigoration of organization studies through engagement with the new pragmatism (see Melles 2008) that highlights ethical and moral dimensions of decision and sidelines unnecessary epistemological debates.

However, closer to our concerns in this text is the meaning of (critical) pragmatism for the design of architectural space. The connection has been explored in terms of the contribution of buildings to their social and physical environment, and their material incorporation of history (e.g., Betsky 1994). Spector (2004) points to the significance in Dewey of embodied (aesthetic) experience, an element central to architecture's work with space. The author suggests that a real engagement with pragmatism offers architecture an intellectually satisfying approach to both aesthetics and social engagement.

Ramroth (2006) adds that the contribution of the building to its environment—social, material, and otherwise—is a measure of its aesthetic truth or value.

The idea that the building is interpreted and reinterpreted over time and therefore does not have a fixed meaning defined by its style is part of what Guy and Moore (2007) signal as an essential feature of critical pragmatism for architecture. Drawing particularly on Richard Rorty's call for a productive pragmatism to eschew theoretical debates and unity, Guy and Moore (2007) suggest pragmatism offers the glue for pluralism and critical theory to inform sustainable architecture and "to design and develop environmental futures that are not only technologically possible but also socially desirable" (p. 18). Some of these suggestions about the cycle of experiencing and interpretation of architecture suggest that the building is itself a social actor. For example, most recently Yaaneva (2009) has claimed that architectural projects mobilize heterogenous actors, convincing, persuading, or deterring them, with building here viewed "as becoming social (instead of hiding behind or serving the social), as active participants in society, design—as a process of recollecting, reinterpreting, and reassembling the social" (p. 18).

Historic Contexts of Material Embeddedness of Spatial Design

History certainly teaches us how the material outcome of architectural work on exteriors and interiors became part of the discourses that configured social thought. Edginton (1997) describes the sustaining and oppositional effects of particular architectural exteriors and interiors on the discourse of the asylum; this discourse most obviously addressed by Foucault (1993). Such an account of the discursive and material embeddedness of spatial design in the society and history of its setting moves us beyond an ideologically neutral philosophy of design concerned with aesthetics and space in account (see, for example, Abercrombie 1990). Interior design in general is still in need of accounts of meaning making that can raise the status and legitimacy of the field in relation to its more established architectural peer (Dickson & White, 1997; Poldma, 2008).

That meaning and meaning construction are materially mediated and sustained is evident not only in socially and ethically significant places like prisons but also in domestic spaces. So Cieerad (2006) notes how meaningful domestic interiors are in relation to the lived experiences of childhood, parenthood, and so on. More contemporary spaces of commodification, such as shopping malls, also offer environments where clear accounts of meaning making and critical analysis are valuable to reducing the danger of architecture's complicitness; while architecture and interior design hesitate, other fields will take over this task (see Goss 1993).

Interior Spaces and Critical Pragmatism/Pluralism: The Way Forward

Interior design is about taking up space and doing so to offer through design different human experiences (Poldma 2009). The intellectual space for critical interior design is being occupied by other fields, including anthropology, cultural studies, and geography, which are developing sensitive critiques of the social meaning making of interior spaces. Nor has interior architecture/design learned much, it seems, from the growing recognition of the power of critical pragmatism to inform current architectural practice and thinking. Two decades after Abercrombie (1990) one may ask if interior design has begun to realize the potential for the design of domestic and residential spaces to exploit the changing experience of embodied meaning making in the architecture of the interior and to examine the kinds of desirable (aesthetic) futures it may create. Desirable futures—interior or otherwise—can arise through the use of good design thinking practices as described above, and even more so, in some cases where critical design ethnography and other participatory practices are employed.

Discussion Questions

1. Melles and Feast suggest that design thinking is a different form of logic from science or humanities. Discuss in light of what it means to design from an aesthetic perspective.

2. Melles and Feast suggest that Buchanan explores the nature of design experience as a parallel to Dewey's ideas about art as experience.
   a. Explore Dewey's idea of experience—how is this pragmatic?
   b. What is it to be pragmatic as a design way of thinking?
   c. Why is a pragmatic experience aesthetic?

3. What is critical design?
   a. Describe critical design ethnography.
   b. How do we use critical design ethnography to empower communities through design?

4. What is the designer's role in this type of design work?

5. How are design meanings uncovered?

References

Abercrombie, S. (1990). *A Philosophy of Interior Design*. New York: Harper & Row.

Antonio, R. J. (1983, Summer). The Origin, Development, and Contemporary Status of Critical Theory. *The Sociological Quarterly, 24*, 325–351.

Barab, S., Thomas, M., Dodge, T., Squire, K., & Newell, M. (2004). Critical design ethnography: Designing for change. *Anthropology & Education Quarterly, 35*(2), 254–268.

Betsky, A. (1994). *James Gamble Rogers and the Architecture of Pragmatism*. MIT Press.

Brown, B. T., & Wyatt, J. (2010). Design Thinking for Social Innovation. *Stanford Social Innovation Review*, Winter, 30–35.

Buchanan, R. (1992). Wicked Problems in Design Thinking. *Design Issues, 8*(2), 5–21.

Cieraad, I. (2006). Introduction: Anthropology at Home. In *At Home: An Anthropology of Domestic Space* (pp. 1–12). Syracuse: Syracuse University Press.

Coyne, R. (1995). *Designing Information Technology in the Postmodern Age: From Method to Metaphor*. Boston, MA: MIT Press.

Cross, N. (2001). Designerly Ways of Knowing: Design Discipline Versus Design Science. *Design Issues, 17*(3), 49–55.

Dewey, J. (1934). *Art as Experience*. New York: Minton, Balch & Company.

Dickson, A. W., & White, A. C. (1997). Interior Design Criticism: Developing a Culture of Reverence for the Interior Environment. *Journal of Interior Design, 23*(1), 4–10.

Duncan, A. K., & Breslin, M. A. (2009). Innovating health care delivery: the design of health services. *Journal of Business Strategy, 30*(2/3), 13–20.

Dunne, A., & Raby, F. (2001). *Design noir: The secret life of electronic objects*. Basel: Birkhauser.

Dunne, A. (2006). *Hertzian Tales: Electronic Products, Aesthetic Experience, and Critical Design*. Boston, Mass; MIT Press.

Dunne, D., & Martin, R. (2006). Design Thinking and How It Will Change Management Education: An Interview and Discussion. *Management Learning, 5*(4), 512-523.

Dym, C., Agogino, A., Eris, O., Frey, D., & Leifer, L. (2006). Engineering design thinking, teaching, and learning. *IEEE Engineering Management Review, 34*(1), 65–92.

Edginton, B. (1997). Moral Architecture: The Influence of the York Retreat on Asylum Design. *Health & Place, 3*(2), 91–99.

Eidson, P. L. (1986). Critical Thinking: Elements of Interior Design Theory. *Journal of Interior Design, 12*(2), 19–24.

Feenberg, A. (1990). The critical theory of technology. *Capitalism Nature Socialism, 1*(5), 17-45.

Foucault, M. 1993. *Surveiller et Punir.* Paris: Gallimard Editions.

Ghaoui, C. (2006). *Encyclopedia of human computer interaction.* Hershey, PA: Idea Group Reference.

Goss, J. (1993). The "Magic of the Mall": An Analysis of Form, Function, and Meaning in the Contemporary Retail Built Environment. *Annals of the Association of American Geographers, 83*(1), 18–47.

Grosz, E. A. (2001). *Architecture from the outside: essays on virtual and real space.* Boston, MA: MIT Press.

Guy, S., & Moore, S. A. (2007). Sustainable Architecture and the Pluralist Imagination. *Journal of Architectural Education,* 60, 15–23.

Held, D. (1980). *Introduction to critical theory: Horkheimer to Habermas.* Berkeley, CA: University of California Press.

James, W. (1907). *Pragmatism.* Cambridge MA: Harvard University Press.

Last, N. (2008). *Wittgenstein's house: language, space, & architecture.* New York: Fordham University Press.

Melles, G. (2008). New Pragmatism and the Vocabulary and Metaphors of Scholarly Design Research. *Design Issues, 24*(4), 88–101.

Poldma, T. (2008). Interior Design at a Crossroads: Embracing Specificity through Process, Research, and Knowledge. *Journal of Interior Design, 33*(3), vi–xvi.

Poldma, T. (2009). *Taking Up Space: Exploring the Design Process.* New York: Fairchild Books.

Ramroth, William G. 2006. *Pragmatism & Modern Architecture.* New York: McFarland & Company.

Romme, A. G. L. (2003). Making a Difference: Organization as Design. *Organization Science, 14*(5), 558–573.

Sanchez, L. A., Hight, T. K., & Gainen, J. (1995). Critical thinking and design: Evolution of a freshman engineering graphics course. *New Directions for Teaching and Learning, 1995*(61), 67–76.

Spector, T. (2004). Pragmatism for Architects. *Contemporary Pragmatism, 1*(1), 133–149.

Wicks, A. C., & Freeman, R. E. (1998). Organization Studies and the New Pragmatism: Positivism, Anti-positivism, and the Search for Ethics. *Organization Science, 9*(2), 123–140.

Yaneva, A. (2009). *The Making of a Building: A Pragmatist Approach.* Bern: Peter Lang.

Note: Gavin Melles thanks Prof. Simon Guy and Albena Yaaneva at Manchester University for an invitation to discuss these issues at a public lecture in 2011, at the Manchester Architecture Research Centre, entitled "Pragmatism in Design and Architecture: Zeitgest Not Method."

It is a simple matter to see the obvious & to do the expected.

the tendency of the individual life is to be static rather than dynamic

and this tendency is made into a propulsion by civilization . . .

where the obvious is only seen and the unexpected rarely happens.

when the unexpected however does happen, and when it is of sufficiently

grave import, the unfit perish. They do not see what is not obvious, are unable to do the unexpected, are incapable of adjusting their well-grooved & defined lives to other and strange grooves.

—Jack London, *The Unexpected*

- Do you know what your daily intake of design food is? Are you getting enough nutrition-based information?
- Do you know how much real design is in all those sugarcoated, unsubstantiated blogs, or oversaturated up-to-minute trends? Do you even have or follow a proper and balanced design regime?
- If you're sluggish and just plain uninspired, don't be too hard on yourself, or even wonder too much! Chances are, you're resource-starved and substance-deprived. Stop the madness! Stop living on zero calories fluff and start getting your duly needed daily design intake.
- There are no miracle solutions, no creative-promising diets or instant-designer pills out there!
- Just like a car with no fuel or the wrong fuel, an empty mind or one without the right type of information will not get you or your ideas anywhere in a hurry.

What goes into a mind comes out in the form of ideas. Think of it like a sponge—whatever information (or disinformation) you absorb is exactly what will come out in your project, once wrung. Consume the right balance/blend of fact and inspiration, and this will hone your every thought/idea, giving you that much needed boost, and arming you with the necessary optics to see far beyond the competition and the plain obvious.

Like spinach to Popeye or sunshine to a flower, your mind needs the right kind of nutrients in order to explode into creativity and flourish. Think of research as a tool to encourage and awaken your spirit of enquiry . . . a tonic of sorts, to rejuvenate curiosity.

Instead of shying away or even avoiding, try instead going at full throttle toward the unknown. Use research and new critical information to veer your mind away from the path of least resistance: mediocrity and complacency. The thing about proper and effective research is that you're continuously absorbing and feeding your critical creative juices, retaining only the useful nutrients, resulting in a very natural and almost automatic creative-solution-design-process. The trick (if there was ever such a thing) is to try and let go of your fears and find the fight in you, to harness any fears or anxieties that you might have about not knowing something and, instead, binge on knowledge.

Curiosity inspires creativity. Creativity generates monsters, and curious, creative monsters are catapulted into absolute brilliance.

How to Research and Boost Your Creative Thinking: 10 Essential Steps

1. **Before that very first click of your mouse, focus, gather all your thoughts, and structure a definitive plan of action/attack.** Establish a target or goal. Figure out what it is that you are trying to find, before you embark on any search. Even if you don't have a final destination, try to at least figure out a close vicinity or "search neighborhood." Your time is valuable, but your peace of mind and not getting frustrated or discouraged is priceless.

2. **Do not suspend your everyday logic, common sense, or rationale.** Just be-

cause you're now delving into something completely new or foreign, it doesn't mean that you should start panicking, close your eyes, and take both hands off the steering wheel. Design logic is not that much different than the logic/reasoning that you would use to figure out, for instance, what you will wear in morning, what you will eat in the afternoon, or even where you will go on vacation next month.

3. **Language is everything.** Be very careful of the choice of words that you use in your searches. Change/replace a word, use a synonym, try another modifier, and you'll immediately notice how it'll affect your results. Quite simply, ask a specific question and you'll get a specific answer. Always be in control. And never surrender a search to an algorithm.

4. **Confirm what you (think you) know.** Go back to the basics, dictionary definitions, universal principles, and so on. Never take anything for granted. Look up even the simplest of words/terms, just to make sure of your own understanding and maintain absolute objectivity.

5. **Eliminate all preconceived notions, ignorance, and prejudices.** Gather evidence from more than one source to ensure that what you base your opinion/conclusions on is reliable, applicable, and valid. Do not go by what you know/don't know, have heard, or have not experienced. This is not about you,

singular exceptions, or even subjectivity, but rather about fact and universal understandings.

6. **Use both *quantitative* and *qualitative* evidence/findings.** Find that perfect balance of combining facts, figures, and measures with observations, quotations, and substantiated/expert opinions. Seek appropriate sources that will inform your preliminary conclusions. Confirm credentials and seek out provenance.

7. **Use the information you find as sources of inspiration.** This is one surefire way of ensuring that your ideas are'"original" and the direction that you assume will be completely your own. Since searches are like fingerprints, each search is entirely personal and reflective of the individual "researcher." That is, of course, unless you decide to cut corners and either simply "copy-paste" or go to the same obvious (first two to three Google hits on the very first page) sources that everyone else is sure to click on. After all, clients will be hiring you for your vision and how you are able to interpret a mandate.

8. **Use different types of searches including the overview search, the historical search, and the current search.** The overview search is to establish a bulletproof understanding of any multidisciplinary design project, brief, or mandate. This phase has two basic functions: (1) to educate/inform yourself about the particular/specific area in which you will be designing and (2) to keep an eye out for anything inspirational—any piece of information, detail, or even a keyword/phrase that might open up your creativity and send you toward a particular concept that will set you apart from everyone else. And, finally, this search is predominantly international and not merely restricted to any specific area, regardless of your project's geographical location.

In a historical search, you're investigating the history of your project type or proposal. You are researching the historical (and chronological) evolution, attempting to identify the very first example—the first time it appears/is documented in history—followed by all the other times throughout history. In essence, what is or has been historically the most important examples of your particular project, including when, where, and by whom.

In a current search, quite simply, you're showing the best examples, the best-of-the-best from around the world of similar concurrent project types. This will give you the proper perspective and a brief overview/appetizer of what your competition might look like, for example, where the bar might be situated in a competitor's restaurant.

Always remember you have to know the rules before you can ever expect/hope to break them. But before any of that, you need to know the following:

a. What has been done—or not done?

b. How was it treated and or made? Aesthetically, fabrication-process, etc.

c. How are you going to be different? What is specific/unique?

d. Revise accordingly. Do you still find your proposal interesting?

e. Modify accordingly.

f. Don't lose sight of how much time you have. Limit your search and ideas accordingly.

g. Narrow down/focus your intention—realistically and within context.

9. **Use other types of searches.** These include scientific, cultural, sociological, psychological, and so on. Next, establish a hierarchy regarding materials, fabrication processes, finishes, furniture, and lighting. Figure out what is the most important right down to the least, within the context of your particular project/mandate. Know what's available on the market, what could be done, and what you could possibly innovate or change to reinforce your own ideas to make your concept/presentation unique and stronger. Your search is only limited by your resilience and creative problem solving. Don't limit yourself by what you don't know or are afraid to ask.

10. **Don't be lazy! Have perseverance and do a thorough search.** It is not about one click or scroll of the mouse or trackball, but rather, about many unrelenting clicks, scrolls, and searches. It is about taking seemingly unrelated information or dots and connecting them together, creating your own picture of your own interpretation and of all the information you've gathered. That is your vision.

Design is a direct product of how you think and see the world around you. Ignore that and your ideas will basically have no substance, effect or distinction from anyone or anything else in the industry.

Insist on yourself! Engage your critical thought and refuse to be spoon-fed. Just because everything you need is a mouse-click away, it shouldn't make you an easy target. Try ducking sometimes; it just might save your brain. Always question the source. Never become desensitized. There's nothing augmented about reality—nor about life itself.

Collaborative Research

Usually research happens when researchers frame research questions, develop methodologies to support that research, and prepare and implement tools to collect data, analyze data, and produce results. These approaches are usually understood to be forms of clinical, basic, or applied research (Friedman, 2003). But what happens when the context within which the research is done begins with the consideration of multiple voices, considering the experiences of the people who are being studied within a framework of personal, social, and physical issues? How does the research and its findings account for the people involved, their multiple perspectives, and a multitude of meanings that they attribute to the issues at hand?

We will examine the context of a project created by researchers from an interdisciplinary research center known as CRIR—Centre for Interdisciplinary Research in Rehabilitation of Greater Montreal—who got together to create a Rehabilitation Living Lab within a real-life setting of an urban public space. This Living Lab allows researchers to experiment together and collaborate with other researchers, users, communities, and various stakeholders within an ecologically valid environment.

This multi-sectorial research project grew out of researcher interest in the issues of people's rehabilitation and their return to participating in society and accomplishing their daily goals, and a desire to collaborate together to solve problems of access for people with disabilities in society. Specifically, researchers partnered with industry, with public agencies and with commercial mall developers to examine the issues of social inclusion and social participation using the real-life setting of the public shopping mall, from the perspectives of both users and stakeholders, in the creation of an innovative Rehabilitation Living Lab.

First, we will present what happens when many people with different aims and goals get together to do research in this real-life setting. Ten principal researchers bring their expertise and generate research, from diverse backgrounds such as interior design, architecture, occupational and physical therapy, optometry and vision, speech and language therapy, audiology, psychology, sociology, and anthropology, among others. Parallel to this core group, periphery projects are explored by allied partners from local, national, and international universities and collaborators, including those from CRIR and from industry. In this context, exploratory, clinical, applied, and basic research is conducted, depending on the project and the situation being studied.

The Rehabilitation Living Lab as an Inquiry Space

The Rehabilitation Living Lab is created to generate research with a cloudlike infrastructure that supports both individual and collective research projects currently being pursued. The Rehabilitation Living Lab is both the physical space of the mall as well as an inquiry space, much like a cloud that is formed "out there" that groups intellectual and cultural capital together with different forms of research essentially project-driven. Within this context, researchers in a broader context include the people who use the spaces daily, people with disabilities, academic researchers experimenting and studying different types of situations, design researchers, and undergraduate, graduate, and postgraduate students.

In particular, the design researchers' roles are to (a) explore the existing conditions of the spaces being used for the Living Lab; (b) understand what exists, the salient issues in the public space that may either be hampering or facilitating access, and the user needs and experiences; (c) analyze these issues; and (d) propose new possibilities for the spaces, informed by the research and the design elements identified as problematic, by the mall owners and the users themselves. This inquiry is considered essential to the vision of the project and serves as the cornerstone for stakeholders.

Furthermore, design students and design researchers also investigate the existing conditions from these three perspectives to understand that *which is* and, in a parallel design project situation, bring the theory into practice by using the preliminary data collection findings to envision that *which does not yet exist* (Nelson & Stolterman, 2003). This offers some practical contexts to ground the baseline work and also help the developer envision potential ideas that align with the research project goals and help bring the research ideas to the corporate stakeholders such as the developer and design team.

Within this framework, dialogue occurs between all participants in a collaborative manner and the different perspectives form the grounding of the research methods. In this essential critical and constructivist approach, sequential, concurrent, and transformative strategies of inquiry (Creswell, 2003, p. 19) are pursued to (a) develop a portrait of the existing issues and conditions of the issues being studied and (b) develop strategies and tools for innovative possibilities for changing the existing conditions. Qualitative, quantitative, and mixed methods in multiple forms draw on all possibilities (Creswell, 2003, p. 17).

We will describe the nature of this project, how the Rehabilitation Living Lab is structured, the research activities pursued, and the salient findings to date. We will also present examples of preliminary findings, what the design inquiry envisions in terms of the visual space, and how working groups such as Communities of Practice (CoP) have emerged as a fundamental part of the project's structure.

The Rehabilitation Living Lab Project: Vision, Aims, and Objectives

The Mall is a Rehabilitation Living Lab, a strategic development project that has been created by the research members of CRIR in collaboration with a real estate developer and owner of the Montreal downtown shopping mall, local community groups, as well as local, national, and international research and industry partners. With the financial support granted in 2011 for four years (2011–2015), the project provides an infrastructure to build a rehabilitation lab that the researchers named "Mall as Living Lab" to promote and develop both the Lab and more developed research grants.

The Concept of a Living Lab

The urban shopping mall emerged as a strategic real-life setting with the concept of the Living Lab, rising out of the researchers' needs to bring together rehabilitation services and the real-time lived experience of the people and how they engage in the daily activities they want to pursue in an urban public place such as the mall. We have used the concept of a Living Lab as a "user-centred, open-innovation ecosystem, often operating in a territorial context (e.g. city, agglomeration, region), integrating concurrent research and innovation processes within a public-private-people partnership" (Living Lab in Wikipedia.org, 2010).

The choice of location in a downtown urban setting as the real-life place is due to the dynamic space of the multilevel mall, with direct access to public transit, the downtown city, schools, hospitals, and local residential neighborhoods of various types. This place is a central hub of activity for social, community, and commercial needs. The combination of the mall, the research project, the location, and the people using the spaces provides "a microcosm of society where complex transactions and activities take place" (Kehayia & Swaine, 2010).

The Vision, Aims and Goals of the Lab

The **vision** of the project is stated in the recent report to the funding organization FRQS, and includes "generating ways to optimize social participation and inclusion for all individuals." The project aims include providing a research space where one can investigate issues relating to how people with disabilities receiving in- and out-patient rehabilitation services move forward into the community and integrate back into society.

With this in mind, the project consists of three streams with the following objectives:

Stream 1—Exploratory and aims at obtaining a comprehensive understanding of the participants and the interrelationships between them

Stream 2—Testing of and training of tools and kits in virtual environments and laboratories

Stream 3—Implementation of the different tools and changes in the actual environment of the mall with assessments of their impact on participation and social inclusion in the transformed environment (Kehayia & Swaine, 2010).

These streams are iterative, as the different research projects allow for observation, creation, and actions that will be implemented, revised, and revisited from multiple perspectives and in multiple iterations. This overarching philosophical approach is an essentially hermeneutic approach (Gadamer, 1976) that allows understanding the different aspects of the situation, and then allows for analysis and a revisiting of issues and fine-tuning of the data analysis and implementation. Each iteration allows time for reflection about the social participation and inclusion issues that arise when people navigate a public environment that is a busy, noisy, dynamic meeting place for various activities such as shopping or meeting people, or as a place of destination for specific activities.

The Context for the Theoretical Framework: Disability, Rehabilitation and the Environment

In Canada, and specifically the province of Quebec, about 12 percent of the population over 15 years of age has a physical disability, and this increases to 32 percent for persons over 65 years and 46 percent for persons over 75 years. Physical disability can result from multiple factors and prevalent conditions such as arthritis, stroke, respiratory problems, and sensory issues, not to mention the effects of deterioration of the senses and capacities due to age-related diseases. Daily challenges include the fulfillment and accomplishment of everyday living, including basic activities such as feeding oneself, communicating, personal tasks we want to fulfill in a day, and/or fulfilling social roles we desire or need, such as running errands, working, or meeting friends for coffee.

While the rehabilitation process prepares people well for organizing their personal lived situation, quite often in rehabilitation, optimum levels of social inclusion are not met, due to factors such as the rehabilitation process not being able to extend beyond the walls of the clinical milieus, gaps in services within the community, or lack of knowledge in public places about the needs of people with disabilities. There are barriers to access and hinder activities, even though environments may be built within local or national accessibility codes and norms (Martel, 2011; Camirand, 2010).

In addition to these issues is the reality of the lived environment itself. Public places such as commercial malls tend to be designed for physical experiences such as walking and buying goods or services, and yet emerging uses of public malls are changing as people increasingly use malls as meeting places. These interior spaces are also places of social congregation, of personal destination, and various other personal and social activities and needs. The interior space thus becomes a place of commerce but also a place of arrival, identity, perception, and reaction (Bachelard, 2001). People experience spaces in the "moment of living, both consciously and unconsciously, in interaction within the space and others in the space" (Poldma, 2011, p. 12) and attribute meanings to both social contact and things they surround themselves with in everyday life (Csikszentmihalyi and Rochberg-Halton, 1981). These meanings and the capacity to comfortably navigate public spaces become compromised when added issues of access or environmental conditions of the space are not optimal. The continuum of rehabilitation practice that can take people with disabilities into such an environment and eventually see their integration into the community would serve to bridge this gap, when the rehabilitation of people with disabilities can be facilitated through an environment free of obstacles, technologies, and innovation that take into account issues within the social and physical environments.

The Research Space: Research Team Composition and Project Management Structure

Two major organizational components to this project include the research team and the project management structure. The research team is composed of the principal researchers and the participants, researchers, collaborators, and stakeholders. The researchers include the (1) Project Scientific Directors: Eva Kehayia (McGill University), Bonnie Swaine (University of Montreal); (2) Co-researchers, in alphabetical order: S. Ahmed (McGill), P. Archambault (McGill), J. Fung (McGill), A. Lamontagne (McGill),

G. Le Dorze (University of Montreal), H. Lefebvre (University of Montreal), O. Overbury (University of Montreal), and T. Poldma (University of Montreal).

A fundamental member of the research team is the shopping complex developer and general manager, Annie Daniel, alongside collaborators and partners such as professors from other universities, various technology industry specialists, clinicians from various rehabilitation clinics, and students allied with the researchers.

The second organization component is the way the project is structured with collaborative groups and working groups that both advise and assist in the project development and evolution. With such a wide range of diverse projects and perspectives, it is essential to structure and coordinate activities to achieve certain goals.

These include an executive committee (the ten principal researchers), an advisory board (external advisors), a biomedical statistical working group (methods analysis), and informal working groups including communities of practice CoP. These various groups are necessary to organize the different participants to get access to the setting, organize and get together to review the project development, launch interactive communication means, develop research projects within the Rehabilitation Lab in years 2 to 4, get perspectives and input from the various stakeholders, and understand and create appropriate mechanisms of evaluation, collaboration, and cooperation throughout project's duration.

The Research Methodology Framework

Due to the nature of the project being an infrastructure grant request at the outset, the research proceeds in two major parts within Stream 1: (a) initial pilot projects to test possible research tools and gather baseline observations about the environments in the mall; and (b) independent research projects developed to test possible situations in the Living Lab setting of the shopping complex.

At the outset, and to generate data for new and innovative tools to be developed, 26 pilot studies were reviewed and funded, and proceed with specific research methods that vary depending on the scope of the work. Most are essentially exploratory in nature, exploring issues of the occupants and users. In particular, focus groups and open-ended interviews are done to provide an overview of the facilitators and obstacles to social inclusion, social participation, and access. The project research methods and structure all frame the study from an essentially constructivist approach, aimed at constructing a holistic and transparent picture of the Rehabilitation Living Lab while supporting the virtual and site specific laboratory experiments that will develop new assistive tools.

Specific Data Collection Methods

Baseline data are collected during Stream 1 in the first year, to understand the various issues and for the development of the tools needed to do the work in the field for the development of Streams 2 and 3. During this initial phase of data collection, it was essential to create multiple baseline data to understand social and physical aspects of the environment, the social issues, and the different barriers and facilitators. Design researchers and students also conduct assessments of existing interior conditions and three researchers with students conducted a thorough assessment of the existing design issues and user needs by visiting and documenting the complex and meeting with various stakeholders. Design students propose possible visions and scenarios based on the evidence collected in the first year.

The research methods combine qualitative, quantitative, and mixed methods approaches. While Stream 1 and Year 1 methods are broad in scope, in Year 2 the focus turns toward researchers' specific development of research tools and strategies using participatory action research (PAR) to engage people within the various studies as active participants. PAR will be used as an overarching method to engage the users, owners, and stakeholders in the various testing and tools that will be used to see what works in the mall, be these technological aids, toolkits, transport aids, and environmental changes, all tested in research labs or in virtual situations first, and then tested in the Living Lab (real-life environment).

About Dialogue and Sharing to Innovate Practices

A final component of the research methods and approach is the underlying nature of the Lab itself as a place of dialogue and sharing of diverse perspectives. There is an ebb and flow between the individual researchers, research teams, the working groups, and the community at large where the users and stakeholders are in the community and within the mall itself. Various committees, working groups, and CoP are formed in the first year with goals that include structuring the projects and researchers, providing data for all to use for their individual or collective purposes, and to capitalize on the rich variety of participants in the project.

The Communities of Practice: Building Knowledge through the Space of Communities of Practice

Finally, various structures are put into place for communication, dialogue, and engagement between the various stakeholders. One example of these structures is the Communities of Practice (CoP). The way to ensure that the project continuing goals and objectives can be transparent, and that voice is given to the issues that emerge, is through the establishment of the CoP. At this stage, these communities of practice are being created to ensure the active participation of all stakeholders in the research process and as projects evolve in the four years of the research project. Let's look at this concept next.

The Concept of Communities of Practice

The communities within which research projects happen are active and engaged places, transmitting knowledge, informing participants, and supporting activities for the benefit of the common good. The concept of CoP is a term attributed to Etienne Wenger, who refers to *communities of practice* as loose organizations of " people who come together to share their experiences and knowledge in free-flowing, creative ways that foster new approaches to problems" (Wenger & Snyder, 2000, p. 139). Notably discussed in business and in health, Wenger's concept proposes a framing of community organization of knowledge that, while tacit and intangible, nevertheless moves decision-making from fuzzy, uncertain ideas and individual concerns toward collaboration, consensus, and solution spaces of benefit to all concerned. As Ash Amin and Patrick Cohendet (2004) also suggest, it is this co-production that adds value and fosters innovation:

> [I]t is the organization's communities, at all levels, who are in contact with the environment and involved in interpretative sense making, congruence finding and adapting. It is from any site of such interactions that new insights can be co-produced . . . the process of generating, accumulating and distributing knowledge—both in sites of informal interaction and informally constituted units such as R & D labs—is achieved through the functioning of informal groups of people . . . or "communities" . . . Communities can be considered as key building blocks of the organization and management of corporate innovation and creativity. (p. 9)

Within this project, CoP will guide the integration of the users and local stakeholders. The CoP will have the purpose of integrating the concerns of local groups, economic needs, political issues, clinical milieus, and social issues and providing a forum for flushing out how these work with the researchers' projects and goals to form cohesive project development for both the objectives and goals of the project.

Preliminary Findings

While this project is still in its development stages, preliminary findings from some of the 26 pilot projects are extensive. Examples of projects results and analysis have revealed challenges faced by various people with disabilities (acoustic assessment, visual impairments, crowd dynamics), issues of navigation, and specific design issues including light, contrast, and material effects. For example, projects focused on the social facilitators and obstacles have revealed issues of entering a mall and of access to services.

In terms of specific findings, an acoustic assessment has revealed challenges faced by individuals with hearing impairments, while for people with low vision, sound becomes a vital identification tool. In a second series of studies on experiences of people with vision impairments, assessments of the environment reveals contrast problems for those with low vision and barriers for others when contrasts are too high. In fact, the lack of certain materials altogether hampers people with vision issues to navigate independently. Finally, in another example, projects focusing on social obstacles and

facilitators have revealed issues of arriving at the mall and using services such as eating counters or elevators.

These are but a few of the findings emerging as the study progresses. These preliminary results from Stream 1 create the framework for further development of the tools and projects that will guide the future research activities.

Design Inquiry and the Potential of the Mall Environment

In a parallel exercise in an interior design academic studio, design students examined the existing spatial features, including understanding the various perspectives of developers, researchers and users from both design and disability perspectives. These analyses revealed new ideas about access, what people actually want, and what design concept for a future mall might look like. Students then created concepts as part of their studio work.

In Figures 9.1 and 9.2, we see the existing mall interior and an example of student visions for the mall, from a design perspective. These examples were presented alongside the first findings from other projects to stakeholders to close off the first year of the study and to provide a vision of the possibilities of what this research could accomplish. Using the findings and understanding the perspectives allowed the students to envision possible ideas already, to inspire the mall developers, and to support the need for the research in Streams 2 and 3. In this way, design inquiry and research work together in the inquiry space of the Rehabilitation Living Lab.

Figures 9.1 Existing mall interior
Photo credit: Courtesy of Tiiu Poldma

Conclusion

Creating accessible spaces for people with disabilities requires understanding the complex situations and issues of access, of social inclusion, and of how communities consider these issues. Through the real-life setting of the Rehabilitation Living Lab, researchers can test and put into practice research ideas, develop creative solutions within communities of practice, and structure activities through working groups that help move ideas forward through research engaged with the realities of the lived environment. This research engages communities, creates collaborative contexts, and promotes experimentation *in vivo* for testing technologies at the forefront of providing autonomy and mobility for those who wish to integrate into the social

Figures 9.2 Concept proposed for the mall. Courtesy students in third year design studio, Université de Montréal, Canada (Julien Caronneau-Gravel, Johathan Conrath, Stefano Giacomello, Nohemie Pont)

environment of public spaces providing social inclusion. This type of inquiry space also brings together design thinking with specific issues in medicine and other fields who participate together to effect change. Dialogues and perspectives come together in a collaborative yet structured research environment that engages theory with practice, helps to make salient people's issues, and promotes social inclusion and social participation to effect transformational change.

References

Amin, A., & Cohendet, P. (2004). Architectures of Knowledge: Firms, Capabilities, and Communities. Oxford, UK: Oxford University Press.

Bachelard, G. (2001). The Poetics of Space. Boston: Beacon Press.

Camirand, J. et al. (2010). Vivre avec une incapacite au Quebec. Un portrait statistique a partir l'Enquete sur la participation et les limitations d'activites 2001 et 2006, Qc, ISQ, 351 p.

Csikszentmihalyi, M., & Rochberg-Halton, E. (1981). *The Meaning of Things: Domestic Symbols and the Self.* Cambridge, UK: Cambridge University Press.

Gadamer, H-G. (1976). In David E. Linge (Trans./Ed.), *Philosophical Hermeneutics.* Berkeley, CA: University of California Press.

Guba, E., & Lincoln, Y. S. (1994). *The Handbook of Qualitative Research.* Thousand Oaks, CA: Sage.

Kehayia, E., & Swaine, B. (2010). A Rehabilitation Living Lab: Creating Enabling Physical and Social Environments to Optimize Social Inclusion and Social Participation of Persons with Physical Disabilities. Project description as submitted to the FRSQ. Montreal: McGill University, Universite de Montreal, and CRIR.

Poldma, T. (2011). Report to the FQRS. Pilot Study 1: Understanding People's Needs in a Public Space Such as a Commercial Mall.

Poldma, T., & Tissaoui, L. (2012). Description of Place Alexis Nihon with Binders 1 and 2 of Baseline Site Documentation. Montreal: CRIR & Université de Montréal, 21 pages.

Wenger, E. C., & Snyder, W. M. (2000, Jan.–Feb.). Communities of Practice: The Organizational Frontier. *Harvard Business Review*, pp. 139–145.

Notes:
1. This Rehabilitation Living Lab is financially supported by an infrastructure grant awarded by the FRQS, Government of Quėbec, Canada, and in-kind funds from rehabilitation Centers in Montreal and the Province of Quėbec, Canada.
2. Living Lab definition is retrieved from http://en.wikipedia.org/wiki/Living_lab.

SUMMARY

Changing spaces of critical design and design thinking are opening up new ways to integrate the systematic aspects of design thinking with both individual and collaborative practices in both research and practice. As designers, not only are we applying our thinking in new ways, but we must also reconsider how we use our innovative thinking in the mediation of new types of spaces and within the ways that we collaborate and work with users, clients, and others whose experiences will be transformed by designers' work. Collaborative and experimental strategies grounded in design thinking and supported by research that inform practices offer possible ways to find new spaces of meaning within design thinking approaches and that raise the level of design inquiry.

Within these new frameworks are inherently subjective and human-situated approaches, and these complex situations require understanding the role of ethics. We will examine ethical approaches within these practices next in Chapter 11.

SUGGESTED READINGS

Dewey, J. (1994). Art as Experience, In S. D. Ross (Ed.), *Art and Its Significance: An Anthology of Aesthetic Theory* (pp. 203–220). Albany, NY: SUNY.

Joannidis, M. (2010). Best of Canada. Michael Joannidis Interview, *KA Magazine, 4,* 157.

Carr, W., & Kemmis, S. (1986). *Becoming Critical: Education, Knowledge, and Action Research.* Philadelphia: The Falmer Press.

Habermas, J. (1981/1987). *The Theory of Communicative Action.* Boston, MA: Beacon Press Books.

OVERVIEW QUESTIONS FOR DISCUSSION

1. Describe the characteristics of design thinking that Melles and Feast propose. What is a critical design approach in the context of design thinking?

   a. What is critical design?
   b. What is pragmatic experience as John Dewey describes?

2. Read John Dewey's "Art as Experience" in light of the theoretical concepts proposed by Melles and Feast, and explore the concept of pragmatic experience as Dewey describes. How is a pragmatic aesthetic experience useful in situating a critical design approach?

3. Compare the idea of critical design by Melles and Feast with the ideas of the practitioner as innovator described by Michael Joannidis.

   a. How are these similar?
   b. How are these different?
   c. What is research for a design project?

4. How would you go about finding out what you need to know?

   a. Using the project of the case study described, list the steps of the project. What are the issues?
   b. What research themes might you need to explore the project and its issues?

5. Examine the idea of critical design as proposed by Melles and Feast. How does innovation happen in the examples that they cite?

6. How does Michael Joannidis achieve "that-which-is-not-yet-existing" using design thinking? What are the characteristics he proposes?

7. How are the critical design and collaborative design approaches put into practice in the case study described by Kehayia, Swaine, and Poldma?

   a. What are the inquiry spaces create by this innovative research lab?
   b. How are the different meanings of the different people organized and why is this important?
   c. What type of research paradigm represents this approach?
   d. What are the issues that arise when stakeholders have different values?

8. Describe how participatory action research and interpretive modes are used to explicitly determine and support the pragmatic experiences that are understood within the context of the case study project.

CHAPTER 10
Mediated Spaces of Practice

transformational change, innovation, discontinuous change, collective intelligence, selective exposure, design thinking, strategic and tactical thinking, experiential and strategic spaces, traditionalists, transformers, focused thinking, broad design thinking, agnotology

AFTER READING THIS CHAPTER, YOU WILL BE ABLE TO:

- Understand concepts of spatial meanings in the context of ongoing emergence of new technologies and virtual tools.

- Assess how the mediation of environments is affected by both people and technology.

- Understand how we are thinking differently and what we use to apply thinking skills using technology.

- Discuss design learning and doing in this multi-digital context and the impact of technology on thinking and doing design now and into the future.

- Understand how technology and its intersections with design changes the realities of design business.

- Understand how new intersecting spaces of practice and design thinking inform innovative meaning-making.

- Decipher new spaces of meaning in digital and third-space contexts beyond space and time.

INTRODUCTION

In Chapter 9 we introduced new critical spaces of thinking that begin to merge practices as both inquiry-based and as catalysts for action. Design thinking was explored in the context of new pragmatic spaces of critical design thinking and how forms of exploration, such as critical ethnography, and collaborative forms of research, such as participatory action research, provide understandings of meanings held in real, lived experiences. We also examined how new forums of research such as collaborative research and/or cooperative and co-research provide avenues for voices to be heard in ways that broaden design decision making, and to be more holistic and in sync with groups that inform practices and that engage pragmatic approaches.

In this chapter we expand these new inquiries and design spaces within contexts of how we actually think as designers, as users, as people using innovative techniques, and as people who now think in a new way as we embrace technological tools daily. We are changing in how we understand our experience, as technology and mediated spaces pervade our lives more than ever before. Whether it is the lived experience of the user interacting in new virtual and technological spaces, chatting with friends 24/7 locally or around the world, or the mediation of spaces that occurs through technological innovation, each changes our perception of the world around us, along with the meanings we attribute to our social lives, the spaces that we navigate, and how we live.

In this chapter, we look at how technology is changing the spaces of mediation of environments we inhabit and the changing ways that technology intersects with design thinking. First, C. Thomas Mitchell examines design thinking as a strategic tool and what this means in terms of reconceptualizing design spaces. Mitchell examines how people's experience drives design thinking and what this means in terms of strategic and tactical design thinking tools. Mitchell also develops concepts about design thinking using technological tools, showing us through examples how these transform business and how technology transforms these interrelationships.

In the Provocation, Charles Burnette speaks to this mediation of environments by provoking ideas about how the emerging mediation of environments is transforming both thinking and doing in spaces in fundamental ways. Not only is design thinking shifting new technologies, but users are no longer recipients of design intentions; rather, mediated environments are changing person-object-space relationships inherently.

Finally, in the Dialogues and Perspectives, Amy Roehl examines user experiences in the context of the emerging technological changes and wicked problem with a provoking dialogue where she specifically discusses Web 2.0 and user interactions. Using the practical mediated world of the Web, Roehl suggests how the Web 2.0 blogosphere opens ways to innovative thinking and what this means for the way we think in mediated spaces. Roehl suggests that discontinuous change is a new space of decision making and explores how this might be integrated with design thinking.

Introduction

When considering design/spaces, the ways we use design thinking are necessary to consider. Design thinking is both a way of using design processes and an emerging trend that uses methods from design disciplines, but in the latter use, it is deployed on a larger, more systemic scale. Tim Brown, CEO of innovative design consultancy IDEO and author of the book *Change by Design: How Design Thinking Transforms Organizations and Inspires Innovation*, suggests:

> Design has the power to enrich our lives by engaging our emotions through images, form, texture, color, sound, and smell. The intrinsically human-centered nature of design thinking points to the next step: we can use our empathy and understanding of people to design experiences that create opportunities for active engagement and participation (Brown, 2009).

The trend toward design thinking as a strategic tool is very prominent in the business world where companies such as Procter & Gamble, GE, Maytag, Philips, and, of course, Apple are turning to it in order to gain a competitive advantage over their rivals. In particular, design thinking is being used to achieve transformative leaps of innovation instead of—as has traditionally been done—incremental improvements.

There are some very specific implications that arise from the application of design thinking to business in terms of different design/spaces and the meanings that emerge. Conceptually, there is a change from what Roger Martin, Dean of the Rotman School of Management at the University of Toronto, Canada, terms the traditional "algorithmic" approach of business to the "heuristic" one of design (Martin, 2004, p. 9). The heuristic approach of design thinking provides methods to work through layers of ambiguity in order to define the nature of a design task and arrive at novel, workable solutions. Ultimately, there is a place for both big-picture thinking and detailed execution. But without disruptive design thinking at the front end of the process, there will be no opportunity for transformative innovation at the conclusion.

Traditionalists versus Transformers Using Design Processes

Interestingly, the application of design thinking by businesses also has implications for designing itself. When those in business describe design, such as Claudia

Kotchka, Vice President of Design Innovation and Strategy at Procter & Gamble, they speak of a process that is highly empathetic and holistic. In particular, they discuss the iterative use of prototypes to model the prospective experiences that might arise for those who will ultimately interact with products or services (Kotchka, 2004, p. 11).

Those of us from the design world may be more familiar with an overriding emphasis on the intuition of the individual designer working on well-defined, aesthetically oriented design tasks. British working group RED addresses this point, noting "there is an emerging split in the industry between 'traditionalists' and 'transformers'" (Burns et al., 2006, p. 25). Traditionalists continue to focus on the individual object or environment—that is, the tactical. Transformers, on the other hand, increase the scope and breadth of design, focusing on the systemic and experiential—the strategic.

New attitudes, approaches, methods, and roles are called for on the part of designers to fully embrace the strategic approach to design. The implication of the transformation that arises from business's application of design thinking is that design goes beyond mere "problem solving." Instead, design thinking serves as a metaphorical new lens through which user experience can be viewed and meaningfully made as the basis for designing. Viewed most broadly, design thinking has the potential to address global challenges of the largest scale.

What Is Design Thinking?

It is important from the outset to identify what design thinking is and to distinguish it from more purely aesthetically oriented design processes. Tim Brown addresses this, noting:

> Design thinking begins with skills designers have learned over many decades in their quest to match human needs with available technical resources within the practical constraints of business.
>
> Design thinking takes the next step, which is to put these tools into the hands of people who may never have thought of themselves as designers and apply them to a vastly greater range of problems (Brown, 2009).

Victor Lombardi concisely sets out the nature of design thinking in his blog Noise Between Stations:

> Based on a review of writing on this topic, I have synthesized for myself what I understand design thinking to be . . .
> - Collaborative, especially with others having different and complementary experience, to generate better work and form agreement
> - Abductive, inventing new options to find new and better solutions to new problems
> - Experimental, building prototypes and posing hypotheses, testing them, and iterating this activity to find what works and what doesn't work to manage risk

- Personal, considering the unique context of each problem and the people involved
- Integrative, perceiving an entire system and its linkages
- Interpretive, devising how to frame the problem and judge the possible solutions (Lombardi, n.d.).

Design thinking, therefore, goes beyond the individual object to take on much larger, more systemic tasks. It necessarily involves many people in the design process, including those who do not necessarily consider themselves to be designers. Further, it endeavors to test, through prototypes, user experience and interactions in a way that doesn't happen through the use of a scale drawing. Design thinking isn't just a way to solve well-defined aesthetic problems; rather, it is a new way of defining and exploring novel solution spaces.

Design Thinking in Business

Design thinking is now a highly prominent trend in the business world. Articles on the subject have appeared in *BusinessWeek*, the *Economist*, the *Wall Street Journal*, *Forbes*, and the *New York Times*. Further, business schools have begun addressing design thinking as well, most notably in the Rotman School of Management at the University of Toronto, the Haas School of Business at the University of California, Berkeley, and the Said Business School at the University of Oxford.

There is even a Design Thinking Boot Camp offered in the summer by Stanford University's Graduate School of Business

(*Design Thinking Boot Camp: From Insights to Innovation.* n.d.). The program is aimed at:

> executives who are responsible for tackling strategic challenges in their organizations. People who are responsible for offerings that are developed for the marketplace, as well as those developed for internal constituencies, are invited to apply for the Design Thinking Boot Camp . . .
>
> Appropriate participant titles include Chief Executive Officer, Chief Operating Officer, Chief of Insights, Director of Research & Development, and Vice President of Product Management.

According to Stanford, the Design Thinking Boot Camp will offer

> executives the chance to learn design thinking—a human-centered, prototype-driven process for innovation that can be applied to product, service, and business design. We believe that innovation is necessary in every aspect of business, and that it can be taught. We invite you to join us here at the HassoPlattner Institute of Design . . . affectionately called "the d.school," for an experience that will enhance your ability to drive innovation in your organization.

The program is intended to provide participants the following "Key Takeaways and Tenets of Design Thinking":

- Develop deep consumer insights.
- Reduce risk and accelerate learning through rapid prototyping.

- Drive toward innovation, not just incremental growth.
- Empower your employees to be innovative.

Given the target audience of business executives, perhaps most important is the method of instruction:

> Our approach is to learn by doing. Your work will be done at the Stanford d.school [HassoPlattner Institute of Design]. Our customized studio space fosters radical collaboration and allows participants to tackle big projects with innovative outcomes.

Why are non-designers and, in particular, business leaders being drawn to the world of design? In an interview with Saj-nicole Joni for *Forbes* magazine, Tim Brown addressed this issue:

> Design thinking is a different way of approaching the big challenges we face. It starts off with really trying to serve people's needs. It connects constraints with creativity, enabling us to look at old problems with new eyes and generate new possibilities. There are many things in our organizations and markets that we can't control, but your mindset and your approach to challenges—those are up to you (Joni, S., 2010).

In essence, design thinking challenges the mindset.

Changing Business Strategies Using Design Thinking

The recognition of the importance design can play in an organization is nicely summed up in the "Danish Design Ladder," produced by the Danish Design Center. In 2007, they found there were four different approaches companies took to design:

1. Non-design: Companies that do not use design (15 percent)
2. Design as styling: Companies that use design as styling appearance (17 percent)
3. Design as process: Companies that integrate design into the development process (45 percent)
4. Design as innovation: Companies that consider design as key strategic element (21 percent)

More and more companies are seeing the need to overcome the merely incremental improvements fostered by methods such as Six Sigma and, instead, find approaches that allow for true transformation of products and services. In an article titled "The Business of Design," Rotman School of Management Dean Roger Martin, suggests that students need to think about "devising clever solutions to wickedly difficult problems (Martin quoted in Breen, 2005)," taking inspiration from Richard Buchanan and his seminal article "Wicked Problems in Design Thinking" (Buchanan 1992). Increasingly, those in business are drawn to design thinking as a way to overcome incremental decision making and jump-start innovation. This is particularly important as companies seek to develop and maintain a competitive advantage over business rivals in an era of globalization.

The importance of using design thinking to gain a competitive advantage and to create innovation and corporate transformation can best be exemplified in the example of Apple Inc. Gary Hamel, in his article "Inspired Design is Essential—and All Too Rare," writes:

> Consider Apple for a moment. How is [it] that quarter after quarter this company has managed to outperform a dreadful economy—given that there are cheaper alternatives to just about everything Apple makes? The answer, of course, is exceptional design. Apple infused everything it does—hardware, software, packaging, retailing, and technical support—with design thinking. Whenever you rub up against Apple you rub up against hip and helpful design (2009).

The tagline "Designed in California" that is present on all Apple products is a key to understanding the unified application of design thinking to the company, and to their products and services.

As is the case with Apple, the shaping not just of individual products but of the overall customer experience is an intangible, but critical, focus of design thinking. This is noted by Vaness Wong when referring to the company Philips and its lighting division, in an article in *Business-Week* entitled "How Business Is Adopting Design Thinking":

> The focus on design-led innovation helped Philips lighting to transform itself over the past decade from a company that simply pushed products into the market into one that designs them with customer desires in mind," says CEO Rudy Provoost. His business, for example, is no longer just about light bulbs, but about designing ambience for consumers. Provoost says the company hopes to provide the bulbs and software to enable consumers to be their own lighting designers.
>
> To support this culture, the company created the role of chief design officer, now held by Philips Design CEO Stefano Marzano, to participate in strategy discussions. Also, Philips Design employees lead workshops that involve case studies and project work about "high design," the company's term for its product development process, which integrates design into other functions such as marketing and technology and focuses on the end user. "We employ disciplines as diverse as psychology, cultural sociology, anthropology, and trend research, in addition to the more conventional design-related skills," says Heleen Engelen, Philips Design's senior design director for lighting (Wong, 2009).

The inclusion of design thinking as a strategic asset necessitates a new organizational structure and the development of new skill sets. As Wong notes, not only are companies such as Philips, GE Healthcare, and Procter & Gamble "hiring design thinkers from schools, they have developed in-house programs to bring people—from all functions of the organization—to think through this lens" (2009).

How Design Thinking Transforms Business

Design thinking provides not just a new lens through which businesspeople can see their world; it also presents a fundamentally different approach than the one conventionally taken in business. Heuristic thinking is a possible means to explore this type of approach.

Heuristic, in this context, according to Dictionary.com, means "encouraging a person to learn, discover, understand or solve problems on his or her own, as by experimenting, evaluating possible answers or solutions, or by trial and error"; whereas algorithms are "a set of rules for solving a problem in a finite number of steps." As Roger Martin of the Rotman School of Business notes:

> Design skills and business skills are converging. To be successful in the future, business people will have to become more like designers—more "masters of heuristics" than "managers of algorithms" (2004, p. 8).

Though using different terminology, Colin Raney and Ryan Jacoby present a similar comparison in their article "Decisions by Design: Stop Deciding, Start Designing":

> A first step is for managers to understand the differences in the ways they and designers go about solving problems. Managers tend to follow a very analytical process. Usually, they make decisions by understanding all of the available options and rigorously determining the best path forward. In contrast, designers tend to prototype and iterate ideas, learning as they go and often developing new ideas along the way. Roger Martin has contrasted "business as usual" and "business-by-design," and Richard Boland and Fred Collopy have contrasted a "decision attitude" and a "design attitude." The net result of these investigations is that the more ambiguous and uncertain the problem, the more suitable design thinking seems to be. The foundational reason is that in a creative process, there aren't automatically a handful of constrained options to analyze and choose among. Instead, the playing field is often broader and the possibilities may appear endless. To make sense of all the options, designers design their way through the problem. (2010, pp. 35–36)

However, this is also risky, as designing from the business manager perspective may not be the same as designing from a design perspective. For designers, the process of building, prototyping, and trying things is the decision-making process. Instead of boiling down a problem to one large decision, designers make lots of little decisions, learning as they go. As they build and learn, something interesting happens: through the iterations, the best option often reveals itself and other less-appropriate options fall by the wayside. By trying things, designers navigate large decisions through smaller trials. Constraints and prototypes help reduce risk and convert decision-making meetings from consensus-building slogs to collaborative, invigorating critique and build sessions. This subtle but significant change in the decision-making process can lead to new avenues that didn't exist at the beginning of the process (Raney & Jacoby, 2010, p. 36).

Design Thinking as an Actual Tool—Issues to Consider

The issue of designing versus the realities of business converge in this new type of thinking space. While there is a place for both the heuristic and the algorithmic—for designing and deciding—it is important to get the metaphorical cart before the horse. The conceptual, systemic, big-picture stuff—the design—needs to come first, and then the detailed execution can follow. Otherwise, there will be no opportunity for innovation—only marginal improvement. *Design Thinking* used as simply a buzzword will not achieve what companies need if not understood in relationship to the business strategies and goals.

Sara Beckman summarizes this issue in the *New York Times*, and examines the relationship between the emerging move toward design thinking in business and the more incremental approaches:

For decades, companies from Cisco Systems to Staples to Bank of America have worked to embed the basic techniques for Six Sigma, the business approach that relies on measurement and analysis to make operations as efficient as possible.

More recently, in the last 5 to 10 years, they have been told they must master a new set of skills known as "design thinking." Aiming to help companies innovate, design thinking starts with an intense focus on understanding real problems customers face in their day-to-day lives—often using techniques derived from ethnographers—and then entertains a range of possible solutions.

Both worlds—the quantum one where designers push boundaries to surprise and delight, and the Newtonian one where workers meet deadlines and margins—are meaningful. The most successful companies will learn to build bridges between them and leverage them both. (2009)

As Beckman suggests, the application of design thinking to business broadens the process. Instead of simply making incremental improvements, each of which will yield less competitive advantage, design thinking provides tools for transformation. Instead of deciding between a series of constrained options, design thinking enables businesspeople to work through ambiguity and uncertainty to define and explore new solution spaces. Thus, through application of design thinking, innovation, and not mere improvement, is made possible.

How Business Transforms Design Thinking

Interestingly, the approach to design thinking taken by those in business is very different from that presented in the studio model of individual designers working intuitively on aesthetic problems. So, in a sense, those in business and at the interface of design and business, like Tim Brown's firm IDEO, are co-creating a new methodology based on some of the tools and approaches of studio-based design, but turned to a different purpose.

Many in the business world seem to have a highly idealized view of how most designers actually approach their work. For example, Procter & Gamble's Claudia Kotchka explains in answer to the question "How do designers think?" that

> [t]here are three keys to it. First, designers are very empathetic. Design is always for somebody else, so if you're designing a product, you start out by getting inside of the head of the user, and determining what they would want or need. The user doesn't usually tell you what they want, because they can't easily describe what they can't see or imagine. So designers have to be able to figure this out by watching, listening and relating to the user. From a

business perspective, if you're trying to structure an organization, for example, it's critical to have empathy for who is going to be working in the organization and not just focus on what the organization is trying to do.

> Designers always ask, "Are we solving the right problem?" If you hand designers a problem, they never just take it and solve it. They always question it, and that comes from empathy—from really understanding the user and being accustomed to questioning models. It's not uncommon for them to come back having reframed the problem, often within a richer and broader context.

> Second, designers problem-solve holistically, not in a linear fashion. While the scientific method for problem solving uses problem-focused strategies and analysis, designers use solution-focused strategies and synthesis. They start with a whole solution rather than break it down into parts.

> That brings me to the next key, which is prototyping. Designers start with a variety of possible solutions, prototype them, get feedback, revisit the problem, and evolve solutions. The process is a continuous loop until they find a solution that works. Often, when business people work on a problem, they spend a long time studying it, trying to identify the best solution, and then rolling it out, rather than using this iterative process of building, testing, and evolving. (2004, p. 11)

While this may, in fact, be the view of design from some in the business community, the reality of most design practices may still be somewhat different.

Back to the Emerging Split Between "Traditionalists" and "Transformers" in Design Thinking

As British working group RED wrote in their white paper on "Transformation Design":

> . . . there is an emerging split in the industry between "traditionalists" and "transformers."
>
> Broadly this is in response to two main developments. Firstly the decline of British manufacturing has led to designers applying their skills beyond the manufactured object and increasingly to the service sector. Secondly, professionals in all sectors no longer have a monopoly over their practice. Just as teachers are no longer the only people who help you learn, and doctors no longer the only people who make you well, it follows that designers are no longer the only people who design. (Burns et al., 2006, p. 25)

And yet there are few designers equipped to work in this way in North America, for example. Design organizations, whether they are consultancies within industry or academic research bodies, have a largely commercial orientation, with a poor understanding of public service issues or the broader government policy context. Most designers and architects deliver tactical outcomes—communications, tools, products, environments. User-centered design, while prolific, is not universal. Designers respond to problem statements, or briefs, and are only beginning to engage with the strategic process of problem definition (Burns et al., 2006, p. 27).

We need to find ways of developing new skills and orientation on the "supply side" of transformation design so that designers keen to work in this way are able to think systematically; apply design thinking in broader social, economic, and political contexts; collaborate fruitfully with other disciplines; and champion a human-centered design approach at the highest levels (Burns et al., 2006, p. 28).

So in a very real sense, the development and application of design thinking in business is charting new territory for the discipline of design itself. As Tim Brown notes:

> Today, rather than enlist designers to make an already developed idea more attractive, the most progressive companies are challenging them to create ideas at the outset of the development process. The former role is tactical; it builds on what exists and usually moves it one step further. The latter is strategic; it pulls "design" out of the studio and unleashes its disruptive, game-changing potential. It's no surprise that designers can now be found in the boardrooms of some of the world's most progressive companies. (2009)

Both RED and Brown identify the key point of transformation in the nature of design that arises from the application of design thinking in business—its scope and nature change from the individual object (the tactical) to something more experiential and systemic (the strategic). It is this latter role that gives design thinking its great transformative power.

Van Erp's View of the Tactical and the Strategic

The relationship between the strategic and the tactical is neatly expressed by Jeroen van Erp, creative director of Netherlands-based firm Fabrique. In Figure 10.1, the Cone Model 2.0 shows that the highest level of activity is the initiation of an activity, next is strategy, then concept, and, finally, on this basis of all this thinking,

is what would commonly be considered design activity. Further, the model shows clearly how this view expands the scope of design activity beyond what is currently contained in tactically oriented design disciplines that focus on the execution of product-oriented designing.

Figure 10.2 shows the interrelationship of the entrepreneur, strategist, conceptualist, and designer as articulated by van Erp and Fabrique. This diagram shows how to achieve a total experience, providing meaning, emotional experience, and aesthetics for the user/consumer together.

Brown articulates the contrast between design as it has been practiced and the broader view of design thinking, noting:

THE CONE MODEL 2.0

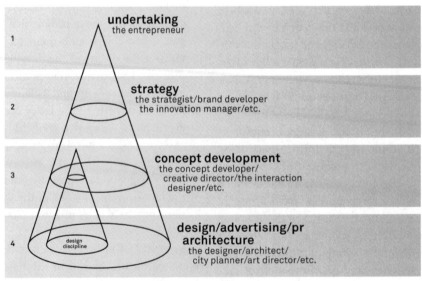

Figure 10.1 Cone model A

THE CONE MODEL 2.0

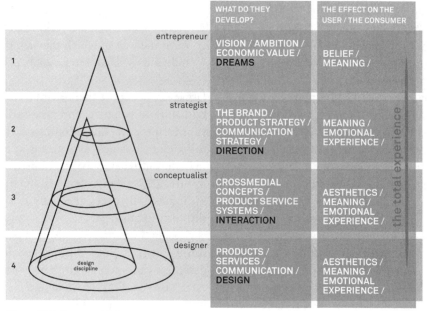

Figure 10.2 Cone model B

Although we will never, I hope, lose respect for the designer as inspired from giver, it is common now to see designers working with psychologists and ethnographers, engineers and scientists, marketing and business experts, writers and filmmakers. All of these disciplines, and many more, have long contributed to the development of new products and services, but today we are bringing them together within the same team, in the same space, and using the same processes. As MBAs learn to talk to MFAs and PhDs across their disciplinary divides . . . there will be increasing overlap in activities and responsibilities (2009).

Conclusion

Roger Martin nicely summarizes the nature of the overlap between business and design that arises from the application of design thinking. He notes:

> [W]e are on the cusp of a design revolution in business . . . Competing is no longer about creating dominance in scale-intensive industries, it's about producing elegant, refined products and services in imagination-intensive industries. As a result . . . business people don't just need to understand designers better—they need to become designers (Martin, 2004, p. 7).

The institutional implications of this overlap are addressed by Coughlan and Prokopoff, who note that there are challenges for business schools to understand design thinking in a broader sense and as the organizational means by which the (ideas) are created and supported (2006, p. 23). As we have seen, Brown, Martin, and the working group RED all articulate the nature and applicability of design thinking as a possible and useful process for developing both tactical and strategic thinking.

Design thinking also has the potential to have a deep and global impact far beyond the worlds of business or design as currently conceived. As RED notes:

[D]esign also goes beyond problem solving. Solutions to today's most intractable issues—such as the rise of chronic health conditions, the impacts of climate change, or the consequences of an ageing population—depend on the choices that people make in their everyday lives: how they eat, consume energy, or form relationships. Good design creates products, services, spaces, interactions and experiences that not only satisfy a function or solve a problem, but that are also desirable, aspirational, compelling and delightful. These

are the qualities desperately needed by organizations in both the public and private sector that are seeking to transform the way in which they connect to individuals (Burns et al., 2006, p. 8).

However, I propose that design thinking is both a transformative, and necessarily disruptive, process. The adoption of design thinking by business as a means of fostering innovation, and not just improvement, in turn, affects design itself as much as the meanings and spaces affects by design, in this case, in business.

Design thinking is serving as a new lens through which both businesspeople and designers can understand their worlds. In each case, application of design thinking leads away from a traditional emphasis on the tactical (individual products/objects) to the strategic (experiential/systems). With this approach, empathy and an overarching user-centered focus guide a collaborative and interactive process.

Design thinking has the potential to transform issues far beyond business and design as currently conceived. The most pressing global issues are ripe for strategic application of design thinking; it has the potential to succeed where other, more tactically oriented approaches have failed.

Discussion Questions

1. What is the nature of the application of design thinking by business that C. Thomas Mitchell presents?
   a. Who are "traditionalists"?
   b. Who are "transformers"?
   c. How are traditionalists tactical and transformers strategic?
   d. Why are these new types of design spaces?

2. What is design thinking in the context of business as described herein?
   a. Why is this not aesthetic according to Mitchell?

   b. Explore Roger Martin's view of design thinking in business.
   c. Compare these views with your idea of design thinking.

3. Describe the four ways that design is understood in the context of business.
   a. Why is design as a process considered to be vital for 47 percent of those who use design?
   b. What does this mean in terms of design spaces in business thinking?

References

Beckman, S. (2009, September 6). Welcoming the new, improving the old. Retrieved February 8, 2010 from http://www.nytimes.com/2009/09/06/business/06proto.html

Breen, B. (2005, April). The business of design. Retrieved July 6, 2010, from http://www.fastcompany.com/magazine/93/design.html

Brown, T. (2009). *Change by Design: How Design Thinking Transforms Organizations and Inspires Innovation*. New York: HarperCollins e-books. [Kindle 2 version].

Burns, C., Cottam, H., Vanstone, C., &Winhall, J. (2006). RED Paper 02: Transformation Design. London: Design Council.

Coughlan, P., & Prokopoff, I. (2006, Winter). Managing Change, by Design. *Rotman Magazine*, 20–23.

Danish Design Center (n.d.) *Danish Design Ladder*. Retrieved July 6, 2010 from http://en.wikipedia.org/wiki/Design_management.

Design Thinking Boot Camp: From Insights to Innovation. (n.d.). Retrieved June 14, 2010, from http://www.gsb.stanford.edu/exed/dtbc/print.html.

Dictionary.com (n.d.). *Algorithm.* Retrieved August 3, 2010, from http://www.dictionary.reference.com/browse/algorithm.

Dictionary.com (n.d.). *Heuristic.* Retrieved August 3, 2010, from http://www.dictionary.reference.com/browse/heuristic.

Intro to Design Thinking: An Interview with David Burney Conducted by Tim Hyer. (2006, May). *Red Hat Magazine, 19.* Retrieved July 6, 2010, from http://www.redhat.com/magazine/019may06/features/burney.

Hamel, Gary. (2009, November 30). Inspired Design Is essential—And All Too Rare. *Wall Street Journals Blogs.* Retrieved February 18, 2010, from http://blogs.wsj.com/management/2009/11/30/inspired-design-is-essential-and-all-too-rare.

Hogan, J. (n.d.). GE Healthcare Technologies CEO Joseph M. Hogan on Design. Retrieved July 27, 2010, from http://www.atissuejournal.com/interviews.

Joni, S. (2010, January 14). The Third Opinion: Why We All Need More Design Thinking. (A conversation with Tim Brown, CEO of the design and innovation firm IDEO.) Retrieved June 15, 2010, from http://www.forbes.com/2010/01/14/tim-brown-ideo-leadership-managing-design.html.

Kotchka, C. (2004, Winter). Designing for Success at P&G. *Rotman Management,* 10–11.

Lombardi, V. (n.d.). *What Is Design Thinking?* Retrieved July 6, 2010, from http://www.noisebetweenstations.com/personal/weblogs/?page_id=1688.

Martin, R. (2004, Winter). The Design of Business. *Rotman Management,* 7–10.

Nussbaum, B. (2005, March 8). The Empathy Economy. *BusinessWeek.* Retrieved August 2, 2010, from http://www.businessweek.com/bwdaily/dnflash/mar2005/nf2005037_4086.htm?chan=db.

Raney, C., & Jacoby, R. (2010, Winter). Decisions by Design: Stop Deciding, Start Designing. *Rotman Magazine,* 35–39.

van Erp, Jeroen. (2010). *Fabrique: Merken & interactie.* PowerPoint presentation.

Wong, V. (2009, November 3). How Business Is Adopting Design Thinking. Retrieved February 18, 2010, from http://www.businessweek.com/innovate/content/sep2009/id20090930_853305.htm.

Architects and interior designers have not yet grasped the potential of new media to transform the environments we live in. They do not think of spatial transformation through media embedded in the surfaces that surround us as we live. Even though the size, high-resolution, and three-dimensionality of imagery, and the variability, translucence, and tactility of physical surfaces has become technically practical, the imagination of designers has not dealt with the possibilities of environments that fully exploit these technologies. In a fully mediated environment, users would be enabled to both select and share the environments they experience.

People want to be where their focus of attention is and experience the environments they are thinking about. Movies bring us into environments that we experience as though we are there. Video imagery of people where they are now embellishes communication. Social networks usually present us where we are to those with whom we are in contact. The ubiquity of both still and video cameras in the world provides images of events when and where they happen. A journalist pictured at the site of the event he or she is reporting is more believable than the same journalist reporting from a studio. Sharing environments through media has become familiar.

From the early days of stereography to today's growing commitment to 3D digital presentations in color on TV, in movies, gaming, or virtual reality simulations, we have constantly tried to develop ways to experience environments that we are not in as though we were in them. Videoconferencing and video telephony have also brought environmental images into face-to-face communications. While present in the background, these environments are not usually focused on or shared in an interactive way. They certainly could be in the future.

In what ways will the desire and capacity to experience distant environments and to share environments with other people influence the design of future environments? Will large-format high-definition 3D television embedded in walls; multiple, automatically tracking cameras; and gestural or behavioral recognition systems begin to make spaces sharable at a distance? Will augmented reality, including enhancements for the visually, acoustically, or physically impaired, become an integral part of such technically enhanced environments? Will larger surfaces displaying situations at their actual scale become a normal feature of people's personal and social environments? Will the large interactive displays in newsrooms become the delivery system for personal exploration of issues and knowledge? Will simulated or transformable spaces be sharable in discussions as well as games? Will it be possible for the occupants of a space to easily switch their environment to support different activities? Will the passive world of the couch potato become an active world in simulated environments controlled by movement and voice as demonstrated by Kinect technology? Will natural voice and gesture begin to control the experiences afforded by technology and spatial enclosures in a more natural way?

To realize the potential of new media in the environments in which we live, there must be a willingness to understand the needs and interests of users in far more sophisticated ways than dictated by the conventional wisdom that has embalmed existing notions of privacy, sociability, and comfort in the cocoon of the average home or work environment. Separate appliances must be replaced by services integrated into spatial enclosures in ways that support change and adaptive use tailored to the needs and interests of occupants. Expression, activity, and social communication must be re-imagined and facilitated through environments that are beautiful, interactive, sensitive to the preferences of users, and global in their reach and knowledge.

Discussion Questions

1. Burnette asks some serious questions about mediation and futuring of the built environment.
   a. How are movies, videos, and alternate dimensions changing how we mediate our environments?
   b. What does this mean for the spaces and designs we create?
   c. What meanings do we attribute to our experiences of them?

2. How is technology mediating our spaces in ways we are still not yet conceptualizing?
   a. What are the questions Burnette asks?
   b. Unpack each one and discuss in terms of your experiences and those of your family, your friends, fellow students.

3. In what ways will the desire and capacity to experience distant environments and to share environments with other people influence the design of future environments?

Dialogues and Perspectives

10.3 Are You Future-Ready? Discontinuous Change and the New Spaces of Practice

Amy Roehl

The world we live in today marks the starting point of a future characterized by unrelenting **discontinuous change**. Discontinuous change is defined as sudden change that cannot be predicted. It threatens traditional authority and power structures, requiring agile shifts in the way that things are currently being done and have been done for years (Martin, 2009). "In an era of constant change [companies] want people who are comfortable with complexity and uncertainty" (Atal & Woyke, 2007). Adaptability and becoming comfortable with the discomfort of uncertainty emerge as crucial skills for current and future leaders in all areas of business (Johansen, 2009). Those who teach and manage with the approach that tomorrow's demand will require only an extension of today's skills and processes quickly fall behind.

What is responsible for this state of unpredictable change? Developments in technology over the past ten years play a major role in the fluctuating conditions we experience. This article reflects on technology's effects on society's perception of information and knowledge, technology's influence on design processes, and how these changes reveal new skill sets necessary for current and future success in business.

Conditions affecting both business in general and design industries in particu-lar will be examined. Design industries include architecture, interior design, and visual communication. The term *designer* is used throughout this essay in reference to professionals involved in all design fields required to create full-scale, three-dimensional space.

The good news is that the future for designers is bright. With wicked problems to solve, design thinkers are essential leaders in untangling the ever-shifting, ever-expanding information accessible on the Web. "Design fluency and literacy will become the newest highly desirable business skill to connect disparate disciplines for maximum effectiveness" (Martin, 2009). The ability to extract pertinent information and organize it both in written and graphic format is essential for all areas of business. Increased expectations for competency in visual communication are fueled by the Web-driven visual nature of daily interactions. Conversations and critique of work both in and outside the design studio are vital to producing the next generation of designers who think equally about design content and quality of visual communication.

In their report for CIDA (Council for Interior Design Accreditation) "Interior Design Trends and Implications," Cindy Coleman and Katie Sosnowchik acknowl-edge the increasingly "strategic and consultative" nature of the design business where "expanded, non-traditional entrepreneurial services are embraced" (Cramer, 2008). Clients expect design solutions to provide positive outcomes for their organizations. Solutions must support their culture by promoting collaboration and innovation. Coleman and Sosnowchik point out "a base in business, behavior, sociology, technology and environmental factors" is essential for success in today's design industries (2006).

For example, the demand for design thinking is evidenced by the global rise of D-Schools merging business and design curriculum. *Bloomberg Businessweek* publishes "D-Schools: The Global List" highlighting the top 60 programs in the world. Tom Kelley, former CEO of design and innovation consulting firm IDEO, founded Stanford's D-School. Kelley encourages master's-level students to participate in classes where design processes are taught and carried out by interdisciplinary teams. "Innovation has become recognized as a pivotal management tool across virtually all industries and market segments" (Kelley, 2005). Business leaders pay hefty sums to attend abbreviated workshops with the intention of cultivating their design-thinking abilities.

Some schools of architecture (where design processes are integral to the education) have responded by offering a combined Master of Architecture and Master of Business Administration. The integration of an MBA reflects both the need for designers to understand business practices and the increasing value of the designer

as a business player. Coming together to problem-solve, the gap is closing between managerial types and creative types who have traditionally butted heads.

As a starting point for understanding context for contemporary problem solving, emerging graduates must be aware of the external forces shaping their minds. Born between 1982 to 1995, the generation currently enrolled in higher education is referred to as *Gen Y* or the *Millennials*. Much has been written about the effects of this highly supervised and overly praised generation. Examining technology as the other key player at work on young people's behavior and thought processes is important to understand this generation's outlook.

Web 2.0 Applications and User Interactions

Web 2.0 (Web applications that enable users to interact with both the site and with each other) was implemented in the early 2000s. This enabled a shift in the way that information is created and disseminated. It is important to understand how the results of this new condition affect the way that young people (and much of contemporary society) perceive information and knowledge.

The initial form of the World Wide Web was primarily a one-way stream outlet set up for passive viewing. The first iteration of the Internet was essentially a vast depository of information that could be accessed and read by the consumer, but presented minimal opportunity of the user to correspond with the authors of the material. It was the introduction of Web

2.0 that moved users beyond passive viewing to complete interactivity.

Consider that in the recent past, information was communicated via one-way stream outlets such as television, radio, and print media. Subject matter generated by a trusted authority such as a news station or newspaper was conveyed from authority to receiver with no interaction between the two. Today's Web 2.0 blogosphere has made it possible for anyone to contribute content in individualized blogs, wikis, personal broadcasts, and chat rooms. News outlets no longer control information communicated to the public. Anyone can create and upload news where viewers comment on content as it is broadcast. A community of participants corresponds with each other around the globe in real time. Content formerly developed by specialists is now generated by anyone, anywhere, anytime. As a result, traditional hierarchies are breaking down, encouraging behavior and systems to evolve. New conditions threaten current power structures, ultimately changing the way business is conducted.

Technology and Collective Intelligence

Collective intelligence, "the aggregate knowledge that emerges from the decentralized choices and judgments of groups of independent participants," is the force driving today's information content (Tapscott & Williams, 2008). As an example, Wikipedia, ranked in the ten most popular sites worldwide (Gutsche, 2009), houses editable Web-based documents that are continuously revised by multiple contributors. On Wikipedia, an article is considered to be complete once participants stop arguing. Unlike traditional information sources such as journals and encyclopedias, Wikipedia's site is filled with disclaimers as users work to collectively negotiate definitions. The public's perception of Wikipedia as a valid resource is explained by Metcalfe's Law, which states that a network becomes more valuable as more people use it (Bruce, 2000). However, Wikipedia has problems of legitimacy among academic scholars.

Do we accept information just because it exists? The ability to add content on the Internet increases public acceptance that multiple contributors collaborate to create knowledge. With the collective increasingly determining content, traditional experts take a back seat. Virtual reality pioneer Jaron Lanier blames software developers on this predicament. He laments that the mere creation of sites editable by the masses implies "that a random crowd of humans is an organism with a legitimate point of view" (Lanier, 2010).

Does our ability to access information anytime, anywhere increase our overall knowledge, or has it led to a perceived sense that we know more than we actually do? In "Manufacturing Confusion: How More Information Leads to Less Knowledge," Clive Thompson cites this era as "the disinformation revolution" (2009). Similarly, Mark Edmunson's *New York Times* article "Geek Lessons: Why Good Teaching Will Never Be Fashionable" considers that "The great enemy of knowledge is knowingness. It's the feeling encouraged by TV and the movies and the Internet that you're on top of things and in charge" (2008). Young people today may perceive that they are well informed without understanding that actually being well informed is a very different condition.

A new phenomenon has arisen from this circumstance. Professor Robert Proctor, a Historian of Science at Stanford, coined the term **agnotology** to describe the study of culturally constructed ignorance. This trend is fueled by easy access to numerous individual opinions on the Internet. Compounding the problem is the barrage of Web-based mass marketing by organizations (and individuals) with specific agendas. In the past, it took money to carry out a marketing campaign. Today you only need access to a blog to preach your beliefs. At the click of a mouse, special interest groups promote and distribute their particular viewpoint.

So why are people confident that they know more than they actually do? The psychological term *selective exposure* gives some insight as to why any given marketing campaign results in buy-in from particular groups. **Selective exposure** describes a human coping mechanism that enables us to tune out information that does not align with our core beliefs (Manjoo, 2008). Studies show that "we steer clear of information that contradicts what we think we know" (Manjoo, 2008). Just about any topic you wish to take a side on has ample backing through communities on the Internet. Whatever it is that you accept as the truth, you can easily find advocates who support and encourage your core beliefs.

The Alternative: Evidence-based Design

In many cases, evidence-based design provides rationale in decision making for clients. Some leading firms now employ PhDs and other interdisciplinary staff focused on research to support design initiatives. IDEO's general manager, Tom Kelley, cites the anthropologist's role as the greatest sources of innovation at his company (Gutsche, 2009). Considering that research supporting positive outcomes for clients is a valuable tool for selling design, it is important to base strategies on accurate information. Emerging designers must understand how to build a research-based case to defend their design decisions. Considering time and budget constraints, knowing where and how to locate accurate findings quickly is imperative.

References

Atal, M. & Woyke, E. (2007, October 4). The Talent Hunt: Design Programs Are Shaping a New Generation of Creative Managers. *Bloomberg Business Week*. Retrieved October 12, 2010, from http://www.businessweek.com/stories/2007-10-04/the-talent-huntbusinessweek-business-news-stock-market-and-financial-advice .

Bruce, B. C. 2000. Credibility of the Web: Why We Need Dialectic Reading. In Nigel Blake and Paul Standish (Eds.), *Enquiries at the Interface: Philosophical Problems of Online Education* (pp. 107–122). Malden, MA: Blackwell Publishers.

Cramer, J. P. (2008, March/April). Compensation Taxonomy and Trends. *DesignIntelligence, 215*, 5–15.

Edmunson, M. (2008, September 21), Geek Lessons: Why Good Teaching Will Never Be Fashionable. *New York Times Magazine*.

Gutsche, J. (2009). *Exploiting Chaos: 150 Ways to Spark Innovation During Times of Change*. New York: Gotham Books.

Johansen, B. (2009). *Leaders Make the Future: Ten New Leadership Skills in an Uncertain World*. San Francisco, CA: Berrett-Koehler Publishers.

Kelley, T. (2005). *The Ten Faces of Innovation: IDEO's Strategies for Beating the Devil's Advocate and Driving Creativity Throughout Your Organization*. New York: Doubleday.

Lanier, J. (2010). *You Are Not a Gadget*. New York: Alfred A. Knopf.

Manjoo, F. (2008). *True Enough: Learning to Live in a Post-Fact Society*. Hoboken, NJ: John Wiley & Sons.

Martin, J. (2009, January/February). A Minor Proposal. *DesignIntelligence*. Report 220, Vol. *15*(1), 31–6.

Tapscott, D., and Williams, A. D. (2008). *Wikinomics: How Mass Collaboration Changes Everything*. New York: Penguin Group.

Thompson, C. (2009, January 19), Clive Thompson on How More Information Leads to Less Knowledge. *Wired*.

SUMMARY

Not only are we, as designers, applying our thinking in new ways, we must also reconsider how people are mediated increasingly in both thought and how they surround themselves with media. We can use our innovative thinking both in the mediation of new types of spaces and within the ways that we collaborate and work with users, clients, and others whose experiences will be transformed by designers' work. Not only are the design thinking tools mediated, so are the spaces we are creating both in virtual and physical realms.

SUGGESTED READINGS

Tapscott, D., & Williams, A. D. (2008). *Wikinomics: How Mass Collaboration Changes Everything.* New York: Penguin Group.

Thompson, C. (2009, January 19). Clive Thompson on How More Information Leads to Less Knowledge. *Wired.* Accessed August 1, 2009, from http://www.wired.com/techbiz/people/magazine/17-02/st_thompson.

Zahedi, M., Poldma, T., Baha, E., & Haats, T. (2012, in process). Design Thinking and Aesthetic Meaning-Making: Interlaced Means to Engage in Collaborative Knowledge-Building. Paper submitted to the NordDesign 2012, August 22–24, 2012, Aalborg, Denmark.

OVERVIEW QUESTIONS FOR DISCUSSION

1. Mitchell presents several case studies to explain the concepts of tactical versus strategic design spaces. Research and locate these examples of Philips, IDEO, and RED by looking up information on these companies, their strategies, and their ideas.

2. Unpack the various case studies: IDEO, Philips, and RED in particular.

   a. How does Philips succeed in capturing lighting as a strategic tool? How are old concepts of fixed spaces changed in this context?

   b. Discuss Mitchell's take on what the British group RED names "traditionalists" or "transformers." Who are these designers, thinkers, and businesspeople? Why is it valuable to distinguish these types in terms of understanding how business and design thinking come together?

    c.   What is special about IDEO? Compare what Mitchell says about IDEO and what Melles and Feast suggested in their reference to IDEO in Chapter 9 and their take on design thinking.

3.   Examine Mitchell's idea of moving from the tactical to the strategic in design thinking and doing. How is design thinking strategic? What are the systemic aspects of design thinking, and how does this change our conceptualization of spaces? For an aesthetic perspective? For business?

4.   Compare Mitchell's ideas and the concepts of technological change as an "equalizer" to how Roehl discusses how technology is changing our spaces of conception. Examine these concepts of technological change of each—what spaces are being mediated and what new spaces of thinking translate into how we might conceive spaces differently as well? How do these approaches compare with Burnette's provocation on the subject?

5.   What meanings of spaces are changing in light of Roehl's idea of discontinuous change? How does Roehl explore this idea in terms of how design thinking occurs with technology?

CHAPTER 11
Ethical and Collaborative Spaces

ethos, cradle to cradle, moral, sustainability, care, greater good, Precautionary list, ethical decision making, standards of care for design spaces, being in service, collaboration, collective action, biomimicry, interdisciplinary practices, sustainable choices, environmental activism, social justice, voice, biophilic design

AFTER READING THIS CHAPTER, YOU WILL BE ABLE TO:

- Distinguish various concepts of care in terms of design services, critical design, ethical decision making, and sustainable choices.

- Interpret concepts of ethics in both theoretical and pragmatic terms.

- Construct meanings in considering ethical and service-oriented thinking with corporate end goals in practice.

- Decipher how the decision making accounts for sustainable aesthetic and material choices.

- Characterize how research incorporated into design choices provides positive impacts on spaces and their conception.

- Synthesize ideas about critical design spaces in light of environmentally sustainable and ethical choices both individually and collectively understood.

INTRODUCTION

As we move toward questions of ethics informing collaborative spaces, it is necessary to understand the roles that service and decision making play in these dimensions. When discussing sustainable concepts and issues, we are often drawn to practical aspects of sustainability wrapped around concepts of providing ethical choices for people, whether in service-oriented designs or built environment projects. For example, in places such as social housing, collaborative spaces are often places where co-construction of activities occurs, such as collective organizations, and all of which are characterized by consensus and by mutual decision making. During any collaborative initiative, many people become involved in the activities and the decision making that drive a particular project. Decision making includes the choices that stakeholders, users, designers, consultants, and others make when coming together for a specific goal, project, or purpose.

These spaces of meaning are expected to construct new social realities, necessarily informed by ethics. Their goal may also be to transform the ways of being within spatial dimensions of various kinds. These concepts of ethical spaces are necessary to grasp, as they are as important a foundational element as aesthetic, historic, cultural, or personal meanings.

Ethics, collaboration, and the spaces within which these occur must also be grounded within the contexts of both the designer and the designed. How do we engage ethical and moral issues of consensus, collaboration, or responsible design decisions? What is the role of ethos in making choices when designing spaces? What is the meaning and role of the designer as *being in service?* This requires understanding the roles of all involved from a perspective of the underlying values governing how people contribute to the choices being made. When it comes to the designers' role as being in service, Harold Nelson and Erik Stolterman state in their seminal book *The Design Way* (2003):

> Artists express their passions, feelings, and understandings of the world out of their own need for self-expression. Their gift is that these insights are shared with audiences who can then make what they will of these personal glimpses into the human condition. The designer, on the other hand, is not self-serving, but *other-serving.* . . . Being in service does not mean being a servant, nor a subservant. . . . It just means that self-expression is not dominant in a design relationship, as it is in the traditions of science and art.

The acknowledgment of a service relationship means that there is a certain responsibility attached to how the designer makes choices, both in how people will live, work, or play, and within what types of spaces these might occur. When designing various spaces, designers create places of living, working, and being in different spatial forms whether interior or exterior, real or virtual, intimate or urban. This is ideally done within the context of an ethical service-oriented relationship in one form or another (Nelson & Stolterman, 2003; Vaikla-Poldma, 2003).

Toward a Collective and Responsible Ethics of Community

This chapter explores the spaces of human social sustainability within a broader and more theoretical context, as these concepts relate directly to values and ethics, and to the changing consciousness of world issues. Paul Hawken (2007) has suggested that in recent years, in part due to new technologies and depleting natural resources, individuals and collective communities have arisen to voice their discontent about the world and unsustainable practices, and those speaking out are part of a movement of change. He suggests that there is a shift developing, wherein emerging sustainable issues are parts of an ethical and holistic being that is collectively challenging a priori assumptions about the world. In his seminal book *Blessed Unrest*, Hawken explains how we might envision this emergence in a metaphor and explains that we are all one in terms of how we live globally. According to Hawken, our world is expanding exponentially and with this, serious considerations are emerging and:

> the movement for equity and environmental sustainability comes as global conditions are changing dramatically and becoming more demanding. We are the first generation to witness a doubling of the population in our lifetime. . . . Every week, 1.4 million people pour into the world's slums to join a metastatic mass of squatters. (2007, pp. 12–14)

Hawken makes some powerful statements that reflect emerging ethical issues of our planet and how what is meaningful to people—what is important to them—plays a major role in determining choices to be made. Juxtapose this concept against the idea of the design as being in service and we begin to understand the necessity for critical design and critical design thinking as an emergent foundational value for the uncovering of ethical and sustainable spaces needed for people and their lived experiences.

Design Thinking, Ethics, and Sustainability

In his influential book *Design Futuring* (2009), Tony Fry reflects on how sustainability, ethics, and new practices must drive the ways that designers consider sustaining an ethical future. He suggests that we must continue to uncover the issues that are driving false ideas about what constitutes sustainability, and how this concept of sustainability places the crisis of natural resource depletion and increasing population in context with current political and economic realities. He suggests that designers can act as a vital and democratic "agent of sustainability" (p. 9). Fry unpacks several issues about the designer, the design act, and problems of the concept of sustainability itself, and suggests that the very terms *sustainable* and *sustainability* have become mired in "rhetoric [that] poses 'sustainability' as a realizable condition gained through the convergence of environmental, social and economic action"(p. 44). He proposes that changes are inevitable and necessary and provides case studies that support ideas of creating sustainment through the democratization of design (pp. 44–49). As Fry suggests, using design as a transformative tool is very complex and difficult, as terms imply meanings that have political and economic implications as much as social ones.

This chapter explores how collective action and ethics can frame the ways that we can make meaning for sustainable spaces. First, we will explore the ideas of collective agency and collaborative practices. Jill Franz et al. examine the new spaces of collective activism, and how design motivations and intentions play out in ethical and sustainable approaches and in design decision making. Franz proposes a collective engagement in designing housing and describes a case study illustrating how design-led activism provides the catalyst for collective engagement for people with disabilities in the creation of social housing.

We then turn to a provocation by Lisa Tucker, who asks fundamental questions about what spaces we chose to design and how we choose to behave in a sustainable—or non-sustainable—approach. She questions to what extent we really know how design affects the planet. The answers are not so simple.

Finally, in Dialogues and Perspectives we contrast two viewpoints on sustainable practices that account for the realities of real-world practices and the issue of ethical choices. First, we return to Harold Nelson for a second installment of our conversation, this time examining the meaning of ethics in the eyes of the working designer. What is the role of the designer as being in service and the role of ethos in designing our lived spaces? We contrast this view with a perspective in practice, in conversation with the international design firm Perkins + Will (USA). Janice Barnes, Peter Syrett, Chris Youseff, and Carolyn Roose discuss their firm's 2009 initiative "The Precautionary List," the work of an inter-disciplinary team composed of researchers, designers, architects, and principals. We have a conversation about the future of design as manifested in both research and collective business strategic decision making.

REFERENCES

Barnes, J. (2011). Personal communication to Tiiu Poldma. February 5, 2011.

Fry, T. (2009). *Design Futuring: Sustainability, Ethics, and New Practice.* Sydney, Australia: University of New South Wales Press.

Hawken, P. (2007). *Blessed Unrest.* New York: Penguin Group.

McDonough, W. & Baungart, M. (2002). *Cradle-to-Cradle: Remaking the Way We Make Things.* New York: North Point Press.

Nelson, H., & Stolterman, E. (2003). *The Design Way: Intentional Change in an Unpredictable World.* Englewood Cliffs, NJ: Educational Technology Publications.

Recognizing the complexity of contemporary issues, organizations increasingly utilize the collaborative effort of individuals and groups (Martin-Rodriguez et al. 2005). However, this appears to be confined to those sectors that have the resources (financial and otherwise) for attracting and sustaining diverse groups of specialists. Of course, complex problems exist everywhere; a reality well known to community-based not-for-profit organizations attempting with limited resources to deal everyday with highly complex social issues such as homelessness, unemployment, and disability, to mention but a few. In addition to service provision, these organizations are being increasingly faced with the need to be involved in research and advocacy (Ansari & Phillips, 2001, p. 354).

Formation of a Collective

Several months ago three organizations formed a collective with the goal of collaboratively developing a more independent and inclusive housing model for people with disabilities and their families. The organizations include a not-for-profit community group (the housing provider and builder—Kyabra); Queensland University Technology, a local university undertaking research and development for the project (QUT); and an advocacy arm of the professional body, the Design Institute of Australia (DIA), coordinating design services such as interior design, industrial design, graphic design, architecture, and landscape architecture, as well as other specialist consultants such as engineers, occupational therapists, and lawyers. Apart from the community group employees, all members and contributors participate on a voluntary pro bono basis.

As illustrated in Figure 11.1, each organization has its own membership of other organizations, departments, and individuals. In terms of the community organization, there is a service arm as well as a social enterprises arm charged with developing and maintaining financially sustainable enterprise businesses and activities that contribute to the overall vision and strategic objectives of the community organization. As a whole, the organization is committed to providing socially just services to enable the sustainable development of individuals, families, communities, and organizations. This is in accordance with its vision of fair, sustainable communities that instill hope, embrace diversity, and promote safety, and in which all people feel a sense of belonging. Values and beliefs explicitly proclaimed by the organization include social justice, respect, cultural recognition, belonging,

Figure 11.1 Collective Structure

participation and inclusion, self-determination, hope, strengths, collaboration, innovation, and accountability.

The Independent Living Project and the Formation of a Collective

The social enterprises arm undertakes activities that contribute to the financial viability of the association as well as producing positive social outcomes. One such activity has to do with property acquisition, the goals of which are affordable social housing, disability accessible housing, and contribution to the financial sustainability of the parent organization. The independent living project forming the focus for the collective arose from acknowledgment of the need of families with an adult son or daughter with a disability to obtain secure, long-term accommodation and support options for their family member. In this respect, there are two components to the project: (1) working with families to explore their hopes and investigate different models and (2) realizing the option once it has been identified. This is the basis upon which the collective was formed.

The vision of the collective is a best practice model of collaboration involving professionals, institutions, community organizations, and people with disabilities and their families to develop environments that advance practices of Universal Design and the right of people with a disability to fully participate in the community. The aim of the collective is to provide a world's best-practice model of Universal Design and Adaptability that is the impetus and basis for government and community to enact their hopes for an inclusive society enshrined in Human Rights and Disability legislation worldwide. The collective will work to achieve this through the development of a process and model of housing design and development that is collaborative, innovative, affordable, and environmentally sustainable.

The family clients, community-support personnel, material and equipment suppliers, and various funding bodies ranging from philanthropic organizations to government departments and banks represent the community group in the project. There are also specialist support people responsible for administration, accounting, occupational therapy, access and mobility, building certification, and town planning.

With respect to the university there are several participants: there is the university representative and research leader, a research assistant, PhD students embedded in the project focusing on various aspects of the project such as policy and design, the university ethics committee as well as its corporate and commercial services departments, the latter which primarily manage issues to do with intellectual property. The inclusion of a research group highlights the speculative and exploratory nature of the project and associated requirements of criticality, rigor, and ethical conduct. In addition, it plays an integral role in recording, reporting, and disseminating process and outcomes, in the process making its

contribution to knowledge accessible and open to critical scrutiny.

The design manager represents the Design Action group in coordinating the contribution of the various design groups as well as external consultants. A project manager at the heart of the collective manages the project and the three organizations. All the individuals and groups mentioned including the client families are considered active members of the collective. In accordance with a hybrid consensus design process developed by (Authors, 2004), it is considered highly important to include the client families (also users), consultants, and others involved throughout the design process as their involvement leads to more positive outcomes (Ansari & Phillips, 2001; Day, 2003), symbolizing in the process the community organization's, and the collective's vision of an inclusive society.

Due to the paucity of research involving collaboration in pro bono situations, research informing the project and this paper on the formation of the collective has been substantially informed by the research on interprofessional collaboration in the institutional health-care sector. Even here, researchers note deficiencies and limitations, particularly in relation to the motivations and intentions of those undertaking collaborative work.

As highlighted by Rocha and Miles (2009), mainstream approaches to collaboration in organizations and across organizations are understood to be driven by self-interest and the challenge of developing cooperative behavior out of self-interest. In an attempt to go beyond this and develop and sustain collaborative capabilities in interorganizational communities, they argue that human nature has the potential to consider the "other" as well as the "self." With a similar focus on intention and motivation, this paper uses the collaborative project just described to more fully understand the nature of the collective as a basis for creative practice and political activism and the theoretical implications and wider application in terms of emerging research in the area of collaborative entrepreneurship and design activism. In terms of design activism, Fuad-Luke (2009), like Rocha and Miles (2009), identifies a lack of understanding in current literature about the intentions and motivations of those involved in collective practice. The study described in this paper actively seeks to address this through the application of grounded theory methodology, establishing the basis for the development of a motivational framework.

The Collective: Formation and Articulation

Based on the work of Drinka (1994), D'Amour et al. (2005) highlights how groups go through five main stages of development: the forming stage where the group is beginning to establish itself; the norming stage where norms, patterns of behavior, and expectations are identified and developed; the confronting stage where team members come together and learn more about each other; the performing stage where they work on the issue or project at hand; and the dissolution stage where team members leave. At this time of writing, the group was experiencing the first four stages, highlighting that the stages are not necessarily consecutive but in fact iterative. In addition, the process revealed strong accord with various dimensions of a process of collaboration developed by D'Amour (1997); namely, a finalization dimension involving the explication of shared goals, recognition of divergent motives, multiple allegiances, and expectations regarding collaboration; an interiorisation dimension where a sense of belonging and trust develops through an awareness of the professionals' interdependency and of the need to manage this interdependency; a formalization dimension where protocols and procedures are developed and set in place; and a governance and leadership dimension giving explicit attention to expertise and connectivity (in D'Amour et al. 2005, p. 123).

Goals of the Collective

As our group started to form, the need to understand it in order to guide its formation and management became increasingly apparent. While a fundamental aspect of this was identifying a shared vision and goals as pointed out above, it also involved working out the type of group we had started to become, wanted to be, and could be. Given our philosophical and substantive focus on inclusion, we very early established the need for the group to be a holistic entity operating in a synergistic way producing outcomes that would be more than an aggregate of parts. In this respect, then, the labels of partnership, team, network, or coalition seemed to fall short of encapsulating the full meaning of what was possible and necessary for our group.

In addition to being an interprofessional, interorganizational, and intersectoral entity (Axelsson & Axelsson, 2009), the group could also be characterized in terms of the relationship between the disciplines. For example, questions were asked as to whether it was to operate as a multidisciplinary group where different professional subgroups work essentially independently but in a coordinated way, or as an interdisciplinary group where there is greater integration and sharing of knowledge and professional responsibility and the potential for enhanced cohesion (D'Amour et al. 2005, p. 120). Given its holistic and synergistic aspirations, and acceptance of a consensus design process, the goal of the group was for the disciplinary relationships to be transdisciplinary involving where possible an opening up and blurring of professional boundaries with the view of developing new knowledge that transcends individual discipline or professional ownership.

It was obvious early on that the scale of the project demanded a complex and adaptive system (Souhbi et al., 2009) and that in effect a new form of community was emerging; a community that had the potential (perhaps, even, obligation) to be a learning organization in its own right, and that through its mandate for social change was also fundamentally an activist group. In this respect, then, and for the

time being, the group was comfortable with the notion of itself as a collective.

Operating as a Collective

Given the above understanding of our group, one of the main aspects to address, as noted generally by various researchers such as Soubhi et al. (2009), was how to transcend professional boundaries in order to integrate distinct professional and disciplinary activities and foster collective capability. In this respect, specific attention had to be given to how members would learn through adaptation, a process involving balancing not only what they know but also what they would be doing collectively (Souhbi et al., 2009, pp. 52–53). An added complexity was how they would do this through the limited time available outside their full-time jobs. As noted by Souhbi et al. (2009), even in situations such as hospitals where professionals are engaging regularly in conversations about their practice, the processes of building knowledge and adjusting practices are severely challenged. In response and in line with Fraser and Greenhalgh (2001), they propose developing an appreciation of the community of interacting professionals as a complex adaptive system where the interdependent parts integrate to form an emergent structure that cannot be predicted from the parts; one where, subsequently, it is essential to give particular attention to the competence, capability, and values of the professionals involved. In terms of values, Soubhi et al. (2009) give emphasis to the relational value of caring for patients with the knowledge value of practice, reinforcing the view of other researchers such as Gilbert (2005) that "improvements in both values are more likely when care is patient-centered, when professionals value the creation and sharing of knowledge, and when their learning activities are geared closely to their needs and interests" (p. 54). Implicated in this is the significance of reflection and of "making visible the group's explicit and tacit knowledge" (p. 54).

Overall, Soubhi et al. (2009) propose that organizing what professionals do requires an understanding of the human as well as organizational factors that facilitate collective work and learning (p. 55). While technical skills are important, so too are emotional factors as well as various ethical and moral factors such as altruism, reciprocity, equity, and fairness (p. 55). Organizationally, attention has to be given to the structure of practice that best aligns and supports these values, possibly one of a continuum ranging from centralized control through to a fattened hierarchy characterized by decentralized communication and coordination, trust, and openness to experimentation (Souhbi et al., 2009, p. 55). For Souhbi et al. (2009), fundamentally what is required is "a balance between head and heart, cognitive and non-cognitive abilities, technical skills and insightful compassion, system design and ethical dimensions of professional practice," the synthesis of which will more likely enable professionals to address the challenging problems of everyday practice (p. 56).

Providing further information on facilitating collective action is earlier research by Martin-Rodriguez et al. (2005), who make the statement that collective action "requires that the parties forego a competitive approach and adopt one based on collaboration" (p. 133), something that, they argue, is more likely to happen when explicit attention is given to interpersonal relationships between professionals (interactional determinants), the organizational context (organizational determinants), and the organization's external environment (systemic determinants). In terms of the latter, these are components of social (for example, social status and stereotyping relating closely to issues of equality/inequality), cultural (for instance, professional values that advocate for autonomy and are therefore in contradiction of the sentiments of inclusion and collaboration), professional (professional organizations implicitly supporting domination and control as opposed to collegiality and trust), and educational systems (occupying a significant position in educating—or not educating—for collaborative practice). With respect to the organizational context, determinants include the structure of the group (with greater support for horizontal structures) and its philosophy (particularly one that values participation, fairness, freedom of expression, and interdependence), resources (especially the availability of time and spaces to meet), and administrative support available to the group to support practice and convey the vision of collaborative practice, as well as mechanisms for communication in and coordination of the group (of significance here being the formalization of rules and procedures, and opportunities for all professionals and participants to meet). Interactional determinants such as willingness to collaborate, trust, mutual respect, and communication skills are also considered significant in facilitating successful collective action (Martin-Rodriguez et al. 2005, pp.134–142).

As highlighted above, literature on interprofessional collaboration gives substantial emphasis to human and relational values. In the health-care context from which the literature is drawn, one of the main barriers to sustaining collaboration is the professional boundary and an inability by professionals to see beyond self-interest and even be willing to give up a part of one's territory if necessary (Axelsson & Axelsson 2009, p. 324). For Axelsson and Axelsson this is exacerbated by the structure of the group. In the case of our collective project, the structure that has emerged due to its complexity and the number of professionals and stakeholders involved demands what Axelsson and Axelsson would describe as a high degree of both vertical and horizontal integration, with integration sought through a combination of coordination and collaboration. Labeled a matrix structure, Axelsson and Axelsson describe how it often leads to conflicting demands and expectations, creates double loyalties, and can contribute to rather than overcome territoriality (p. 324). As a response to this they suggest exploring the concept of altruism as an alternative; altruism being based on a concern for others and for society as a whole and understood as the "ability to transcend and sacrifice

particular interests for a common purpose" (Krebs & Miller, 1985, in Axelsson & Axelsson, 2009, p. 324).

In understanding how this might be addressed and actioned in the project, our research turned to the work of Rocha and Miles (2009) in the area of humanistic management and collaborative entrepreneurship. They argue that "in order to develop and sustain collaborative capabilities in inter-organizational communities, a set of assumptions that takes both self-regarding and others'-regarding preferences as ends is required to avoid any kind of instrumentalization of collaboration, which is an end in itself" (p. 457). Despite the fact that all participants in the project had volunteered their services and were undoubtedly driven by altruistic goals, articles such as that by Rocha and Miles (2009) and Ansari and Phillips (2001) prompted us to consider that these may not be the only goals, and that a motivational framework should be developed that recognizes a range of motivations and seeks to address the needs of its members while at the same time contributing to successful outcomes for the project and the collective as a whole. In terms of design activism, Fuad-Luke (2009), like Rocha and Miles (2009) and Ansari and Phillips (2001), identifies a lack of understanding in current literature about the intentions and motivations of those involved in collective practice recognizing that "personal motivation may embrace needs, desires, goals, a certain philosophical approach, or other intrinsic factors. Activities can also be driven by a strong sense of altruism or morality, aimed at delivering benefits for the greater societal good (although there may not be consensus on what this 'good' constitutes). Aside from these intrinsic factors, external circumstances can provide strong motivational forces" (p. 18).

Given the significant role of designers in this project, an empirical study was planned that would first externalize their intentions and motivations. This would then be followed by similar studies of all other participants. The following section reports on the findings for two groups of designers: the interior design group and the architecture group.

Designers' Motivations and Intentions

Data from the two design groups were collected via two focus groups, one for each discipline group. Each group involved approximately five to six participants. Using a semi-structured approach the members of each group were asked the same questions about their reasons for joining the collective, what they perceived as their contribution, and what they saw as challenges and benefits. The focus group interviews were recorded with the permission of group members and analyzed in accordance with Grounded Theory methodology, which involves the researcher working with the participants to actively construct the data and arrive at multiple levels of meaning (Charmaz 1995), an inclusive approach that aligns with the vision and mission of the collective. Specifically part of the data analysis, the analytical approach included open coding, involving categorization, and axial

coding, involving identification of relationships between categories. Given that the focus group interviews are yet to be finalized for other participant groups, selective coding analysis aimed at theory formation was not undertaken.

Data Analysis and Interpretation

Several categories emerged from the analysis in terms of the participants' motivation. A significant motivator for all participants was the opportunity for personal enjoyment, satisfaction, and spiritual growth reflected in the following extracts:

- Participate in something exciting and meaningful
- Be able to enjoy one's work and revitalize oneself
- Experience design/architecture in a more fundamental way
- Experience it as a journey—through immersion at various levels and looking at things from different angles
- Have the potential to grow it and take ownership
- Be involved in cutting-edge work
- Be accepted and considered as an equal despite extent of knowledge and experience—no experts, act on an equal basis
- Be part of an open-ended process where things are not defined at the start
- Have opportunities to push boundaries and challenge, opportunity for new experiences
- Experience something life changing and discipline changing, to be a part of pushing things further, reignite belief

in interior design—compliment the vacuous, to do something inspiring (creative potential)
- Get out of the rut, be less frustrated, fill the void, be liberated, step back
- Do something you actually *want* to do—not *have* to do as in paid work

Aligned with the above was the expectation for professional growth involving the opportunity to learn more about the role of research in design and to do research, to have an introduction to academia and how it operates, to learn by doing and by participating with all involved, with all stakeholders, by getting it out there, and to integrate the theoretical and the practical. In addition, participants identified developing networks, consolidating skills (communication and collaborative skills), enhancing career development, learning the language of design, and learning more as reasons to be involved. Some participants also highlighted a social dimension in their desire to be a part of a group, of belonging to a group that was pushing things further.

The above are reasons for involvement based on personal goals and satisfaction; however, participants are also motivated altruistically to contribute to the community and society including their own profession. Responses include the following:

- Do something positive, to help others, to give back to the community.
- Be proactive, to contribute something of value, do something genuine.
- Provide some balance to a mainly nongenuine world.
- Walk the talk.

- Raise the profile of the profession and the activist role of design.

In terms of what they could contribute, participants cite the following cognitive and emotive contributions:

- Complementing the range of skills, knowledge (content and procedural), and experiences—generic as well as discipline specific, for example, good listening skills, guidance regarding best practice, specific knowledge in the area, younger/fresher views, knowledge that is transferable, personal experience of having a sibling with a disability
- Empathy, enthusiasm, passion, energy, open minded, not blinkered

Challenges in the Work of the Collective

The main external challenges to realizing their goals, and that of the collective, include the following:

- Time
- Flow of communication through the group without too much structure
- Communication with other design teams
- Creating and maintaining a non-threatening environment
- Maintaining equality and equity
- Working with different levels of age, skill, and experience

Following are some of the internal personal and professional challenges:

- Lack of experience
- Preventing your input from being diluted

- Maintaining ownership
- Being interdisciplinary and, at the same time, maintaining professional deference
- Making expertise available to the group
- Dealing with new processes such as research and contexts such as academia
- Dealing with preconceptions about the other design disciplines
- Throwing off past behaviors
- Having an open mind in a new way
- Enjoying the process of working together
- Understanding your place in the group
- Dealing with prejudgments
- Maintaining energy
- Having fun with the group
- Managing the personal commitment

Discussion

Overall, these responses appear to support the theories proposed by McAdam et al., 2001, in Thorpe (2008) as to why people decide to participate in collective action. They are as follows:

- Resource mobilization/mobilizing structures: People participate in social movements when organizations and individuals step forward to mobilize resources on behalf of a cause.
- Political opportunity: People participate in social movements when viable opportunities appear.
- Collective action frames/collective identity: People participate in social movements because of the way the issues and actors are framed culturally and emotionally by the movement and because participants in movements can help frame issues and actors.
- Social paradigm: People participate in social movements because they are concerned about the greater good. (pp. 4–5)

The responses also point to a visionary type of desired change—one that is about looking forward and inventing new visions, in this case, of more inclusive housing for people with disabilities, which then becomes the demonstration artifact of what is better (Thorpe 2008, p. 5). While this should not be surprising given that designing by definition is about imagining new or alternative scenarios, the business reality of design and architectural practice often means that profit is put before, or seriously impinges on, concerns for human welfare. As pointed out by Collier (2006), "empathy between end-users and architects is an essential but not always realized part of morality in architecture ... and when extended more widely than a given situation, may lead architects to question the social, political and ecological contexts of their work and thus motivate them to prioritize the 'ethical' in all the choices they make" (p. 307). For the designers involved in the collective, it appears that the project, in contrast to their paid employment, enables them to more fully exercise "moral imagination" and be more faithful to their mandate of creating appropriate places and contexts of social life, the purpose of which is by definition ethical (Collier 2006, p. 307).

Added to this, it seems, is the opportunity to more fully realize "interdependence, affiliation and the quality of the human and communal relationships" such as trust, integrity, and concern for others (Collier 2006, p. 310). In this sense, then, it is important to be aware of how the project provides for "good" practice and a context of and for communal "flourishing" (Collier 2006, p. 310). The responses for the interior design and architecture groups also highlight how the participants have been drawn together by common challenges, opportunities to "develop and share the capacity to create and use knowledge" (Collier 2006, p. 310) and a passion to make a difference in people's lives at a fundamental level.

Acknowledging and Addressing Intentions and Motivations

This section draws together the findings of the empirical study with the literature in an attempt to develop a conceptual base for acknowledging and addressing the intentions and motivations of the project participants. Design is the central mechanism to this conceptual base. According to Fuad-Luke (2009), "design is already 'activated' in trying to address contemporary issues" (p. 20) albeit that "while it is acknowledged as a powerful communicative force it has failed to communicate its own social and environmental ambitions to society and so remains perceived as merely a servant to powerful economic imperatives" (p. 50). As identified through the focus groups, the project offers participants a way of actively countering a "history of egoism" (Fuad-Luke 2009) and of undertaking a journey that is personally transformational, as well as contributing to a greater social good.

In this respect, then, it makes sense to invite participants to focus on design and collaboratively explore how the project can capitalize on its moral and creative potential. "Moral deliberation is exploratory when it reflects on situational possibilities; artistic reflection is investigative when it suggests design and enactment possibilities"—both are forms of creative self-expression (Collier 2006, p. 314). This can be facilitated through keeping at the forefront of the participants' consciousness the vision and values of the collective and the need for empathy for all involved. In part this can be supported through the provision for dialogue, sharing points of view, recognizing what each member brings to the project, and generally developing a context that promotes and sustains belonging and trust (D'Amour et al. 2005). For individuals and their personal growth, there is the need for a clear idea of purpose and intention and critical and creative self-reflection involving individual and collective intentions and outcomes and assessment of outcomes with intentions (Collier 2006; Fuad-Luke 2009). Such considerations can be further supported and facilitated through the design of effective management, operational, and governance processes including behavioral protocols, formalization of rules, and the provision of resources and services that support the members and assist in the design and operation of collaboration, induction, and training (Rocha & Miles, 2009) as well as the explication and dissemination of shared goals and knowledge. In part, this is being addressed in our current project through the development of a website as well as an in-house repository.

In all, there is need for intentions and motivations to be externalized and articulated, for the human as well as the organizational factors to be addressed, and for recognition of divergent motives, multiple allegiances, and expectations (D'Amour et al., 2005). For our project, this has been addressed through the formal inclusion of research—of our collective practice as well as of the substantive issues of the project. In summary, adopting an all inclusive action research ethos incorporating various research projects using different methodological lenses aids in the externalization and documentation of the process; invites experimentation, critical exploration, and rigor; enables generic skill development; makes visible explicit and tacit knowledge as well as intentions and motivations (as exemplified in this paper); and reminds us continuously of our ethical roles and obligations.

Conclusion

In conclusion, this project responds to several deficiencies noted in literature, namely, the absence of a user perspective in interprofessional collaboration; the lack of empirical data providing a finer grain understanding of the relationship between systemic, interorganizational and interactional determinants; and the lack of a motivational framework for interprofessional, interorganizational, and intersectoral collaboration. While the study is currently limited by its focus on a small group of designers, it does demonstrate the relevance of interprofessional collaborative theory for the pro bono sector and the potential of design activism to address potential conflict between self-regarding interests and other-regarding interests (Rocha & Miles, 2009).

Discussion Questions

1. Explore the ways that the designers worked with the various stakeholders to collectively engage in the design project.

2. What were the designers' motivations and intentions?

3. How is this interdisciplinarily and collectively a sustaining project for the people who will live within the housing project?

References

Ansari, W., & Phillips, C. (2001). Inter-professional Collaboration: A Stake-holder Approach to Evaluation of Voluntary Participation in Community Partnerships. *Journal of Interprofessional Care, 15*(4), 351–368.

Axelsson, S., & Axelsson, R. (2009). From Territoriality to Altruism in Interprofessional Collaboration and Leadership. *Journal of Interprofessional Care, 23*(4), 320–330.

Charmaz, K. (1995). Grounded Theory. In J. A. Smith, R. Harre, & L. V. Langenhove (Eds.), *Rethinking Methods in Psychology*. London: Sage.

Collier, J. (2006). The Art of Moral Imagination: Ethics in the Practice of Architecture. *Journal of Business Ethics, 66*, 307–317.

D'Amour, D. (1997). *Structuration de la collaboration interprofessionnelle dans les services de santé de premiere ligne au Quebec*. These de doctorat. Universite de Montreal, Montreal, Québec, Canada.

D'Amour, D., Ferrada-Videla, M., Martin-Rodriguez, L., & Beaulieu, M. (2005). The Conceptual Basis for Interprofessional Collaboration: Core Concepts and Theoretical Frameworks. *Journal of Interprofessional Care, 1*, 116–131.

Day, C. (2003). *Consensus Design*. Oxford, UK: Architectural Press.

Drinka, T. (1994). Interdisciplinary Geriatric Teams: Approaches to Conflict as Indicators of Potential to Model Teamwork. *Educational Gerontology, 20*, 87–103.

Fuad-Luke, A. (2009). *Design Activism*. London: Earthscan.

Freeth, D. (2001). Sustaining Interprofessional Collaboration. *Journal of Interprofessional Care, 15*(1), 37–46.

Gilbert, J. (2005). Interprofessional Education for Collaborative Patient-Centred Care. *Nursing Leadership, 18*, 32–38.

McAdam, D., Tarrow, S., & Till, C. (2001). *Dynamics of Contention*. Cambridge: Cambridge University Press.

Martin-Rodriguez, L., Beaulieu, M., D'Amour, D. & Ferrada-Videla, M. (2005). The Determinants of Successful Collaboration: A Review of Theoretical and Empirical Studies. *Journal of Interprofessional Care, 1*, 132–147.

Rocha, H. & Miles, R. (2009). A Model of Collaborative Entrepreneurship for a More Humanistic Management. *Journal of Business Ethics, 88*, 445–462.

Soubhi, H., Colet, N., Gilbert, J., Lebel, P., Thivierge, R., Hudon, C. & Fortin, M. (2009). Interprofessional Learning in the Trenches: Fostering Collective Capability. *Journal of Interprofessional Care, 23*(1), 52–57.

Soubhi, H. (2007). The Greatest Challenge of Interprofessional Education. *Network Toward Unity for Health, 26*(14).

Thorpe, A. (2008). *Design as Activism*. Milton Keynes, UK: The Open University.

Note: The authors of the paper wish to thank the participants of the study and acknowledge the support and endorsement of Kyabra, QUT, and DIA.

This article was originally presented as a paper at the Alternative Practices in Design Symposium, Melbourne, Australia, July, 9, 2010. We acknowledge RMIT Design Research Institute and RMIT Design Archives, the conveners of the symposium, and thank them for their permission to publish the paper in this book.

11.2 Living Our World
Lisa M. Tucker

It is incumbent upon designers to learn how human design can work within the world habitat. This essay explores the need to design in a way that human habitats can be sustained for years to come. We are at a crossroads in our evolution and have begun to damage our ecosystems beyond what they can handle. It is our ethical responsibility as designers to design only that which works in harmony with the world.

It is a well-known fact among biologists that a species that destroys is own ecosystem will go extinct. We are in the process of destroying not only our own ecosystem but also that of many other species—plant and animal. As I wrote these thoughts, we were experiencing what may be the single worst man-made disaster in our history—the Gulf oil spill, courtesy of British Petroleum (BP) in the USA. We will not know the full impact of this disaster for decades, but the immediate consequences seem dire.

Mankind requires shelter from the elements. Early on in this pursuit of shelter, man also expressed the need for meaning through building, as evidenced by the pyramids, cathedrals, and stone formations around the world. Over time, we have come to believe it is our due as a species to build wherever and whatever we want for a variety of purposes. We are exhausting our natural resources in the pursuit of man-

made goods and materials. We are polluting our skies and waters. Any number of websites, books, conferences, and other media attest to these facts. As design professionals, we are amongst the guiltiest of parties because we contribute to the consumptive nature of our society. It is hard to veer from the current course and question all that we do. Yet we claim we protect the health, safety, and welfare of the public. Isn't it, therefore, our ethical responsibility to challenge design and designers to work within the ecosystems in which we find ourselves?

Waste and disregard for resources begins early in our design education. How many among us has built a model—out of foam core no less—only to later throw it out? How many sheets of mat board, foam core, balsa wood, and other materials have we been responsible for during the four or five years of our education? As teachers, do we ask ourselves before we make an assignment that uses these valuable resources: How many of us really apply recycle, reuse, and reduction when it comes to a school project? Or in our real lives?

This process is continued throughout the life of the professional. How many offices throw away boxes of samples each year? How many manufacturers request their outdated samples be returned? How many reams or rolls of paper does an average office expend during the course of a year?

Furthermore, we do this so we can achieve things for our clients such as building the tallest building in the world. How many termites do you suppose are running around saying "my termite mound is bigger than yours"?

So, what can we do? How can we change course? It has always been the job of the designer to educate the client. Perhaps it is time for us to educate ourselves and fully reevaluate our position on materials and resources, the reasons for building, and our professional position with regard to all of these complicated issues. Only then can we hope to educate a client. We must engage with complexity and unanswerable questions to even begin to tackle the paradigm shift required to rethink humans' relationship with the built environment. What do we truly need? What can we do without and not feel deprived? How do other species cope? The advent of **biomimicry** and **biophilic design** begins to answer some of these questions. **Cradle to cradle** is a proposal that challenges us with a new design assignment (McDonough & Braungart, 2002). Biomimicry looks to nature as a model. Biophilia asks us as designers to look to nature for answers. Perhaps our own consciences can challenge us to ask whether we need to build a particular project at all.

Reference

McDonough, W. & Braungart, M. (2002). *Cradle to Cradle: Remaking the Way We Make Things*. New York: North Point Press.

Dialogues and Perspectives

11.3 Ethics and Design: Issues in Practice
Harold Nelson and Janice Barnes with Peter Syrett,
Chris Youssef, (Perkins + Will), and Carolyn Roose

In this Dialogues and Perspectives, we pull together concepts of ethics, sustainability, and collaborative practices in the context of the real world. We examine ethics in the context of business practices in conversation with Harold Nelson to understand the relative contexts and goals of business against issues of ethics and intention. We then examine the ways that architectural practice might consider how ethical choices in interior spaces are put into practice in a firm, promoting sustainable choices as a foundational component the material choices made in the production of design projects, in conversation with Janice Barnes, Peter Syrett, Chris Youseff, and Carolyn Roose of Perkins + Will.

Perspective I: Dialogue with Harold Nelson

As we continue the second part of our conversation with Harold Nelson, we discuss issues of ethics and intention in the context of business goals, goals that are often economic. Harold Nelson suggests that we must, as designers, have accountability and understand that the people we design for are real and subjective people. Consequently, design must be in sync with broader goals of ethics accountability as the counterpoint to business practices.

Harold Nelson: We cannot treat another individual as a means only, in the Kantian sense. Think about the example of the use of placebos in medical science, as opposed to real medicine. When you experiment with a placebo the individual people are treated as objects, set up as merely a means to an end that is not found within themselves. This is why action research is risky. In action research, when using real people in real situations, there is little or no accountability to the individual as an end, unless this is situated in ethical transparency.

Think about business and the bottom line. An example is housing, when this is framed as a business venture played out through real estate development and developer's business interests. In terms of ethics, business too often still runs on the Darwinian model of survival of the fittest. Whatever survives in the market place is considered to be a good product or service. In business, ethical issues are thus removed unless they make good business sense, since business has its natural checks and balances.

Generally, designing in the context of business, as for example web design or industrial design, focuses on doing what the company wants done, although to some extent, the designers may be forced to respond to public welfare and safety standards, such as code requirements for accessibility in building construction, standards for development of drug safeguards and automobile crash ratings, etc.—i.e., governmental intervention. Design activity does not typically revolve around professional codes of behavior. Some professional associations do adhere to professional and ethical codes of conduct when they are of a certain self-reflective level of development, but such codes are primarily meant to influence and not control the conduct of designers working for business interests.

On the business side, design is emerging as a tool for management. If you enter a web search for *managing as designing*, you will find a number of authorities on this burgeoning concept, such as a book edited by Boland and Collopy (2004) titled *Managing as Designing*—on how design thinking and methods can improve management and managers by shifting the focus from management as a science to management as a type of designing.

When designers successfully become part of the decision-making process in business, government and other types of social institutions, then there is a substantial change in creative thinking and innovative action and this is positive. . . . the most successful leaders are designers by definition.

Perspective II: Conversation with Peter Syrett, Chris Youseff, and Carolyn Roose, Perkins + Will, New York City, USA

We now turn to an example of practices incorporating this type of thinking

with our second conversation with Peter Syrett, Chris Youseff, and Carolyn Roose of the New York City-based internationally renowned architectural firm Perkins + Will. I spoke to Janice Barnes of Perkins + Will, who introduced me to her team. They have developed their "Precautionary List" of materials and a way of reconceptualizing the material choices made in the composite of space we live and work within interior spaces. Their list is an open-source resource that provides hard-hitting data about the materials we use in our interior spaces and the impact of carcinogens on our quality of life, and how the choices we make are intrinsically tied to ethics.

An example of forward-thinking designing for interior environments is the work of the international architecture/design firm Perkins + Will (USA). Peter Syrett, Chris Youseff, and Carolyn Roose discuss their 2009 initiative the Precautionary List, the work of an interdisciplinary team composed of researchers, designers, architects, interdisciplinary specialists, and principals at the design firm.

Tiiu Poldma: In listening to your backgrounds and expertise, it seems to me that Perkins + Will combines (and is concerned about) how to successfully integrate business strategies and environment strategies with design. I have read your Precautionary List that you published on your website and am impressed with the work and research Perkins + Will has done. I would like to acknowledge that here is a large design-architecture firm taking a stand to move this kind of necessary thinking forward. In light of your business strategies, what are the reasons Perkins + Will created the Precautionary List?

Peter Syrett: Let's begin with the reason for and the genesis of the Precautionary List. Chris [Youseff] and I have had a long interest and passion for issues of sustainability. We have been wrestling for a long time with how material issues impact on the environment. For example, in 2002 we were designing a cancer centre. We naively thought we could design a place that was carcinogen-free. We found out very quickly not only was this audacious and difficult, but this work went a long way to uncover latent health issues with materials and how these materials impact people and the environment.

Our research uncovered a lot of commonly used materials that are carcinogenic. We realized that there was a disconnect between the Hippocratic oath mandate to "do no harm" and the materials being used in buildings. In other words, a building's design approach needed to align at every level with the health mission of an organization in order to be successful. This simple realization opened our eyes to the need to better understand what buildings are composed of.

The reason for the research: In this opaque world, there is no tool to guide the public in understanding what the materials are made of and their potential health impacts. Here at Perkins + Will, we created the Precautionary List as an open source, to open the discourse and gather knowledge. This is the tip of the iceberg. We want to share with peers and influence how business is done. We want to work with the manufacturers and people involved in the built environment to bring it in line with healthy and sustainable environments. Buildings are instruments of public health—the built environment affects us from the exterior to the interior.

Through our research, we also discovered that the indoor environment is polluted on a molecular level. The statistics in the United States bear this out. First, here in the U.S. the Environmental Protection Agency (EPA) states that we spend 90 percent of our time indoors. Second, the Center for Disease Control (CDC) has published the statistic that approximately 25 percent of all U.S. housing units are unhealthy. There is clear quantifiable data on negative issues of the built environment.

Chris Youseff: I would add that making the issue even more complex is the fact that we are conversely increasing the energy efficiency of our buildings, and this is having a major impact on what the interior materials are doing to the interior environment.

As the interior designer here, I am very concerned about the coming together of two major issues. First, energy efficiency is driving the sealing of buildings to control energy and lower costs for the consumer/client.

Second, while we improve the interior in terms of energy performance, we are also sealing the interior and selecting materials where we do not know the impact on health and well-being. We do not know, for example, the effects of selected materials and what off-gassing occurs with materials, and the impact that has in a 10 foot x 10 foot sealed room.

The bigger problem then becomes that we are selecting materials without knowing their pollutant properties. If we identify what any material is made of and understand the impact of mixing various materials together, we can also see what impact this has on health and welfare.

Syrett: The impacts on health are enormous. The footprints are significant, in that we are not considering the impact of materials on people's health as we are designing. A closed room with no ventilation, for fresh air, is like the interior of an airplane. Both are tight spaces with a lot of synthetic materials that are constantly exposing occupants to numerous substances that are not comprehensively tested for their impact on human health. To date, there has not been significant research on the effects of these design decisions on health and welfare of people.

A Design Tool for Design Community

Poldma: Why did you choose the Precautionary Principle as your guide for this initiative? Can you elaborate about how you came to know about this principle and what this means for you?

Youseff: The Precautionary Principle Environmental movement is a sound principle we discovered through our research into materials and for approaching health issues.

We are neither scientists nor biologists; we are architects and designers— lay people in the world of science. When faced with a scientific uncertainty we looked at the Precautionary Principle as a guide that makes perfect sense for the design community.

Impossible to Navigate Waters with Certitude

Poldma: Would you suggest that designers and architects must be ethically responsible for choices we make?

Syrett: Yes absolutely. For example, as design professionals we have a professional and contractual responsibility to provide standards of care. We are responsible to ethically perform and assess the impact of all the decisions we make.

We also need to sit back and think about the greater good—actions individually add up to collective results. We need to understand that although one specified product may have a small impact, 100 people specifying the same product with small off-gasses, for example, creates a problem that becomes magnified, and if 1,000,000 people make this choice, then the problem is again exponentially magnified.

Youseff: It was in the interests of Perkins + Will to make the list public, to share with owners, students, clients and users— to create transparency and to develop this as the business concept of today and tomorrow.

We want to share in order to advance— [as for] competitive issues—there are none. We want and need everyone to embrace this. The good design principles are these principles of sustained choices for our lived environment.

Syrett: This level of thinking is holistic,

where we approach the design as an inter-disciplinary one and one that is empirical and data driven. We need to use knowledge and react to it. Environment is a part of our DNA and we need to really grasp what this means.

Poldma: How are you involved, Carolyn?

Carolyn Roose: Well, Peter and Chris are the drivers of the Precautionary List. My role is to mobilize and structure strategy, and how to implement the ideas.

Syrett: Carolyn provides us with health research on a wide range of topics, and she brings forward vital issues through her research. Her research and expertise helps to inform our thinking.

Poldma: So you use knowledge to help inform your thinking?

Syrett: Yes . . . Research is what the profession is about today. Without research design we cannot provide the solution that best suits the needs and circumstances of our clients. Different perspectives from both the interior designer and the architect provide different views, research completes the ideas with evidence-based and sound solutions; and from our client perspective, this adds the conscience for the client.

Youseff: Research is the future. Research is not yet a fundamental part of design but it is a necessary part. This becomes an education tool. Not every alternative exists; every space still needs to meet code requirements. In health care or signage there are certain requirements needed to get to certain rooms—sometimes not always an alternative. There is a black list of certain materials, and the choices made depend on adherence to this list, and the requirements, and learning to balance the two while putting pressure on [suppliers] to improve the material quality when it is not there.

Reference

Boland, R. J., Jr., and F. Collopy (Eds.). (2004). *Managing as Designing.* Stanford, CA: Stanford University Press.

Note: The authors are inspired by the Precautionary Principle, a general principle that the authors use in terms of guiding choices for prudent environmental decisions. This principle originated as a movement and its applications here is specifically applied to architecture and design. In this book it is referred to as an inspiration by the authors for prudent choices in architecture and design.

For specific definitions and additional references, refer to the principle and the Precautionary Principle Movement more specifically in environmental science and policy-making in Europe and the US.

SUMMARY

We can no longer ignore how collective agency, collaborative practices, interdisciplinary knowledge, and design knowledge all work together to provide meanings for sustainable and ethical spaces. Whether it is the individual designer making choices, collective agency at work, or world conditions driving practices, each is a type of what Melles and Feast noted in Chapter 9 as a form of a new "aesthetic of experience," where critical design empowers communities and embraces social change. As we have seen with Franz's case study, there is a potential for new ways of doing design where motivation and intention can be directed through interdisciplinary and cross-disciplinary work on community action. As Nelson, Perkins + Will, and Tucker all note, we cannot ignore the ethical and sustainable choices we must make for living in our world. While space is still the catalyst for the project, the ideas of what constitutes space become broader, supported by ethical choices, and encompassed by the actions of multiple actors working together to define the spaces of living in the community, living sustainably, and in devising ways to make choices that support collective values and diverse voices.

We return to the ideas of spaces and places as equal parts social and aesthetic, where the aesthetic is about experiences of places and not just the material elements. Embodied meaning includes the experience of, and sustainability of, the spaces created within the context of pragmatic realities of business and commerce.

ADDITIONAL READINGS

Kant, I. (1992). Critique of Judgement. In S. D. Ross (Ed.), *Art and Its Significance: An Anthology of Aesthetic Theory* (3rd ed.; pp. 95–142). Albany, NY: SUNY.

Fry, T. (2009). *Design Futuring: Sustainability, Ethics, and New Practice.* Sydney, Australia: University of New South Wales Press.

McDonough, W., & Baungart, M. (2002). Cradle to Cradle: Remaking the Way We Make Things (chaps. 1 and 2). New York: North Point Press.

OVERVIEW QUESTIONS FOR DISCUSSION

Drawing from Chapters 9 and 10, explore here in Chapter 11 the relationship between design thinking goals, business goals, and ethical goals as spaces of meaning. In discussion groups, explore the philosophy of Immanuel Kant as proposed by Harold Nelson, the new "design futuring" concepts of Tony Fry, and the conversations you have read in the Dialogues and Perspectives about how these ideas are put into practice by firms.

1. What is the Kantian sense of "an individual as a means" evoked by Harold Nelson?

2. Find examples in practice of efforts to both live sustainably and practice sustainable practices. Who and how are these practices happening and what actions are occurring to provide for the collective good?

3. Define the concept of "care" that is evoked in theory by both Fry and Nelson/Stolterman, and in the example of practices that Perkins + Will's design team discusses.

4. What are concepts of care from the perspective of spaces?

5. How do we include meanings of care in spaces of design that provide meaning and account for necessary choices of sustainability and what forms might this take?

6. How do Tony Fry and Harold Nelson discuss ideas about ethics and contexts?

    a. What are the ways we must re-materialize what we choose when making design decisions?
    b. What are design ethical and sustainable spaces of practice?
    c. How are ethical spaces to intersect with cultural, collaborative, and physical spaces?
    d. How do ethical spaces incorporate concepts of care, collaboration, and material choices?

6. How are Perkins + Will taking first steps to change design thinking?

    a. What is sustainable, ethical, and valuable in their ideas about the Precautionary List they have created?
    b. How is the initiative by Perkins + Will and others another excellent example of collective action?

CHAPTER 12

What Next? The Future of Design and Knowledge Spaces

global meanings, meaningful spaces, fourth-dimensional space (experience), doctoral education, interdisciplinary stances, business culture, cross-cultures, practice/academic cultures, cultural sphere, design scholarship, global sensitivity, global form and context, leap creativity, adaptive creativity, meaningful design innovation, sustainable path

AFTER READING THIS CHAPTER, YOU WILL BE ABLE TO:

- Consider future spaces of designing.

- Analyze how diverse, dynamic approaches to global challenges impact future ways of thinking and doing.

- Appraise design in practice and scholarship in the light of emergent meanings such as the fourth dimension of space (experience), transdisciplinary spaces, knowledge spaces, and global contexts.

- Examine the future for scholarship, practice, and design research.

- Develop knowledge spaces by challenging engagements of theory, research, and practice.

INTRODUCTION

The future is now, and yet we cannot predict the future. How do we navigate uncertain change? What are meanings of space in this global context, especially when we play, work, and live 24/7 around the world and in modes that cut across time and space?

Global contexts and future issues are explored in this last chapter. We can consider futures and knowledge spaces from two perspectives. For example, Franco Berardi Bifo (2011) suggests that the future is not only unpleasant, it is unsettling and uncertain. He suggests that we are already in an era of "post-future." Conversely, designers are inevitably hopeful as they employ change as a transformative agent that is used to explore new spaces and dimensions when combined with design thinking.

We explore these possibilities with a taste of ideas from three authors who engage in considering what is necessary and desirable for the future's meanings in designed spaces. We have used interiors as the thread throughout the book and will now use interior space to frame these last perspectives as a way of closing the conversation, but in a broader sense, of also considering alternative views. The authors in the final chapter propose practices, academic spaces, and research as catalysts for change in light of changing worldviews. Possible scenarios include inter- and multidisciplinary approaches, new spatial dimensions linked to human experience, and rethinking understandings of lived space from both academic and professional perspectives.

First, from the academic arena, Joy Dohr considers what research tools are necessary to promote designerly scholarship that represents design practice and process through various voices and knowledge construction methods.

Michel Dubuc, President of Aedifica (Canada), provokes us with a perspective from practice. He provides a pragmatic view of the changing world of design and its position in the world as a profession and a discipline. How does experience contribute to cultural capital, and what role does experience play as the fourth dimensional space?

In Dialogues and Perspectives, Janice Stevenor Dale offers a practice-based view of futuring, following up from her earlier ideas about commercial design and cultural capital in Chapter 8 and those of Dubuc, but from a different perspective. Here Stevenor Dale asks fundamental questions about our future and the future of spaces in design from the perspective of commercially designed interiors and the knowledge required for business from an American perspective of efficiency and innovation.

REFERENCE

Bifo, F. B. (2011). In G. Genosko & N. Thoburn (Eds.), *After the Future*. Oakland, CA/ Edinburgh: AK Press.

The marketplace for scholars and scholarship is now thoroughly global.
—From *The Formation of Scholars,*
2008, p. 2

The above quoted premise forms the basis for a Carnegie Foundation study on rethinking doctoral education for the twenty-first century, authored by George Walker, Chris Golde, Laura Jones, Andrea Bueschel, and Pat Hutchings. The work further documents global meanings and takes the position that scholarship and graduate programs of every ilk must face fundamental questions of purpose, vision, and quality. It further holds that while graduate education remains a local process, the models of the past—the silo mentality or a single methodology or even a single advisor—no longer serve the kind of complexities and types of questions that need to be asked and explained in this century.

Introduction

Some design scholars and practitioners express an affinity for position of the opening quote. The universal observation above could be paraphrased: "the marketplace for designers and design scholarship is now thoroughly global." Over the past decade, this premise fits evidence and a line of work that examines the future of interior design issues and graduate education (Hasell & Scott, 1996; Friedman, 2001; Guerin & Thompson, 2006; Dohr, 2007; Pable, 2008, Martin & Guerin, 2010; Dohr & Portillo, 2011). The premise fits observations and experiences of design practitioners and design academics whose lives exists across, between, and within multiple cultural spheres. Such spheres can be different cultures of design scholarship, for instance, creative performance, research-based practice, and design research (Dohr, 2007). They can be different professional and business cultures (e.g., in-house design, large firm, small firm, dealerships, governmental and institutional design, experience design), and/or different geographic and ethnic cultures. What is common to cross-cultural and between-cultural realities is a design perspective by which one discerns distinctions of spheres—what is unique to each—while integrating parts from each that blend to a new form or movement. As an example, one design professor operates in Chinese and North American cultures, in professional cultures of practice and academe where he shares his exploration in visual venues, as well as written and verbal scholarship. One design practitioner operates in Western and Middle East cultures and in a large firm practice culture where an interdisciplinary, global view of the field is demanded. She shares her knowledge and practice skills in built projects involving colleagues and clients, in speaking, and in leading a movement of what branding means for the field. Another design practitioner operates in a small firm culture and primarily within a 200-mile radius of his firm's location. But advancements in sustainability research and a global sensitivity to materials and resources are his catalyst to returning to graduate school and to a new career in academe. One design student garners core knowledge and skill in her program, but seeks added international experiences related to interior design and architecture. Learning also includes service learning and evidence-based design that augments lecture and studio classes, again different aspects of development. Each of these individuals—academic scholar, practice scholars, and student—speaks of global opportunity as life-changing experiences for themselves and the field.

Knowing our times and community, a profile emerges of a design community that is globally savvy, locally sensitive, and innovative and skilled in the execution of design projects. Further it is a community that asks substantive questions about design issues and articulates how a global context or movement changes the way we work. The community is in conversation about design research and assessment of building and interior design. While this general statement sounds correct to some and daunting to others, let us consider specifics that undergird it. In other words,

what meanings of global form a context and move us into the future? What type of design scholarship are we talking about? What agenda of issues and what new types of research methods might fit this context and might catapult us forward? If the marketplace is global publics, how might interior design share its scholarly force as world knowledge with the marketplace? How might this force be a vision that has a clear formation through design research?

To address these questions, interpretations of three major themes shape this essay:

1. Meanings of global views with local sensibilities
2. Innovation in interior design as an issue for scholarship in a global, holistic context
3. Design research models that anticipate the interdisciplinary and multidisciplinary reality of practice and scholarship of the field (e.g., collaborative models as narrative inquiry and analysis, action research, and transference research—sometimes also termed translational).

In summary, integration of these themes brings interior design to a new platform and to an energy or force for readers' consideration. Moving the field into the future with its contribution to knowledge in the world stands as our challenge. Having dialogue about integrative methods for studying design and interiors of humans, I suggest, become a critical factor in the journey of finding new meanings and understanding.

Meanings of a Global Context

Global: as Worldwide Human Environmental Condition

When space in a global context is referenced, the first line of thought is thinking about how people of the world shape their space based upon their living style, functions, and values. The image before us is the architectural interiors—concrete and virtual. We think of geographic conditions, natural elements, historical artifacts, and cultural ways. We use systems frameworks in the shaping, such as Ken Friedman's domains of learning and leading, the human world, artifact, and environment from which root disciplines and applied disciplines offer meanings. All demand study, but the domains of learning and leading inherently suggest scholarship and communication patterns.

We use the Body of Knowledge (BoK) categories (Martin and Guerin 2006) or professional standards to shape content and processes of what we examine and claim. We question and learn from ways of others and connect with players around the globe. General global movements occupy thought and action, such as sustainability. We think of and act on sustainability related to human comfort and traditional approaches to energy or thermal comfort, for example, within cultural/social definitions, as well as technological. Such thinking introduces knowledge about the interior that pulls from global knowledge, yet has local reference. The observations remind us that a global view doesn't mean designers and design scholars operate at a global sphere alone. It means that designers and design scholars have the capacity to know global in terms of time and place and equally know its impact on local interests and even push-backs that make localization a movement as well. Common human needs suggest examination of a menu of factors of comfort and what gets selected and what does not. Reflecting on the local and the global intertwine.

Another meaning is studying a global human condition, such as homelessness. The question isn't about geographic and ethnic culture. It is about a phenomenon of shelter and displacement that can be experienced anywhere. Across the globe, space has a very different meaning for those homeless or displaced from those in place. The narrative goes like this:

A single man has lost work and earning potential in a large city. The results are he no longer has an apartment or work setting to anchor his day. He has to move. He travels to a medium-size community where he has heard of a social agency that provides both daily shelter and two meals—a supper and a breakfast. The shelter is a physical gathering space in a downtown, Gothic Revival church that is 150 years old. The space is open to him from 6 p.m. to 8 a.m., but availability is only for three consecutive weeks. Then he must move again. While staying there, the agency assists him in finding work and/or another place to stay. But finding work anticipates his physical well-being, as well as social background and preparation.

What interior attributes hold integrity of individual and effort of the agency in this process?

The church as a stakeholder wasn't originally planned and built with this service in mind. The security of a group of individuals staying and sleeping in its interior was not in an original plan. Neither does the church or nonprofit agency have funds today to convert spaces to fit the needs of these homeless, single men who come daily. The space is made do, but the space could do more.

Present in this situation are the following: a single, homeless man among other homeless men; a social agency with hired staff and volunteers; and a common place where they come together. Where they come together is powerful and primary to success and the journeys of both. This shelter in a historically designated building offers a voice to draw upon another connection. The place has a stature that others draw upon. A corporation in the community comes to assist the place. But the executives and gift hold to some basic expectations. The funds must go for a knowledgeable designer and construction crew to first address the common space—the tie to the community, to the individual, and to the social agency. The agency is sound and has a strong track record; the men are ever present.

But where and what types of person-in-place conditions are to be addressed?

As it turned out in this case, the primary condition was not focused on space for cooking and serving meals; it was not even space for sleeping or space for counseling and preparation for interviews. The corporation, designer, and crew devoted their knowledge and their action to enlarging and designing spaces where the homeless man's experience gives an order to a day and to his personal hygiene—showers, vanities areas, private toileting, and dressing places. Maslow's hierarchy comes into play. Designers' knowledge of civility and empathetic design with its sensory and environmental behavior attributes is evident (Dohr and Portillo 2011). Again, a global reality has individual and local meanings of interior place.

Global as Interdisciplinary Mindset

Another common meaning of global view is a standard index in interior design connoting the capacity to see the big picture, the gestalt (Lawson 2005). Such a connotation is joined by translation and interpretation that moves back and forth with concrete specifics. The fact that interior design is held to be an art and science, to be explained and be known from a number of schools of thought, again anticipates a capacity that it is studied and practiced using a spiraling of economic, social, cultural, technological, and aesthetic filters (Ziesel, 2006). Thus, when we speak of global meanings, holistic thinking and worldwide human conditions and interior places merge.

Innovation in Interior Design and Questions to Explore

In taking the global meanings as a world-wide connotation and an interdisciplinary mindset connotation, we can ask, "What issues emerge for moving interior design and its scholarship forward?" For purposes of this essay, I've selected innovation in interior design as an example of a global, holistic issue based upon four reasons. First, in studies of interior design over the past decade, innovation has been shown to be a marker of impact when design as memorable experience is sought (Dohr and Portillo 2011). Second, from a world standpoint, innovation and connections that produce innovation are held to be a global economic driver. Third, innovation has affinity to local design and new potential forms for the field. And local innovation informs global movements and vice versa. Fourth, it is my opinion that our field might more fully (to a greater extent) celebrate and make known our genre of innovation as a capacity and identity often unknown to others.

In earlier writings, innovation is shown to be action related to the creative process—an inherent knowledge topic in design. Creativity has been written about as a leap creativity type as well as an adaptive creativity type (Kirton, 1994). Leap creativity offers entire new paradigms and new originality of discovery such as observed in the late twentieth century through open-office planning, systems furniture and accompanying infrastructure, or through computer and Internet technology. Adaptive creativity is that character of discovery—that elaborative component—often found in engineering, business, education, and interior design where the individual and the team refresh or bring new development to spatial elements, as well as to interpretation and refinement of processes and experience. It operates with a different time cycle, yet offers everyday impact. The field talks about such innovation as customization, recycling of materials, design-build with contributed materials and objects, life cycle of interiors, and new mental models for new research and practice models (Budd 2000).

If earlier work is assumed, how and where does the interior design field articulate and share its knowledge of customization, or of recycling materials or portrayal of design-build interiors or new interdisciplinary processes in gathering information? What models of research could move us forward where these issues are examined and become known as world knowledge?

Design Research Models Fitting Global Connotations of Interiors

Given a global context that equally anticipates local input and sensibilities and given that an agenda of holistic issues are known, we have new opportunities to converse and consider how we study something and come to understand in new ways. Traditionally our community will study and act upon scholarship through three general scholarly cultures. There are scholars who know and act in creative, experiential ways, sharing knowledge in visual and experiential forms. There are practice scholars who take research and apply it in practice cases. There are design research scholars who observe and study issues from views of art and design, environment and behavior, planning and design, or business. There are some design scholars who view interior design holistically. These have been shared in verbal and written venues (Dohr 2007).

But new research methods and formations and today's technologies suggest there may be ways to better integrate our own community, as well as work in multidisciplinary collaborations. I identify three collaborative models that might contribute to new force for our field:

1. **NARRATIVE** inquiry and analysis I, among others, maintain the narrative method permits creative performance, research-based practice, and design research to work simultaneously together. The work stems from narratives based upon cases selected by specific identifiable criteria and multiple information-gathering techniques. A collaborative team of creative performance scholar, research-based practitioner, and design research are engaged. Each scholarly culture may take the narrative; give interpretation that informs the other and the whole. Together they offer a reliable and valid knowledge that taps global context and critical issues and offers exciting presentation with current technologies. For example, a written format shared online or in text may have a visual streaming component and a practice application. The increasing use of video and film for sharing a holistic and innovative knowledge presents another format for narrative. The richness of the field is evident in persons-in-place stories. It further offers the ability to ask new questions.

2. **ACTION RESEARCH** anticipates a holistic view of a phenomenon or situation and opportunity where researchers and community work together. The common intent is to discover new knowledge and gain immediate feedback for changing direction and policy. Community members and the research team focus on topic and conceptual frameworks. Team members bring different experiences of knowledge and a collaborative intent to questioning and testing. For example, the infrastructure of where architecture meets interiors is an example issue where this model is particularly effective (Dohr and Portillo 2011) Infrastructure-type issues can be physical in terms of data or HVAC, or they might be social and organizational in nature where spatial arrangements and/or social-focused differentiation of work is anticipated or needed.

3. **TRANSFERENCE RESEARCH** is a term used recently related to a new discovery center's mission. One might also see a similar idea of translational research used. In general, a basic finding or theory forms the center from which multidisciplinary teams of researchers are brought together to seek how it transfers and transforms findings to their areas of study and design.

Innovation underlies its purpose. For example, using basic research findings on biomechanical technology, scholars from engineering, nursing, textile design, and interior design are exploring new discoveries and applications of the biomechanical interface in their own areas of study and practice. While outcomes offer new knowledge for a field, it also opens one field to another. This has precedence in academic-industry consortiums of the 1990s where industry might have membership in a consortium and be provided basic findings for their own application prior to general publication. Collaborative and transference research also underlie the development of centers and institutes where a topic may be explored from different disciplinary backgrounds. While there are challenges of language, methods, and technology, the basic research grounds further study.

Summary

The essay assumes a global context and argues global equally requires local knowledge and sensibility in movement as well. Further global fits the very nature of design and design thinking. Global meanings suggest holistic thinking in design scholarship, a cross-cultural and multicultural activity of design, and observation of common human conditions in general and in specifics. We move back and forth. Persons-in-place concerns where people and properties are in transition also form a turning point.

Such global meanings anticipate questioning design issues that are holistic in character and innovation serves as one example. Importantly, when we consider global context and holistic views with the collaborative reality of our design work, we need to explore opportunities and pursue research methods that fit such realities. We are at a threshold point, where intentional new forms of collaborative research exist for our adaptation. The essay briefly offers narrative inquiry and analysis, action research, and transference research as three such methods. By joining and acting from such collaborative models of scholarship, I suggest a new force is in the offing and certainly, now is the right time to move.

References

Budd, C. (2000). Narrative Research in Design Practice: Capturing Mental Models of Work Environments. *Journal of Interior Design, 26*(2), 58–73.

Dohr, J. H. (2007). Continuing the Dialogue: Interior Design Graduate Education Inquiry and Scholarly Cultures. *Journal of Interior Design. 33,* (1), v–xvi.

Dohr, J., & Portillo, M. (2011). *Design Thinking for Interiors: inquiry + experience + impact.* Hoboken, NJ: John Wiley & Sons.

Friedman, K. (2000). *Creating Design Knowledge: From Research into Practice. IDATER* (pp. 5–32). Loughborough, UK: Loughborough University.

Friedman, K. (2001). Creating Design Knowledge: From Research into Practice. In E. W. Norman & P. H. Roberts (Eds.), *Design and Technology Educational Research and Development: The Emerging International Research Agenda* (pp. 31–69). Loughborough, UK: Department of Design and Technology, Loughborough University.

Guerin, D., & Asher Thompson, J. (2006). Interior Design Education in the 21st Century: An Educational Transformation. *Journal of Interior Design, 30*(1), 1–12.

Hasell, M. J., & Scott, S. (1996). Interior Design Visionaries: Explorations of Emerging Trends. *Journal of Interior Design, 22*(2), 1–14.

Kirton, Michael (1994). *Adaptors and Innovators: Styles of Creativity and Problem Solving* (Rev. ed.). London/New York: Routledge.

Lawson, B. (2005). *How Designers Think: The Design Process Demystified.* Burlington, MA: Architectural Press.

Martin, C., & Guerin, D. (2010). *The State of the Interior Design Profession.* New York: Fairchild Books.

Pable, J. (2008). Interior Design Identity in Crossfire: A Call for Renewed Balance in Subjective and Objective Ways of Knowing. *Journal of Interior Design, 34*(2), v–xx.

Walker, G., Golde, C., Jones, L., Bueschel, A., & Hutchings, P. (2008). *The Formation of Scholars.* San Francisco, CA: Jossey-Bass.

Ziesel, J. (2006). *Inquiry by Design: Environment/Behavior/Neuroscience in Architecture, Interiors, Landscape, and Planning.* New York: W. W. Norton & Company.

Provocation

This article is a view of how the discipline of design is evolving in reaction to a changing world. Is it really evolving . . . or are we finally considering design in its rightful perspective?

Design has become a buzzword, appropriated in many circles through the concept of design thinking, design intelligence, service design, organizational design, and so on. Now (business) management is looking at design and design thinking as a way out of its traditional methodology in an effort to leverage creativity and incorporate intuition as an equally important aspect of a business plan, beyond the black-and-white metrics of a business case or market forecast. Design is the new battleground in the democratization of our societies: "Everyone is a designer; design is everywhere."

The future of design doesn't lie in its appropriation by the layman or in its elevation to the textbooks of management schools. We are conveniently confusing design with strategy (the skills with the process), with lateral thinking, with brainstorming. The future of design still lies in the material world, in the understanding that it is reaching its full potential in being the key to meaningful experiences.

We see the future of design taking shape in what we could define as the fourth dimension of space: experience. In science, the fourth dimension is time. In design, we would rename it "the experience of an XYZ object or environment as we interact with it over time," or in a more succinct way, design needs to integrate the experience variable in the equation: what is known as the brief, the concept, needs to broaden to include experience.

This is about shifting the focus from the act and object of design to the purpose of space, to an intimate (and generous) understanding of how people draw meaning and usefulness from it. We usually think that design will define itself around three attributes:

- User-centered, collaborative, and interactive
- Innovative
- Meaningful

This view of design is not new. It lives in the world of industrial design, where the rules of mass production have made those attributes conditions for success—namely, establishing value in use.

Web design is showing us increasingly how design will evolve according to these lines with technically complex dynamic user interfaces, customizable skins, and interactive effects and transitions that engage the user. What is new and necessary is the need to revitalize this concept of meaning through experience.

Retail interior design is already embracing this framework as corporations strive to speak to and interact with their customers, and begin to see creativity as a tool to define their uniqueness and promote their brand. The market and business are pushing design to its future, and that future is to be meaningful.

Design thinkers have proposed concepts around how design contributes to enhancing one's life experience. Dave Norton (consultant at Stone Mantel and contributor to the DMI, the Design Management Institute) has lectured extensively on how space and experiences must be designed to contribute to people's "cultural capital."

Although design in the past decades has been pervasive, for many years it took a back seat to the deeper social and cultural changes that were going on. The popular television series *Mad Men* epitomizes the 1960s, where design played a supporting role in a social fresco and where people were defined by the role they played in society.

Two decades later, the ready-to-wear fashion industry blossomed as people were defined by what they wore. Today, individuality is expressed by which spaces one goes to and by which technology and applications one aggregates. We have gone from the worker, to the consumer, to the user.

More recently, Bernard Cesvet, of Sid Lee, coined the concept "Conversational Capital" as a stealth strategy to reinforce brands. Combining codes drawn from anthropology and marketing, he proposes a toolbox of experiential triggers that are carefully blended to create the fourth dimension of space that will elevate space and objects to the status of memorable and self-defining experiences.

More often, space is created as the result of a series of differentiated and disconnected decisions relative to its components. The act of design is too often focused on the designer him- or herself or defined and limited by a functional brief. But design is now evolving to become the process by which a rich experience is created. Here, design takes on meaning by becoming multidimensional, connected, interactive, collaborative, and even democratic.

Design cannot be a commodity, and it goes beyond entertainment, beyond design for design's sake. At one end of the spectrum, design is defined today by the fact that you can purchase a logo on the Internet for a few dollars. But the future hopefully lies at the other end, in the designers' ability to see the world through the filters of anthropology, psychology, and sociology— and to create meaningful spaces and objects that become the building blocks of people's lives.

Discussion Questions

1. What type of designing is Dubuc referring to? Why are experiences driving how we define and determine fourth space and its use?

2. What are the issues of design turning into a commodity?

Will the continuum of aesthetic evolution continue in the face of increasing alternate officing and virtual officing practices? Will locations failing to take advantage of alternative officing cease to exist, or will they learn to compete in a different way? Will the efficiencies expected by American companies lead to future success in the global world, or will different cultures less interested in efficiency outpace American business? How does efficiency relate to innovation, or are they enemies? How does an aesthetic that creates a sense of freedom connect to innovation?

Aesthetic evolution will continue, the complex interior spatial forms align with their businesses—large-volume outdoor-inspired spaces for REI, a retail sporting goods store in the United States, complete with pick-axe custom door handles, or sensuous curves connecting people within large law firms complete with interconnecting stairs offering a crescendo to elevated conferencing centers with a view.

Those businesses that refuse the competitive edge and cost savings that alternative officing offers have either suffered the effect of mergers or acquisitions. Virtual officing continues to be explored by corporations that have been open to human resourcing solutions, job sharing, and employee needs for flexibility. Drive for the virtual officing often stems from the female population and her need to work while caring for younger or older family members.

What American business has that others could benefit from, should they choose to, is a high regard for efficiency in practice. From the manufacturing sector, we utilize employee repetitive motion studies to minimize the health concerns associated with a task and to speed the process. Efficiencies are researched by all the leading furniture officing systems to showcase their products' ability to increase health of employees and aid in recruitment/retention, if not additionally to assist with carbon footprint and office productivity itself. What is in question is whether the culture of global neighboring countries will consider efficiency in as high regard as the American culture does. If efficiency is not a driver, then how is a benchmarked cost analysis completed? How is a comparative analysis completed? The answers to these questions will lead us perhaps to a new norm for the built environment, and an understanding of non-American cultures will be key.

In America, we speak much of STEM (science, technology, math) education and the need for innovation. Colleges and universities are incorporating the wisdom of Tom Peters and the inspiration of the

Aspen Design Conference to inspire even the most left-brained engineers to begin thinking toward innovation. Considering the unimaginable wasn't always allowed. More and more, design thinking is being integrated into top business schools. Design is beyond good business; it's known as a key factor in business success from techno devices to corporate offices. For example, clients can build a $15 million business from a garage start-up. That can only be accomplished with a great office space as part of the business strategy.

Central to interior design thinking is interior design education, leading the way for future professionals to lead thought-provoking responses to new problems, whether the problems of their clients or problems of their own workforce and workspace, both virtual or bricks and mortar. How do professionals respond to the round-the-clock nature of client expectations and the possibilities of work in the workplace? If efficiencies can be imagined, why not executed?

How is the interior design educational community producing a sustainable path for interior design? For our purposes, a **sustainable path** is defined as a long-term projection of continuous growth based on sustainable principles and practices. When we regard the body of knowledge that we closely protect and that exists as a foundational component of our very professional being, is it growing rapidly to build a database of reference material for all interior designers and associated professionals to utilize to build smarter spaces? How is the body of knowledge changing and evolving

to capture more intelligence areas to support the design of the built environment?

Important to the sustainable path is collecting the many facets and parts of the practice, from tripping hazards associated with particularly shaped door thresholds to the latest color psychology or the predictable emotional impacts of the way a hospital room might be designed.

How do we sustain interior design as an American phenomenon, and how is it evolving relative to the practices of architecture in Europe or Asia? How will these issues be manifested in the global environment? A global perspective and vision for the profession remains elusive, and currently there is no formal (American) professional organization with its mission statement and focus keen on leading the profession toward a global vision.

What think tank group leads thought innovation in educational environments for interior design? And when those innovations occur, which ones are qualified as legitimate and accepted as practice experimentation? Who determines? Are those people who serve on the visiting teams at accreditation visits truly trained in the nuances of collegiate scope creep? With universities facing serious cost issues, how is the merging of interior design departments into those of architecture, or worse, construction management, being addressed by the profession or its accreditation board? We must ensure that teaching includes the traditional body of knowledge together with collaboration with related professions, and an opportunity for diverse innovation that will make each institution unique. And, we must do so with a global view and global professional standard in mind.

Does sharing classes with an architectural department truly benefit interior designers? At first glance, it seems obviously beneficial. However, with greater study, one finds that the content of each interior design class is specifically designed to carry different informational content toward a different educational scaffold and summative knowledge area. Under closer scrutiny, we find that only a few instructional periods within a normal 16-week curriculum in one or two classes can offer shared content without degree impact. Degree impacts can be measured by attrition of interior design majors into different program majors, such as architecture, or worse yet, misunderstanding of the interior design profession to the point of renaming it interior architecture in order to bolster its perception in the marketplace.

If mergers continue despite the above, the loss is fully the burden of the body of the knowledge of the interior designer profession. Interior design is known by the educators and unknown by students. On one level, part of what is missing in the overall equation is the maintenance and continuous upgrading of an accreditation system that demands standards of interior design, quality of teaching, and qualifications of interior design educators, and defines and allows for market-driven innovation. Many today question the teaching standards made available within online design programs. Are they truly endeavoring to produce top-quality interior designers? Are they oriented

to weeding out a freshman class, or more likely to have a corporate mandate toward student retention?

Consulting with an on-campus and online university this summer, we've had a chance to review this first hand. Adding to the argument toward a global view, many of the online students were from countries other than America. Some came to the United States to live abroad for a time and experience America, and others remained in their home country to complete their degree. While the university offered language courses, their communication abilities were greatly compromised. Some had difficulty creating a final presentation of their concept statements and explanation of the projects as a result of the divergent language skill sets.

Beyond communication problems, there are new problems of design context. While the student may solve the problem with aesthetics representing the context of the project, student-centered and chosen, the instructor may be less than familiar with the cultural norms of the foreign location. This inability to render culturally relevant design guidance presents a dilemma of right and wrong. For example, is the American aesthetic standard of clean lines and less texture correct for a project in Singapore? If the local standard is for mixed and clashing textural contrasts, should that be considered well done by instructors in America? Or does it beg for an international design staff in which the American standards of design can be reinterpreted with open-mindedness toward cultures other than our own?

As a result of their attempts to blend architecture and interior design, the essential component of teaching space planning was highly compromised—so much so that it had to be re-taught in the thesis class as senior-level students were preparing their portfolios for job searching. Space planning had been obviated by the intent to teach interior design students spatial organization utilizing leading architectural iconic buildings as case studies (by an architect). While certainly there are spatial organizational models—block planning used in the formulation of those buildings—the practice of arriving at the final spatial shape is clearly dominated by exterior goals rather than interior, functional, people-oriented goals.

Others say that we stand at the crossroads. I think we are soon to be swept on a tsunami of technological change, changing education of all types, particularly beneficial to the technologies surrounding interior design and its practice. I trust that the foundational components of the interior design practice have the leadership and strength to lead us into the future and withstand the forces of nature that present themselves at this dynamic time and within our current global context.

The continuum of aesthetic evolution now faces a global revolution, as American interior design education goes online at a rapid speed. Alternate officing and virtual officing practices, while practiced modestly to save costs in corporate America, have not been received as culturally acceptable. The efficiencies expected by American companies and contributed to their success may not play in the global world, as different cultures less interested in efficiency outpace American business through their sheer desire and thirst for innovation and market edge. Innovation may be the enemy of efficiency, and perhaps both are required for success. Those who recognize that and provide that happy balance within a well-designed and inspirational corporate headquarters reap the benefits. By effecting efficiency through a study of the functional and business culture through aesthetics, interior designers impart entwined tendrils to a project, creating a sense of freedom that leads to innovation.

WHAT NEXT?

What is the future? As we have seen, we cannot predict the future—all we can do is think about how dialogue and conversation, supported by meaningful and considered thinking, can move forward with possibilities for new and informed futures. New spaces will be envisaged through social transformation, design intention, creative design thinking, and new pragmatic practices. Our experiences will also change with time and as future ways of living and working evolve.

We conclude here with a challenge, and a caveat of sorts. The presence of dialogue and your ability to use these texts as a means of engagement in developing theory and concepts about design/spaces depends on you.

Whether it is engaging in theory, understanding theory practice through pragmatic and theoretical lenses, or understanding how these various concepts are put into practice in both business and academia, each chapter engages you, the reader, in issues current in our society, as a means to make meaning. We are all engaged in finding new ways to express what is actually happening in the world and how we might facilitate understanding. We do not pretend to have the answers here, and throughout the book we have been explicit in contextualizing the discussions, theories, and provocations with context and case-based ideas and projects with the view to starting the conversation, not defining it. Yes, we have used interior spaces as our thread, but we have also engaged in larger ideas about design, design research, fluid stances, and emerging contexts. We have engaged in theory to understand practice, while learning about practices to reflect back into theory. Hopefully you can engage in the questions and issues that are of concern to you, and move meaning and understanding forward.

This book is the continuation of an ongoing conversation, offering new perspectives, foundational thinking, and grounded ideas about space, meanings, experience, design spaces, multiple spaces, and a host of other ideas that you can unpack in your engagement of your respective disciplines.

Consider, collaborate, explore, and engage in discussing possibilities, researching and designing future spaces, and changing things for a designed world that needs your critical and enthusiastic engagement in meanings of design/spaces!

SUMMARY

Global meanings, meaningful spaces, and expansive dimensional possibilities all speak to futures of knowledge that will expand the discourse for meanings of design/spaces. Whether it is collective knowledge-making with various perspectives or collective meaning elicited from contexts yet to be realized, designing and the spaces explored will continuously expand.

ADDITIONAL READINGS

Fry, T. (2009). *Design Futures: Sustainability, Ethics, and New Practice.* Sydney: University of New South Wales Press.

McDonough, W., & Braungart, M. (2002). *Cradle to Cradle : Remaking the Way We Make Things.* New York: North Point Press.

OVERVIEW QUESTIONS FOR DISCUSSION

Explore some of the major themes uncovered in this final chapter:

1. How do designers have the ability to see "the big picture" and add creative thinking
   a. As Dohr suggests?
   b. As Dubuc proposes ?

2. What "futures" might people in all disciplines consider for new types of spaces
   a. Beyond conventional dimensional spaces into new spaces such as fourth dimensions of experience or fourth-order design?
   b. That are cultural capital spaces and cultured spheres?
   c. That cross cultures and intersect with cultures of knowledge, practice, and design?

3. Joy Dohr asks questions that harken us back to Drew Vasilevich in Chapter 1.
   a. What issues does Dohr uncover?
   b. How do spaces take on new meanings in this current global context?

4. How does Dubuc challenge designers to act?
   a. Why is experience a fourth dimension for Dubuc? How is this similar to the fourth-order design and collective/collaborative concepts explored in earlier chapters?

5. What is Stevenor Dale saying about new design contexts?
   a. What are emerging issues of communication and design context?

6. What are some of the fundamental aspects of design learning that Dohr, Dubuc, and Dale all ask?
   a. How are they similar?
   b. How are they different?

Index

BIM (building information modeling), 59–60, 235–236, 238

Biomimicry, 432

Biophilic design, 432

Blessed Unrest, Hawken, 415

Bloomberg Businessweek, 406

Bloomingdale's, 219

Blossom, Nancy, 290, 293–299, 317

Boccioni, Umberto, 180

Body in motion, Ciné-torsion, 299–304

Body-object-space relationships, experiences, 289–291

Body of Knowledge (BoK), 49, 144, 445

Boland, Richard, 394

Bonaventure Hotel, 92

Book composition, 6–7

Borden, Iain, 185, 187

Boudon, Philippe, 209, 211

Bousbaci, Rabah, 205, 207–212, 244

Boys, Jos, 258

Brazilian society, cultural space, 267–268, 271–274

Brideshead Revisited, 218

British Petroleum (BP), 431

Brown, Denise Scott, 221

Brown, Tim, 239, 361–362, 389, 390, 396, 397

Buchanan, Richard, 321, 350, 351

Bueschel, Andrea, 443

Buildings, places of living, 233–235

Built environment, design in, 146, 147

Bunge, Mario, 37

Burnette, Charles, 388, 403–404, 411

Business, design thinking in, 391–394

Business ethics, interior design, 134–135

Business management, cultural contexts and spaces, 321–322

BusinessWeek, 391, 393

Cache, Bernard, 229*n*.11

Cameron, Julia Margaret, 279

Carnegie Foundation, 443

Carroll, Lewis, 279, 283

Cartographers, place, 113

Catalyst for change, design wisdom, 322–323

Centre for Interdisciplinary Research in Rehabilitation of Greater Montreal (CRIR), 374–383

Cesvet, Bernard, 452

Chadwick, Whitney, 263

Change by Design, Brown, 239, 389

Chicago marketplace, building design, 327–328

Chicago's Catalog Distribution Center, 189

Choreographers, movement-space-time, 293–295

Chronophotography, 300–302

Ciné-torsion
    dimensions and spatial perceptions, 303
    installation, 301–302
    Muybridge and altering perception, 300–301
    Vallée, 291, 299–305

Cinema-Ballroom, Café L'Aubette, 181

City dweller, 208

Civil War, 160

Clapham, Christopher, 269*n*.10. 270*n*.14

Clemons, Stephanie, 37

Client perspective, 349

Clinical research, 26

Close, Susan, 247, 278–285

Code, Lorraine, 261

Coded language, space as form, 256–257

Codesign, critical design ethnography, 364–365

Codman, Ogden, 160

Designer
  intention, 102, 103
  term, 405
Designerly ways of knowing, 42
Design foundations, understanding, 42
Design Futuring, Fry, 415
DesignGeographies, 332
Design heuristics, specialty, 43
Design history
  innovation, 325
  specialty, 44
Design inquiry
  building information modeling,
    59–60
  scientific inquiry vs., 59–60
Design Institute of Australia (DIA), 417
Design intention, 82, 103
Design logic, specialty, 43–44
Design Methods, Jones, 231
Design problematics, specialty, 43
Design process
  Buckminster Fuller's idea, 10–11
  doing, inquiry and action with
    intention, 308–309
  service-oriented process, 320–321
  space, place, meaning and, 79–80
  specialty, 43
Design professions, 235–238
Design research
  confusing issues, 27
  future, 443–449
  knowledge, 16
  making arguments for, 38–41
  proposal for functional specialties,
    42–44
Design systematics, specialty, 42–43
Design territories
  lesson of Prévert's glazier, 209–212
  user's obstinacy, 207–212

Design thinking, 29–30, 307, 360–362,
    390–391
  beyond design problem, 357
  in business, 391–394
  business transforming, 396–399
  changing business strategies, 392–394
  ethics and sustainability, 415–416
  issues to consider, 395–396
  research, context and pragmatic
    thinking, 357–358
  researching and futuring, 453–457
  strategic and tactical, 398–399
  symbolic, 322, 325
  systematic nature of dialogue with, 310
  systematic process, 309
  traditionalists vs. transformers using
    design processes, 389–390,
    397–398
  transforming business, 394–395
  voices, 309
Design Thinking Boot Camp, 390
The Design Way, Nelson and Stolterman,
    11, 30, 320, 414
Dessau Bauhaus, Gropius, 231–232
Dewey, John, 94, 120, 358, 361, 384
de Wolfe, Elsie, 221
Dialogue
  aesthetic value, 310
  communication, 307–308
  meaning-making, 308
  systematic nature of, 310
Dictionary.com, 394
Disciplinarity, 33, 50–52, 56
Disciplinary development
  existing models, 47–48
  interior design, 48–50
  liquid design, 52
  multidisciplinarity, 51–52
Disciplines, 121–122, 139–140

Service-oriented process, design process as, 320–321
Seventh Art, 300
Sexual orientation, 263
Shamir, Ronen, 267*n*.2
Sherman, Cindy, 283
The Shock of the New, Hughes, 231
Sir George Watson Lectures in 1939, 168
Situatedness, 140
Six Sigma, 392, 395
Skills, learning to design, 145
Smith, Lindsay, 280
Social construction, human ecosystem, 75–76
The Social Construction of Reality, Berger and Luckmann, 104
Social constructions
    space, 259–260
    space and place, 259
Social equalizer, ornament as, 163–167
Social identity, space, body, gender and, 258–259
Social impact, space, 72
Social justice, human ecosystem, 75–76
Social maps, women and space, 257
Social qualifier, ornament as, 160–163
Social reality, 256–257
Social sensitivity, ornament as, 167–169
Social theory, space, 255–256
Sociological theory, space vs. place, 71–73
Socrates, 261
Sosnowchik, Katie, 405
Space
    aesthetic values, 261–262
    feminism, postmodernism and social constructions of, 259–260
    gender and social identity, 258–259
    social and political value construction, 258

Space, Time, and Perversion, Grosz, 260
Spaces, 4, 14, 243. *See also* Alternative spaces
    alternative, of experience, 204
    change and complexity, 4–5
    communication and coded language, 256–257
    critical science and critical thinking, 75
    design and creation of interiors, 121–122
    designing significant living, 251–252
    design process, 79–80
    development of idea, 66–84
    experiences, 245–247
    human ecosystem theory, 75–77
    interdisciplinarity in design of, 139–141
    interior design perspective, 77–79
    interiors, 213–222
    interiors in historic context, 213–222
    as inter-story, 156
    material culture, 155
    new, of practice, 405–408
    ordinary, 189–199
    philosophical frameworks, 63–65
    poststructuralism and meanings of, 104–105
    relative vs. absolute, 68–70
    semiotics and visual reading of, 80–82
    understanding design, 42
    versus place, 70–74
Space-time concepts, 293
Spain, Daphne, 255–256, 259
Sparke, Penny, 92
Spatial design, historic context, 366
Spatial rationality, 207
Speaks, Michael, 95
Spielberg, Steven, 220
Stanford University, Design Thinking Boot Camp, 390
Steelcase, case study, 240–241